In memory of
Elio Alberto and Maria Quarina,
my parents

POST-TRAUMATIC STRESS DISORDER

Diagnosis, Treatment, and Legal Issues

Second Edition

C.B. Scrignar, M.D.

Clinical Professor of Psychiatry
Tulane University School of Medicine
Adjunct Professor
Tulane University School of Social Work
New Orleans

BRUNO PRESS – New Orleans, LA

Library of Congress Cataloging in Publication Data

Scrignar, C. B. (Chester B.)
 Post-traumatic stress disorder: diagnosis, treatment, and legal issues/C. B.
 Scrignar. — 2nd edition.

 Bibliography: p.
 Includes index.
   1. Post-traumatic stress disorder. I. Title. [DNLM:
1. Stress disorders, Post-traumatic. WM 170 S434p]
RC552.P67S37 1988   616.85'21—dc19   87–33808

ISBN 0–945032–00-5 (Hardcover)
ISBN 0–945032–01–3 (Paperback)

Publishing History:

   First Edition 1984 Prager Publishers, New York, NY

   Second Edition 1988 Bruno Press (A Division of B.T.C., Inc.)
   2627 General Pershing Street, New Orleans, LA 70115 USA
   (504) 899-2367

Printed in the United States of America

FOREWORD

Just what is a Post-Traumatic Stress Disorder, and what are its clinical and legal implications? It has long been known that traumatic events can produce serious emotional reactions. Indeed, the history of humankind is marked with trauma. When Chicago went up in flames, many people came down with PTSD, as it is now called. The victim of a mugging or a rape is left with psychological damage. As many as a million Vietnam combat veterans are claiming a delayed PTSD.

To be sure, trauma has always been with us, yet the literature has been lean and the conceptualization poor. As recent as two generations ago, emotional distress of any kind was considered the result not of any environmental factors—social or psychological—but of such unsavory agents as witches, the devil, "humors," or masturbation.

There has been much progress in understanding trauma, but there is still a question of PTSD as a clinical entity, and how to deal with it. Until very recently, few mental health professionals, and even fewer attorneys, understood PTSD and its ramifications. Following World War II, professionals who endorsed the concept spoke about "traumatic neurosis" or "neurosis following trauma." It was not until 1980, with the publication of the American Psychiatric Association's third edition of its *Diagnostic and Statistical Manual* (DSM-III), that PTSD entered the official nomenclature. The DSM-III describes PTSD as a constellation of characteristic symptoms that develop "following a psychologically traumatic event that is generally outside the range of usual human experience." Prior to 1980 the symptoms that are now grouped under PTSD were not included under a single diagnostic heading. The original edition of the DSM, published during the Korean War in 1952, included a diagnostic category for "Gross Stress Reaction" that referred to combat as one of a number of precipitating factors. The DSM-II, in 1968, dropped "Gross Stress Reaction," and categorized the symptoms under "Transient Situational Disturbances."

Is PTSD a valid or reliable concept? With the advent of PTSD as a diagnostic entity, some victims of severely stressful events are now regarded as suffering from a specific mental disorder etiologically related to a precipitating stressor. Some argue, however, that PTSD lacks clinical specificity and valid diagnostic criteria, or that it relies too heavily on a self-report of the individual, and that it can be readily abused as a legal defense in criminal cases or as an element of damages in negligence cases.

PTSD is among the few psychiatric disorders listed in the DSM-III that are defined in part by environment. The event context, described as "outside the range of usual human experience," poses the question of just what is included and excluded. Freud separated the war neurosis from the ordinary neurosis of peacetime, but he cautioned, "The war neurosis may proclaim too loudly the effects of mortal danger and may be silent or speak only in muffled tones of the effects of frustration in love." The DSM-III excludes from PTSD such common experiences as simple bereavement, chronic illness, business losses, and marital conflict; it includes rape, assault, military combat, floods, earthquakes, car accidents with serious physical injury, airplane crashes, large fires, bombing, torture, death camps, and other disasters. DSM-III-R expands and clarifies: "The stressor producing this syndrome would be markedly distressing to almost anyone." Physical injury need not occur as a result of the trauma. "The most common traumata involve either a serious threat to one's life or physical integrity; a serious threat or harm to one's children, spouse, or other close relatives and friends; sudden destruction of one's home or community; or seeing another person who has recently been, or is being, seriously injured or killed as the result of an accident or physical violence. In some cases the trauma may be learning about a serious threat or harm to a close friend or relative, e.g., that one's child has been kidnapped, tortured, or killed."

Is a diagnosis in relation to a stressor event a distinction without a difference? The death of a loved one is an experience facing all of us, a common life event, leaving many in a pathological state. Is it any different from that resulting from events generally outside the range of usual human experience? What measure is to be taken of preexisting personality characteristics? What are the clinical and legal consequences of the disorder?

In this book Dr. C. B. Scrignar discusses the diagnosis, treatment, and legal issues of PTSD. Dr. Scrignar brings to the task a background of over 25 years of teaching and practical experience. In his career he has treated several hundred patients suffering with the disorder, and he has frequently been called upon as an expert witness in both criminal and civil cases. All too often, books written by academics have little practical value, and books by practitioners tend to be a mere telling of "war stories." This book is a wonderful integration of theory and practice. It is helpful to both clinician and lawyer and is, without doubt, the definitive work on the subject.

In both clinical and legal practice, PTSD is a relatively new way of describing and explaining behavior. The potential for creative and responsible applications of the concept is just being realized. Dr. Scrignar's pioneering text will educate, and his case examples will illuminate. He examines the diagnostic criteria for PTSD. He analyzes the legal issues. He discusses ways of testifying in court. He unravels the delayed PTSD. And he does it all superbly, with utmost clarity. As lagniappe, he gives us witticisms we are not likely to forget.

Dr. Scrignar sets out, in a fascinating way, what he considers to be the sources for the production and maintenance of pathological anxiety—namely, the environment, encephalic events, and endogenous processes. They are called, for easy reference, the Three E's. The category Post-Traumatic Stress Disorder, Dr. Scrignar observes, could have been called Post-Traumatic Anxiety Disorder, since stress and anxiety involve the same psychophysiological systems and for all practical purposes, are the same. Following a trauma the interaction of the Three E's determines whether or not a state of pathologic anxiety is maintained. Pathologic anxiety may be said to emanate from the Three E's—these factors interact to determine whether the anxiety will be maintained. Anxiety is described as pathologic when the autonomic nervous system discharges so quickly or unpredictably that the person is rendered seemingly incapable of thought or movement.

As Dr. Scrignar explains, the initial feature in determining whether a PTSD develops is the impact of the trauma on the individual's autonomic nervous system. Any outside stimulus, if perceived as dangerous, can be regarded as a trauma and precipitate a PTSD. A common misconception by lawyers and others is that a PTSD is dependent on physical injury, and that if no physical pathology is present, a PTSD is not valid. These days, however, litigation increasingly involves injuries having psychological components or claims that are based entirely on psychological harm. The courts, by and large, no longer require physical injury or impact in an action for negligent infliction of emotional distress, for instance.

Persistence in the habit of thinking and visualizing scenes directly and indirectly related to the traumatic event is one of the most important factors in maintaining a PTSD. These encephalic processes result in retraumatization of the patient when confronted with environmental stimuli that the patient associates with or that resemble the initial traumatic event. Dr. Scrignar describes this process as the Spiral Effect.

Because PTSD is a multifaceted disorder involving not only post-traumatic stress but disruptions in other areas of personal functioning as well, Dr. Scrignar has developed a broad range of appropriate treatment techniques. The goal of treatment is the gradual lessening and modification of stimuli from the Three E's through various anti-anxiety schemes. Usually a return to normal functioning is slow and tedious, but when the person begins to cope adequately with the stresses of everyday life, treatment is considered to be successful. As demonstrated through the case studies presented here and through his many other successes in private practice, Dr. Scrignar's treatment methods are worthy of critical acclaim.

It is an especial honor to introduce this book because Dr. Scrignar is a cherished friend. I met Chet, as he is affectionately known, in the early 1960's when I, though a law professor, was invited to do a residency in the Tulane University Department of Psychiatry and Neurology. Chet was a resident at the time. Even then, he was challenging old ideas and seeking new and more effective therapy. He was not afraid to look at the new for the sake of the old. He was innovative then, always probing, as he is now. He was a pleasure to behold.

After a few years of practice, Dr. Scrignar found that traditional therapy was costly and ineffective for a considerable number of patients. His training in psychodynamics and psychoanalysis seemed inadequate for treating the types of patients discussed in this book. One is reminded of the characterization of psychotherapy as "an undefined technique applied to unspecified cases with unpredictable results—and for this technique, rigorous training is required." Dr. Scrignar turned his sights to behavior therapy. In 1968, after studying under Dr. Joseph Wolpe, Dr. Scrignar began applying behavioral concepts to patients with "traumatic neurosis." He found behavior therapy best suited to conceptualize and to treat those involved in a traumatic incident. He has developed the therapy to a fine art. His behavior therapy center in New Orleans is a byword.

Dr. Scrignar is a prominent academic as well as practitioner, excelling in both word and deed. In fact, his academic achievements are so many that one might assume that he is full-time in academia. He began teaching at Tulane University after finishing his residency, and currently he is Clinical Professor of Psychiatry in the Tulane University School of Medicine, Adjunct Professor of Law and Psychiatry in the School of Law, and Adjunct Professor in the School of Social Work. In 1964 he initiated a course in forensic psychiatry in both the Tulane University Department of Psychiatry and the then tradition-bound School of Law. At that time only a handful of law schools around the country offered a course in forensic psychiatry, and even those tended to focus primarily on issues of criminal responsibility.

Dr. Scrignar explored the psychological impact of trauma, and he turned it into a fascinating subject.

Dr. Scrignar is the author of more than 30 articles and an earlier book in the area, *Stress Strategies*. He has been active, giving generously of his time, in many professional and civic organizations. Friends love to have a coke or beer with Chet and to talk with him. He radiates with optimism and good cheer. He has been an inspiration. He has enriched my life, and for his friendship I am forever grateful. His wonderful spirit will be found in this book.

Ralph Slovenko
Professor of Law and Psychiatry
Wayne State University School of Law

PREFACE TO THE SECOND EDITION

Since the first edition of this book was published, my knowledge about personal injury litigation, workers' compensation claims, and criminal defendants has been enhanced by conducting seminars on PTSD throughout the country for attorneys and forensic clinicians. My life-long love of teaching has been rewarded by the repartee and cross-fertilization of ideas from astute audiences. Information I have gained while teaching seminars on the diagnosis, treatment, and legal issues relating to PTSD and other psychological sequelae of trauma has found its way into this book.

Continuing contact with patients and consultations with lawyers have been other important sources of data. Evaluating and treating traumatized patients and testifying as an expert witness sharpens one's clinical skills and increases expertise in court. I still ascribe to old-fashioned notions that patients teach doctors and experience is the greatest teacher. During the writing of the second edition, I have drawn upon my clinical and forensic experience to illustrate theoretical concepts, recommend treatment approaches, and suggest guidelines for testimony in court. Case histories and examples gleaned from clinical practice are liberally sprinkled throughout this book.

This edition contains five new chapters. "The Traumatic Principle and The Three E's," concepts mentioned in edition one, have been expanded into a separate chapter because of their significance. Recent interest in the psychological reaction to toxic-waste disposal sites, the Three Mile Island accident, the disaster at Chernobyl, and cases involving AIDS, stimulated a new chapter titled, "Invisible Trauma and PTSD: Toxic Substances, Radioactivity, and Pathogenic Microorganisms." The section on group therapy has been expanded into a separate chapter. Another new chapter, "The Forensic Evaluation," was written in response to colleagues who requested a format upon which to organize clinical observations leading to an expert opinion. The interest among lawyers and forensic clinicians in the chapter on legal issues led to its expansion and division into two chapters—civil and criminal.

Many articles and several books on the subject of PTSD have appeared since the first edition. An analysis and distillation of current information has led me to conclude that the best theory available for understanding and treating PTSD patients is a cognitive-behavioral one. This opinion has some basis in animal experimentation and clinical research, as is described herein. Learning and conditioning not only explains the onset of PTSD, but also provides the basis for therapeutic interventions which impact on the key symptoms as described in DSM-III-R. Of course, other theoretical orientations offer alternative explanations and propose treatment which improves some PTSD patients. This is the nature of contemporary psychiatry, as the behavioral sciences strive for a more scientific and objective foundation. Ultimately, I have no doubt that basic brain research will unravel current unfathomable issues relating to PTSD.

I end this preface with the same sentence from the first edition—"It is my hope that this book will contribute to a better understanding of PTSD and improve treatment for those suffering from this disorder."

ACKNOWLEDGEMENTS

Professor Ralph Slovenko of the Wayne State University School of Law has been a very special friend and colleague for over a quarter of a century. During the writing of this book, he has shared his scholarship, and his encouragement and comments have been invaluable. Ralph is one of those rare individuals who unselfishly give more than they receive, and I am thankful for his continuing friendship. Professor Michael Vitiello of Loyola Law School of New Orleans was especially helpful during the writing of the chapters on legal issues, and I am indebted to him for his perceptive suggestions. Another attorney, Judy Gic, was also helpful while formulating the chapters on legal issues, and her thoughtful suggestions led to the inclusion of a new chapter related to toxic torts. I sincerely thank Michael Duffy for his scholarly examination of the entire manuscript, and his imprint is to be found in the final version. Dr. Aris Cox shared his clinical expertise and contributed to the chapter on the forensic evaluation. Dr. Daniel Winstead, Chairman of the Department of Psychiatry at Tulane University School of Medicine, has been particularly supportive of my work, and I am most appreciative. Drs. Bill Bloom, Dave Mielke, Frank Silva, and Dan Sprehe are friends and forensic colleagues who have enriched my knowledge. I thank all of the people who have been an important part of my professional life, including my relationship with numerous plaintiff and defense attorneys and my continuous contact with countless patients. They have added an element of reality to this book.

I wish to express my gratitude to Deborah Moncrief, a former student now a practicing social worker, for her editorial assistance. John and Lorraine Hamwey of ABC Publications, Inc., Westwood, Massachusetts, were extremely helpful in the design and printing, and I am grateful to both for shepherding this book to its final form. A special thanks goes to Mrs. Eileen Ferniz, my secretary, for her untiring efforts, good cheer during trying times, and her enthusiasm and determination while learning the technology of computers. The writing of this book has been made easier by Eileen and a word processor, the former being the most important.

Finally, I wish to thank my loving and devoted wife Mary for her patience and support and for tolerating the role of a writer's widow for over a year.

CONTENTS

ONE

HISTORICAL PERSPECTIVE: TRAUMA AND STRESS

Since the inclusion of Post-Traumatic Stress Disorder (PTSD) in the American Psychiatric Association's Diagnostic and Statistical Manual (DSM) in 1980, Vietnam veterans, victims of criminal assaults, survivors of natural or man-made disasters, and accident casualties have come under closer scrutiny. There has been a plethora of articles, books, and public media presentations about trauma and stress. Different psychological syndromes have been brought under the umbrella of PTSD, as it became apparent that rape, torture, criminal coercion, toxic substances, and the "invisible" trauma of radioactivity produce similar symptoms in victims.

Psychotraumatologists have invaded the heretofore inviolate territory of the child psychiatrist, and this trend will accelerate with the recent publication of DSM-III-Revised (1987), which for the first time includes several specific references to children and PTSD. Forensic psychiatrists and lawyers embrace PTSD to explain the psychological sequelae of trauma in personal injury cases and to formulate an insanity defense in criminal cases. Politics and PTSD merge when terrorists seize hostages and the deadly serious melodrama plays to a world-wide television audience. Domestic disputes erupting into the battering of women, children, or the elderly involve physical abuse and PTSD.

Some have criticized the concept of PTSD, especially the publicity which emphasizes its ubiquity, but it is hard to deny the environment's potential for causing physical and psychological harm. To place the issue in perspective, most people who are exposed to situations which pose a serious threat to life or limb do not develop PTSD, but in the past this stress disorder has been overlooked and underdiagnosed.

WARS AND PTSD

Wars, the most intense and destructive of human enterprises, traumatize and damage minds and bodies of antagonists. The battlefield, a microcosm of trauma, is a ghastly place which assails all five senses. The sounds of battle—the discharge of weapons, the fierce shrieks of soldiers, the wailing of the wounded—all merge into a terrifying cacophony. The sights and smells of war assault the eyes and insult the nose and are no less frightening. The maniacal look on the faces of the enemy, together with the sight of broken and bloodied bodies of combatants and the pervasive stench of death, overpower the minds of soldiers and civilians alike. Battles inflame thoughts of imminent death or impending injury, so the trauma of war becomes firmly embedded into consciousness.

Unquestionably some soldiers throughout history—to say nothing of the civilian victims—have been emotionally affected by war, either temporarily or permanently, whether they received a physical injury or not. Yet, the relationship between war trauma and psychopathology received little attention until the late nineteenth century.

In the United States, Dr. Jacob Mendes DaCosta (1871) was the first physician to study a group of physically-sound, yet symptomatic Civil War veterans. He noticed symptoms, similar to those described earlier among British troops in India and during the Crimea. The young Civil War veterans (two-thirds of his 300 patients were 16 to 25 years old) complained of palpitations, increased pain in the cardiac region, tachycardia, cardiac uneasiness, headache, dimness of vision, and giddiness. With clinical astuteness, DaCosta theorized that since there was no evidence of myocardial disease, the condition was due to a disturbance of the sympathetic nervous system. He labeled the condition "Irritable Heart," and it became known as DaCosta's Syndrome (Wooley, 1982).

Sir Thomas Lewis (1919) observed symptoms of chest pain, breathlessness, palpitations, tachycardia, and fatigue in soldiers of World War I and called this "Soldier's Heart and the Effort Syndrome." Summing up, Lewis said, "It is because these symptoms and signs are largely, in some cases wholly, the exaggerated physiological response to exercise...that I term the whole the 'Effort Syndrome'." While noting that nervous manifestations were "more or less prominent," Lewis wrote that "a proportion of the patients whom I include in the group, Effort Syndrome, sooner or later acquire a diagnosis of Neurasthenia." Oppenheimer (1918), a contemporary of Lewis, noting the psychoneurotic and cardiac manifestations of soldiers, preferred the term "Neurocirculatory Asthenia" to characterize the disorder (Dalessio, 1978).

Nonpsychiatric physicians of the early 20th century were usually generalists who concentrated on the cardiac manifestations of soldiers exposed to combat during World War I. Nervousness was noted but not emphasized by these cardiac-oriented physicians. As the 20th century advanced, wars continued to serve as a laboratory of stress, but psychiatry and the other behavioral sciences evolved to include the effect of non-war trauma upon living organisms. Research took three separate, but related, directions: psychoanalysis (traumatic neurosis), stress ("flight-or-fight" and the "alarm reaction"), and behavioral psychology (learning and conditioning).

NEUROSIS AND TRAUMATIC NEUROSIS

Sigmund Freud (1895) wrote a paper titled "On the Grounds for Detaching a Particular Syndrome from Neurasthenia Under the Description 'Anxiety Neurosis'." Freud's perspicacity led him to sort out anxiety from the melange of symptoms found in patients suffering from neurasthenia. The concept of anxiety neurosis gained acceptance and by the 1940's, psychiatrists applied this new knowledge to World War II veterans who broke down following a battle. Although the soldiers' symptoms were the same as observed by DaCosta (1871), Oppenheimer (1918), and Lewis (1919), the diagnostic labels "Irritable Heart," "Effort Syndrome," and "Neurocirculatory Asthenia" were abandoned in favor of "Traumatic War Neurosis" and "Combat Neurosis" (Kardiner and Spiegel, 1947). The symptoms were considered to be manifestations of anxiety and neurotic in origin. Some clinicians, however, preferred the concept of stress and wrote about "Combat or Battle Stress," "Battle Fatigue," "Combat Exhaustion," and "Acute Combat Reaction" (Grinker and Spiegel, 1945).

In the 1950's, the theory of neurosis gained ascendancy and was the conceptual framework within which civilian trauma was viewed. The term "traumatic neurosis" came into popular usage (Kaiser, 1968). A high percentage of persons developing a traumatic neurosis had premorbid personality problems, and this observation raised the possibility that a latent neurotic illness was made manifest by the traumatic incident. Perplexingly, clinicians also observed that apparently healthy individuals with no neurotic predisposition also developed a traumatic neurosis. This conundrum was not solved but merely restated by Robitscher (1966) who, summarizing an American Psychiatric Association Round Table discussion, "Neurosis and Trauma," (1960), wrote that all categories of incapacity can be "boiled down to these main types":

1. Traumatic Neurosis: A healthy individual becomes mentally ill as a result of an overwhelming stress.
2. Compensation or Triggered Neurosis: The individual has a latent illness triggered or precipitated by trauma and held onto by the patient for largely unconscious reasons.
3. Malingering: The individual consciously deceives.

This classification fitted the facts as observed by clinicians, but it fitted poorly into the nosology of neurosis. Neurosis is generally considered to be a developmental disorder. Unresolved, unconscious conflicts with parents or significant others during childhood are considered to be etiologically significant, while in traumatic neurosis, the disorder is precipitated by an environmental event later in life. According to the APA Round Table classification, only a healthy (non-neurotic) individual can become neurotic as a result of an environmental stress (trauma). Persons presumably neurotic or emotionally unstable can, following exposure to a trauma, have their neurosis "triggered" for unconscious reasons related to compensation. This unclear and somewhat judgmental classification was perhaps one reason why the label of "traumatic neurosis" was never accepted in the Diagnostic and Statistical Manual of Mental Disorders (DSM) of the American Psychiatric Association (APA).

Eschewing the term "neurosis," Herbert Modlin (1967) proposed "post-accident anxiety syndrome" as a more suitable label to describe the effects of trauma attributed to an accident. The grouping of symptoms into a syndrome under the rubric of anxiety added clarity to a post-traumatic clinical entity that was not to emerge again until 1980 (DSM-III).

STRESS — FLIGHT–OR–FIGHT RESPONSE AND THE ALARM REACTION

In the late 1920's the psychophysiologic aspects of trauma ("emergency situations") were studied by Walter Cannon and Hans Selye. Cannon (1929) wrote about the phenomena he termed "homeostasis" and the "flight-or-fight" response. When a living organism was confronted with a threat to its physical integrity, or homeostasis, it responded to the "traumatic stimulus" by an activation of the sympathetic nervous system and a stimulation of the neuroendocrine system, especially the adrenal medulla. The physiological response that ensued (increased heart rate and cardiac output, exaggerated respiration, dilation of the arteries to the skeletal muscles, etc.), Cannon concluded, prepared the organism for flight or fight as an adaptation for survival.

Hans Selye (1946, 1950, 1956) also conducted experiments and described an organism's reaction when it was suddenly exposed to traumatic stimuli to which it had not adapted. Selye, who first introduced the word "stress" as a physiologic concept, described "the alarm reaction," the first stage of a response he called "general adaptation syndrome." The alarm reaction, as an endocrine response to emergency situations, was associated with alterations in cardiovascular functioning, respiration, and muscle tone. Selye observed that if the stress was chronic, the arousal becomes a health hazard. The observations of Cannon and Selye were strikingly similar to those described by DaCosta, Lewis, Oppenheimer, and Freud, but this is not surprising since all were studying the response of the same physiological system.

Stress researchers concentrated their efforts on the study of environmental influences on the nervous and endocrine system as they affected various organ systems of the body. This proved to be a more pragmatic approach to the study of stress than that of most psychiatrists and psychologists who observed stress but called it "anxiety" and postulated intrapsychic theories of neurosis. Stress thus stood apart from anxiety in the minds of researchers and clinicians, although both terms were used to explain the same psychophysiological response (Scrignar, 1983). This divergence created considerable confusion in formulating a unified concept concerning the effects of trauma upon an individual. Even today, stress and anxiety, although physiologically identical, should be interchangeable terms, but they are not because they connote different frames of reference for clinicians, researchers, and the public.

BEHAVIORAL PERSPECTIVE

From Pavlov (1927) to Skinner (1938), behaviorists, sharing a scientific orientation, had a natural kinship with stress researchers, since both delved into psychophysiological responses to environmental stimuli. Unlike stress investigators, behaviorists were more clinically oriented and developed a technology that could be applied toward the treatment of pathologic symptoms and behavior in humans.

Behavior therapy became a significant development in clinical psychiatry when Joseph Wolpe published *Psychotherapy by Reciprocal Inhibition* (1958). The basis of the book rests on Wolpe's attempt to create, then treat "experimental neurosis" in laboratory animals. Cats, while standing in a special cage, were made "neurotic" by a series of electrical shocks to their feet. The expected response of fear (anxiety, stress) continued long after the electrical shocks ceased, thus in Wolpe's mind establishing an experimentally-induced neurosis. Wolpe's experiment was really an analogue for traumatic neurosis or Post-Traumatic Stress Disorder. The environmentally-induced trauma (the electric shock) was administered randomly and elicited a response of fear (stress, anxiety) in the cat. After a while, the cat, anticipating danger in the form of pain, became agitated and anxious ("neurotic") when exposed to the cage in the absence of any electrical shock. In this classical conditioning experiment, Wolpe clearly demonstrated that traumatic stimuli could elicit a response in the cat similar to anxiety in humans.

This Pavlovian experiment was not new, but the extrapolation of results to humans led to a different way of conceptualizing neurosis and, more importantly, opened a new avenue of treatment- systematic desensitization (Wolpe, 1982). Since neurotic habits in humans were largely learned and conditioned, Wolpe hypothesized that relearning and deconditioning could occur when neurotic persons were gradually exposed to anxiety-evoking situations. The stimulus-response relationship between environment and anxiety following trauma sparked a trend toward a more objective analysis of post-traumatic behavior.

Following up on Wolpe's work, recent investigators have described PTSD symptoms as essentially a learned response to an antecedent traumatic conditioning event (Keane, Zimering, and Caddell, 1985). A traumatic event (unconditioned stimulus) becomes paired with a previously neutral stimulus which then acts as a conditioned stimulus. Through the principles of classical conditioning, the conditioned stimulus may elicit adverse cognitive, physiological, and emotional reactions in traumatized individuals. By the principle of instrumental (operant) conditioning, traumatized patients may then learn to avoid and escape traumatically-conditioned stimuli as a means of reducing the conditioned adverse state. It is specifically this learned avoidance response that is viewed as critical to the maintenance of many of the symptoms of PTSD (Fairbank and Nicholson, 1987). Although a growing body of research is providing indirect empirical support for a conditioning model of arousal and avoidance in PTSD (Kolb and Mutalipassi, 1982; Fairbank and Keane, 1982), critics have expressed concern that this model does not adequately account for the potential mediating influence of PTSD patients' cognitive response to trauma on adaptation and symptom development (Saign, 1985).

The development of cognitive behavior therapy clarified the relationship between covert mental processes (intrusive thoughts, flashbacks, nightmares) and post-traumatic symptoms. In PTSD, cognitions, commonly called "videotapes of the mind," could now be correlated with anxiety and analyzed in terms of trauma. The sequence—traumatic event, cognitions, anxiety (stress)—explains what is observed clinically in traumatized patients. Persistence of symptoms beyond the traumatic event by "imaginal retraumatization" and "flashbacks" fits well into cognitive theory. Cognitive restructuring to control and diminish symptoms has important therapeutic significance as will be discussed in Chapter 8.

In summary, our knowledge about PTSD has evolved from several separate but related sources. Internists, psychiatrists, psychologists, stress researchers, and behaviorists have studied the same phenomena, but have emphasized only those aspects common to their training, interests, and experience. Like the proverbial blind men of Indostan touching the various parts of an elephant, clinicians and researchers had been studying the same elephant but drawing different conclusions when touching the trunk and then the tail. The confluence of these parallel perspectives were influenced by a historic event—the Vietnam conflict. The laboratory of war once again furnished clinicians with hapless victims to study and treat. In response to the large numbers of Vietnam-era veterans with stress symptoms, clinicians with different professional backgrounds converged, new theoretical and therapeutic practices emerged, and PTSD entered our nomenclature.

REVISION OF NOMENCLATURE

As behavioral, cognitive, and pharmacologic approaches to the treatment of anxiety made steady advances, a reevaluation of terminology was necessary. It became increasingly apparent that neurosis was inadequate to describe anxiety, for under this diagnostic heading a conglomeration of disparate psychiatric disorders were grouped—anxiety, depression, hysteria, dissociative reaction, hypochondriasis, depersonalization, and even neurasthenia (DSM-II, 1968). In 1974 the Council on Research and Development appointed an advisory committee on Anxiety and Dissociative Disorders. The committee labored for five years, eventually deciding that there was no consensus concerning the definition of neurosis. The group noted that psychoanalytic, social learning, cognitive, behavioral, and biological models all attempt to explain the development of the various neurotic disorders. Rather than endorse any theoretical conceptualization, the task force wisely decided to eliminate the term "neurosis" and employ the atheoretic heading "anxiety disorders." Some of the psychiatric disorders formerly subsumed under neurosis were now included under this new generic heading. In 1980, for the first time a category called Post-Traumatic Stress Disorder was included in the DSM and in 1987 the diagnostic criteria were refined and expanded.

DSM-III-R AND PTSD

During the preparation of DSM-III-R, insight and information gathered over a period of seven years has added specificity and precision to the criteria for PTSD (Table 1-1). The nature of the stressor (Section A) has been expanded and clarified: the traumatic event would be markedly distressing to almost anyone; physical injury need not occur as a result of the trauma; witnessing destruction or violence can precipitate a PTSD; a serious threat or harm to one's children, spouse, or other close relatives and friends; sudden destruction of one's home or community or seeing another person who has recently been, or is being, seriously injured or killed as the result of an accident or physical violence.

A persistent re-experiencing of the traumatic event, is the *sine qua non* of the disorder, as noted in Section B of DSM-III-R. At least one of the following must be present before a PTSD can be diagnosed: recurrent and intrusive distressing recollections of the event, recurrent distressing dreams, dissociative episodes (flashbacks), and intense psychological distress at exposure to events that symbolize or resemble the traumatic event.

Recognition that many traumatized persons develop phobic avoidance related to their trauma is noted in Section C of DSM-III-R. Efforts to avoid thoughts, feelings, or activities and situations associated with the trauma characterize most PTSD patients. Symptoms related to a numbing of general responsiveness, not present before the trauma, include a variety of responses associated with depression (e.g., marked diminished interest in significant activities, feeling of detachment or estrangement from others, restricted range of affect, and a sense of foreshortened future).

Persistent symptoms of increased arousal, not present before the trauma (Section D of DSM-III-R), indicates autonomic hyperactivity and anxiety. Difficulties falling or staying asleep, irritability or anger, difficulties concentrating, hypervigilance, exaggerated startle response, and psychological reactivity upon exposure to events that symbolize or resemble the trauma result from chronic increased arousal. Phobic behavior occurs when traumatized persons avoid situations similar to the trauma because of high anxiety, and this can prove to be very costly, especially if the trauma were work-related and the patient avoids work.

The DSM-III-R criteria for PTSD represent an improvement over the old, but it is a pity that the classification of acute and chronic has been abandoned. PTSD, like any other illness or disorder, does have a progressive course with prominent symptoms occurring at each stage. Anxiety symptoms are more apparent during the acute phase, while depressive symptoms become pronounced during the chronic stage. The inclusion of specific symptoms involving children acknowledges that all humans, regardless of age, can have an adverse psychological reaction to trauma. The Manual also states that the duration of symptoms must be at least one month before a diagnosis of PTSD can be made; symptoms usually subside before one month in the "normal" response to trauma.

TABLE 1-1
DSM-III-R Diagnostic Criteria for 309.89 Post-Traumatic Stress Disorder

A. The person has experienced an event that is outside the range of usual human experience and that would be markedly distressing to almost anyone, e.g., serious threat to one's life or physical integrity; serious threat or harm to one's children, spouse, or other close relatives and friends; sudden destruction of one's home or community; or seeing another person who has recently been, or is being, seriously injured or killed as the result of an accident or physical violence.

B. The traumatic event is persistently   reexperienced in at least one of the following ways:
    (1) recurrent and intrusive distressing recollections of the event (in young children, repetitive play in which themes or aspects of the trauma are expressed)
    (2) recurrent distressing dreams of the event
    (3) sudden acting or feeling as if the traumatic event were recurring (includes a sense of reliving the experience, illusions, hallucinations, and dissociative [flashback] episodes, even those that occur upon awakening or when intoxicated)
    (4) intense psychological distress at exposure to events that symbolize or resemble an aspect of the traumatic event, including anniversaries of the trauma

9

TABLE 1-1, continued

C. Persistent avoidance of stimuli associated with the trauma or numbing of general responsiveness (not present before the trauma), as indicated by at least three of the following:
   (1) efforts to avoid thoughts or feelings associated with the trauma
   (2) efforts to avoid activities or situations that arouse recollections of the trauma
   (3) inability to recall an important aspect of the trauma (psychogenic amnesia)
   (4) markedly diminished interest in significant activities (in young children, loss of recently acquired developmental skills such as toilet training or language skills)
   (5) feeling of detachment or estrangement from others
   (6) restricted range of affect, e.g., unable to have loving feelings
   (7) sense of a foreshortened future, e.g., does not expect to have a career, marriage, or children, or a long life

D. Persistent symptoms of increased arousal (not present before the trauma), as indicated by at least two of the following:
   (1) difficulty falling or staying asleep
   (2) irritability or outbursts of anger
   (3) difficulty concentrating
   (4) hypervigilance
   (5) exaggerated startle response
   (6) physiologic reactivity upon exposure to events that symbolize or resemble an aspect of the traumatic event (e.g., a woman who was raped in an elevator breaks out in a sweat when entering any elevator)

E. Duration of the disturbance (symptoms in B, C, and D) of at least one month.

Specify Delayed Onset if the onset of symptoms was at least six months after the trauma.

Source: Diagnostic and Statistical Manual of Mental Disorders, Third Edition, Revised 1987. Reprinted with permission of the American Psychiatric Association.

TWO

THE TRAUMATIC PRINCIPLE AND THE THREE E'S

A 26-year-old welder was one of a gang assigned to repair the conveyor belt system within the hold of a ship designed to carry ore. The five-foot wide conveyor belt was propelled by huge motors and arranged in such a fashion so that ore could be transported in or out of the hold of the ship. Prior to the start of the repairs, it was an established rule that power to the conveyor belt system must not be activated. The young welder had just finished his job within the hold of the ship and was on deck, leaning over the open hatch, pulling up his torch hose, hand-over-hand, onto the deck of the ship. As he retrieved his welding equipment the young welder heard the humming of machinery and saw the conveyor belt system beginning to move. Just minutes before he was walking on the five foot-wide conveyer belt, and he felt relief which immediately turned to horror when he saw a co-worker and friend lose his balance and fall on the slowly moving, but gradually accelerating conveyor belt. The co-worker was frantically trying to get off of the conveyor belt, but to no avail. His feet had become inextricably wedged between two steel rollers, one along each surface of the conveyor belt. Despite desperate efforts to free himself, the trapped welder was drawn into and crushed between the closely-spaced rollers. Shouts of alarm resulted in a shutdown of power, and the young welder scrambled into the hold of the ship to help rescue his friend. When he arrived at the scene of the accident, he saw the bloodied and mutilated corpse of his friend. In a state of anguish and incredulity, the young welder became nauseated and vomited, thinking if the power had been turned on a minute or so earlier the dead body would have been his own. Later, he experienced insomnia, nightmares of the accident, flashbacks, and extreme nausea and vomiting whenever he attempted to eat meat which was cooked rare. The young welder developed PTSD.

A 42-year-old married ticket agent for a travel agency was driving his car down a highway as he was returning home from work. The next thing he remembered was opening his eyes in an ambulance and the attendant telling him he was going to be okay. Then he again lapsed into unconsciousness. Several days later he was told that a large 18-wheel truck had run a red light and broadsided his car. His automobile was totaled, and doctors told him that he was lucky to be alive. He sustained the following injuries: three broken ribs; fracture of the lower right arm, involving muscles and nerves; hairline fracture of the pelvis; trauma to the left knee; multiple lacerations and bruises of the face and head; two broken teeth and dislocation of the jaw. The ticket agent required surgery to reset bones and to sew up the lacerations. He remained in the hospital for three weeks and returned to work six months following the accident. He did not develop PTSD.

From the foregoing case histories, it is evident that the development of a PTSD depends upon factors which may not be clearly evident on superficial examination. Questions come to mind regarding the nature of the stressor, duration of the traumatic event, the awareness of the victim, the vulnerability and predisposition of the affected person, and the extent of physical injury. Both patients in the preceding clinical vignettes were exposed to stressors which satisfy DSM-III-R criteria: the young welder, "seeing another person who has recently been, or is being seriously injured or killed" and the ticket agent, "experiencing an event that is outside the range of usual human experience and is psychologically traumatic"; yet only the first patient developed PTSD. What are the essential factors associated with the development of PTSD?

THE TRAUMATIC PRINCIPLE

In psychiatry, the word "trauma" has a generic meaning which encompasses all insults to the personality, but does not necessarily involve a threat to life or limb. Divorce, death of a loved one, loss of a job, or bankruptcy can be considered "traumatic," but are not life threatening. Trauma, in psychodynamic formulations, includes any disruption of family life which impacts upon a developing child. Although psychologically painful, trauma in this sense does not constitute a serious threat to one's physical integrity. Poverty, racism, overpopulation, and oppression are pernicious and "traumatic," but do not pose an immediate threat to life. When defining "trauma" as a stressor which precipitates a PTSD, specific and precise guidelines are required.

DSM-III-R refines the definition of trauma by the inclusion of statements such as "outside the range of usual human experiences," "markedly distressing to almost everyone," "serious threat to one's life or physical integrity," "serious threat or harm to one's children, spouse, or close relatives and friends," "destruction of one's home or community," or "seeing another person who is mutilated, dying, or dead or the victim of physical violence." Although one may debate what is "outside the range of usual human experience" or the meaning of the words "serious" or "markedly distressing," the DSM-III-R criteria for PTSD adds specificity and precision to the definition of trauma.

Clearly, the range of responses to any of these stressors mentioned in DSM-III-R would vary, depending upon the perception of the trauma and the susceptibility of the victim. In an estranged marriage, serious threat or harm to one's spouse might be perceived with relief or even joy. Destruction of one's insured but heavily-mortgaged home could be viewed as a godsend by a debtor. Seeing mutilated bodies of an enemy by a soldier following a victorious battle might be accompanied by exhilaration. Any attempt to predict the impact of a stressor upon an individual is, therefore, fraught with difficulty. Anxiety, hysteria, agitation, phlegmatism, or even indifference are possible reactions to the same traumatic event. Since the trauma or stressor is the key event in initiating PTSD, how it is perceived by a person via one or more of the five senses, determines whether a stress disorder will develop. Actually, any stressor which poses a realistic threat to life or limb could induce a PTSD in some individuals. How can this general statement help the clinician and the lawyer sort out the truly traumatized from others? The answer is: by application of the "Traumatic Principle."

The "Traumatic Principle" is: any environmental stimulus which poses a realistic threat to life or limb, impacting on one, or more likely a combination of the five sensory pathways to the brain, if perceived as a serious threat to one's life or physical integrity, whether it produces physical injury or not, can be regarded as a trauma and precipitate a PTSD in a vulnerable individual. The central factor in the development of PTSD is not necessarily the type or duration of the environmental trauma, but whether the trauma poses a realistic threat to life or limb and a person is consciously aware and has a full appreciation of the potential for serious injury or death to self or others. Also vital and a natural consequence is an intense activation of one's autonomic nervous system following exposure to the traumatic event. The sequence: realistic traumatic event—perception of potential danger to life or limb—intense activation of the autonomic nervous system—may occur before, during, or after the trauma. Sufficient time is necessary for the life-threatening nature of the trauma to be impressed upon a person's mind. Sometimes only seconds, but more often longer exposure to the "dangerous situation" are required. No physical injury need occur, although one may result, but a neurophysiological response to the trauma must eventuate before a PTSD can develop. Viewing victims of physical violence or the destruction of one's property, if connected to self by the process of identification, also fulfills the criteria of the "Traumatic Principle." In most cases, the anxiety associated with autonomic discharge diminishes with time and no PTSD results; however, when anxiety symptoms persist or intensify after one month, PTSD has developed. Clinically, the application of the "Traumatic Principle" assists in the diagnostic evaluation by eliminating those disorders which do not fulfill this basic criterion.

PATHOLOGIC ANXIETY

In DSM-III-R, PTSD is classified as an anxiety disorder; therefore, an understanding of pathologic anxiety is necessary to understand the genesis and maintenance of symptoms which typify this stress disorder. Anxiety is always pathologic, no matter what the circumstances, if it is of extremely high intensity, occurs frequently, or persists. A subjective interpretation of whether anxiety is pathologic or not can be avoided if anxiety is conceptualized strictly in terms of autonomic nervous system functioning. In this context, anxiety is pathologic when the autonomic nervous system discharges: (1) so intensively that it renders an individual incapable of speech, movement, or of thought; (2) unpredictably and frequently in an attack-like manner, and (3) so regularly that chronic anxiety is the result. Although autonomic activity is but one of the many neurophysiological and endocrine events associated with anxiety, it correlates closely with phenomena that can be observed clinically and reported by patients. Imprecise labels that refer to anxiety as adaptive or maladaptive, appropriate or inappropriate, or realistic or unrealistic, can be avoided if anxiety is considered to be pathologic when the autonomic nervous system discharges frequently, intensively, or for long duration. These three parameters of pathologic anxiety can be defined and described in terms of symptomatic behavior (Table 2-1).

TABLE 2-1
Levels of Anxiety Chart

Level	Symptoms of Anxiety
Level 5 (panic)	Acute, intense, dysphoric symptoms include feelings of impending loss of physical or mental integrity, depersonalization, derealization, and incorrect encephalic statements, e.g., thoughts of impending doom, going crazy, going out of control, dying, or other thoughts of a cataclysmic nature. Panic attacks occur suddenly, without apparent warning, and are followed by severe anxiety symptoms. Autonomic hyperactivity is a prerequisite for the development of a panic attack.
Level 4 (severe)	Acute, intense symptoms include palpitations, dyspnea, hyperventilation, tightness or pain in the chest, trembling or shaking, sweating, dizziness, vomiting, fainting, tingling sensations in the hands and feet, cold, clammy feeling, and hot flashes or flushing. Symptoms usually occur abruptly and unpredictably in the form of an anxiety attack.
Level 3 (moderate)	Chronic, moderate anxiety includes somatic symptoms usually affecting the gastrointestinal, cardiovascular, respiratory, genitourinary, or musculoskeletal systems. When persons are in this level for most of their waking state, they are suffering from a Generalized Anxiety Disorder.
Level 2 (mild)	Subclinical mild symptoms are characterized by statements from persons that they are uptight, edgy, high strung, tense, or nervous.
Level 1 (normal)	Non-symptomatic.

Source: Stress Strategies: The Treatment of the Anxiety Disorders (Scrignar, 1983).

The effect of trauma upon a person's autonomic nervous system is an important factor. When the trauma stimulates high levels of pathologic anxiety, PTSD can develop. PTSD patients experience periodic intense anxiety symptoms or, more commonly, persistent moderate levels of anxiety following their trauma. Persistence of pathologic anxiety beyond one month distinguishes PTSD from a "normal" response to a stressful event. In the latter case, anxiety quickly diminishes and does not materially affect a person's life. In order to understand, then, why it is that for some victims of trauma, pathologic anxiety is a sequela and for some it is not, it is essential to identify the three sources of pathologic anxiety—the "Three E's."

THE THREE E'S AND PTSD

The environment, encephalic events, and endogenous processes, the Three E's, are the sources for pathologic anxiety and are responsible for the production and maintenance of the symptoms which comprise PTSD. The interplay among the stimuli from the external world, the cognitive activities of the brain, and the internal physiological processes of the body determine whether a state of pathologic anxiety is maintained. An understanding of the etiological concept of the Three E's, therefore, clarifies the mechanisms that lead to the development of PTSD and directs the clinician to ask the right questions during a mental status examination.

Environment

The stressor which precipitates a PTSD always originates from the environment. DSM-III-R lists a variety of stressors which can precipitate a PTSD: rape, assault, military combat, natural disasters (e.g., floods, earthquakes), accidental disasters (e.g., car accidents with serious physical injury, airplane crashes, large fires, collapse of physical structures), deliberately-caused disasters (e.g., bombing, torture, death camps), and direct damage to the central nervous system (e.g., malnutrition, head injury). Psychotraumatologists have studied the effects of environmental trauma upon children, and for the first time in DSM-III-R there are several specific references to children. The environmental stressor must be outside the range of usual human experiences and be markedly distressing to almost anyone. The stressor must pose a serious threat to one's life or physical integrity. Exceptions to this criterion include a serious threat or harm to one's children, spouse, close relatives, or friends; witnessing the destruction of one's home or community; or seeing another person who has recently been seriously injured or killed.

A homogeneity of symptoms exist among persons who have been exposed to an environmental trauma. A subdivision of PTSD into groups according to the commonality of stressors has emerged. "Rape trauma syndrome" (Burgess, 1983), a synonym for PTSD, designates women who have been sexually assaulted. "Vietnam combat neuroses" (McKinnon, 1984) has been a term used to describe a soldier's response to war trauma. Family violence can precipitate PTSD, and it is estimated that between five and six million children, spouses, and elderly individuals are neglected, battered, and beaten in the United States each year (Rosenbaum, 1986). Another source of environmental trauma is reflected in the alarming increase of crime statistics which parallels the growing number of criminal assault victims, many of whom develop a PTSD. The aphorism, "Man's inhumanity to man," takes on realism when victims of terrorism, many of whom have been subjected to torture, display psychological symptoms following their ordeal (Ochberg and Soskis, 1982). Trauma centers, which cater primarily to the physical needs of patients who have been injured in industrial or vehicular accidents are now beginning to recognize and to meet the psychological needs of injured patients. The environment's potential for imposing a serious threat to an individual's life or physical integrity is almost limitless.

Perhaps the most common environmental stressor which causes a PTSD is a vehicular accident; automobiles, trucks, airplanes, boats, or any conveyance can pose a serious threat to one's life or physical integrity. Another important source of accidents involves the work-place, especially industries. Factories, refineries, construction sites, or any place where heavy machinery or equipment may go awry through negligence or happenstance, represent potential sources of trauma which may impact upon workers. Chemicals and toxic substances, whether inhaled, ingested, or absorbed through the skin, have the potential for producing physical as well as psychological pathology. An "act of God" (earthquakes, tornadoes, hurricanes, volcanic eruptions, floods, a bolt of lightening) can cause psychological turmoil and a PTSD, as can man-made disasters, collapse of a large building, sudden sinking of a ship, explosion or malfunction at a nuclear power plant, or any of the myriad possibilities involving modern technology). Rescuers at a disaster site are subjected to the trauma of viewing and handling corpses and this experience can precipitate PTSD. A new area of interest, the psychological effect of exposure to "invisible trauma" (radioactivity, toxic industrial wastes, pathogenic microorganisms), is discussed in Chapter 4. In these cases, the awareness of danger to self is not necessarily coincident with exposure but may occur many months and possibly years later. When analyzing the effect of the environmental stressor, one must always keep in mind the "Traumatic Principle." The types of environmental trauma and PTSD will be discussed more fully in Chapter 3.

Encephalic Events

Encephalic events, commonly called cognitions, are those functions of the brain which have to do with thoughts, visual images, flashbacks, assumptions, beliefs, perception of external events, and dreams. In DSM-III-R, Section B of the diagnostic criteria for PTSD includes encephalic events: "(1) recurrent and intrusive distressing recollections of the event, (2) recurrent distressing dreams of the event, (3) sudden acting or feeling as if the traumatic event were recurring (includes a sense of reliving the experience, illusions, hallucinations, and dissociative [flashbacks] episodes, even those that occur upon awakening or when intoxicated), and (4) intense psychological distress at exposure to events that symbolize or resemble an aspect of the traumatic event, including anniversaries of the trauma." Encephalic events are the *sine qua non* for PTSD and distinguish it from other anxiety disorders.

Following a trauma, encephalic events play a major role in the development, furtherance of symptoms, and the sustainment of PTSD. Anxiety rises and is maintained when intrusive thoughts and frightening visual images related to the traumatic incident periodically erupt into consciousness. These upsetting memories, like the sounds and images on a tape cassette in a video recorder, are extremely vivid and realistic. When these "videotapes of the mind" are activated by stimuli reminiscent of the trauma, the resulting scenario, portraying the themes of serious injury and death, generates and sustains pathologic anxiety, thereby retraumatizing the victim. The traumatic "videotapes," which contain macabre visual images projecting dangerousness, may be played back in the mind several times each day for months or even years. The fragility of life and the tenuousness of existence become dominant thoughts during the waking states, as elaboration of the traumatic theme includes such self-statements as, "I could have been paralyzed, blinded, maimed, or killed," and, "But for the grace of God or luck or both, I should be dead."

Patients tend to ruminate and speculate on the possibility that a more dire or potentially fatal consequence could have resulted from the traumatic incident. These intrusive thoughts take on the power of an obsession, seemingly uncontrollable but to the patient quite rational. The victim of trauma experiences flashbacks during the day and nightmares during sleep, and neither provides reassurance of survival, for the scenarios always end in anxiety-evoking images depicting ongoing danger. A woman who was involved in a automobile crash which was frightening, but resulted in only minor physical injury, experienced flashbacks portraying her death, had dreams involving her funeral, and during waking hours presaged a short life. In the clinical vignettes at the beginning of this chapter, the young welder who witnessed the accidental death of his friend and co-worker later visualized his own death and had nightmares that he had been horribly mutilated. The 42-year-old ticket agent was amnesic about his accident and had no "videotapes of the mind"; therefore, encephalic retraumatization could not occur and he did not develop a PTSD.

Why PTSD patients remain preoccupied with their trauma is a question open for research. Some investigators (Kolb, 1984; Fairbank and Nicholson, 1987) propose a conditioning hypothesis. Thoughts and visual images related to the trauma become conditioned to the surroundings where the trauma occurred. When the patient encounters similar stimuli post-traumatically, cognitions, anxiety symptoms, and behavior associated with the trauma are triggered. Another investigator (van der Kolk et al., 1984) has proposed an "addiction" to the trauma, based on neurochemical changes in animals exposed to inescapable shock. He postulated that both the central noradrenergic system and central nervous system opioid peptides play an active and reciprocal role in the initiation and maintenance of post-traumatic stress states. Whatever the actual mechanism, persistence in the encephalic activity of thinking and visualizing various aspects of the trauma is one of the most important factors contributing to the chronicity of PTSD. Imaginal re-exposure to the traumatic event sensitizes patients to elements of the original trauma and perpetuates the maladaptive theme of danger in the absence of a realistic threat. To a casual observer, the victim of PTSD appears to be an irritable complainer or a moody, withdrawn ruminator overly concerned with a trauma long past. In reality, however, the intrusive and seemingly uncontrollable encephalic activity of thinking, visualizing, and elaborating on various aspects of the traumatic event keeps the trauma fresh in the mind.

As time passes, the PTSD patient's encephalic processes may not dwell entirely upon the traumatic event. As an old medical aphorism states, "Sickness enlarges one's self to one's self," correspondingly the emphasis of thoughts switches to the current incapacity believed to have been a consequence of the trauma. Distressing thoughts now include reference to an inability to work, financial problems, marital conflicts, sexual dysfunction, and vague generalized self-statements contrasting lifestyle before and after the trauma. Depression is a common accompaniment to PTSD as negative encephalic events or cognitions include thoughts of self-reproach and remorse.

Endogenous Events

Some patients become organically oriented and concentrate on pain, physical discomfort, or psychophysiological symptoms. These endogenous events, if cognitively interpreted as pathological, result in the activation of the autonomic nervous system and the production of pathologic anxiety and additional somatic symptoms. Despite negative findings during medical examinations, patients attribute these endogenous sensations to the original trauma and cling obdurately and erroneously to the conclusion that there is something physically wrong with them. Such a conclusion is not entirely spurious, since the source of uncomfortable endogenous sensations can result from: (1) residual soft tissue damage to muscles and ligaments as sequelae from the original trauma; (2) motor tension due to chronic anxiety, or (3) visceral symptoms associated with stress. In all cases, pathologic anxiety either initiates or accentuates these uncomfortable somatic symptoms. An apprehensive expectation and increased vigilance and scanning, also characteristic of a Generalized Anxiety Disorder, together with a hyper-awareness of endogenous sensations further increases pathologic anxiety and physiologic sensations. Pain, another endogenous event, focuses a person's mind on his body and the possibility of physical defect. Such people are loath to listen to alternative explanations for their physical discomfort. In fact, if a clinician persists with a psychophysiological explanation for pain, the patient may question the competence of the physician.

When patients fail to appreciate the relationship between stress and somatic symptoms and blindly adhere to a belief of organic causality, they suffer the consequences. As will be seen from the following case history, skepticism can lead to an unsuccessful therapeutic outcome.

20

A 38-year-old truck driver was involved in a traffic mishap that resulted in his ejection from the cab of his truck onto the pavement. Following the accident the truck driver was stunned but not hurt seriously. Complaints of back pain prompted medical attention, but examination including x-rays disclosed no serious physical injury. A diagnosis of sprained muscles was made, and the patient was sent home with prescriptions for an analgesic and a muscle relaxant. The truck driver's back pain persisted, and symptoms of headache, nausea, and malaise added to his discomfort. Insomnia, nightmares, nervousness, sexual problems, dizziness, lack of interest in life, and a phobia of driving a truck complicated the clinical course. Not reassured by repeated negative examinations, the truck driver sought medical verification for his physical discomfort as he went from doctor to doctor, but no physical cause for his symptoms was ever discovered. As time passed family relations disintegrated and his wife divorced him, taking their three children with her. An inability to work led to financial insolvency, and the truck driver was forced to live with his grandparents. Still complaining of pain, wearing a back brace, and using a walking stick, the truck driver continued to trek to doctors' offices, where x-rays, a myelogram, a discogram, and a computerized axial tomographic scan failed to convince him that he was structurally sound. A recommendation to see a psychiatrist was greeted with skepticism and, as he predicted, psychological treatment proved ineffective. Even following a successful lawsuit, the patient continued to complain of somatic symptoms and remained disabled, firmly convinced that he had something physically wrong with him.

When patients constantly complain of endogenous sensations, it is a bad omen and presages a poor prognosis. A fixation on somatic symptoms in lieu of objective physical findings prevents the patient's acceptance of therapeutic principles which can ameliorate or resolve a PTSD. As will be discussed in Chapter 9, group treatment may resolve this impasse to recovery.

THE SPIRAL EFFECT

Endogenous sensations also remind the patient of the traumatic incident and stimulate encephalic activity. Following the perception of pain or physical discomfort, thoughts and visual images pertaining to the trauma activate the autonomic nervous system, producing anxiety, thus increasing motor tension and somatic symptoms. This magnification of physical symptoms alarms the patient and stimulates additional encephalic activity, consisting of thoughts concerning bodily damage. More anxiety results, physical sensations intensify, and a feedback loop occurs, a "Spiral Effect," (Figure 2-1). The cycle continues, compounding the anxiety-evoking effect of encephalic and endogenous events, further increasing the uncomfortable physical sensations. In this manner, somatic symptoms can persist in the absence of organic disease for months, years, or a lifetime following the trauma. These patients may still believe that they are suffering from the residual physical effects of the traumatic incident, rather than from the Spiral Effect.

Frequently, patients with PTSD report an intensification of symptoms for no apparent reason. A careful history, however, reveals that the patient may be quietly ruminating about the trauma or its aftermath, and this encephalic activity causes autonomic hyperactivity, increased motor tension, with hypervigilance and scanning. The physiological (endogenous) sensations caused by increased pathologic anxiety or stress further reminds the patient of the traumatic incident, setting into motion the Spiral Effect.

FIGURE 2–1
THE SPIRAL EFFECT

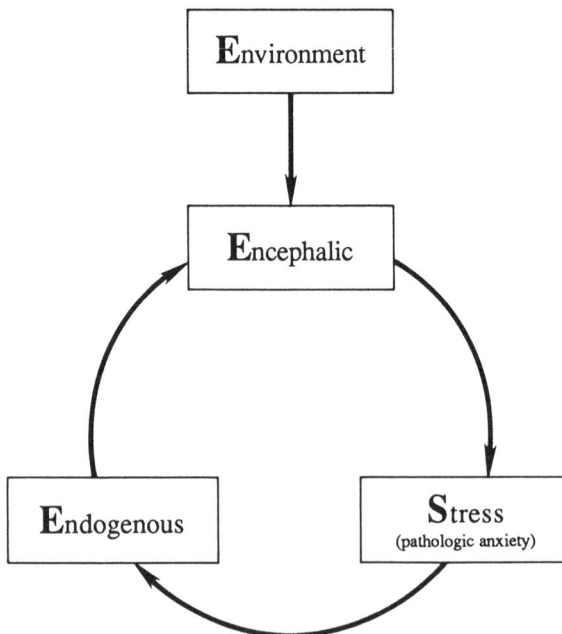

The Spiral Effect can be initiated by either exposure to environmental events which resemble or symbolize the original traumatic incident or the perception of uncomfortable physical sensations (endogenous events) attributable to the original trauma. Once the Spiral Effect is set in motion, environmental events lose importance, and the cycle is maintained by the interplay of encephalic and endogenous events. The Spiral Effect explains why certain patients, despite negative physical examinations and tests, continue to complain of somatic symptoms and are unresponsive to various therapies. Unless the Spiral Effect is explained to patients, they may continue to believe that they are suffering from residual physical effects of the traumatic incident, rather than from surges of anxiety.

RETRAUMATIZATION

A perplexing question concerning PTSD is why and how the disorder is maintained following the acute trauma. The presence of symptoms, seemingly in the absence of specific stimuli, may puzzle a casual observer or even an experienced clinician, especially when symptoms fluctuate for no apparent reason. A careful analysis of the time when patients experience maximal symptoms usually reveals retraumatization—encephalic replaying of the mental tapes involving the trauma. As the patient relives the trauma in imagination (flashbacks, vivid visual recollections, intrusive thoughts), the autonomic nervous system is activated and pathologic anxiety results.

Encephalic retraumatization is usually put in motion by environmental stimuli. When the PTSD patient encounters any stimulus that resembles and brings to mind the traumatic incident, encephalic activity, portraying the original trauma or some variant usually occurs. For the victim of an automobile accident, screeching tires, traffic noises, the accident site, the sight of speeding vehicles, or the smell of gasoline may elicit frightening images of the original accident. The sights, the sounds, and the smells associated with any trauma are environmental stimuli that are capable of initiating anxiety- evoking encephalic activity.

Retraumatization also occurs when PTSD patients perceive pain, physical discomfort, or unpleasant psychophysiologic symptoms which are associated with the original trauma. These endogenous events stimulate encephalic activity during which the patient visualizes the trauma or some frightening aspect of it. The ensuing stress or anxiety which is generated intensifies endogenous symptoms, thus increasing the tendency towards a revivification of the trauma. Retraumatization may occur several times a day and, untreated, last for a lifetime. It constitutes the most important factor in the prolongation of symptomatic behavior.

THE THREE E'S—INTERPLAY IN PTSD

Conceptualizing a trauma in terms of the Three E's allows the clinician a framework upon which to understand and treat the patient's symptoms. Following all environmentally-induced traumas, there is always a relationship between encephalic activities and endogenous sensations which is particularly pronounced when patients develop PTSD. The following case history typifies what is encountered in clinical practice and illustrates the application of the Three E's to PTSD.

> The patient, an attractive girl in her early twenties, was in an automobile driven by her boyfriend when she felt a slight bump, "like we had a blowout." She turned and looked out the rear window of the car and gasped with fright, as the entire window was filled with the grill of a huge truck. Her fear turned to terror as the rear end of the car was lifted up by the huge truck, and the car turned end over end. Her body was propelled forward and her face struck the dashboard of the car. She felt the crunch of her teeth loosening, followed almost immediately by "an explosion of pain" and the salty taste of blood. The car then careened against the expressway railing, and as she looked out the side window, she saw the ground about 30 feet below the elevated expressway. "I am going to die," she frantically said to herself while the car bounced off the railing and rolled over and over "as if it was in slow motion." The patient was thrown to her left against her boyfriend, and her head slammed against the left window. As the car continued rolling, the patient was then thrown violently to the opposite side of the car, and she felt an awful pain in her scalp. The patient related later that she was wearing her hair, which was waist length, in a ponytail and that somehow it got caught outside of the car. The car, now upside down, was sliding along the ground, and the patient's ponytail was between the pavement and the top of the car. As the car continued to skid, she felt intense scalp pain as some of her hair was pulled out. Simultaneously, her head was pulled by the hair tightly against the door opening, immobilizing her. Not knowing her hair was tangled between the automobile and pavement, she thought she was paralyzed.

Smelling gasoline and fearing that the car might explode, she tried desperately to extricate herself from the car; however, she was helplessly immobilized. As she looked out the car window, she saw the enormous front wheels of the truck and believed erroneously that the truck, which had actually stopped, was moving toward her and would crush her. She screamed hysterically for several minutes, believing that she was paralyzed and death was imminent. Later, when help arrived, she was reassured that her hair was tangled beneath the wreckage and that she would be freed momentarily. A passerby produced a hunting knife, and her hair was hacked away "in a sawing motion", and she was freed. During the rescue she looked about the interior of the car and noted blood splattered all over. She became panic stricken and felt that she must be seriously injured. Eventually she was removed from the car, placed in an ambulance, and taken to a hospital.

Probably because she was young and athletic, the woman miraculously sustained no irreversible physical injuries. Examination at the hospital revealed that she was bruised and battered but not seriously injured. Her teeth were loosened, her jaw was bruised, several large tufts of hair had been pulled from her scalp, and she had numerous small lacerations over her face, arms, and legs. After her wounds were treated, the patient insisted that she be allowed to go home with her mother, who was a nurse.

She began experiencing nightly bad dreams in which she relived her awful accident or some variation of it. Often the patient would wake up screaming, struggling, and sweating profusely. After a while she began to fear sleep because of horrible nightmares. She became extremely anxious and obsessed about the possibility of another accident. These ruminations lasted for hours and occurred daily. Physical symptoms dominated her consciousness as she experienced backaches, joint pain, and a variety of muscular aches. A new malady, headaches, began to plague her along with dizzy feelings and a tendency to lose her balance. Although she had never had any problems with nocturnal teeth grinding, she experienced bruxism on a nightly basis. She was "jumpy," extremely sensitive to noise, and easily startled. Upon viewing television or movies portraying accidents or violence involving humans or animals, she became anxious and agitated and experienced nausea. Her accident occurred in a compact-sized car, and she developed a phobia of driving or riding in small cars, which she considered unsafe. She also had phobic anxiety of expressways, heavily trafficked streets, and enclosed places, especially if exit from the small enclosure was impaired or blocked.

After the acute crisis had passed and the physical effects of the trauma had gradually subsided, the young woman continued to experience anxiety symptoms. During the day she was pathologically preoccupied with the accident and at night she had nightmares. The patient's memory for the details of the auto crash was remarkable, and she frequently fantasized the horrifying aspects of the entire traumatic incident, often elaborating and speculating upon a more devastating outcome. At the end of these rampant reveries, she often experienced an anxiety attack or intense discomfort. She was hypervigilant when encountering situations she thought dangerous, and for the first time in her life was cautious and restrained. Competition in gymnastics was discontinued since she felt weakened by her traumatic experience. She felt ugly and unattractive and was hypersensitive about minute scars on her face and body. Headaches, pain, and physical discomfort were a constant reminder of the traumatic incident, and she was puzzled by the persistence of these body aches. As time passed, these physical symptoms attenuated to some extent, but they were still present in varying degrees 18 months following the accident. She was suffering from symptoms of anxiety and depression, but the patient did not discuss this with any of her physicians, fearing they would think her insane. She confided in her attorney who was familiar with PTSD, and he referred her for psychiatric consultation.

During the psychiatric evaluation, the patient in the above history was asked to fill out a Symptom Inventory Checklist (Chapter 10) and an Anxiety Source Profile (ASP-Tables 2-2 to 2-4) and to check only those ASP items that caused anxiety following the accident. The ASP helped to identify those environmental, encephalic, and endogenous events that still served to stimulate and maintain pathologic anxiety.

Environmental Events

On the Environmental section of the ASP (Table 2-2), the patient in the above history checked the following items that elicited much (4) or very much (5) anxiety: being alone; crossing streets; journeys by car, train, airplane, bus, or boat; weapons; sick people; being in an elevator; enclosed places; doctors; being seen unclothed; leaving home; physical examinations; heavy traffic; expressways; noises; courtrooms; and judges or law-yers (she was involved in a personal injury suit and frequently had to relate the history of her accident to her attorneys and others).

The trauma that the young woman experienced impacted on all five of her senses. Stimulation of proprioceptive pathways initiated her traumatic experience when she felt a slight bump, "like a tire blowing out." Visual impressions impacted traumatically when she turned and looked out the rear window of the car and saw huge headlights within an enormous truck grill. Proprioceptive pathways were again stimulated when the truck hit the vehicle, tumbling it end over end. Pain and the taste of blood suffused her mind when her body and face violently struck the dashboard of the car. As the car careened against the guardrail of the elevated expressway, more visual impressions increased her fear as she saw the ground 30 feet below and imagined the car plummeting through the railing, killing her. As the car bounced off the railing and began to roll over and over, she was tossed "like a rag doll" from one side of the automobile to the other, further aggravating her proprioceptive trauma. The environment begot more proprioceptive trauma when her hair became tangled beneath the wreckage of the car, causing intense scalp pain and immobilization. Olfaction, the smell of gasoline, contributed to the trauma as the overturned car began leaking fuel and she feared an explosion and fire. Finally, the sight of the enormous front wheels of the truck and the automobile interior splattered with blood caused her to scream hysterically. During the accident the rending and scraping of metal and the sound of glass breaking were auditory sensations associated with the trauma. Visual, auditory, olfactory, taste, and proprioceptive stimuli impacted greatly upon the patient during the course of her accident. Although the accident lasted only about a minute, all five of her senses were stimulated and constituted the environmental trauma.

Encephalic Events

On the Encephalic Section of the ASP (Table 2-3), the patient checked that she spent much (4) or very much (5) time thinking about or visualizing the following subjects: dying; death or illness; being out of control; panic; injury; violence; being trapped; explosions; accidents, and impending doom.

Although the accident lasted a short time, the patient related that "the entire incident appeared to be in slow motion." The temporal sequence and the minute details of the accident were firmly and almost indelibly im-

TABLE 2–2
Anxiety Source Profile I: Environmental Events

Check the appropriate column by marking an O to indicate the degree of anxiety (nervousness, discomfort, or fear) that the item cuased you *before* the accident or traumatic incident. Next check X for the degree of anxiety (nervousness, discomfort, fear) that the item has caused you *following* the accident or traumatic incident.

	1. *Not at All*	*2.* *A Little*	*3.* *A Fair Amount*	*4.* *Much*	*5.* *Very Much*
1. Being alone					
2. Speaking in public					
3. Urinating in public bathrooms					
4. Eating in public					
5. Writing in front of others					
6. Crossing streets					
7. People who seem insane					
8. Taking a test					
9. Dentists					
10. Storms					
11. Worms					
12. Receiving injections					
13. Strangers					
14. Journeys by car					
15. Journeys by train					
16. Journeys by airplane					
17. Journeys by bus					
18. Journeys by boat					
19. Crowds					
20. Cats					
21. Birds					
22. Dogs					
23. Harmless snakes					
24. Mice or rats					
25. Insects					
26. Harmless spiders					
27. Fish					
28. Sight of deep water					
29. Weapons					
30. Dirt, germs					

TABLE 2–2, continued

	1. Not at All	2. A Little	3. A Fair Amount	4. Much	5. Very Much
31. Fire					
32. Sick people					
33. Being critized					
34. Being touched by others					
35. Being in an elevator					
36. Angry people					
37. Parting from friends					
38. Enclosed places					
39. Darkness					
40. Nude men					
41. Nude women					
42. Doctors					
43. Making decisions					
44. Being with a member of the opposite sex					
45. Large open spaces					
46. Being seen unclothed					
47. Taking medicine					
48. Ministers or priests					
49. Funerals					
50. Police					
51. Leaving home					
52. Physical examinations					
53. Marriage					
54. Insecticides					
55. Vomiting					
56. Bridges					
57. Lights					
58. Heavy traffic					
59. Expressways					
60. Odors or fumes					
61. Static electricity					
62. Being in public places					
63. Attending meetings					
64. Waiting in lines					
65. Swimming					
66. Courtrooms					

TABLE 2–2, continued

	1. Not at All	2. A Little	3. A Fair Amount	4. Much	5. Very Much
67. Judges or lawyers					
68. Body excretions (mucus, urine, feces)					
69. Telephones					
70. Procrastination					
71. Food					
72. Failure					
73. Noises					
74. Poisons					
75. Masturbation					
76. Heights					

Source: Adapted from *Stress Strategies: The Treatment of the Anxiety Disorders* (Scrignar 1983).

pressed upon her mind. Each day she spent considerable time thinking about and visualizing various aspects of the trauma, with the addendum that she might have been more seriously injured or killed. Like the replaying of a video tape, she reexperienced the trauma many times in her imagination. Retraumatization, the constant replaying of the video tapes in her mind, resulted in a hyperactive autonomic nervous system and a chronic state of anxiousness. Her encephalic activity served to perpetuate the effects of her trauma, thereby maintaining symptoms of PTSD. Even her sleep was plagued by negative encephalic activity (nightmares) that reflected her preoccupation with the trauma during the waking state. As the young woman visualized, talked, and thought about the accident or various aspects of it, anxiety was generated. The patient, however, did not make this correlation. Like a moth attracted to flame, the patient, it seemed, could not escape from her obsessions about the accident. Many things reminded her of the trauma. The sight of large trucks or small automobiles, expressways, sudden noises, the screech of tires, the sight of blood, television programs or movies portraying accidents or violent acts, and many other associations to the surroundings where the accident took place elicited anxiety-evoking encephalic activity. Like a cat in an experimental cage, the young woman

TABLE 2–3
Anxiety Source Profile II: Encephalic Activities

Check the column O that most accurately indicates the *time* you spent thinking or visualizing about the following subjects *before* the accident or traumatic incident. Next check the column X which most accurately indicates the *time* you spend thinking about these subjects *following* the accident or traumatic incident.

	1. *Not at All*	*2.* *A Little*	*3.* *A Fair Amount*	*4.* *Much*	*5.* *Very Much*
1. Dying					
2. Disease or illness					
3. Insanity					
4. Homosexuality					
5. Being out of control					
6. Panic					
7. Injury					
8. Being contaminated					
9. Violence					
10. Making mistakes					
11. Being trapped					
12. Embarrassment or humiliation					
13. Making decisions					
14. Being unworthy					
15. Explosions					
16. Being assaulted (or raped)					
17. Being victimized by a criminal					
18. Rejection or disapproval					
19. Sexual performance					
20. Evil					
21. Accidents					
22. Going crazy					
23. Impending doom					

Source: Adapted from *Stress Strategies: The Treatment of the Anxiety Disorders* (Scrignar 1983).

responded predictably and adversely to these stimuli and, as if on cue, automatically played the video tapes of her mind, repeating the traumatic experience. As retraumatization occurred, replete with the signs and symptoms of PTSD, her condition became chronic.

Endogenous Sensations

On the Endogenous sensations section of the ASP (Table 2-4) the patient checked that she experienced the following sensations or feelings much (4) or very much (5) of the time: nausea; heart beating fast; tightness of the chest; headaches; pain; dizziness; feelings of fainting; trembling; crawling sensations on the skin; feeling unreal or like another person; feeling angry, and light-headedness.

Immediately following the accident, pain and discomfort were significant sequelae. The young woman suffered from numerous cuts, bruises, and puncture wounds. Her jaw was bruised, teeth were loosened, one hip joint was extremely tender; muscles throughout her body were extremely sore. With the passage of time, headaches and nausea were an almost daily occurrence and joint and muscular pain continued. Any experience of pain or discomfort in any part of her body acted as a pernicious reminder of disability owing to the accident. Endogenous events, even normal physiological sensations, were misinterpreted as residual, perhaps permanent, injuries sustained in the accident. Pain augured thoughts and images of her trauma and permanent disablement. The uncomfortable endogenous sensations, whether due to soft tissue damage or to anxiety, stimulated encephalic activity that resulted in more anxiety and additional physical discomfort. The interplay between endogenous and encephalic events served to heighten and maintain anxiety, thus setting up a vicious Spiral Effect. The patient's symptoms became chronic, as did her PTSD.

CONCLUSIONS

Following exposure to trauma, there is a likelihood that a person may develop PTSD. Clinicians and lawyers when evaluating patients/ clients post-traumatically should apply the Traumatic Principle to sort out those persons who may have developed PTSD. Once a potential PTSD patient has been identified, the application of the concept of the Three E's further clarifies a person's psychological response to trauma. During the evaluation, the Spiral Effect, the concept of retraumatization, the ASP and

TABLE 2–4
Anxiety Source Profile III: Endogenous Sensations

Check the appropriate column by marking an O to indicate the *frequency* with which you experienced the following sensations or feelings *before* the accident or traumatic incident. Next check the appropriate column X to indicate the *frequency* with which you experienced the following symptoms *following* the accident or traumatic incident.

	1. *Not at All*	2. *A Little*	3. *A Fair Amount*	4. *Much*	5. *Very Much*
1. Smothering					
2. Choking					
3. Nausea and vomiting					
4. Heart beating fast					
5. Tightness of chest					
6. Headaches					
7. Pain					
8. Dizziness					
9. Tingly feelings					
10. Feeling faint					
11. Trembling					
12. Blurry vision					
13. Buzzing or ringing in ears					
14. Feeling hot or cold					
15. Crawling sensations on skin					
16. Feeling dirty					
17. Feeling unreal or like another person					
18. Sweating					
19. Urinating unpredictably					
20. Defecating unpredictably					
21. Feeling angry					
22. Light-headedness					

Source: Adapted from *Stress Strategies: The Treatment of the Anxiety Disorders* (Scrignar 1983).

the SIC assist the clinician in making the proper diagnosis. Reference to DSM-III-R refines the diagnosis, as criteria for PTSD are matched with the patient's symptoms. Not all persons develop PTSD following a trauma, but those that do must be identified and treated. In workers' compensation claims and personal injury suits, lawyers familiar with PTSD are best able to protect their clients' interests (Chapter 11).

THREE

TRAUMA AND PTSD

During the summer of 1928, a woman from Georgia and her two children attended the Christy Brothers Circus. Together they sat in the front row viewing an equestrian act. The show horses were prancing around the ring, nose to tail in a circle, responding to the ring master's exhortations and commands. As part of the act, the horses stopped, turned toward the center of the ring facing the trainer, and in unison reared up on their hind legs. One of the animals stopped in front of the woman, and with tail raised high, deposited unceremoniously several highly odoriferous pellets onto her lap. The horses continued the act, leaving the lady gasping. Was this sufficient trauma for the development of a PTSD?

The lady from Georgia was undeniably surprised, embarrassed, and flabbergasted when the horse defecated onto her lap. Her vexation may have turned to chagrin, and no doubt the horse's action ended her visit to the circus that day. An appeals court upheld "damages for humiliation and mental suffering when the defendant's horse evacuated bowels in her lap, verdict of $500 was authorized" (Christy Brothers Circus v. Turnage, 1928). In this oft-quoted case, it is hard to judge what psychological effect the deposit of horse feces had upon the woman, but it seems unlikely that a PTSD developed.

In the following case history involving another woman, the "trauma" was tragicomic. Did this lady develop a PTSD?

A graying middle-aged woman wishing to look younger purchased a nationally advertised hair rinse which was guaranteed to restore the normal color and luster of aging hair. Following the instructions on the label, the woman applied the hair rinse, carefully checking the time allotted by the manufacturer. While waiting for the hair rinse to impart a "natural color" to her hair, the woman noticed an itching sensation in her scalp which gradually grew uncomfortable. The intense itch progressed to a burning sensation, then to an almost unbearable searing pain throughout her scalp. Upset and alarmed, the woman quickly placed her head under the full force of the water faucet in an attempt to quench the pain. Eventually, her discomfort subsided and she lifted her head and stared at her image in the mirror above the basin. She saw an almost entirely bald scalp punctuated by several tufts of hair protruding at irregular angles.

This woman, attempting to curb Father Time's effect on her hair, experienced progressive discomfort leading to intense scalp pain and the loss of much hair. The proprioceptively perceived pain, together with visual evidence of damage to self, stimulated the autonomic nervous system, producing symptoms of pathologic anxiety. Subsequently, each time she looked at herself in the mirror or felt the remaining tufts of her hair, the traumatic incident was replayed in her mind. The "Traumatic Principle" was operative, and the woman developed the signs and symptoms of PTSD.

In the next case history the plaintiff's attorney pleaded that the junior executive developed PTSD. If you were a member of the jury, would you award damages?

A junior executive of a large corporation was attending a management seminar in New York City. Awakening in the morning, the 32-year-old executive went to the bathroom to perform his morning ablutions. After completing his bath, the junior executive attempted to open the door of his bathroom, but the door would not budge. Irritated because he desired to dress and make himself ready for a morning management session, the junior executive turned and twisted the doorknob, yanking it forcibly. The door still would not open. Annoyance turned to alarm as the man wrestled with the door, placing one foot on the

door frame and both hands on the doorknob which he twisted and
yanked violently, but to no avail. Panic stricken, the young
executive began to hyperventilate and feared that he might
suffocate and die. His heart began to pound wildly in his chest and
he struggled with his breath. Noticing a glimmer of light beneath
the door, he slumped flat on the floor and placed his lips against
the crack, sucking in air hungrily. Periodically he frantically
hollered and thumped the door. Finally, after two hours had
elapsed, a hotel maid opened the door from the outside.

Although true, the history involving the junior executive appears
unbelievable and the jury awarded no damages. In this case, the stressor or
trauma involved confinement in a hotel bathroom. Could this situation
cause the symptoms of suffocation and a fear of dying? The answer is yes,
but the mental disorder is a Panic Disorder, not a PTSD. The young man's
past psychiatric history revealed pre-existing panic attacks and claustro-
phobia. The young executive's symptoms were genuine as they related to
a Panic Disorder. Being locked in a hotel bathroom is annoying, inconven-
ient, and uncomfortable but hardly represents a realistic threat to life or
limb.

The following case history involved five bridge construction workers,
a cofferdam, a string of barges, and a tug boat. The scenario comprising this
trauma caused considerable chaos, but did it precipitate a PTSD in the
construction workers?

Five bridge construction workers were welding supports
within a cofferdam, a large cylindrical caisson-like structure used
to construct piers upon which a bridge is supported over water.
The cofferdam was about 80 feet in diameter and over 150 feet
high. After the cofferdam was built and securely fastened to the
bottom of the river, the water was pumped out so that men could
work within it, fastening steel rods preparatory to the pouring of
concrete. Moored to the side of the cofferdam was a rig barge,
upon which was set a 150 ton crane which was used to deliver
men and materials in and out of the cofferdam. The crane
operator, sitting high up in his cab, looked upstream and saw a
tugboat attempting to maneuver a string of barges between the
cofferdam and the eastbank of the Mississippi River. With fright,
the crane operator realized that the current of the river had caught
up the barges and a collision with the cofferdam was inevitable.
To avert a catastrophe, he alerted the men and they quickly exited

the cofferdam and clambered onto the deck of the rig barge. The men put on life jackets and looked with alarm at the oncoming barges. Moments before the collision, all of the men jumped into the Mississippi River. The barges struck and collapsed the cofferdam and the workers were sucked into the vortex of the swirling, muddy water. The men, tumbling in all directions, became disoriented in the darkness of the muddy Mississippi and their lungs were almost bursting from lack of air. Unexpectedly but fortunately, the buoyancy of the life jackets brought the men to the surface. Relief concerning survival was only momentary; the 150 ton crane toppled off the capsizing rig barge, causing a second suction which again drew the men under the water, but this time cables and debris from the crane and rig barge accompanied them. The men struggled to free themselves from the flotsam and cables, thought that their luck had run out and they would die by drowning. The second submersion mercifully was brief, and the life jackets lived up to its name. The survivors were collected by a passing boat and brought to shore where an ambulance awaited them. None of the men received any serious physical injuries and were discharged from the emergency room after examination.

Even the skeptical would have no difficulty diagnosing PTSD in the construction workers. The alarm sounded by the crane operator alerted everyone to danger. The sight of the barges bearing down on the cofferdam reinforced the idea of danger to life or limb. Submersion in water and lack of oxygen sent emergency proprioceptive impulses to the brain. The smell and taste of the muddy water containing petroleum products further increased fright. All five sensory modalities to the brain signaled a threat to existence. Although none of the men suffered any significant physical injury, all developed a PTSD.

An undramatic accident involving a fall from a slowly moving freight car caused injury and pain in a middle-aged railroad switchman. Examinations and laboratory tests were negative, causing doctors to conclude that the veteran railroad man was malingering. Was this man faking or suffering from PTSD or another disorder?

A 42-year-old switchman for a railroad had just signaled the engineer to start the train. As the freight cars began moving, the switchman put his foot on the first rung of the steel ladder attached to one of the freight cars and reached for the hand hold to pull himself up. The hand hold broke, sending the switchman sprawling backwards onto the ground. The small of his back hit the steel rail, and his head whipped backwards striking a railroad tie. Dazed, the man hollered for help and was assisted by fellow workers and taken to the supervisor's shack. He reported the accident to his superiors, stating that he felt okay but was experiencing some pain in his lower back. He was taken to a hospital where a physical examination, various x- rays, and laboratory tests revealed no fractures or serious injury. Subsequently, the man developed a partial paralysis of both lower extremities, but doctors were at a loss to explain the cause. All examinations, x-rays, and tests were negative. After 18 years of service on the railroad, the man could not return to work.

The seasoned railroad switchman did experience trauma to his back and head, and initially physicians thought that the partial paralysis of his lower extremities was due to a concussion of the spinal cord. Subsequent examinations failed to disclose any evidence of organic pathology. Malingering was suspected; however, the patient's character was not consistent with feigning, and a private investigator hired by the defense failed to disclose any evidence of malingering. When a symptom is judged not to be under voluntary control and cannot, after appropriate investigation, be explained by a known physical disorder or pathophysiological mechanism, the diagnosis of Conversion Disorder is warranted. PTSD would have been the wrong diagnosis for the railroad man.

THE IMPACT OF THE TRAUMA

The nature of the environmentally-induced stressor and especially its impact upon the body can vary according to the circumstances of the traumatic event. The trauma may result in severe, moderate, slight, or no physical injury. When severe injury results from a trauma and particularly when surgery or medical treatment is required, clinicians and casual observers have no difficulty comprehending the relationship between trauma and injury as it relates to pain and mental suffering. More difficult to understand are those cases which involve no or slight physical injury and yet persons continue to complain of incapacitating symptoms. This appears enigmatic because the patient's complaints and symptoms seem out of proportion to the actual trauma. Emphasis is one-sided, however, when one considers only the nature of the trauma and its impact on the physical structure of the body. Actually, a trauma impacting upon an individual may produce one of three possible effects: (1) physical injury with no PTSD; (2) PTSD with no physical injury; or (3) physical injury and PTSD (Figure 3-1).

Trauma and Physical Injury

Commonly following a trauma, if the victim consults a doctor or lawyer, there is evidence of physical injury. Pain and physical discomfort in these cases represent the subjective or psychological response to injury. Ordinarily, as recovery occurs, pain and suffering diminish with treatment and time. In those cases of incomplete recovery, the residual disability may include physical limitations, chronic pain, mental suffering, and possibly depression. Pain and suffering in and of itself, however, do not constitute PTSD.

Trauma and PTSD

If the conditions of the Traumatic Principle (Chapter 2) are fulfilled, any trauma can precipitate PTSD. The individual must have experienced an event that is psychologically traumatic, involving a realistic threat to one's life or physical integrity. Following exposure to the stressor, the victim develops the cluster of signs and symptoms as listed in DSM-III-R (Chapter 1). Physical injury is not essential and sometimes only brief exposure to an environmental trauma can initiate PTSD. If the environmental stimulus impacts one or more of the five sensory pathways to the brain and is perceived as dangerous by the victim, it can be regarded as a trauma which can precipitate PTSD in a vulnerable person without evidence of physical injury.

Physical Injury and PTSD

It has been seen that a trauma can inflict physical injury involving pain and suffering but not a PTSD, or it can precipitate PTSD without physical injury. Commonly, a trauma produces both physical injury and PTSD. The physical injury and the stress disorder are produced by the same trauma, but are independent of one another. When physical injury and PTSD coexist, confusion often arises when clinicians or lawyers mistakenly equate the emotional sequelae of physical injury with the signs and symptoms of PTSD. Physical limitations, pain, suffering (mental anguish), and depression correlate with physical injury. Although sharing the trauma as a precipitant, PTSD is an independent mental disorder characterized by specific symptoms. However, a relationship does exist between pain associated with physical injury and PTSD. Pain and physical discomfort remind patients of their trauma, and these endogenous sensations stimulate encephalic activity (intrusive thoughts, flashbacks) causing retraumatization and intensification of PTSD symptoms. Because of this mechanism, chronic pain portends a poor prognosis. Unless pain can be controlled, ameliorated, or eliminated, it is extremely difficult to treat the companion problem of PTSD.

It is the clinician's responsibility to sort out the symptoms during a mental status examination and explain the relationship between physical injury and PTSD to patients during treatment and to lawyers, judges, and juries during forensic proceedings. The use of the Three E's construct and

FIGURE 3–1

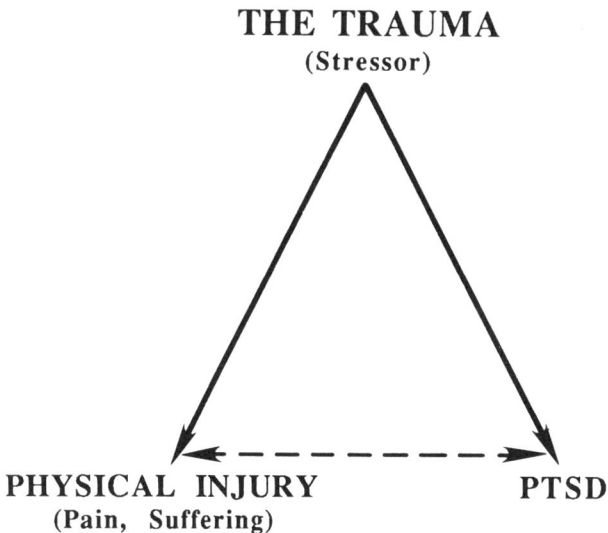

THE TRAUMA
(Stressor)

PHYSICAL INJURY   PTSD
(Pain, Suffering)

Figure 3-1 helps to explain the relationship between physical injury and PTSD. At the same time the chart illustrates that the two disorders are distinctly different and may occur independently of one another.

TYPES OF TRAUMA

PTSD may be precipitated by many different types of trauma. DSM-III-R states that the type of trauma or stressor producing this syndrome would be markedly distressing to almost anyone and is usually experienced with intense fear, terror, and helplessness. The psychologically distressing stressor should be outside the range of usual human experiences and common occurrences such as simple bereavement, chronic illness, business losses, and marital conflict are excluded as precipitants. The most common stressors which cause PTSD involve a serious threat to one's life or physical integrity or a serious threat or harm to one's family and friends. Sudden destruction of one's home or community or seeing persons who have been seriously injured or killed as the result of an accident or physical violence is also sufficient trauma to precipitate PTSD. Sometimes learning about a serious threat or harm to a close friend or relative is enough trauma to initiate a PTSD. DSM-III-R states that, "The trauma may be experienced alone, or in the company of groups of people. Stressors producing this disorder include natural disasters, accidental disasters, or deliberately caused disasters. Some stressors produce the disorder frequently, and others produce it occasionally. Sometimes there is a concomitant physical component of the trauma which may even involve direct damage to the central nervous system. The disorder is apparently more severe and longer lasting when the stressor is of human design." The following types of trauma with clinical examples illustrating a person's response to trauma may be helpful to clinicians and lawyers in identifying potential patients or clients.

Vehicular Trauma

Traumas involving vehicles such as automobiles, trucks, airplanes, or boats, may result in death or serious injury. Many survivors later develop PTSD, particularly if the trauma represented a realistic threat to life or limb and the person was fully aware of the potential for death or injury to self or others. The recognition of danger may precede, occur concurrently, or follow exposure to the traumatic incident.

Case Illustrations

(1) A middle-aged secretary encountered a severe thunderstorm with violent winds and torrents of rain while driving home from work. She was driving on an expressway when suddenly her car engine stalled. She had been driving very slowly owing to poor visibility, and thus her automobile did not have enough momentum for her to switch lanes. She was stranded in the middle of the expressway. Realizing the precariousness of her situation, the secretary turned on the flasher lights and also pumped the brake pedal, hoping that both would alert oncoming drivers and prevent a rear end collision. At the same time, she frantically tried to restart her automobile. As she looked in the rear-view mirror, she saw a car rapidly approaching, the driver apparently oblivious to her plight and not responsive to her signals of distress. With mounting fear she braced herself for the inevitable collision that occurred a few seconds later. Unhurt except for some strained muscles, the secretary experienced severe palpitations, labored breathing, and extreme trembling as she marveled that she was still alive. Following this experience she displayed the signs and symptoms of PTSD with phobic anxiety about driving, especially on expressways, at night and in the rain.

(2) A middle-aged businessman returning home from a meeting was a passenger on a commercial jet. The jet had taxied to the end of the runway and was commencing its takeoff when suddenly the landing gear collapsed and the airplane began skidding down the runway. The piercing sound of metal collapsing and rending and the frenzied screams of frightened passengers filled the air as the jet slid to a stop. Efficiently and calmly, the flight attendants opened all safety exits, prepared the exit chute, and authoritatively instructed all passengers to disembark. Escape from the damaged airplane was conducted without any loss of life or serious injury to anyone. As the passengers were herded into a nearby hangar, the disabled aircraft suddenly exploded and burst into flames. The businessman, shaken by the entire experience, looked upon the flaming wreckage with horror that escalated into panic when he considered that "but for the grace of God" he could have been inside the airplane at that time. The smoke and flames of the burning jet, suggesting Dante's inferno, became etched in the mind of the man. He later accepted free drinks from the airline but declined the offer of a ticket on the next flight and returned home by train. He developed PTSD with a phobia of flying.

(3) A 26-year-old seaman was aboard a jack-up barge which was in an oilfield about a mile and a half offshore in the Gulf of Mexico. The jack-up barge was underway, and the seaman was sleeping on a bunk located in the middle deck of the boat. The barge lurched and rolled to the left, causing the sailor to fall out of his bunk onto the deck. Sleepy and dazed, he looked out of the window, "to verify my senses," and saw that the barge was leaning about thirty to forty degrees. The young man, who had worked for most of his life on boats, immediately sensed that something was seriously wrong. He scrambled to his feet and opened the door leading out of the crew quarters. Water surged into the room, and he quickly closed the door and climbed to the high side of the jack-up barge, his eyes frantically searching for some means of escape. The barge suddenly shifted so that the beam was vertical to the water, and a window on the submerged starboard side of the barge burst. The pressure of the entering water slammed up against the young seaman's chest, pinning him to the wall. He remembers thinking to himself, "I can't move and I know I am going to die." He called on God and Jesus Christ, and he held his breath as the water filled the room. Somehow the door leading out of the crew's quarters burst open, and the sailor miraculously was swept out into the hallway, and he floated to the top of the passage which was above the level of the water. As he gasped air hungrily, thanking God for his salvation, he apprehensively surveyed his situation. He was still trapped and there appeared to be no way out of the barge. "I was scared, shaking, panicky, and very cold," reported the young man. After he calmed down somewhat, he noticed a board floating on the water. Grasping it, he managed to pound against the walls of the crew house, creating an opening. He climbed out and clung to the side of the barge, which was rolling and pitching in three to six foot seas. Within an hour, a Coast Guard vessel arrived and rescued the young seaman. He was taken ashore to a hospital where a physical examination disclosed a laceration on the middle finger of his right hand, which was sutured and bandaged. He was given some medication for pain, discharged, and sent home. Subsequently, symptoms of nervousness, insomnia, nightmares, flashbacks of the traumatic incident, and a phobia of working aboard a ship led to a psychiatric consultation and the diagnosis of PTSD.

These case histories illustrate how a car, an airplane, and a boat can serve as the setting for accidents which precipitated a PTSD. Although none of the victims sustained serious physical injuries, all were incapacitated to some extent by the PTSD. In addition, all three suffered from stress symptoms which interfered with work and pleasurable living. The secretary began to miss work because of her refusal to drive in the rain. Even on dry days, the secretary avoided expressways and traveled on service roads, which lengthened her drive to and from the city. The businessman's refusal to fly led to missed business opportunities and loss of income. Unemployment was the lot of the sailor who refused to go aboard ships even though he knew no other line of work except the sea.

Industrial Trauma

Industrial settings such as manufacturing plants, oil refineries, construction sites, and many other blue collar work sites are places with a high potential for accidents. Heavy equipment, moving machinery, flammable gases or solvents, caustic chemicals, together with the carelessness of others are environmental influences that can be harmful or deadly to workers. Although safety regulations and procedures are mandated and monitored by private and public agencies, accidents still occur with regularity. When a worker is injured, it is understandable that the physical needs of the patient generally supersedes attention to the psychological sequelae of the trauma. After the physical injuries have been treated, however, clinicians must not ignore any symptoms of PTSD which may be present. Unfortunately, some clinicians fail to appreciate the psychological after-effects of trauma and may grow disdainful of patients who complain of emotional symptoms, especially when physical injuries have healed.

> An oil refinery worker in his early twenties was told by his foreman to unbolt a valve cover on a pipeline that connected two large petroleum storage tanks. The young man proceeded to unscrew the bolts, and when the last bolt was removed, the valve cover blew off, narrowly missing him. A blast of hot, flammable gas struck him in the chest and arms. In shock, the worker looked down and saw his clothes on fire and the skin of his chest melting "like candle wax." He was a human torch, screaming in pain and fright, haphazardly running in circles. He was pursued by his fellow workers who corralled him, doused his flaming clothes, and called for medical assistance. Many months later, when he had recovered from his burns and was pronounced physically fit by his doctors, he was told he could return to work. Overlooked,

45

however, was the patient's extreme anxiety and phobic avoidance of all things flammable. Even the sight of a burning cigarette or an unlit match caused flashbacks, tachycardia, hyperventilation, and hyperhidrosis. Work in an oil refinery was impossible since he had developed PTSD with a severe phobia of fire and all things potentially flammable.

Chemical Substances

The environment contains many chemical substances that can act as traumatic agents if inhaled, ingested, or absorbed by the skin. It must be remembered that any chemical substance which has the capacity for harm is capable of precipitating a stress disorder. In accidents involving aromatic chemicals, pungent and toxic gases may be inhaled, causing irritation of the lungs. Following exposure to noxious fumes, some persons exhibit emotional symptoms after physical symptoms have cleared.

A 38-year-old supervisor working in a Texas oilfield was investigating a broken pipe at a pump station. With an assistant, the supervisor waded through a foot of water attempting to locate the source of the rupture. Hydrogen sulfide gas had suffused the atmosphere of the pump house. When the supervisor noticed the gas, he ordered his subordinate to leave the building. Eyes streaming tears and coughing violently, the supervisor cleared his head and lungs in the open air. When his helper did not appear outside the pump house in a few minutes, the supervisor re-entered the hydrogen sulfide-filled room and saw his assistant lying on the floor unconscious. Grabbing the man under his arms, the supervisor attempted to drag his helper out of the pump house, but he was overcome by the toxic gas and collapsed. By chance, the supervisor's wife who worked for the same company was in the area looking for her husband as a lunch companion. Upon entering the pump house, she saw the still forms of her husband and his helper and immediately sounded an alarm. The two men were rescued and brought out into the open air. An emergency vehicle arrived, and the men were revived with respirators and taken to a nearby hospital where they were treated for hydrogen sulfide intoxication and discharged two days later.

Following the toxic gas incident the supervisor lost enthusiasm for his job. He refused to carry a beeper and became anxious whenever the telephone rang in his house, fearing that he would be told to investigate an emergency in the oilfield. For the first time in his life, the supervisor hated going to work. He experienced sleep disturbance, nightmares, and high anxiety and was extremely irritable. Marital conflicts, diminished sexual desire, and family problems developed as the supervisor dwelled on the accident, frequently commenting that he easily could have died. The gassing incident morbidly preoccupied the supervisor and he became depressed. Because his training and work experience did not prepare him for any other vocation, the supervisor saw no solution to his dilemma and he trudged to work each day feeling very hopeless. Despite the fact that he had several acute anxiety attacks while at work, the supervisor refused to see a physician. Five months after the accident the supervisor committed suicide.

The preceding case history was pieced together utilizing techniques of a psychiatric autopsy. The wife, children, and co-workers were interviewed at length to determine the state of the supervisor's mind, both before and after the trauma. No neurological evaluation was performed before his death, and at autopsy the brain was grossly intact, but microscopic examination was not done. The retrospective diagnosis in this case was PTSD with possible Organic Mental Syndrome. Phobic anxiety of the workplace and severe depression were secondary diagnoses. No psychiatric diagnosis was made while the supervisor was alive. Proper diagnosis and treatment could have prevented this suicide.

A 53-year-old nurse with a terminal illness developed renal failure that required kidney dialysis. The nurse accepted her illness philosophically and remained optimistic. Although her twice-weekly trips to the renal dialysis unit interfered with life to some extent, she managed to function as wife and mother to her family. One day while being dialyzed, the nurse noted a "formaldehyde taste" and reported this to clinical personnel at the unit. It was discovered that by mistake formalin had been introduced into the dialysate solution. The dialysis was immediately terminated for that day. The nurse became extremely agitated, and upon hearing of the error wondered how such a mistake could have been made. Her plight was such that she could not drive home and her husband was summoned. Following the incident, the nurse became gravely disturbed and was unable to carry on with her usual household duties. She complained of intense anxiety, insomnia, nightmares, and other symptoms related to her trauma. A "personality change" was noted by members of her family, and she never functioned normally again. She could not drive her car, cook meals, or care for the house. With great difficulty and in a state of intense anxiety, the nurse was forced by necessity to continue dialysis. Her condition quickly deteriorated and she died within two months. She had developed PTSD following the accidental addition of formalin into the dialysis solution. Although she was suffering from a terminal illness, one can deduce that the stress disorder probably hastened her death.

Chemical substances emanating from the environment can act as primary traumatic stimuli (Chapter 4). These substances, of course, produce certain physiological changes within the body and act directly on the nervous system to produce symptoms of anxiety and on occasion organic pathology. A combination of environmental and endogenous events better defines the traumatic stimulus; however, since chemicals must be inhaled, ingested, absorbed by the skin, or injected, it seems appropriate to list environment as the primary source of the trauma.

Criminal Assaults

The unlawful use of coercion or battery upon an individual is an odious act that creates anxiety and is capable of initiating PTSD. A blow to the body by fist or bludgeon, the sight of a weapon aimed at one's head, or verbal outbursts threatening injury or death constitute environmental traumas that are associated with criminal conduct. Burglars, armed robbers, rapists, and other miscreants who impose their will by force can terrorize their victims. When perceived as a threat to life or limb, assaults stimulate the victim's autonomic nervous system, producing high levels of anxiety and in some people a PTSD may result.

> Following a party late one night, a 23-year-old medical student was walking down a darkened street, attempting to locate his car, when he encountered a stranger. The man reached into his pocket, withdrew a handgun, pointed it at the medical student's chest, and menacingly demanded money. The frightened student desperately attempted to explain that he never carried much money and was merely trying to find his automobile in order to drive home. The gunman raised the pistol to the medical student's head and with penetrating expletives threatened death unless money was produced. The medical student urinated in his pants as he helplessly pleaded with the armed robber, begging him not

to take his life. The gunman again demanded money and pulled back the hammer on the pistol. The medical student, now trembling violently, offered the hold-up man all of his possessions. The robber rifled through the student's pockets, taking keys, coins, and a wallet. He then ordered the student to turn around and start running as fast as he could, warning him not to look back. The student complied and began running, fearing a bullet in his back. The medical student subsequently developed PTSD.

Sometimes a criminal assault can result in physical injury and PTSD.

A 32-year-old man was awakened late one night by the sound of a roaring car engine. The man put on his bathrobe, told his wife to watch their two children, and left to investigate. His condominium was surrounded by a wall punctuated with a large, solid gate and a window at eye level. The man stepped from the house, walked to the gate, peered out, and saw a shotgun protruding from the passenger window of a car, pointing at him. He heard the blast of the shotgun and felt stinging, burning sensations in his body. He turned and ran to the open door of his home and remaining outside slammed it to prevent any intruders from entering and harming his wife and children. Running to the side of the house, he heard the automobile accelerating and feared that his unknown assailants were tracking him. In response to the noise of the shotgun, a neighbor opened his side door and the wounded man hurried inside. Although not seriously injured, the man was bleeding freely from superficial wounds caused by shotgun pellets. In addition to the physical injury, the man also developed PTSD with a phobia of darkness and weapons.

Clinicians and attorneys should suspect PTSD in those crime victims who remain obsessively preoccupied with the criminal assault beyond one month. Flashbacks of the criminal act, nightmares portraying violence, and a phobia or avoidance of the place where the criminal assault occurred usually develop. Disruption of family life and diminished productivity at work are often reported post-traumatically by a crime victim. The following case history illustrates a type of criminal assault which has become much too common—armed robbery in one's home.

Ray, a 46-year-old married accountant, had been reading a book in his study and had fallen asleep when he was aroused by the sounds of an automobile driving past his house. He rose from his chair and walked drowsily across the hall. Looking up, he was abruptly confronted by a man wearing a ski mask and wielding a chrome-plated 38-calibre pistol. Crouching in a marksman stance, the robber pointed the gun at Ray and blurted, "Don't make me kill you!" Quickly, without thinking, Ray bolted forward and seized the man's hands and wrestled with the intruder. The weapon discharged; the bullet harmlessly penetrated the wall of his bedroom. The scuffle continued and Ray struggled to get possession of the gun. The armed assailant tried to force the pistol towards Ray's abdomen. Terror- stricken, Ray thought, "He's trying to shoot me in the stomach." Looking closely at the man's masked face, he recognized a neighbor's 17-year-old son. In a strong, commanding voice, Ray ordered the boy to stop struggling and to give him the gun, which surprisingly the subdued robber did. The police were called; the young man was arrested and taken to jail.

That night Ray could not sleep. As he ruminated about the incident, he had "chilling thoughts" that he or a member of his family could easily have been murdered. Later, Ray experienced "flashbacks" of the incident, nightmares, distress when in the room of his home where the incident took place, feelings of detachment, diminished interest in life, and a sense of a foreshortened future. Decreased productivity at work, irritability, and marital tension soon developed. Ray's symptoms continued and intensified when he testified at the criminal trial against his neighbor's son. He ignored pleas from the defendant's grandfather and father to drop the charges and was determined to seek retribution. The youth was found guilty and sentenced to prison. Ray also filed a civil suit against the boy's father and the third party insurer, and was awarded damages. After the civil trial, Ray's symptoms continued and he remained in psychotherapy.

Sexual Assaults

Rape, whether it be heterosexual or homosexual, constitutes a horrendous invasion of one's privacy and person, with consequences that are injurious to mind and body. The element of unwilling submission to another person's sexual demands sets the stage for a traumatic experience. Failure to comply with a rapist's commands has deleterious consequences ranging from fear, pain, injury, mutilation, to death. Even the verbal threat of violence in the absence of any visible weapon can activate a victim's nervous system, producing panic or extreme anxiety. There is no question that all rape victims suffer emotionally and some bear physical as well as mental scars. Rape trauma syndrome (Burgess, 1983), a term applied to the emotional sequelae of rape, is actually a PTSD precipitated by a sexual assault. Rape fulfills the requirement of the Traumatic Principle and the PTSD criteria of DSM-III-R. Intrusive thoughts and nightmares centered around the rape theme interfere with normal living and affect future sexual behavior. The case history in Chapter 14 illustrates the extensiveness of rape trauma and its impact on a woman's life.

Sexual assaults upon children can be divided into two distinct categories. The first is similar to coercive rape and involves the use of physical force or even torture. In these cases strangers usually abduct unsuspecting children, take them to an isolated place, and inflict sexual violence. It requires no imagination to appreciate the traumatic effects of such an experience upon children. The signs and symptoms exhibited by physical and sexually abused children fall clearly into a pattern of PTSD. More complicated and less obvious are the traumatic effects of sexual activity subtly imposed on children by trusted friends or relatives. In this latter category, the sexual assault is disguised by an atmosphere of friendliness, gifts or money, and is presented in the form of a sex game or play. The willingness to please adults and pleasurable sexual stimulation which sometimes occurs, may soothe the child-victim's apprehension (Swan, 1985). In many cases, it is only when the pedophiliac's unlawful behavior comes under scrutiny, arrests are made, and children are brought forward to bear witness against the defendant that stress occurs. Police interrogation, a criminal trial, and the label "victim of a child molester" may prolong anxiety and stress related to the sexual encounter (Scrignar, 1968). Incest is essentially a family problem (Renshaw, 1982) which may involve coercion or persuasion and precipitate PTSD or it may not. A careful appraisal of children involved in sexual assaults by relatives or friends will reveal guilt, a sense of betrayal, feelings of rejection, and an expectation of punishment. Incest always produces psychopathology but not necessarily a PTSD. The application of the Traumatic Principle helps to sort out the responses of children to sexual assaults.

Terrorism

Terrorists impose upon hostages a display of irresistible strength with the threat of annihilation. This stressor is magnified by the unpredictability of physical force which is made worse when random, unprovoked, and meaningless outbursts of violence aimed at one member of a hostage group erupts. Terrorization is the systematic application of this force which overwhelms the victim's capacity for willing their own behavior. The fear of imminent destruction is accompanied by a sense of powerlessness and unpredictability (Fields, 1982). Four basic threats have been described which are common to all acts of terrorism: (1) threat to life; (2) threat to bodily integrity; (3) threat to security; and (4) threat to self-image (Lazarus, 1971). These threats, redefined as stressors, certainly can precipitate PTSD, not only in a hostage but in relatives who later learn about the threat or harm from news sources.

The following is a summary of a well-publicized terrorist-hostage incident which began on June 14, 1985, and ended 17 days later (Washington Post, 1986).

> Navy diver, Clinton Suggs, was one of the passengers aboard TWA's Flight 847 when it was hijacked on June 14, 1985. Suggs, apparently because he was a member of the U.S. Armed Services, was beaten and threatened with death by terrorists. Bound and blindfolded, he and a fellow Navy diver were singled out of the group of passengers, physically abused and pistol whipped. To emphasize the seriousness of their demands, the terrorists shot and killed Suggs' buddy and threw him out of the airplane onto the tarmac. The terrorists then pointed a gun at Suggs' head and yelled, "Another one in five minutes." Only the intervention of the flight purser saved Suggs' life.
>
> A year after the incident when he was reassigned to Iceland, Suggs said he was "seized with a sense of becoming unglued." He feared the airplane flight and said, "I had thought I was back to a place where I was comfortable, but I found that as I reached the point of deployment, the stress, the anger, the terror started to come back. I found myself drinking to numb myself. I found myself getting into a shell, snapping at my wife." Boarding the airplane for Iceland, Suggs said he was terrified. "You imagine the worse, you know it's not going to happen again, but you still imagine it will. You feel it. You work your way up to a panic." No doubt Navy diver, Clinton Suggs, developed a PTSD as a result of the hostage incident. A phobia of flying, marital disharmony, detachment, extreme anxiety, alcohol abuse, dissociative episodes, and irritability all plagued Suggs following the hostage incident.

Torture

If one were to devise a fiendish laboratory experiment to determine the effects of various stressors upon an individual, systematic torture would be the undisputed choice. Although enemies have tortured one another since the dawn of civilization, the so called "Torture Syndrome" as a clinical entity has only been recognized for the last 30 years in the national and international systems of classification of diseases and in the standard textbooks of psychiatry (Allodi and Cowgill, 1982). Methods of torture are divided into physical and psychological, and the variety of torture techniques is limited only by the macabre imagination of the torturer. In a preliminary report titled, "Medical and Psychological Sequelae in Latin American Survivors of Torture", the authors (Quiroga, Deustch, and O'Grady, 1982) described the following methods of torture as related by survivors. Examples of physical abuse include: severe and prolonged beatings, electric torture ("Picana Electrica"), stretching ("Potro"), submersion ("Submarine"), hanging-suspension ("LaBandera"), burns of the skin, . . . holding weights in the hands and standing in the same position for hours ("Planton"), sexual torture, soles of the feet are beaten with a cane or stick ("Phalanga"), the saw-horse—the victim straddles an iron bar which is moved violently back and forth for hours ("El Caballete"), blows to the external ear with cupped hands ("Telephone"), and amputation of nonessential body parts.

METHODS OF PSYCHOLOGICAL ABUSE *

1. **Isolation**
   Isolation must last for at least three days or longer. It may be complete or semi, or an entire group may be cut off from the external world.
2. **Induced Disability**
   Exhaustion, fatigue, and weakness may be induced by depravation of food (for at least three or four days), water (for 48 hours or more), or sleep (for several days).
3. **Monopolization of**
   a. Perception—movement is restricted, darkness (hooded, blindfolded), bright lights, or monotonous sounds.

---

* Source: Quiroga, Deustch, and O'Grady, 1982

    b. Threats—threats of death to the victim. Threats of death against the victim's family. Vague threats. Sham executions. Witnessing torture.

    c. Degradation—personal hygiene is prevented. There is a denial of privacy. Insults (verbal abuse). Overcrowding. Excrement in food. Infected surroundings (lice). Undress.

4. **Occasional Indulgence**

Reward for partial compliance. Granting of occasional favors. Fluctuations in interrogative attitudes.

5. **Alteration of Consciousness**

Use of mind-altering drugs and occasionally hypnosis has been reported by some torture victims.

As reported in various studies, all torture victims suffered from a similar disorder characterized by severe anxiety, insomnia, nightmares (about persecution, violence, or their own torture experience), somatic symptoms of anxiety, phobias, suspiciousness and fearfulness (Allodi, 1982). Most torture victims in Allodi's study had physical damage as evidence of torture; surprisingly no patients exhibited hysterical elaborations of anxiety or dramatic and histrionic presentations of symptoms. The health of the victims prior to the persecution, imprisonment, or torture without exception was excellent, and no one reported previous psychiatric symptoms or treatment (Allodi and Cowgill, 1982). In addition to basic PTSD criteria, the investigators concluded that another basic diagnostic criterion of "Torture Syndrome" should include the lack of any apparent predisposition to a mental disorder. This is an interesting observation which lacks substantiation and requires further study.

According to Alllodi (1982), symptoms after torture fall into the following categories: (1) psychosomatic (pain, headaches, nervousness, insomnia, nightmares, panic, tremors, weakness, fainting, sweating); (2) behavioral and personality changes (withdrawal, irritability, aggressiveness, impulsiveness, suicidal intents, sexual dysfunction-severe), affective symptoms (depression, crying, fear, and anxiety); and (3) mental functioning impairment (confusion, disorientation, memory disturbance, loss of concentration, and attention). Torture victims can also suffer from physical damage including scars, burns, fractures, central nervous system symptoms, weight loss, and miscellaneous damage to physical integrity including broken feet, missing teeth, torn tendons, and skin rash.

Symptoms following torture clearly fit the diagnostic criteria of PTSD in DSM-III-R and the International Classification of Diseases of the World

Health Organization (ICD-9). Few clinicians would deny the existence of the "Torture Syndrome". Like a laboratory animal in a cage, the stressors and consequences of torture upon a victim are clear-cut. Worse than war, torture is an intentional trauma deliberately conceived by vile men to systematically cause pain and suffering to a selected individual and ultimately ending with the physical and psychological collapse of the victim. A sterile clinical term like PTSD seems inadequate to describe the horrifying aspects of the torture experience and its aftermath, but it is the mental disorder which results.

The Holocaust

A variant of torture, though less systematized, involves the political persecution and wanton disregard of life and human dignity of minority groups. Holocaust, which means "a thorough destruction especially by fire," is a term used almost exclusively to describe the extermination of six million Jews by Nazi Germany. The term could equally be applied to Cambodians, hundreds of thousands of whom were executed and still others who died of starvation and disease in brutal labor camps during the regime of Pol Pot from 1975 to 1979. It has been estimated that one to three million of Cambodia's seven million people died during this time, victims of a brutal government (Kinzie, 1986).

Holocaust victims are subjected to numerous stressors including: isolation and imprisonment, physical and psychological torture, malnutrition, exposure to extremes of temperature, degradation by captors, sexual abuse, and other deliberately inflicted torments. The stressors are almost constant. Survivors witness the disappearance and death of companions while waiting for their own death. Severe protracted stress of human design, whether it occurs in the death camps of Nazi Germany, the tropical forests of Cambodia, or in the Bataan death march in the Philippines during World War II, has a devastating effect upon survivors. Guilt about surviving when others have not or about behavior required for survival is a group phenomenon found in holocaust survivors. The psychological reactions of death camp victims is best described and defined under the heading—PTSD. The longevity of PTSD symptoms reported by Jewish holocaust victims, Cambodian refugees, and released POW's from World War II (Kluznik et al., 1986) attests to the malignity of the stress disorder. Among Jewish survivors and World War II veterans, some victims still display symptoms 40 years after their trauma.

War Trauma

As has been mentioned, throughout history wars have traumatized large numbers of people. The casualties of all wars include a significant number of soldiers and civilians who sustain not only physical injuries but also PTSD (Grinker and Spiegel, 1945; Kardiner and Spiegel, 1947; Figley, 1978). From DaCosta's Syndrome of the Civil War era to Post-Traumatic Stress Disorder of the Vietnam conflict, clinicians have observed and described the psychological signs and symptoms due to war trauma. There is abundant material available in the literature concerning the detrimental psychological effects of war upon combatants and civilians, and no attempt will be made to review them here. The machines of war, however, are not silent during peacetime, and accidents occur when military personnel are engaged in training exercises. The following case history illustrates a tragedy which could have been prevented if PTSD had been diagnosed.

Rick was a helicopter pilot and a captain in the U.S. Army. He had logged over 3,000 hours in Cobra helicopters and had served two tours of duty in Vietnam. Because of his expertise with helicopters, Rick was nicknamed "Captain Cobra," and following the Vietnam conflict, trained Army pilots to become instructors. One day while on a routine war training exercise, Rick's helicopter malfunctioned and began yawing violently. Flying at a low altitude, time was of the essence and Rick, who had experienced similar malfunctions, swore to himself and fought to gain control of the helicopter. Losing altitude, the ground loomed large and, despite Rick's efforts, the helicopter crashed. Upon impact, the shoulder harness failed and Rick's body was propelled forward against the control panel. Stunned but not unconscious, Rick felt intense pain in his left shoulder and back. Smelling smoke, he turned and saw flames leaping from the engine compartment. Frantically, he yanked at his seatbelt and with some difficulty pried open the door of the pilot's compartment and tumbled to the ground. Painfully crawling away from the burning helicopter, he feared that an explosion might engulf him in flames. When he had reached a safe distance, Rick looked back at the burning helicopter, thinking that he could easily have been burned alive.

In the hospital, Rick was treated for a fracture of the left clavicle, hairline fracture of the fourth lumbar vertebra, and bruises to his body, mainly in the chest area. Within six weeks his physical wounds healed, but Rick began to feel apprehensive about flying helicopters. A career soldier with over 18 years service, the Captain's identity was that of an Army helicopter pilot and he secretly loved his nickname, "Captain Cobra." A military colleague had recently been killed in a helicopter accident, and Rick began to obsess about the safety of the whirlybirds. He continued to suffer from pain, anxiety, insomnia, nightmares, and headaches. Whenever he would hear a helicopter flying over the hospital, flashbacks of his accident sped through his mind. Because his symptoms did not clear after six months, he was removed from flight status and assigned to ground duty.

Rick applied for reassignment to fixed wing aircraft, and he became unhappy and despondent when his request was denied. He began to drink excessively, marital problems ensued, and for the first time in his military career his performance was judged unsatisfactory. After a talk with his commanding officer, Rick was hospitalized in an alcohol and drug abuse center. Following discharge from the center, the Captain did very well for several months. However, he continued to obsess about the unreliability of Cobra helicopters, blaming the manufacturer for defects in certain servo systems. He lamented his loss of flight status, but was ambivalent about flying again. On one hand he wanted desperately to be a pilot, the only thing he had ever done well in his life; on the other hand physical pain and anxiety precluded the fulfillment of this goal. Rick's marriage failed, and shortly after his divorce he began to abuse alcohol again. Two years had elapsed since his helicopter accident and no connection was made between the trauma and current symptoms. Although PTSD was considered after his accident, clinicians now concentrated on his alcohol abuse, which was not responding to treatment. Rick was eventually discharged from the Army and several months later he committed suicide. A tragic end to a career officer's life which may have been averted if the proper diagnosis had been made and appropriate treatment rendered.

Natural or Man-Made Disasters

The traumatic effects of disasters are like war, except the cause is due to nature, engineering defects, or the errors of man (Fredrick, 1981). The unleashed fury of nature in the form of floods, earthquakes, tornadoes, hurricanes, volcanic eruptions, or lightening can produce great destruction of property and impose physical injury, psychological trauma, or death to victims. The collapse of large buildings, bridges, or dams due to structural defects also claims a share of victims each year. A well-studied disaster involved the inhabitants of Buffalo Creek, West Virginia.

> Nature and man, in the form of unceasing rain, flooding, and a man-made slag dam became partners on February 26, 1972, when the large slag dam collapsed and unleashed thousands of tons of water and mud into the Buffalo Creek valley in southern West Virginia. In less than 15 minutes, the ensuing tidal wave of mud and water destroyed everything in its path, killing 125 people and leaving 4,000 homeless. The torrent carried away human bodies, houses, trailers, cars, and assorted debris (Titchener and Kapp, 1976). The Buffalo Creek disaster has been thoroughly investigated and there is documented evidence that adults, adolescents, and children suffered severely from PTSD. Those who were closer to the actual path of the tidal wave and experienced or witnessed firsthand its terrible effect on people and property seemed to suffer most. Researchers also noted that persons who had lost loved ones had more severe psychological symptoms than survivors who lost only property. On July 5, 1971, 29 months after the disaster, an out-of-court settlement was reached, awarding the litigants 13.5 million dollars. Over half of this amount was for psychic injury, the remainder consisted of settlement of claims for lost real and personal property, business or salary losses, and "wrongful death." Follow-up studies over a three-year period after litigation revealed a brief period of euphoria followed by a rebound in anxiety and depression, and then a more gradual reduction of symptoms. However, approximately a third of the sample continued to suffer symptoms as severe as when seen initially (Gleser, Green, and Winget, 1981).

Disasters, whether produced by acts of God or by the failing of man, certainly are capable of causing psychological distress in almost everyone. However, not all people who are involved in a disaster develop PTSD. To determine who develops PTSD following a disaster, it is helpful to remember the guidelines expressed in the Traumatic Principle. In the two clinical histories which follow, a mother and son were exposed in different ways to a disaster involving a railroad train derailment. Tank cars carrying deadly chemicals exploded and caught fire, and toxic gas fumes spread throughout a sparsely-populated rural community, causing inhabitants to evacuate the

area. The nature of the trauma varied for the mother and son, and only one
developed a PTSD.

> The mother, a woman in her mid-40's, was at work when she
> received a telephone call informing her of the train derailment.
> She was told that her house was on fire but received no news
> concerning the safety of her teenage son. Immediately, the
> mother rushed to the disaster site, but roadblocks prevented her
> from driving directly to her house. Thinking that her young son
> may have been injured or killed, the mother was frantic. State
> troopers at one of the roadblocks told the mother that her son was
> safe and could be found at a neighbor's house. A joyful reunion
> took place when the mother discovered that her son was safe and
> sound except for a minor shoulder injury. Later she learned that
> her house with all of its possessions had been burned to the
> ground. At no time did the mother experience a threat to her life
> or limb. Although the telephone call stirred up thoughts about her
> son's safety, the reality was that he survived with minimal injury
> and this was confirmed shortly after she learned about the
> derailment. There is no question that the mother suffered emo-
> tionally from the trauma and its aftereffects, but she did not
> develop a PTSD.
>
> The son, Teddy, was awakened by the booming noise of an
> explosion. Rolling out of bed, he fell ungainly to the floor.
> Looking up he saw the ceiling of his bedroom on fire, and he
> quickly scrambled to his feet and rushed down the hall towards
> the back door. Running past the living room, Teddy saw a
> burning railroad tank car through the collapsed wall. The odor of
> toxic gas was everywhere and Teddy, coughing, choking and
> with eyes tearing, ran quickly out of the house, banging his left
> shoulder against the door frame as he sped towards the nearby
> woods. Scared and shaken, he sought the shelter of a neighbor's
> house where he was reunited with his mother an hour later. The
> Traumatic Principle fitted Teddy's case, and he did develop a
> PTSD.

Rescuers at a Disaster Site

Rescuers charged with the task of gathering and identifying the bodies
of disaster victims are often confronted with horrible scenes of carnage. The
environment, strewn with disfigured corpses and body parts, acts as a
traumatic stimulus for many rescue workers. Even experienced rescuers

under the proper circumstances can be traumatized by the sights, sounds, and smells of a disaster scene.

A coroner's assistant was told to report to the scene of a jet aircraft crash where more than 150 people were believed to have perished. Upon arriving at the scene of the disaster, he and others set up a makeshift morgue where the victims of the plane crash were taken for identification. As the black zippered body bags arrived at the temporary morgue, the coroner's assistant was assigned the task of photographing the human remains with close-up shots of bodies and body parts to assist in identification. The body bags contained dismembered torsos, smashed skulls, an assortment of arms, legs, intestines, and fragments of human flesh. The coroner's assistant had viewed death and mutilated bodies before, but not on the magnitude presented by this disaster. He did his job in a competent and professional manner until he viewed the corpse of a boy who reminded him of his grandson. Although he had been working steadily for four hours and was fatigued, he had no symptoms until then. He hesitated in his work and began to feel extremely apprehensive and mildly nauseated. He managed to photograph the dead boy and went on with his work. The next body bag he opened was smoking and steaming, since the clothing on the body was still burning when it was put into the black bag. As the coroner's assistant bent over to take a close-up photograph, the stench of burning flesh assailed his nostrils, causing him to retch. Shortly afterward, he trembled, shook violently, felt his heart pounding, had difficulty breathing, and vomited. Feeling wretched, he asked to be excused from duty. The sights, sounds, and smells of the disaster stimulated intense autonomic activity and pathologic anxiety and precipitated a PTSD. Viewing the dead boy, then thinking of his grandson personalized the traumatic scene. The stench of burning flesh in the next body bag was overwhelming and reinforced the reality of the awful tragedy, involving a large loss of life.

CONCLUSIONS

Clinicians and attorneys must be alert to the fact that almost any environmentally-induced trauma which poses a realistic threat to life or physical integrity can precipitate PTSD. Conscious awareness of danger to self or others occurs as information is processed through the five senses and stored encephalically in the form of cognitions. Later these memories manifest themselves as intrusive thoughts, flashbacks, and nightmares. If emotional symptoms persist after one month, a PTSD must be suspected and clinicians, utilizing diagnostic criteria from DSM-III-R, must rule in or rule out the disorder. Physical injury or disease may or may not be associated with PTSD which is an autonomous mental disorder not dependent upon organic pathology. Most cases of PTSD are clear-cut and can be easily delineated by application of the Traumatic Principle, the concept of the Three E's, and DSM-III-R diagnostic criteria. All traumas certainly do not precipitate PTSD, but for those that do, it is imperative for medical and forensic purposes that clinicians and lawyers become familiar with the types of trauma which produce a stress disorder.

FOUR

INVISIBLE TRAUMA AND PTSD: TOXIC SUBSTANCES, RADIOACTIVITY, AND PATHOGENIC MICROORGANISMS

Some traumatic stimuli are not visible to the naked eye or ordinarily perceived by the other senses. Harmful chemicals or "technological toxins" which seep into water supplies, leech into topsoil, or float invisibly in the air are potential sources of trauma producing illness, disease, or even death. Accidents at nuclear power stations, x-rays or radioactive materials improperly used during diagnostic medical procedures, and natural occurring elements (e.g., radon) release invisible radiation which can cause sickness or death. "Germ warfare," the accidental discharge of lethal microorganisms into the water supply or air, and exposure to persons suffering from contagious diseases such as AIDS call forth mental images of plague, pestilence, and panic. How can these unseen and unperceived potentially lethal sources of trauma produce symptoms of stress in an unsuspecting person? Applying the Traumatic Principle, the invisible trauma may pose a realistic threat to life or limb; however, the five sensory pathways to the brain are circumvented and no causal connection between the unseen trauma and danger may be made. Invisible trauma represents an anomaly to the Traumatic Principle, since common sense and medical knowledge have demonstrated that the invisible trauma of toxic substances, radiation, and pathogenic microorganisms can produce serious illness or even death and should, at some point, evoke symptoms of stress.

Before symptoms of pathologic anxiety or stress can occur, a person must know, understand, appreciate, or be cognitively aware that they are in danger. Cognition links any threat from the environment to a person's nervous system, resulting in symptoms of stress. Ordinarily, when the trauma or stressor is perceived by one or more of the five sensory pathways to the brain and the cognition of danger to self or others is registered in the mind, autonomic arousal occurs and the exposed person exhibits stress symptoms. Following exposure to any of the "invisible traumata," cognitions concerning danger may be absent and it can be anticipated that no significant symptoms will become manifest unless or until physical illness develops. For example, Madam Marie Curie, co-discoverer with her husband, Pierre, of the radioactive properties of radium, was unaware of its lethal properties and, as far as we know, never developed psychological symptoms following exposure to this radioactive element. Ultimately, she developed and died of radiation sickness. Every medical student has learned about the investigative work of physicians in the 1920's, which was prompted by the deaths of nine young female luminators who worked in the same New Jersey dial factory. The women, who died within three years of one another, applied radium paint to the tiny numerals encircling watch dials. Dial painting required a deft hand and a finely pointed brush which was achieved by a quick touch to the lips or tongue, "lip tipping." The unsuspecting luminators developed osteomyelitis, aplastic anemia, osteosarcoma, mastoid carcinoma, and necrosis of the mandible. Until the connection between the ingestion of radium paint by the "lip tipping" method and disease was discovered in 1924, the luminators had no knowledge that this practice was hazardous to their health. In 1925, an article entitled, "Some Unrecognized Dangers in the Use of and the Handling of Radioactive Substances" (Martland et al., 1925), reported cases of radiation burns and dermatitis in chemists, aplastic anemia and cancer among radiologists, and osteomyelitis among workers in luminous dial factories. Prior to this time, an absence of premonitory symptoms and lack of information about the deleterious effects of radiation resulted in no cognitive awareness of danger to self, and hence no symptoms of stress and certainly not a PTSD.

Cognitive awareness of danger following exposure to toxic substances, radioactivity, or pathogenic microorganisms is related to the development of a stress disorder. Like any other trauma, knowledge that an environmental stimulus, albeit invisible, poses a realistic threat to one's self or others is sufficient to activate the stress mechanisms of the brain and body. Knowing that one has consumed, breathed, or absorbed through the skin toxic substances, radioactive materials, or pathogenic microorganisms would evoke symptoms of stress in almost everyone. As in other traumata which are perceived by one or a combination of the five senses, a variety of emotional responses can be expected. Some persons with good coping skills and a solid social support system would adapt quickly and experience no significant stress symptoms after four to six weeks. Others, who are "worriers" and may have been suffering from a Generalized Anxiety Disorder prior to knowledge of exposure to invisible trauma, may have an exacerbation of their GAD or possibly develop a PTSD. Persons who develop a PTSD would have intrusive thoughts centering around exposure to the invisible trauma and its damaging effect upon their bodies, avoidance of all things believed to have been contaminated, and symptoms of increased arousal (anxiety). Encephalic events (cognitions) vivify the trauma, stripping away the cloak of invisibility. Official notification by governmental or medical officials of the hazards to health and the visible efforts and publicity attendant to populations in the danger area (warnings, evacuation, preventive measures, etc.) flesh out cognitions of dangerousness in the "videotapes of the mind." Accuracy of information and adequacy of preventive measures play an important role in a person's ultimate response to invisible traumata (Chapter 13).

Irrational cognitions have the same impact upon the nervous system, as do those based on fact and reality. For example, during the early days of radio transmissions, many people erroneously believed that radio waves caused sickness or even death. Farmers attributed the sudden death of cattle to the arcane invisible radio waves. Misconceptions and erroneous beliefs can lead to emotional outbursts or even mass hysteria. Orsen Wells, in his famous "War of the Worlds" radio program, broadcast a fictional account of extraterrestrial creatures invading the U.S. Hysteria abounded when many people ignored the disclaimer at the beginning of the program that it was make-believe. The emotional reactions of the "martian believers" was based on fantasy, not fact, posing no realistic threat to listeners. Hysteria, not PTSD, was the result of this Mercury Theater production. In the same way, persons who have not been exposed to the source of the invisible trauma, may develop irrational attitudes, false beliefs, and maladaptive behavior. Although the invisible trauma could not, according to accepted scientific data, impact adversely upon a human, some people may ignore this information and react as if they were in danger, denouncing official explanations.

It becomes apparent that cognitions have an important role in determining the effect of invisible trauma upon a person. Absence of any cognition to link a realistically dangerous invisible trauma to the nervous system means no stress symptoms and no PTSD. Cognitions of danger based on fantasy or false information may produce emotional symptoms or even stress, but since no realistic threat was present, a PTSD cannot develop. Exposure to a dangerous invisible trauma, verified by scientific data, coupled with a cognitive awareness of it as a realistic threat to life or limb, results in symptoms of stress and possibly a PTSD.

TOXIC SUBSTANCES

Adverse health effects can be produced by a variety of organic and inorganic chemicals. Organic compounds, usually pesticides, herbicides, or industrial effluents (Lindstron, 1973), and inorganic chemicals, especially those containing heavy metals (arsenic, copper, lead, manganese, and mercury) (Grandjean, Arnvig, and Beckmann, 1978), are toxic to the central nervous system and other organ systems of the body. Chlorinated hydrocarbons (polychlorinated biphenyls [PCB], chlorinated benzenes, chlordecone [Kepone], chloroform, ethylene dichloride, chlorinated naphthalenes), heavy metals and phosphorus-containing compounds can produce liver dysfunction, pathologic effects on the reproductive system and fetus, abnormalities in the hematopoietic and lymphatic systems, genitourinary disease, pathology involving the lung and respiratory tract, diseases and injury in the alimentary tract, cardiovascular complications, and skin lesions. Depending upon route of entry, concentration of chemicals, and length of exposure, toxic substances can adversely effect virtually all organ systems of the body, as is well documented in the literature, and will not be elaborated here (Buffler et al., 1985).

Behavioral changes resulting from exposure to toxic substances range from neurasthenia to psychosis and may involve direct damage to the central nervous system. The nervous system is particularly sensitive to toxic substances, and peripheral neuropathies, seizures, Parkinsonism, impaired visual acuity, increased intracranial pressure, and neoplasm (Baker, 1983) are some neurological complications which have been reported.

Most investigators studying the health effects of populations exposed to toxic chemicals concentrate only on the direct toxic effects upon biological systems of the body (Buffler, Crane, and Key, 1985). Physical disease or injury is the impetus for action, and a health study develops from either of two events: (1) evidence of release of chemicals into the environment; and (2) a real or apparent excess in the occurrence of a relevant health outcome, such as a "cluster" of reported diseases or illnesses in the community. If the disease cluster cannot be explained by confounding factors or chance, then the more difficult task is to determine if there is an association between the chemical exposure and the real or apparent disease cluster.

To determine the effect of toxic substances in the environment upon individuals, an epidemiological study requires documentation of the number, type, and volume of chemicals disbursed, the time period of exposure, and the particular chemicals and quantities currently present. Air, water, or direct contact are the most likely methods for the spread of toxic substances to human populations. Whether the source of contamination is well publicized as in the chemical plant explosion in Bhopal, India, the carcinogenic effect of toxic substances in the Love Canal area (Heath et al., 1984; Janerich et al., 1981), or an accidental spillage of toxic chemicals upon a worker, information regarding the type and amounts of toxic materials and its impact upon humans must be collected and analyzed. Medical examinations, toxicology studies, quantitative biological assays of human tissue or body fluids give some estimate of the degree of exposure and ensuing pathology. When the results of all examinations are negative, suspicion of disease is not erased. The question of future physical disability remains unanswered in many instances, and this uncertainty produces psychological symptoms which must be assessed by psychiatric consultation.

The situation is quite different when a "cluster" of diseases leads to a retrospective analysis and an epidemiological study searching for the cause of illness. This is the case when a disease cluster occurs near a waste disposal site and adjacent residents are warned of a hazard to their health. A two-step statistical procedure for monitoring routinely reported health effects (deaths, births, etc.) in populations has been outlined for communities adjacent to waste disposal sites (Heath, 1983). Use of this monitoring procedure calls for an initial "alert" status when a number of relevant events exceeds a specified level during a given interval of time with follow-up observation being continued for one or more time periods. "Action" status is established if the excess of diseases continues to be apparent in the second time period. The system also allows for immediate action to be taken if the observed number of events greatly exceeds expectation in the first time period. Such a procedure may be useful in assessing the health effects of exposure to chemical waste disposal sites when exposure data are limited or unavailable, and the anticipated health effects are unknown. Clusters of cancer cases, birth defects, or infant deaths can alert health officials and residents to the potential of toxic chemicals for producing hazardous health effects at concentrations sufficiently low that the public is not likely to be aware of their presence. Short-term, very low exposures are far less likely to induce any of the health effects identified, whereas chronic exposure to low concentration and acute high exposure may produce a wide-range of pathology. Population exposures resulting from chemical waste disposal sites are usually much lower than those observed in work environments or accidental environmental exposures.

Some prominent physical health effects are predictable on the basis of data from occupational health studies. In high-dosage situations, disorders involving the skin, central nervous system, liver, kidney, and reproductive system predominate. Following moderate exposure, hematologic abnormalities were frequent. In long term low-dosage situations, central nervous system, liver, and reproductive abnormalities were more likely. Investigators understandably have been concerned mainly with physical effects following exposure, but there can be no question that significant emotional sequelae result from exposure to toxic substances.

Psychological Reaction to Toxic Substances

No so well documented as the physical effects are the psychological reactions following exposure to toxic substances. After acute exposure to toxic substances, an individual's psychological response is observable and easily predictable. When, by accident or explosion, toxic gasses permeate the air, high concentrations of dangerous chemicals suddenly enter the drinking water, or toxic compounds directly contaminate a person's body, exposure to the toxic substance becomes a traumatic event which poses a definite threat to one's physical integrity or life. During acute exposure, the essential criteria for the development of PTSD are fulfilled when one applies either the Traumatic Principle or DSM-III-R. If the victim were present at the site of the explosion or accident, perception of danger occurs almost immediately. Additionally, the smell, taste, or tactile contact with the toxic substance alerts exposed individuals to danger. The emotional response to the trauma would be identical to visible traumatic events, producing symptoms of stress and in some individuals, a PTSD.

As with exposure to low dosages of radiation or pathogenic microorganisms, uncertainty plagues persons who have been exposed, either short-term or long-term, to very low concentrations of toxic chemicals. Uncertainty translated into psychological mechanisms means rumination, or in terminology of the "Three E concept of stress", excessive encephalic activity. Thinking about exposure to toxic chemicals, visualizing the trauma, and presaging a deleterious effect on health, invariably results in increased stress. Those persons with a propensity to worry will worry more, and this encephalic activity will further intensify stress and anxiety. In many ways, adapting to uncertainty is more difficult and more anxiety evoking than coping with realistic danger. Persons feel helpless and powerless when confronting invisible trauma, especially when the circumstances are mysterious and the outcome is questionable. The knowledge of being involuntarily subjected to hazardous chemicals engenders fear, anxiety, stress, anger, bewilderment, and a myriad of dysphoric emotions. Physiological symptoms of stress can in turn be misidentified as an indication of disease produced by the toxic substance. The Spiral Effect (Chapter 2) further intensifies stress, producing more psychophysiological symptoms which seemingly confirm the idea of a hazardous chemical damaging the body. This same sequence can happen even in the absence of any evidence of exposure to significant concentrations of toxic chemicals. When symptomatic behavior occurs within the context of a lawsuit, persons who ruminate about exposure, presage bodily damage, and suffer from a stress disorder, may be inappropriately dismissed as malingerers.

There is a paucity of information concerning the psychological reactions of individuals exposed to toxic substances. An interesting and important study (Lopez-Ibor, Canas, and Rodriguez-Gamazo, 1985) described the psychopathologic aspects of toxic oil among residents who lived in the outskirts of Madrid, Spain. In May of 1981 this new disease caused by widespread food-poisoning (probably with adulterated rape-seed oil) affected more than 20,000 people, causing over 350 deaths. The Toxic Oil Syndrome (TOS), as it was called, consisted of pulmonary, neuromuscular, and systemic symptoms which evolved to produce mild to severe physical disabilities. Although TOS is not primarily a psychiatric disorder, more than 6,000 patients were referred to psychiatrists. The psychopathologic symptoms present in these patients in decreasing order of frequency were: anxiety, depression, irritability (dysphoria), insomnia, lability of affect, feelings of personal inadequacy, loss of recent memory, loss of concentration, loss of vitality, vegetative symptoms, hopelessness, mistrust, fear, anorexia, social withdrawal, restlessness and agitation, sexual problems, aggressivity, obsessions, lack of drive, poverty of affect, bulimia, hysterical symptoms, amnesia, ambivalence, and inhibition of thoughts. Many of these symptoms certainly indicate stress, and although the authors failed to mention it in their report, the symptoms are definitely suggestive of PTSD.

Uncertainty concerning long-term effect of high, moderate, or low dose exposure to toxic chemicals breeds anxiety and one would expect an increase in psychophysiologic reactions and symptoms suggestive of stress, e.g., tension headaches, gastrointestinal upsets, sexual dysfunction, sleep disturbance, irritability, depression, and preoccupation with illness. Two generalizations emerge: (1) persons exposed to acute situations involving a sudden dispersal of toxic substances in the air, water, or directly onto the surface of the skin have a high probability for developing PTSD; and (2) persons who have been alerted that they have had long-term exposure to either high, moderate, or low concentrations of toxic chemicals which may be a risk to health are more likely to develop a chronic stress syndrome (Generalized Anxiety Disorder) than a PTSD.

RADIOACTIVITY

Radiation may be emitted from a variety of sources including: radon 222, a ubiquitous noble gas arising from decay of radium 226; radioactive isotopes used in medicine; roentgen rays from diagnostic machines used in radiology; nuclear power plants, or explosions of nuclear devices. In 1945 following the dropping of the atomic bomb on Hiroshima, the magnitude of the harmful effects of radiation upon survivors became evident. Robert Lifton (1967) has written about the survivors of Hiroshima and the "radiation response syndrome" in which people very quickly sensed that they were in a situation that could not be controlled. Terrifying rumors containing varying degrees of truth were part of the radiation response syndrome. Survivors accurately or inaccurately attributed various symptoms to the aftereffects of the nuclear explosion. Lifton has pointed out that Hiroshima survivors tended to associate any illness or discomfort with radiation effects. General fatigue, a cut that does not quickly stop bleeding, and a common cold were attributed to radiation exposure. Survivors obsessed about an endless chain of potentially lethal impairments that, if it did not manifest itself in one year or in one generation, might well make itself felt in the next.

In peacetime, the spread of radiation by nuclear power plant accidents is not as devastating but no less traumatic. Waves of anxiety spread over the world following the Three Mile Island incident and especially after the more serious Chernobyl nuclear power plant accident in the Soviet Union on April 26, 1986. As Gale (1987) has commented, "We should take one lesson from Chernobyl: a nuclear accident anywhere is a nuclear accident everywhere." At Chernobyl it has been estimated that the amount of radioactive cesium discharged into the environment was three hundred times more than at Hiroshima. Cesium has a half-life of about 30 years and has entered the air, water systems, and food chains in the Soviet Union, southern Europe, and as far away as Lapland. Airborne radioactive cesium has been found within lichen, a complex thallophytic plant which is a food for reindeer. An important commodity and food for Laplanders, reindeer have become contaminated with radioactive cesium, and entire herds are scheduled for elimination or already have been destroyed. The gallimaufry of situations involving radioactivity following a nuclear plant accident makes it difficult to predict a uniformed physiological or psychological response of persons caught up in the chain of events resulting in acute or chronic exposure.

Appropriate medical and psychological treatment of persons exposed to radiation depends upon accurate assessment of radiation dose. There are two basic approaches—physical and biological dosimetry (Gale, 1987). Physical dosimetry involves the use of environmental monitoring devices or individual radiation meters or badges. However, at Chernobyl, many of these environmental monitoring devices were either destroyed or unrecoverable due to the circumstances of the nuclear accident. In the future, remote monitoring of dosimeters and the use of special badges and thermoluminescent dosimeters will improve the monitoring of radiation. Biological dosimetry improves the reliability of the radiation dose received by victims (Eisert and Mendelsohn, 1984). Biological dosimetry at Chernobyl involved serial measurement of levels of lymphocytes and granulocytes in the blood and an analysis of dicentric chromosomes in spontaneously dividing and phytohemagglutinin-stimulated blood and bone marrow derived hematopoietic cells (Barabanova, Baranov, and Guskova, 1986). Calculation of dose was based on data relating these parameters to dose in prior radiation accidents, and using these variables, it was possible to estimate the dose of radiation received. Biological dosimetry is effective, but it demands considerable medical and technical expertise.

Medical treatment and prognosis depend, to a large extent, upon an accurate assessment of the dosage of radiation received by victims. Information concerning dosage also becomes the basis for cognitions, as exposed persons consider the consequences of radiation to themselves. Visible evidence such as thermal injury to the skin or symptoms due to toxic effects to the lungs, liver, gastrointestinal tract, and other organs clearly indicate to the victim that a serious threat to life exists. In these cases, the development of stress or PTSD is quite understandable and the psychological course parallels individuals who have been exposed to an ordinary visible trauma.

Not so clear-cut are the psychological effects of victims who have been exposed to lower dosages of radiation and manifest no visible or perceived radiation injury. Physical and biological dosimetry in these cases may give some evidence of expected impairment and future development of radiation-related pathology.

The medical effects of ionizing radiation and the hematopoietic impact of radiation exposure has been determined as follows: with less than 1 Gy (less than 100 rad), survival is virtually certain; with 1 to 2 Gy (100 to 200 rad), survival is probable; with 2 to 4.5 Gy (200 to 450 rad), survival is possible (especially with medical treatment); and with 5 to 6 Gy (500 to 600 rad), survival is virtually impossible (Mettler and Moseley, 1985). Distilling this data in relationship to short-term and long-term effects of radiation and speaking as a physician called on by a patient or a family to provide prognostic information following radiation exposure from a nonmilitary radiation accident, Adelstein (1987) raises two questions which he answers affirmatively: (1) is there significant uncertainty in the estimate of risks associated with radiation exposure? and (2) will physicians have difficulty in explaining these risks to patients and their families? Adelstein, reminding readers that a physician's job is "to comfort always", also points out that providing prognostic information to patients who have been inadvertently exposed to radiation reduces anxiety by conveying a realistic and comprehensible estimate of the projected harm and long-term consequences of radiation exposure, namely cancer and genetic defects. The perception of risk is contextual and the fear of radiation received from a nuclear accident is greater than the fear of that received from natural and medical sources. Granting that there are uncertainties in predicting long-term outcome from radiation exposure, Adelstein proposes that patients be informed concerning the probabilities of the development of leukemia, other forms of cancers, and genetic risks. Patients are sometimes reassured when radiation risks are compared to other hazards of everyday living. In general, short-term response to high-dose exposures can be explained as a deterministic acute illness for which the pathophysiology is understood and the natural history is dose dependent, but as with other illnesses is individually variable. The potential consequences of low-dose exposures, which are probablistic rather than deterministic, are more difficult to describe, and although there will be no residual damage, there is a chance that cancer or a genetic abnormality will develop.

Despite uncertainties in the estimates, physicians have an obligation to help their patients understand the outcome of radiation exposure. As physicians proffer prognosis, patients ponder the perils to their existence. Scientific explanations based on the most accurate available evidence become incorporated into the cognitive apparatus of the mind. When the news is bad, anxiety and depression can be expected, as patients presage incurable illness and their demise. Acute radiation exposure, whether it produces physical illness or not, can precipitate a PTSD. Uncertainty envelopes the prognosis of long-term risks of developing leukemia, other types of cancers, or genetic and chromosomal diseases. In this latter case, chronic stress is the most likely response; however, PTSD is still a possibility. Preventive interventions can reduce psychiatric morbidity, and some patients can adapt to projected risks with minimal impairment due to stress.

PATHOGENIC MICROORGANISMS

Pathogenic microorganisms have the capacity to produce acute illness, chronic disability, and death. Major groups of infectious agents for humans include: viruses (AIDS, infectious hepatitis, influenza, measles, and mumps), bacteria (staphylococci, streptococci, neisseria gonorrhoea, etc.), mycobacteria (tuberculosis and leprosy), spirochetes (syphilis, Weil's disease, and leptospirosis), rickettsia (typhus, Rocky Mountain Spotted Fever, and tsutsugamushi fever), chlamydia (trachoma, lymphogranuloma venereum, and psittacosis), fungi (histoplasmosis, coccidioidomycosis, cryptococcosis, etc.), and animal parasites (malaria, amebic dysentery, schistosomiasis, etc.) (Berk, 1983). Pathogenic microorganisms can be inhaled, ingested, or absorbed through defects in the dermis. Each infectious agent has its own properties relating to: epidemiology, entry into the host, length of time before symptoms become manifest, organ systems affected, and lethality. Similar to the acute effects of radiation or sudden exposure to toxic substances, some pathogenic microorganisms produce an almost immediate effect upon an unsuspecting person who, for example, may become violently ill after ingesting food contaminated with staphylococcus. Pathogenic organisms can be introduced into the environment by weapon systems during wartime, accidentally by improper filtration and purification of sewage, randomly by contact with infected persons, or by passage through intermediate hosts such as insects.

Some infectious agents take longer to produce pathologic symptoms. A relatively benign primary lesion at the site of entry of a pathogen, a chancre, is often the initial symptom in syphilis which can progress over time to tertiary syphilis involving the central nervous system. Leprosy, or Hansen's disease, has a wide clinicopathologic spectrum ranging from mild to severe lepromatous leprosy involving the skin, peripheral nerves, and internal organs. The wide range of outcomes and the mode of transmission which, even today has not been well-established (Lefford, 1983) had in part been responsible for the isolation and shunning of lepers, a phenomenon we are currently observing with AIDS patients.

Exposure to a pathogenic microorganism does not necessarily lead to overt disease. Outbreak of illness varies, depending upon previous exposure, inoculations, or the integrity of a person's immune system. Few people, however, are immune to alarm which occurs upon notification of a contagious disease in the community, as is epitomized by the growing epidemic of AIDS in the United States and other parts of the world. The discussion in this text will center on AIDS because it is a contemporary crisis and raises issues inherent in all infectious diseases.

Acquired Immune Deficiency Syndrome

Since its description in 1981, (Gottlieb et al., 1981) acquired immune deficiency syndrome (AIDS) has become a modern plague. By January of 1986, almost 30,000 cases of AIDS had been reported in the United States and at least one to two million persons were thought to be infected with human immunodeficiency virus (HIV). The Institute of Medicine predicts that 270,000 cases of AIDS will be diagnosed by 1991, with 74,000 cases identified in that year alone. Deaths caused by AIDS are expected to reach 179,000, with 54,000 occurring in 1991. During the next four years, pediatric cases of AIDS will increase ten-fold to a total of 3,000, and cases that result from heterosexual transmission of HIV will increase from 1,100 in 1986 to 7,000 in 1991 (Institute of Medicine, National Academy of Sciences, 1986).

The cause of the disease has been conclusively shown to be the third human retrovirus: human T-lymphotropic virus III (HTLV- III), which is also called human immunodeficiency virus (HIV) (Gallo, 1987). It is believed that the virus originated in central Africa and probably spread to the Caribbean and then to the U.S. and Europe. Seen mainly among young homosexual men, the virus is believed to be transmitted by sexual contact and recent reports reveal heterosexual spread of AIDS by intravenous drug users. HIV is spread by the exchange of body fluids, principally (probably exclusively) blood and blood products, semen, and vaginal secretions. Medical personnel who deal with AIDS patients and come into contact with their body fluids (mainly blood) have contracted the disease. Since blood can be tested for HIV, transfusions have been virtually eliminated as a source of infection. The major transmission models are sexual intimacy, parenterally from mother to child, and exchange of blood by needle sharing among drug abusers.

Once inside the body, HIV invades the host white blood cell, a T4 lymphocyte, that has a central role in regulating the immune system. The virus may remain latent for years until the lymphocyte is immunologically stimulated by a secondary infection. Then the virus bursts into action and the T4 lymphocyte dies. The resulting depletion of T4 lymphocytes—the hallmark of AIDS—leaves the patient vulnerable to "opportunistic" infections, brain disease, and several types of cancer (Selwyn, 1986).

Redfield and associates (1986) have developed a six-stage system of classifying AIDS beginning with a positive blood test and ending with a full-blown syndrome. They used the system to follow a group of patients for as long as thirty-six months and found that about ninety percent of them progressed from the stage in which they began the study to a subsequent stage. These results suggest that there may not be a large group of infected people who remain without symptoms. Although much progress has been made in the last three years—identification of the virus which causes AIDS, formulation of a blood test, a promising therapy (azidothymidine or AZT), and the beginning of vaccine development—AIDS is still a lethal disease (Gallo, 1987). Many of the millions of persons already infected with HIV will become ill and die before treatment is available.

Psychological Reactions to AIDS

Polio, the last important infectious disease to succumb to the onslaught of medical scientists, was conquered decades ago. For most Americans, fear of contracting a deadly contagious disease with no known predictable and effective treatment is a new experience. A pandemic of emotionalism surrounds AIDS, partly because of its incurability leading to death and partly because AIDS is primarily a disease contracted by homosexual men and intravenous drug users. Prejudice against these risk groups inflames fear, sometimes to the point of hysteria. Misinformation about AIDS also contributes to irrational fear and anxiety. The death of celebrities such as Rock Hudson, Liberace, and Michael Bennett focuses public attention on the utter helplessness of modern medicine to deal effectively with AIDS. Inaccurate or incomplete public media presentations which highlight sensational aspects of AIDS further fans fear and anxiety. What are the possible psychological reactions to AIDS from the standpoint of persons in the high-risk group and those who are not?

The High-Risk Group

Persons engaged in unsafe sex practices and intravenous drug use are in a sense addicted to these practices because the pleasure associated with each reinforces this behavior. Educational programs aimed at prevention, as has been reported recently in San Francisco (Institute of Medicine, 1986), may reduce high-risk behavior, but until a cure for AIDS is developed, the number of people infected with HIV will increase. Uncertainty and anxiety must plague the minds of persons in the high-risk group; thoughts about developing AIDS increase stress even though no discernible disease may be apparent. An unrealistic fear of AIDS has been termed "AIDophobia" (Freed, 1983). Weight loss, unexplained infections, and physical symptoms signal apprehension even in the absence of a positive blood test. Anxiety may be temporarily allayed by a negative serological test, but the future is filled with doubt, as high-risk individuals consider the future.

One can imagine the psychological impact of a positive blood test. Coming to grips with the possibility of an untimely death due to a mysterious virus for which there is no known effective treatment is the ultimate emotional experience. Uncertainty concerning one's existence dominates thinking, producing stress and depression. Serologically positive persons may be considered a pariah, further intensifying anxiety and alienation. As HIV positive persons progress down Redfield's six-stage system of classification ending with full-blown AIDS, anxiety escalates and depression deepens. Persons with AIDS probably suffer more emotionally than do victims of other incurable fatal illnesses. In addition to coping with a shortened lifespan, AIDS patients also have to contend with diminished social support during the time of greatest need. Ostracism occurs, not only because of fear concerning the contagious nature of the disease and its incurability, but also because of prejudice against homosexuals and intravenous drug users. AIDS patients are the modern-day lepers. Persons with leprosy were carted away to leprosariums, and it was believed by many that God had visited the disease upon the sinful as punishment. The thoughtful words of Gallo (1987) places the issue of AIDS in perspective: "AIDS is not a disease of homosexuals or drug addicts or indeed of any particular risk group. The virus is spread by intimate contact, and the form of contact seems to be less important than the contact itself."

The emotional reaction of persons in the high-risk group varies in accordance with the following factors: (1) unsafe sex practices and intravenous drug use does not always result in infection with HIV; (2) even when the AIDS virus is transmitted during intimate contact, there is an undetermined latent period before symptoms may develop. Unless a blood test is performed, persons may not know if they are infected; (3) knowledge of a positive blood test is more ominous and is the first indication of a definite threat to life. Notification of a positive blood test may be accompanied by high levels of stress and possibly PTSD. With time, anxiety is accompanied by depression; (4) a positive blood test is not equated with AIDS, but is a step along a continuum which could lead to florid symptoms. The proportion of serologically positive persons who go on to become ill is unknown but may be considerably higher than was once thought (Redfield et al., 1986). During the stages before AIDS is definitively diagnosed, anxiety continues to mount, symptoms of PTSD, if present, may intensify, and dysthymia is a likely possibility; (5) following the diagnosis of AIDS, depending upon coping skills and social support system, a victim may become panicky, severely depressed, and suicidal. After the acute crisis has passed, patients, especially those who receive emotional support from professionals and friends, will adapt—perhaps with a greater appreciation of life. As the disease progresses, the presence of opportunistic infections, central nervous system involvement, or tumors complicate the psychological response. A wide variety of psychological symptoms ranging from anxiety, depression to psychosis or dementia may occur before death, but as energy wanes and the end nears, physical symptoms take precedence over psychological ones. Hope should never be abandoned. Promising treatment such as AZT is currently available, and there is intense activity in the scientific community in the search for a vaccine.

Exposure to Persons in the Risk Group

Potential exposure to a lethal infectious agent should instill fear and anxiety in most people. Medical personnel or others who work with AIDS patients on a regular basis must harbor a fear of becoming infected. Doctors, medical students, nurses, laboratory technicians, or anyone who handles body fluids of AIDS patients frequently engage in the practice of masking, gowning, goggling, and double-gloving primarily to prevent infection and secondarily to decrease their anxiety. Although accidents or mishaps are uncommon, they are highly publicized and it is difficult for members of the health profession to be dispassionate about the possibility of infection. The stress level of persons working with AIDS patients is high, not only because of the possibility of infection, but also because patients ultimately deteriorate and die. Some medical personnel refuse to work with AIDS patients, while others labor under considerable stress, and still others may develop PTSD. Most medical personnel who are accustomed to dealing with disease and death carry on, performing the duties of their chosen profession without undue psychological problems (Zuger and Miles, 1987).

The AIDS patient does pose a potential threat to life, thus fulfilling the qualification for a stressor as described in DSM- III-R. Intrusive thoughts about contracting AIDS, an avoidance of physical contact with AIDS patients, and symptoms of increased arousal (anxiety), fulfill criteria B, C, and D of DSM-III-R. The development of a stress disorder among medical personnel or persons who are regularly exposed to AIDS patients, is, therefore, a distinct possibility, especially among those people who are vulnerable to developing PTSD under any circumstances.

There can be no doubt that exposure to infectious agents of any type can produce stress and in some individuals a PTSD. In the case of AIDS, emotionalism mixed with misinformation cloud the realistic danger and heighten anxiety, similar to the situation with radiation and toxic substances. There is a defined risk when working with AIDS patients, as there is with personnel within a nuclear power facility or workers in a petrochemical plant.

CONCLUSIONS

Invisible traumata—toxic substances, radiation, and pathogenic microorganisms—usually bypass the five senses. However, the cognition of current or impending danger is the "sixth sense" which links the unseen traumata to the nervous system, producing symptoms of stress or PTSD. The impact of invisible traumata upon a person can be summarized as follows: (1) in order for a PTSD to develop, the invisible trauma must pose a realistic threat to life or limb which must be verified by scientific data from reliable sources; (2) stress, though not necessarily a PTSD, would be the most common response to an invisible stressor; (3) following exposure to invisible trauma, those individuals with good coping skills and a solid social support system would adapt within a short period of time. Other persons, especially those with a preexisting mental disorder or inadequate coping skills and social support system, would suffer from symptoms of chronic stress and could develop a PTSD. Still others, especially those with physical manifestations (illness or injury) due to the invisible trauma, would develop PTSD in the same way as those exposed to ordinary visible trauma; (4) persons who have verified knowledge of possible long-term effects of the invisible trauma but no demonstrable physical evidence of illness or injury would have to cope with the uncertainty associated with the future. Many of these individuals would probably adapt with minimal psychiatric symptoms, some would develop a chronic stress syndrome, but a PTSD would be unlikely; (5) there will always be a segment of people who have not been directly impacted by the invisible trauma who complain of psychiatric symptoms or claim psychological distress. These complaints and claims can result from hysteria or malingering. The former is usually associated with a history of previous mental disorder, while the latter with Antisocial Personality Disorder (Chapter 7).

FIVE

PREDISPOSITION AND CLINICAL COURSE

Winston Churchill developed a PTSD. In *The Last Lion*, William Manchester (1983) wrote that on December 12, 1931, Churchill was in New York, and Bernard Baruch had invited him to dine that evening with mutual friends. Churchill, riding in a taxi, could not remember Baruch's exact address, and the driver who was new to Manhattan was of little help. Growing increasingly exasperated, Churchill told the driver to let him out on the Central Park side of Fifth Avenue. He believed that he could recognize Baruch's house from the sidewalk. Stepping off the curb to cross Fifth Avenue, Churchill made two mistakes. The red signal light meant nothing to him because they had not yet been introduced in Great Britain. Also, forgetting that American's drive on the right, he looked the wrong way and, seeing no automobiles, believed that his way was clear. Immediately, he was struck by a car traveling over thirty miles per hour. He was dragged several yards by the car, and then flung into the street. Churchill later wrote: "There was a moment of a world aglare, of a man aghast...I do not understand why I was not broken like an eggshell, or squashed like a gooseberry." Although in shock and in great pain, Churchill wiped the streaming blood from his face and assured the driver of the car that he was blameless. Another taxi stopped, and Churchill was helped into it and taken to Lenox Hill Hospital. Although he was in pain, the hospital receptionist, adhering to policy, asked Churchill his name and then how he was going to pay for treatment. "I am Winston Churchill, a British statesman," Churchill stated and then added,

"I do not wish to be hurt anymore. Give me chloroform or something." Churchill had only a few dollars in his pocket, and treatment was delayed until Clementine, his wife, was called at the Waldorf Hotel and produced additional money. After examining Churchill, Dr. Otto C. Pickardt's findings were: "Head scalp wounds severe, two cracked ribs, simple slight pleural irritation of right side, generally much bruised. Progress satisfactory." Initially Churchill's recovery was swift. He cabled his friend in Great Britain, Professor Lindemann, asking him to calculate the shock to a stationary body weighing 200 pounds, of a car weighing 2,400 pounds and traveling between thirty and thirty-five miles per hour. Professor Lindemann quickly replied, "Collision equivalent with falling thirty feet on pavement. Equal 6,000 foot pounds energy. Equivalent stopping 10-pound brick dropped 600 feet or 2 charges buckshot point-blank range. Rate inversely proportional thickness cushion surrounding skeleton and give of frame. If assume average one-inch your body transferred during impact at rate 8,000 horsepower. Congratulations on preparing suitable cushion and skill in bump." In a piece for the Daily Mail, Churchill wrote, "I certainly suffered every pang, physical and mental, that a street accident or, I suppose, a shell wound can produce. Dr. Pickardt prescribed rest, and Churchill and his wife packed for the Bahamas, where they arrived on New Year's Eve. In Nassau, Churchill suffered from severe aftershock and depression. "Vitality only returning slowly," Churchill wrote on January 3, 1932. Five days later a nervous reaction struck. He wrote Dr. Pickardt that he had experienced "a great and sudden lack of power of concentration, and a strong sense of being unequal to the task which lay so soon ahead of me." Churchill, attended by a nurse, fought insomnia with nightly sedation and forced himself to exercise a few minutes each day. His easel was there, but did not attract him. He wrote his son: "I have not felt like opening the paint box, although the seas around these islands are luminous with the most lovely tints of blue and green and purple." His wife, Clementine, also wrote their son: "Last night he was very sad and said that he had now in the last two years had three very heavy blows. First the loss of all that money in the crash, then the loss of his political position in the Conservative Party, and now this terrible injury—he said he did not think he would ever recover completely from the three events." Dr. Pickardt, when Churchill returned to the United States, was aware of prohibition and also of the medicinal properties of alcohol, and wrote on his stationery: "This is to certify that the post-accident convalescence of the Honorable Winston S. Churchill necessitates the use of alcoholic spirits, especially at meal times. The quantity is naturally indefinite, but the minimal requirement would be 250 c.c. (slightly over 8 ozs.)." (Manchester, 1983).

It may be hard for people to imagine that Sir Winston Churchill, the "Last Lion" and certainly one of the great politicians of the 20th century, lay on a litter in the emergency room of Lenox Hill Hospital whimpering, "I do not want to be hurt anymore. Give me chloroform or something." The biographical data seems to suggest that Churchill undeniably was affected both physically and mentally as a result of the December, 1931 auto accident. In Churchill's own words, "I certainly suffered every pang, both physical and mental, that a street accident or, I suppose, a shell wound can produce." Lady Churchill suggests a predisposition when she writes to her son, Randolph, that the auto accident was the last of three very heavy blows Churchill experienced over the past two years. In 1931, neither PTSD nor traumatic neurosis had entered the medical nomenclature, but it can be surmised from documented evidence that Churchill not only suffered from physical injuries as a result of the car accident, but developed PTSD as well. Unlike most commoners, Churchill was able to quit work (depart from his lecture tour) to rest and recuperate in the Bahamas with his wife, personal secretary, a nurse, and the rest of his entourage. Utilizing his prodigious personal resourcefulness and assisted by a strong social support system, Churchill soon made his way back to the lecture circuit as he moved steadily towards a prominent place in history.

PTSD AND PREDISPOSITION

An individual's predisposition to PTSD has intrigued clinicians over the years. Not all soldiers in the same battle, persons in the same automobile accident, or workers exposed to an identical explosion develop PTSD. Why similar traumas impact differently is not known with certainty, but clearly there must be dissimilarities between the individual who develops a PTSD and the one who does not.

A common conclusion of psychotraumatologists, whether studying the effects of war or civilian stressors, is that persons who develop and maintain symptoms following exposure to a traumatic incident seem to be predisposed or vulnerable. Investigators have noted a pre-traumatic history of neurotic traits and various psychiatric disorders in patients (Brend, 1939; Brill and Beebe, 1951; Lewy, 1941; Slater, 1943). Some researchers have studied the hereditary predisposition of anxious persons (Crowe et al., 1980; Cloninger et al., 1981). When this tendency was present pre-traumatically, a minor stressor could precipitate a stress disorder, whereas a major stressor was needed to produce a breakdown in non-susceptible persons (Robitscher, 1966; Cohen, 1970). Correspondingly, those who are anxious and insecure cope less adequately and display more symptoms following a trauma than more emotionally healthy persons. Although there is a paucity of reliable statistics relating to PTSD and predisposition, hypotheses based on clinical observation may furnish a framework for future research.

The Stressor and the Response

The intensity and duration of the stressor and the reactivity of the nervous system are important factors in determining the ultimate response to a traumatic event. The trauma must be of sufficient severity to pose a realistic threat to life or physical integrity and the duration must be long enough for the victim to perceive danger. Traumatic situations involving exposure to a stressor for an indeterminate time (e.g., torture, sexual assaults, entrapment in a burning building) allow the idea of danger to self or others to be perceived and to become firmly fixed in the mind, increasing the potential for the precipitation of PTSD.

The anxiety level (Table 2-1) or reactivity of a person's nervous system, especially the autonomic nervous system, prior to the trauma is another factor. In order for a PTSD to develop, the anxiety level at the time of the trauma must reach Level 4 (severe) or Level 5 (panic). Episodes of high anxiety or panic are associated with intense dysphoria and a feeling of impending loss of physical and mental integrity (Scrignar, 1983). For example, patients suffering from a Panic Disorder frequently have thoughts of impending doom, going crazy, being out of control, or of dying. A panic attack is unforgettable and becomes firmly fixed in the mind of the patient. Similarly, in the context of PTSD, high levels of autonomic activity at the time of the trauma concentrate the victim's perception of danger so that the "videotapes of the mind" become vivid and unforgettable.

The relationship between the stressor and the preexisting level of anxiety can be expressed in a simple equation. The anxiety produced by the stressor plus the pre-traumatic (baseline) anxiety equals post-traumatic anxiety. The relationship between the strength or intensity of the stressor and the anxiety level existing at the time of the trauma also explains what is observed clinically and stated in DSM-III-R, "Several studies indicate that preexisting psychopathological conditions predispose to the development of this disorder. However, the disorder can develop in people without any such preexisting conditions, particularly if the stressor is extreme." If the anxiety level is low (Level 1) as in a normal individual, the intensity of the stressor must be high so that Levels 4 or 5 are reached, the level which is necessary to precipitate a PTSD. If the victim's baseline of anxiety is at Levels 2 or 3 (mild to moderate), a less intense stressor is required to reach Levels 4 or 5.

Predisposition to PTSD is, therefore, correlated with preexisting autonomic hyperactivity or anxiousness. It would be expected that anxious people, especially those suffering from an anxiety disorder, would be more vulnerable to develop PTSD. Data concerning anxiety disorders cite familial incidence (McInnes, 1937; Cohen, et al., 1951; Noyes, 1978a) and twin studies (Shields, 1962; Slater and Shields, 1969; Torgersen, 1978) to support a strong genetic component related to etiology. Environmental factors cannot be ignored—for a large number of psychosocial stressors in the absence of a genetic factor can raise an individual's anxiety to Levels 2 or 3. Psychoactive Substance Use Disorders, either through direct stimulation to the brain (e.g., amphetamines) or during withdrawal (e.g., alcohol), may also result in the increase of a one's anxiety level. Other biological factors such as chronic sickness or extreme fatigue may predispose persons to anxiety. From a clinical standpoint, it matters not whether vulnerability is interpreted genetically, psychosocially, or biologically, the fact remains that an increased baseline anxiety (Levels 2 or 3) coincident with a traumatic event makes it more likely that a person will develop a PTSD. Observations made over the course of years reflect the conclusion that most people who develop persistent mental symptoms following a trauma appear to be predisposed (Brend, 1939; Brill and Beebe, 1951; Lewy, 1941; Slater, 1943). Clinicians have described "unstable, labile, latent, nervous, immature, dependent, neurotic" traits among traumatized civilian patients. In the analysis of traumatized combat soldiers, evidence for a pre-traumatic personality predisposition received some support (Worthington, 1978; Kadushin, Boulanger, and Martin, 1981; Laufer, et al., 1981); however, other investigators support the view that it is essentially the combat experience itself that triggers the onset of PTSD, pointing out that Vietnam veterans who saw heavy combat are more likely to develop a PTSD (Figley, 1978; McDermott, 1981; Card, 1983). It must be concluded that no carefully controlled study has ever been conducted which definitively demonstrates that certain personality characteristics predispose a person to PTSD. Individuals with a higher than normal pre-morbid anxiety level apparently are more likely to perceive danger and develop PTSD. Whether a patient appears for psychiatric treatment depends more upon their personal coping skills and social support system.

Coping Skills and Social Support System

Almost everyone who is confronted with a trauma which involves a threat to life or limb will respond with symptoms of distress such as anxiety, intrusive thoughts, and a tendency to avoid situations associated with the trauma. The individual's ability to cope with these psychological sequelae of trauma depends upon his personal coping skills and social support system. Normally, psychological symptoms subside within a month and most trauma victims seldom appear in a mental health professional's consulting room for diagnosis and treatment. A few may consult their family physician because of somatic symptoms due either to physical injury or stress but manage recovery without formal psychiatric intervention. Others who have inadequate coping skills and a limited social support system may continue to complain of symptoms in the absence of demonstrable organic pathology and eventually end up in a psychiatrist's office, where PTSD may be diagnosed. Theoretically, two patients with identical pre-morbid personalities, subjected to identical stressors, may deal differently with stress depending upon their coping skills and existing social support system. One may be identified as a PTSD patient, and the other may not.

To summarize, the ability or inability of victims to cope with the psychological sequelae of trauma determines whether they solicit psychiatric treatment and are identified as patients. Trauma victims who do not seek psychiatric treatment obviously do not come under scrutiny, and are not included in any study concerning predisposition. Apart from the severity and duration of the stressor and the reactivity of the nervous system, the ability to cope post-traumatically may be the most important factor in the ultimate development of PTSD. The vignette at the beginning of the chapter involving Sir Winston Churchill revealed a man of immense personal resourcefulness with an extensive social support system. Retrospectively, Churchill was diagnosed as suffering from PTSD. He never required psychiatric treatment, although he did receive medical attention for physical injuries and alcohol, the world's oldest tranquilizer, for emotional symptoms.

CLINICAL COURSE

Like all diseases or mental disorders, PTSD has an acute and chronic course. As time passes, the intensity and character of symptoms change, and it is unfortunate that in DSM-III-R the distinction between acute and chronic PTSD has been eliminated. Actually, there are three time periods which bear analysis: Stage I — Response to Trauma, Stage II — Acute Phase, and Stage III — Chronic Phase. Conceptualizing PTSD in this manner allows for a description and discussion of salient symptoms and issues which predominate at each phase.

Stage I — Response to Trauma

Phlegmatism is seldom a response to trauma. Most people subjected to situations that have the potential for causing injury or even death react with alarm or fear. On impact with the incursive trauma, irrespective of any physical injury, one or more of the five senses are stimulated, which activates the autonomic nervous system and related stress mechanisms, producing symptoms of anxiety. After impact, the victim may shake, tremble, experience tachycardia, palpitations, hyperventilation, nausea, vomiting, or even pain. Some trauma victims go into a state of shock, not due to physical injury, and appear dazed, numb, and unresponsive. Depending upon the victim's ability to cope and adequacy of social support system, the symptoms may abate within a month or crystallize into PTSD.

Although frightened by the experience, persons who do not become psychiatric patients do not dwell or speculate on the more dire consequences of the trauma. During treatment or hospitalization for a physical injury resulting from the trauma, patients exude optimism, comply with therapy, and adapt to any disability. After the acute crisis has passed, the symptoms are followed by a philosophical and grateful period of reflection. Victims thank God, fate, or both for their survival and move on with the business of life. Over the course of years, the traumatic incident may intrude in consciousness or in dreams, but this is not a frequent or recurrent problem and, more importantly, does not disrupt everyday living. The acquisition of a successful coping style, together with family support, improves prognosis and diminishes future disability. Psychiatric intervention is not necessary unless the physical injury is very severe and irreversible. Organic mental disorder, dismemberment, loss of sight, or other serious injuries such as extensive burns or multiple fractures requiring long periods of convalescence may necessitate psychiatric consultation or treatment, but the mental disorder is more likely to be depression rather than PTSD.

Those who develop PTSD respond differently to trauma during Stage I. The affected person's baseline of anxiety is above normal and the response to trauma is, therefore, heightened. In part, this explains why a susceptible person reports a higher degree of anxiety in response to a trauma than the non-susceptible person. Furthermore, vulnerable individuals invariably perceive the stressor in an intense fashion and react to all real or imagined dangers inherent in the trauma. The wheels of rumination are set in motion, and intrusive thoughts about the trauma dominate the mind of the victim. Differences in perception leading to an obsessive preoccupation with the trauma sets apart a pathologic response from a "normal" one. In some cases when the stressor is extremely intense and prolonged, perception and preoccupation are pronounced, and PTSD may develop in almost anyone regardless of predisposition.

Stage II — Acute Phase

If symptoms related to the trauma intensify or persist beyond one month, the patient is in the acute phase of PTSD. When symptomatic patients reflect back to the time of their trauma, they admit to a feeling of powerlessness and an inability to control or influence events. Symptoms of an intense autonomic nervous system discharge and a "state of shock" are commonly reported, and just before impact, patients believed that they were about to die or suffer serious injury. Following the trauma, victims exhibit surprise about survival, but not much relief.

The trauma becomes the focal point of patients' existence. Talk becomes catharsis as patients relate the history of the trauma to relatives, friends, and acquaintances and usually in greater detail, with their doctors and lawyers. During the day, patients relive the trauma through flashbacks. At night, sleep is interrupted by nightmares that portray the traumatic incident or a more macabre variant. Patients often awaken abruptly, disturbed and thrashing about, their night clothes drenched with sweat; further sleep is impossible as they ponder their bad dreams. As daylight

TABLE 5–1
Cardinal Characteristics of Post-Traumatic Stress Disorder

Nervousness
> The person is apprehensive, on edge, tense, jumpy, easily startled, and fearful.

Preoccupation with the trauma
> The person talks a great deal about the accident, speculating that more serious injury or even death could have occurred.

Pain or physical discomfort
> The person complains of pain or physical discomfort that appears disproportionate to the actual injury incurred.

Sleeplessness
> The patient complains of insomnia with resultant tiredness and fatigue.

Flashbacks and nightmares
> The person relives the trauma during flashbacks or nightmares with similar emotional reactions as if the accident were happening again. Intrusive thoughts related to the trauma are common.

Deterioration of performance
> The person experiences inability or difficulty in carrying out usual life activities such as work, family responsibilities, social/recreation, or any activity engaged in before the trauma.

Phobia
> The person experiences fearfulness and avoidance of the place where the accident occurred or extreme apprehension associated with some activity related to the trauma.

Personality change
> The person becomes withdrawn, moody, irritable, distracted, forgetful, and unlike his or her usual self.

Dudgeon
> The person gives expression to frequent unprovoked outbursts of anger with complaints about the carelessness of others and a retributive attitude. Quarrelsome behavior may be evident.

TABLE 5–1, continued

Depression

At some point following the trauma the person feels "blue" or "down in the dumps." A loss of self-confidence, a pessimistic attitude, brooding about past events, or feeling sorry for self may be noted. Social withdrawal, lack of pleasure, and a look of sadness on the face of a person formerly cheerful and outgoing may be extant.

Source: Compiled by author

approaches, patients are not rested but remain frightened and fatigued. Imaginal retraumatization (flashbacks) takes place, and this encephalic activity reexposes and sensitizes the patient to various aspects of the trauma. In this way, retraumatization continues unchecked over the course of months or years, unless interrupted by treatment.

A state of anxiousness continues throughout the day, and autonomic hyperactivity and increased motor tension produce psychosomatic symptoms or aggravate existing pain. The mind's eye turns inward, and patients frequently attribute their physical symptoms to some organic process. The endogenous sensations of pain and physical discomfort also stimulate intrusive distressing thoughts (encephalic activity) which remind patients of their trauma. The Spiral Effect of endogenous and encephalic events is set in motion, further intensifying anxiety. At times, anxiety may surge, producing feelings of unreality, depersonalization, and/or derealization.

During Stage II, patients' lives become centered around the trauma. Family and friends are relegated to a position of lesser importance as patients' self-centeredness contribute to an alienation from other people. Patients become preoccupied, introspective, and withdrawn; this change of behavior is noticed by friends and relatives who conclude that the patient has experienced a "personality change." Lifestyle alters as anxiety intrudes and interferes with usual activities. An inability to return to work is a bad omen, as occupational impairment affects finances and frequently entails a role reversal which is not conducive to harmonious family relationships. When a breadwinner is out of work, lack of money and uncongenial communication erodes a marriage. Unemployed people with a PTSD do not leave for work each morning, but remain home with the spouse. This increased togetherness does not lead to enhanced intimacy, but rather to increased opportunity for unpleasant confrontations. As marital satisfaction wanes, so does the frequency of sexual intercourse (Scrignar, 1987), along with a decline of shared pleasure from recreational and social activities.

Episodes of high anxiety impact on patients who encounter environmental stimuli closely resembling the scene of the trauma. Even depictions of accidents, injury, or death on television and in movies cause agitation and anxiety. For example, many persons involved in an automobile accident become highly agitated and anxious when viewing television programs which involve automobile crashes, chase scenes, the screeching of tires, and

FIGURE 5-1

Acute Post-Traumatic Stress Disorder (PTSD). Predisposed persons are at Level 2 prior to the impact of the environmental trauma (ET). The trauma poses a realistic threat to life or limb, is perceived as dangerous, and causes intense activation of the autonomic nervous system and a rise in anxiety. The traumatized person experiences severe anxiety that gradually diminishes after the trauma is over. In those persons who develop PTSD, anxiety does not return to a pretraumatic baseline but remains elevated at the moderate range (Level 3).

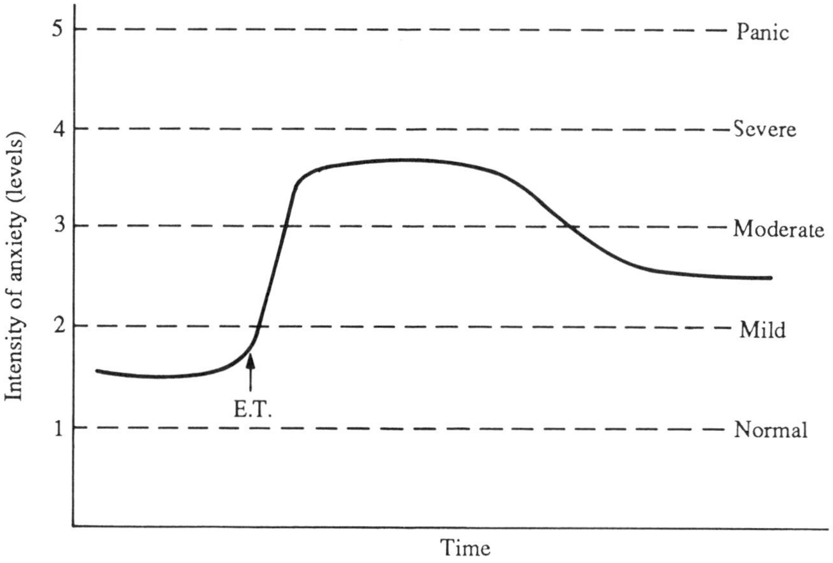

the sound of police sirens. Some patients develop a phobia and avoid surroundings similar to the traumatic scene. For instance, patients may avoid going to work if that is where the trauma took place. Others may avoid driving or riding in automobiles following an accident. Phobic behavior is often viewed by relatives and friends as peculiar, and contributes to the conclusion that a personality change has occurred. Persons are high-strung and overly sensitive to quick, unpredictable stimuli such as sudden noises, fast-moving objects, and commotion of any type.

FIGURE 5–2
Acute Post-Traumatic Stress Disorder (PTSD) — Prolonged Trauma. The environmental trauma (ET) poses a realistic threat to physical integrity, impacts on a vulnerable person, and is perceived as dangerous. The autonomic nervous system is stimulated, causing anxiety to rise into the intense range (Level 4). When the trauma is continuous (CT), such as in natural catastrophes or war, anxiety slowly escalates to Level 5, where it may remain for a period of time. At this point victims seem "numb" and in a "state of shock." Anxiety diminishes over time but does not return to pretraumatic levels, remaining instead at the high range of moderate anxiety (Level 3).

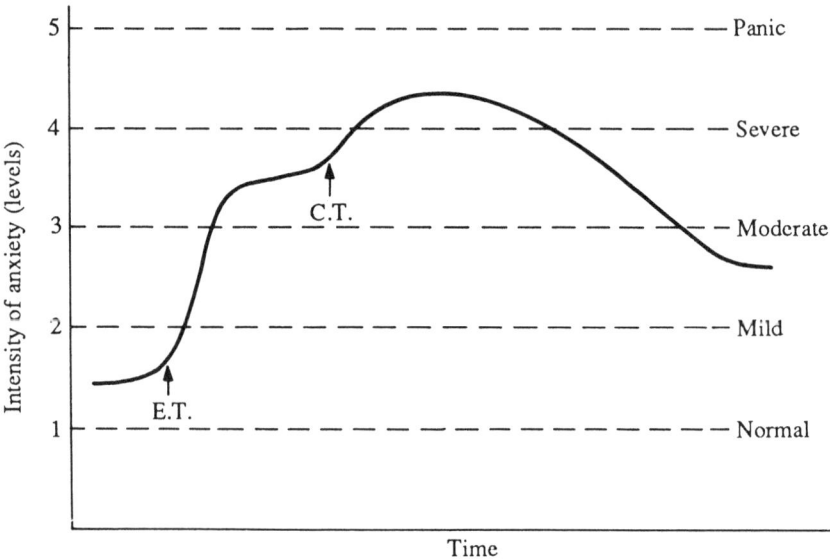

FIGURE 5–3

Chronic Post-Traumatic Stress Disorder (PTSD). Patients in the Chronic phase of PTSD are at the moderate level of anxiety (Level 3) throughout most of their waking hours. Environmental stressors (ES) not necessarily related to the original trauma may elevate anxiety to the severe range (Level 4). Persons in the chronic phase of PTSD are extremely vulnerable and sensitive to environmental stressors, since less intense stimuli are required to elevate anxiety into the severe range. Patients or clinicians may incorrectly ascribe symptomatic behavior to the original trauma when current life stressors are responsible for the elevation of anxiety.

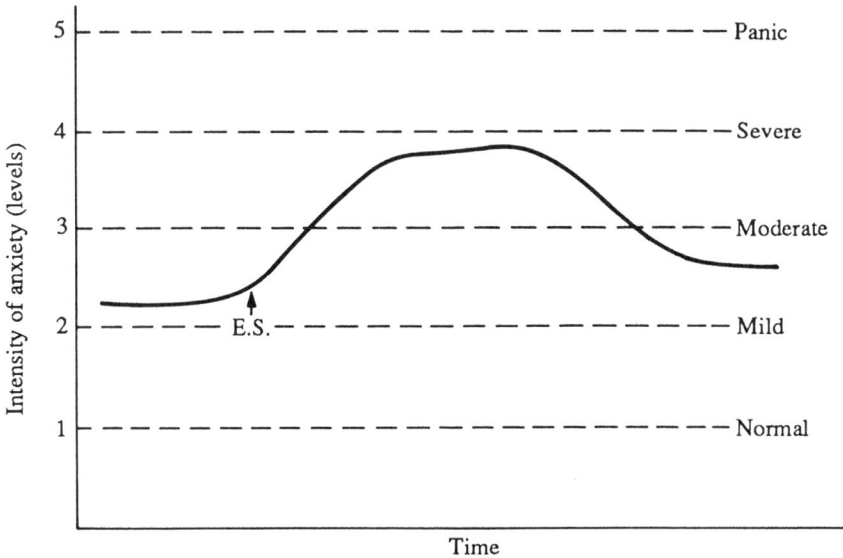

Fear and frustration are intermittently replaced by anger, irritability, and ill humor. An unpleasant disposition increases social isolation—people who dwell on the unpleasant side of life tend to be poor companions. A negativistic attitude concerning treatment also develops, especially if numerous visits to different doctors have produced no improvement. A retributive attitude solidifies and, in some cases, a visit to an attorney results in a personal injury lawsuit or similar form of legal action.

Stage III — Chronic Phase

There is no sharp delineation between the acute and chronic phase of a PTSD. After several months, however, the patient's emphasis and orientation gradually change from a preoccupation with the actual trauma to an obsessive concern with disability attributable to it. Disablement, demoralization, and despondency characterize Stage III. An inability to function lies at the core of the patient's thoughts and actions. Somatic preoccupation and ruminations relating to injury dominate the patient's waking hours. In their trek from doctor to doctor, patients dolorously declare that they only want to be the way they were before the trauma. In many cases, a comparison of lifestyle before and after the trauma is quite striking. Changes from being employed to unemployed, physically active to sedentary, good natured to grouchy, fun-loving to depressed, solvent to indebtedness, self-sufficient to dependent, and potent to impotent reflect but a few unpleasant extremes in lifestyle and status experienced by patients during the chronic phase.

Clinically, patients complain of many of the symptoms referable to motor tension, autonomic hyperactivity, and vigilance and scanning, which are characteristic of a Generalized Anxiety Disorder (GAD); however, a history of a precipitating trauma at onset distinguishes PTSD from GAD. Mood Disorder (Major Depressive Episode, Dysthymia) secondary to chronic anxiety and disablement are commonly manifest during Stage III; despair and a pessimistic mood can cloud and dominate other symptoms (Bromberg, 1979). Sometimes suicidal ideas emerge and coalesce into action, but suicidal attempts are seldom fatal. Some patients seek solace by resorting to alcohol or other drugs. Psychoactive substances, however, offer only short-term relief and severely complicate the course of PTSD. Breakdown in family relationships, financial problems, inability to work, and all of the other issues mentioned in Stage II continue in Stage III and worsen with time.

Although disability is the hallmark of Stage III, litigiousness does not lag far behind. Frustration and irritability escalate to a choleric mood, which eventually erupts into anger and a retributive attitude aimed toward those believed to be primarily responsible for the trauma and subsequent disability. Civil lawsuits, although prompted by anger and reprisal, are seldom specious, for in most cases a well-documented trauma precedes disability. The legal action once filed becomes the hub of patients' lives, and they frequently vilify their traumatizers, feeling completely justified in a bid to seek compensation for injuries incurred. Some patients become quasi lawyers, familiarizing themselves with pertinent laws and legal procedures.

Still others become impatient with the slowness of the legal process and phone their lawyers frequently in an attempt to hasten civil proceedings. Although patients who are involved in litigation may embellish and exaggerate their symptoms, it is the experience of the author that most malingerers have been weeded out by lawyers and doctors before cases come to court.

Many physicians and jurists are of the opinion that traumatized patients with significant psychiatric illness will recover following successful litigation. However, Daniel Sprehe (1984) in a follow-up of 108 patients over a ten-year period has reported that seventy-eight percent of his patients with significant psychiatric illnesses were "no better" and fifty-eight percent were not working following successful adjudication of their cases. The "greenback poultice" is more fantasy than fact. As Valliant (1981) has pointed out, continuing psychiatric therapy following settlement of the legal issues is required if traumatized patients are ever to return to the workplace.

During Stage III many patients become notoriously resistant to usual medical treatment and begin to believe that their condition is beyond the comprehension and therapeutic skills of their physicians. Disenchantment with medical therapy grows until patients become convinced that they are incurable and chronically disabled and have reached an end-stage in their illness. Lack of response to medical treatment reinforces and confirms this belief, and patients tend to shun a psychiatric referral because of the implication of "craziness." Disablement owing primarily to PTSD is an important concept and must be carefully explained to all patients.

It is interesting to speculate about how attorney and physician attitudes contribute to the patient's self-image as a disabled person. Lawyers, of course, see an advantage in manifest pathology at the time of the trial and may indicate this to patients either directly or indirectly. Physicians, frustrated by patients who turn plaintiff and whose emphasis seems more on tort than therapy, may dismiss such recalcitrants and label them laggards or malingerers who appear more motivated by money than cure. The treatment of patients with chronic PTSD offers an unusual challenge to physicians and requires patience, understanding, and tenacity. It is professionally rewarding when patients are rescued from a possible lifetime of unproductivity.

DELAYED ONSET

The reporting by patients or the observation by clinicians of stress symptoms of PTSD many months or even several years following the original trauma is called Delayed Onset. According to the DSM-III-R, Delayed Onset is specified if the onset of symptoms was at least six months after the trauma. This seems to suggest that the original trauma lies smoldering in the mind, like a ticking time bomb waiting to explode. Indeed, some clinicians conclude that the emotional effects of the original trauma had remained latent or dormant, only to surface at a later time (Kolb and Mutalipassi, 1982). Why and how this should occur and the mechanisms underlying a delayed response to trauma are never made clear by commentators. Lack of clarity, however, has not modulated interest in Delayed Onset PTSD, perhaps because the concept fits well into traditional psychiatric beliefs of conflict, repression, and defense mechanisms.

In the experience of the author, Delayed Onset is actually a term used to describe chronic PTSD which later is identified, possibly because symptoms have been made more manifest by subsequent stress. The delay, therefore, has been in recognizing, diagnosing, and treating an existing PTSD. An examination of the patient utilizing the concept of the Three E's usually reveals that an increment of anxiety at a later time is due to environmental stressors not directly related to the original trauma. Patients with inadequate personal resources, poor coping skills, and an absent or limited social support system fail to deal effectively with the additional stress and develop symptoms of anxiety, often taking on the coloring of the long-past trauma. To an untrained eye, it appears that the patient is having a delayed response to the original trauma, rather than symptom intensification owing to additional stress.

Delayed Onset PTSD can also be misapplied when a person has encountered two separate and discrete traumas at two different periods of time. Just as a person may fracture the same arm twice or contract the same illness on two or more occasions, an individual subjected to two different traumas can develop PTSD on each occasion.

A 59-year-old World War II combat veteran was driving his truck down a narrow highway that was shrouded with fog. Visibility was poor and the man slowed his truck. Suddenly, through the fog, he saw the dim outlines of headlights coming straight toward him. He slammed on the brakes and attempted to swerve away from the oncoming headlights, but a collision was unavoidable; he braced himself for the impact. At the last second, the oncoming vehicle swerved, too late, to the right, and the truck driver hit the other vehicle on the side, knocking it off the road and head-on into a tree. Unharmed but shaken, the truck driver got out of his cab and hurried to assist the stricken driver of the other vehicle. Looking into the wrecked automobile, he saw the battered face and broken body of the driver, apparently lifeless. Attempts to open the door of the car to rescue the driver were fruitless, and the truck driver went back to his vehicle and radioed for assistance. The state police arrived, conducted an investigation, and concluded that the dead man had been intoxicated, thereby exonerating the truck driver. Subsequently, the truck driver developed the typical signs and symptoms of PTSD.

Past history revealed that in 1943, when he was a 19-year-old Marine Corps private serving in the South Pacific, he was involved in fierce combat. Under constant fire from the Japanese, the young soldier and his platoon were pinned down and had to remain in a foxhole for a day and a long night. Frightened and fatigued, he fell into a deep sleep later that night as the fire lessened. Upon awakening the next morning, he tried to rouse his best friend who lay huddled against him. When he shook his friend by the shoulders, his head lolled back, revealing a large, bloodied cavity where the face had been. Panic stricken, the young private leapt out of his foxhole and ran to the rear to find a medic. Sobbing hysterically and speaking almost incoherently, he told the medics where to find his friend. He then was given an injection that calmed him. Later, he was shipped back to the United States and placed in the psychiatric ward of a military hospital. He received an honorable discharge for medical reasons from the U.S. Marine Corps and reentered civilian life. During the next three years he was in and out of Veterans' Administration hospitals because of extreme nervousness, sleep disturbance, incessant nightmares about war, and an inability to adjust to civilian life. Finally his symptoms subsided and he returned to activities he had enjoyed prior to the service. Over the course of the next thirty years, he did not require any further psychiatric treatment. Occasionally, memories of war intruded upon his consciousness and on rare occasions he dreamed about his combat experiences, but these symptoms never interfered with daily living.

Following the accident, which occurred thirty-five years after his last psychiatric hospitalization, the truck driver again developed nervousness, sleep disturbance, nightmares, and other symptoms of a PTSD. Ruminations and dream content were primarily related to his vehicular accident and the death of the driver. The second trauma also reminded him of his combat experiences and another physician made the diagnosis of delayed PTSD, but the previous war trauma remained at the periphery of the driver's mind. The second trauma precipitated a second PTSD and was not a Delayed Onset PTSD related to his war experience.

When people develop PTSD long after the time of the traumatic incident, it is important to search out the source of symptoms. One can discover a chronic untreated PTSD, symptoms of stress not directly related to PTSD, or, if another trauma has occurred, a second PTSD unrelated to the first. One must be cautious before applying the label Delayed Onset because of the implication that all subsequent stress symptoms are directly related to the original trauma.

Survivors of major catastrophes, rather than victims of unspectacular accidents, are more likely to receive the diagnosis of Delayed Onset. Wars, natural disasters, explosions, fires, or nuclear power plant malfunctions involving a huge loss of life and injury to many people make large impressions upon the minds of survivors and observers than do more mundane traumas. The patient and physician may, many months or years later, attribute any stress symptoms or pathologic behavior to the disaster. This assumption, of course, is not necessarily accurate, but it reinforces the "festering wound" or "ticking time bomb" hypothesis that the effects of a trauma can be delayed and appear at any time in the future.

Combat veterans of all wars carry within their minds terrible memories of death and destruction. When recalling battle scenes, most veterans may experience momentary anxiety, but not the persistent symptoms characteristic of PTSD. The celebrated author William Manchester described in his book *Goodbye Darkness: A Memoir of the Pacific War* scenes of World War II violence that included personal accounts of killing a Japanese soldier and being wounded himself. Manchester reported that the mental images related to his killing the Japanese soldier remained forever embedded in his mind and occasionally he still dreams about this incident. He required no psychiatric treatment and his subsequent life, judging from his success as an author, has not been adversely affected.

Veterans of the Vietnam conflict epitomize what is called Delayed Onset PTSD; however, the real delay was the acceptance by the government of the traumatic effects of war on the combat soldier and prisoner of war. Undeniably, if veterans, especially combat soldiers, had been examined prior to discharge, a significant number of them would have displayed signs and symptoms of PTSD. However, upon returning to the United States, many Vietnam-era veterans with PTSD were processed and discharged from the armed services, their stress disorder undetected, minimized, or ignored. The affected veterans, upon returning home, were plagued with memories and nightmares of wanton death and needless destruction. Ashamed and afraid, many of these veterans of the early post-Vietnam era neither sought treatment nor considered their symptoms and behavior to be pathologic. Biased emotionalism had distorted the effect of the Vietnam conflict on combat veterans, but as time passed, it became increasingly obvious that this conflict, like any other war, had left its mark on certain veterans. Symptoms typical of Stages II and III of PTSD experienced by veterans were endured or self-treated with alcohol or sedative-type drugs. In Vietnam many combat soldiers had easy access to unlimited quantities of inexpensive alcohol, opium, and hashish. Upon discharge, self-tranquilization learned in Vietnam was simply transferred to the United States, where these drugs had to be obtained illicitly, forcing some veterans to resort to antisocial behavior (Friedman, 1981). Substance abuse disrupts family life, increases suicidal risk, affects job performance, fosters antisocial behavior, and together with the debilitating effects of PTSD, severely incapacitates the veteran (Figley, 1978; Goodwin, 1980; Walker, 1981; Card, 1983). Statistical studies indicate that Vietnam combat veterans had more difficulties in readjustment than would be expected in a comparable population of veterans not exposed to combat (Fischer et al., 1980; Wilson, 1980; Keane and Fairbank, 1983). Later, when the Vietnam conflict was placed in perspective and the combat veteran received appropriate recognition for service to the country, PTSD was also recognized as a legitimate psychiatric sequela to war. The condition is, of course, service related and treatable.

SIX

DIAGNOSING PTSD

In PTSD what appears to be a potpourri of symptoms is really a complex and a well-organized set of pathologic behaviors interlaced with multiple issues occurring at different periods of time. At the onset when symptoms persist beyond one month, the clinician's chief concern may consist of sorting out the patient's complaints and determining whether the basic cause is physical, mental, or fraudulent. When physical factors are ruled out, the clinician must make a judgment about whether the symptoms are genuine (a mental disorder) or fake (malingered). As time passes even the relatedness of symptoms to trauma may be subject to question. Issues of laziness versus sickness may enter the clinical picture when a workers' compensation claim is initiated by the patient. When financial reward is tied to symptomatic behavior, the sincerity and character of the patient comes under scrutiny, as questions of primary and secondary gain are raised during a personal injury suit. Depending upon the personal and paradigmatic proclivities of the clinician, value judgments concerning the patient's symptoms may distort the clinical picture and result in an incorrect diagnosis. In truth, pejorative adjectives describe many post-traumatic behaviors, and clinicians must be aware of their own attitude towards chronic patients who claim disability, do not respond to treatment, and are involved in litigation.

The stage of the disorder at the time a mental status examination is conducted, determines which set of symptoms is observed. PTSD is a multi-faceted disorder, but pathologic anxiety always lies at the core. Anxiety symptoms persist throughout all three stages of PTSD, but they are more obvious during Stage I and during the earlier part of Stage II. Concern about somatic symptoms and depression, on the other hand, are more likely to occur during Stage III. A tendency toward exaggeration of symptoms occurring during the height of legal action must be differentiated from malingering and Factitious Disorder. Addiction to alcohol or other psychoactive substances begins in Stage II, but may become malignant during Stage III, completely obscuring other signs and symptoms of a PTSD. Patients obsessively preoccupied with pain may orient the clinician toward a physical problem or a Somatoform Disorder. Despondency and depression may be misinterpreted as a Mood Disorder unrelated to the original trauma. Disillusionment with medical treatment often found in patients during Stage III may be shared by physicians who have become upset with patients who do not respond to treatment, resulting in a referral or refusal to continue therapy. These are some of the pitfalls that await clinicians who evaluate and treat traumatized patients. A recognition of the signs and symptoms present in each of the three stages of PTSD and an appreciation of DSM-III-R diagnostic criteria direct the clinician to a correct diagnosis and appropriate treatment.

STAGES AND SYMPTOMS

Stage I — Response to Trauma

Most everyone responds emotionally to traumatic situations which pose a threat to life or limb. An airplane accident, an encounter with an armed robber, or an exposure to toxic gas would produce similar psychophysiological reactions of alarm and fear in most people. The trauma must be perceived and interpreted as dangerous to self or others and be followed by intense stimulation of the autonomic nervous system, producing symptoms characteristic of an acute anxiety reaction, as can be seen in Table 6-1. Patients describe the experience as a "spurt of adrenaline throughout my entire body." Feelings of fear are accompanied by an accelerated heartbeat, exaggerated and increased breathing, nausea (sometimes accompanied by vomiting), tremulousness, shaking of the entire body, dizziness, and a feeling of numbness and "shock." The number, type, and intensity of anxiety symptoms vary with the trauma and the individual. Sometimes persons experience a dissociative reaction with feelings of unreality or depersonalization. Subsequent to the trauma, patients may complain of sleep disturbances, bad dreams, pain, nervousness, and irrita-

TABLE 6–1
Characteristics and Symptoms of Stage I

Characteristics

History of a specific trauma from the environment which poses a realistic threat to life or limb has impacted on one or more of the five senses, has been interpreted and perceived as dangerous, and has resulted in a sudden discharge of the autonomic nervous system.

Almost everybody who is involved in a traumatic incident will respond in the fashion described above. For most persons these symptoms subside within a few weeks, and there is no impairment of family, vocational, recreational, or social life; treatment is not required and time usually heals. Stage I is not an anxiety disorder but a reaction to environmental stress. Pathologic behavior becomes manifest during Stage II.

Sources of Stress

Environmental

The environmental stimulus, the trauma, impacts on one or more of the five senses. The environs where the trauma took place frequently become a phobic stimulus, and, depending upon the nature of the trauma, similar settings may elicit anxiety. Any environmental event that is identical to or resembles any part of the traumatic incident may also stimulate anxiety.

Encephalic

The patient's encephalic activities consist of visualizing and thinking about the traumatic incident. Intrusive thoughts (flashbacks) of the trauma, highlighting closeness to death or serious injury, may occur. Dreams portraying the actual traumatic incident, some variant of it, or any situation involving danger are also frequent.

Endogenous

Endogenous events consist of pain or physical discomfort in any part of the body. The uncomfortable endogenous feelings were not present before the trauma, and the perception of them stimulates encephalic activity related to the initial trauma. Endogenous sensations may also be the result of chronic anxiety.

TABLE 6–1, continued

Symptoms

Helplessness, powerlessness
Increased heart rate
Dyspnea
Hyperventilation
Nausea
Vomiting
Extreme trembling or shaking
Excessive sweating
Dizziness
Feeling faint (light-headedness and unsteadiness)
Blurry vision
Hot flashes or flushing
Tingling sensations
Diarrhea
Urinary or fecal incontinence
Nervousness
Ringing in the ears
Outbursts of anger
Inability to remember recent events
Headaches
Pain
Restlessness
Hypersensitivity to sudden or rapidly changing stimuli (noise, light)
Sleep disturbance
Nightmares
Irritability
Difficulties in concentration
Feelings that familiar things are strange or unreal

Source: Compiled by author

bility. Patients may ponder the trauma and speculate about death and the impermanence of life. Exposure to environmental stimuli similar to or resembling the surroundings in which the original trauma took place also evokes anxiety. Loud noises, sudden kaleidoscopic visual phenomena, and abrupt changes in almost any stimulus irritate and make patients "jumpy" and apprehensive.

Interestingly, amnesia seems to protect people from the dysphoric emotional effects of a trauma. A failure to perceive impending danger correlates with diminished psychiatric morbidity. When persons are rendered unconscious as a result of the trauma and develop amnesia, post-traumatic anxiety is much less. A possible explanation is that in the absence of the "videotapes of the mind" retraumatization cannot take place.

For most a trauma produces only temporary discomfort and inconvenience. Even if the trauma was severe, people who are not predisposed to PTSD usually cope with the psychological reaction within a month. Memories of the traumatic incident may linger in the mind for years or even for a lifetime, but they do not intrude significantly on daily functioning. Transient symptoms of anxiety, sleeplessness, and even nightmares may occur sporadically, but no major disruption of life results. Stage I is the end point for most individuals who have encountered an environmental trauma. Vulnerable persons predisposed to PTSD or those subjected to an overwhelming trauma move on to Stage II.

Stage II — Acute Phase

A failure to cope with the trauma after one month signifies PTSD. Patients may be puzzled by the presence of intrusive thoughts, flashbacks, nightmares and complain of sleeplessness, fatigue, irritability, and a sense of estrangement (Table 6-2). Although pathologic anxiety lies at the heart of PTSD (Linn, 1975; Horowitz et al., 1980), patients mention nervousness as an aside, concentrating instead on the possibility that they could have been more seriously injured or killed. General appearance belies the minimizing of fear, as moist palms, apprehensive facies, and hyperactive motor movements clearly indicate anxiety. Because it is emotionally painful to discuss the details of the trauma, a patient relating the history often glosses over anxiety-laden material. Often, it becomes necessary to direct the patient's attention to events just prior to and shortly following impact. Questions regarding what the patient was thinking and feeling at that time usually reveal thoughts about annihilation and feelings of intense fear. As patients recall and relate the history, anxiety increases and talk becomes animated. Some patients will report the entire traumatic episode in great detail, pointing out that it seemed as if it were happening in slow motion. During impact and immediately thereafter, patients report symptoms relative to the thorax, including tachycardia, palpitations, dyspnea, tightness or pain in the chest, and at times hyperventilation. Tremulousness

TABLE 6–2
Characteristics and Symptoms of Stage II

Characteristics

Morbid preoccupation with the trauma marks this stage. Patients are obsessed with all aspects of their trauma and constantly speculate upon more dour consequences that could have resulted. Symptoms from Stage I are maintained beyond 4 to 6 weeks, and there is definite impairment of family, vocational, social, and recreational life.

Sources of Stress

Environmental

Environmental stimuli that are identical to or closely resemble the surroundings where the trauma took place may elicit pathologic anxiety even after a considerable amount of time has elapsed since the original trauma. The environs of the trauma frequently become a phobic stimulus, and, depending upon the nature and place of the trauma, similar settings may be avoided. Environmental settings that the patient considers to be dangerous may also elicit pathologic anxiety and may be avoided even though there is no similarity to the initial traumatic situation.

Encephalic

The hallmark of Stage II is a total preoccupation with the trauma. Patients spend endless hours daydreaming, fantasizing, thinking, or talking about various aspects of their traumatic experience. Frequently, speculation and elaboration include a more devastating trauma than the one experienced. Nightmares depicting the trauma or some variant of it cause patients to awaken suddenly in a state of alarm. Because of the noxious nature of nightmares, patients may dread sleep. Encephalic activity (obsessions and ruminations) generates and sustains pathologic anxiety, so that patients remain in a very uncomfortable state throughout most of their waking hours. Retraumatization, whereby the patient repeatedly visualizes the traumatic incident, is a pernicious part of PTSD and helps explain why patients remain symptomatic long after the trauma has passed.

Endogenous

Pain or any uncomfortable physical sensation is a common concomitant of PTSD and reminds patients of the original trauma. Endogenous sensations that were not present before the trauma focus the patient's mind on damage to self and stimulate encephalic activity in which the traumatic incident is replayed in the mind, further increasing pathologic anxiety. The Spiral Effect is set in

TABLE 6–2, continued

motion, contributing to more anxiety and more physiological sensations that are interpreted erroneously, thus completing the cycle.

Symptoms

Patients experience a generalized feeling of nervousness with occasional surges of higher anxiety. Any of the symptoms listed in Stage I may be noted in patients during Stage II. In addition, the following symptoms may also be present.

Phobic anxiety
Phobic avoidance
Physical discomfort
Disinterest in sex
Ruminations about the traumatic incident
Marital problems
Inability to work
Retributive attitude
Litigiousness
Feeling that personality has changed
Feeling detached from others
Not being able to express or show feelings
Thoughts of death
Thoughts about accidents, injury
Guilt feelings for or about the trauma
Feelings as if the accident were happening again
Feelings of discouragement (subclinical depression)
Disinterest in life (family, recreational activities, work)
Feeling of unreality (depersonalization, derealization)
Episodes of terror or panic
Difficulties in making decisions
Fatigue and weakness

Source: Compiled by author.

may be accompanied by nausea and vomiting. Dizziness and unsteadiness of gait may force patients to sit immediately after the trauma because they fear falling. Hot flashes or flushing may be accompanied by excessive sweating. Patients invariably report that the entire trauma was an extremely frightening experience.

If physical injuries require hospitalization, the PTSD process is put "on hold" since the patient's mind may be distracted by physical pain or blunted by sedative medication. When the patient is discharged from the hospital, a thread common to all sufferers with a PTSD emerges—obsessive preoccupation with the trauma. Retraumatization occurs by the repetitious playback of the "videotapes of the mind." Intrusive thoughts, flashbacks, and nightmares highlight the horrifying aspects of the trauma, but curiously downplay the fact of survival. The high levels of anxiety generated in this way sensitize the patient to various elements of the traumatic scene. The propensity of patients to ruminate, visualize, and talk about their trauma as if it were to be repeated soon, encephalically maintains symptoms and sustains the stress disorder.

As time passes, anxiety does not diminish but is heightened and maintained by the action and interplay of the Three E's. Patients continuously feel on edge, tense, jumpy, and look unwell. Commonly, patients complain of frontal or occipital headaches, tightness of the chest, nausea, and difficulties in concentration. Feelings of dizziness, giddiness, and unsteadiness are coupled with thoughts about fainting or abruptly losing consciousness, falling, and incurring injury. Episodes of depersonalization or derealization may occur during periods of increased stress.

Disturbed sleep invariably occurs at the onset of PTSD and leads to fatigue. At night patients ruminate over their trauma and related worrisome subjects, hence peace of mind leading to sleep becomes impossible. Patients tumble restlessly throughout most of the night, awakening the next day in a state of unrest and ill-temper. Nightmares depicting the traumatic event or a similar frightening variant frequently awaken patients from a shallow sleep. Sleep is dreaded because disturbing dreams may erupt unpredictably, reawakening unpleasant memories of the trauma. Following a night of broken and inadequate sleep, the patient is frazzled and unable to cope effectively with the events of the day.

When patients are exposed to the traumatic site or environmental surroundings that closely resemble it, anxiety becomes more apparent and intense, at times escalating into a panic attack. The sudden appearance of palpitations, tachycardia, shortness of breath, as well as other acute anxiety symptoms, terrifies patients and reinforces the idea that something is terribly wrong with them. Scenes of accidents, death, or injury on television or movie screens evoke high anxiety, frequently leading patients to close their eyes, turn off their television sets, or leave the theatre. Phobic avoidance of situations resembling the traumatic setting often develops and prevents a return to useful activities.

Although anxiety, flashbacks, and avoidance behavior are prominent, patients may feel offended if their physician or friends suggest that they consult a psychiatrist. Instead, the somatic manifestations of anxiety are interpreted by the patients as an indication of bodily damage or ongoing disease. An organic orientation blocks any insight into the psychological manifestations of PTSD, and some patients relentlessly continue their trek from doctor to doctor in search of a remedy. If the physical symptoms persist in spite of medical treatment, patients gradually conclude that the trauma has resulted in an incurable condition that has rendered them permanently disabled.

At some point during Stage II, some patients dwell on culpability for their trauma. Thoughts about negligence and carelessness of others spur anger and incite legal action. Clinicians must sort out exaggeration of the patient's complaints when litigation is pending. The Symptom Inventory Checklist (SIC) and the Anxiety Source Profile (ASP) help to assess the extent to which the patient is embellishing symptoms. Interviews with family members or friends also help to place the patient's symptoms in context with the trauma. Past medical or psychiatric records will give some indication of preexisting illness and pretraumatic personality and will shed light on the patient's coping skills. There is no question that litigation colors the symptomatic picture of PTSD, but in the author's experience outright conspiracy or malingering is infrequent. A retributive attitude may inspire litigation, but a lawsuit usually results from an honest assessment by the patient that he has been wronged and should receive compensation for injuries because of the carelessness of others.

In summary, patients who reach Stage II have developed PTSD. Anxiety does not recede but is maintained or increased by a combination of the Three E's. Obsessive concern for the traumatic incident characterizes Stage II, and as patients relive the trauma during flashbacks, conversations, ruminations, and in dreams, this process of retraumatization sustains the disorder. Environmental settings closely resembling the scenes of the trauma also stimulate pathologic anxiety, and patients frequently develop a phobic avoidance of these situations. The somatic manifestations of anxiety, along with any symptoms owing to physical injury, focus patients' attention on their bodily processes and increase anxiety vis-a-vis the Spiral Effect. If anxiety and physical symptoms persist, patients tend to attribute them to organic factors even if there is no objective evidence to support this conclusion. Towards the end of Stage II, patients become concerned with chronic disability and litigation.

Stage III — Chronic Phase

Emphasis shifts during Stage III from a preoccupation with the actual traumatic incident to an overzealous fixation on disability believed to have resulted from the trauma (Table 6-3). Patients become somatically preoccupied and pain, physical discomfort, fatigue, and a generalized feeling of malaise are likely chief complaints. Various aches and pains are described in minute detail, and patients tend selectively to glean ambiguous statements from their previous physicians and combine them with the results of inconclusive laboratory procedures to support the notion of physical impairment. The patient is not easily dissuaded from the erroneous belief that organic pathology is responsible for symptoms. If the physician dismisses the patient's symptoms cursorily without explanation, this is often interpreted as a lack of understanding and erodes the doctor-patient relationship. From the onset, patients must be told of the connection between stress and somatic symptoms, for this is often a pivotal point upon which success or failure in treatment may well be determined.

Beneath the somatic preoccupation and worry about physical disablement, a mental status examination will reveal chronic anxiety and symptoms similar to those of a Generalized Anxiety Disorder: motor tension, autonomic hyperactivity, and vigilance and scanning. Without a history of onset related to a specific traumatic event, PTSD might easily be mistaken for GAD. However, the SIC and ASP quickly reveal the type, severity, and scope of anxiety symptoms. Generalized feelings of nervousness, irritability, restlessness, inability to relax, tension headaches, upset stomach, worrying, and tiredness in the context of a trauma suggest PTSD. Feelings of unreality (depersonalization/derealization) may occur as anxiety increases. Less prominent, intermittent anxiety symptoms such as dizziness, blurred vision, ringing in the ears, tingling sensation, and vague physical sensations in almost any part of the body are usually not interpreted by patients as an indication of nervousness. A phobia or phobic anxiety of places or settings closely resembling the scene of the trauma is common.

TABLE 6–3
Characteristics and Symptoms of Stage III

Characteristics

During this stage the patient's preoccupation with the actual trauma recedes, being replaced by an obsessive preoccupation with the adverse consequences attributed to the trauma. Disability becomes the focus of the patient's life, and all pain, physical discomfort, and deficits of behavior are attributed directly to the traumatic incident. Changes in life-style and status result from impaired functioning and affect family, work, social and recreational activities. In this stage patients feel that a personality change has transpired because of the trauma. Chronic anxiety and problems attributed to disablement frequently lead to a secondary depression. During periods of stress, flashbacks can be associated with episodes of disassociation and feelings of unreality. A legal settlement of the patient's tort action occurs during Stage III but in most instances this has little effect on the course of the stress disorder.

Sources of Stress

Environmental

A wide variety of environmental stimuli perceived as dangerous may produce pathologic anxiety. Phobic anxiety or a phobia of the surroundings and situations related to the trauma may still exist. The patient's perceived disablement may adversely affect interpersonal relationships, participation in work, and social and recreational activities. Withdrawal from the environment is associated with depression.

Encephalic

The patient's central concern consists of disablement believed to have been caused by the original trauma. Although from time to time thoughts about the actual trauma cross the patient's mind, the traumatic incident no longer occupies a central place in thinking. The persistence of physical symptoms, nonresponse to treatment, incurability, permanent disablement, litigation, and the inability to resume usual life activities are themes that overshadow the actual trauma during Stage III. Depression is abetted by self-statements that impugn one's self-worth. Thoughts about death and suicide are not common but if present are indicative of depression. Patients become very self-centered and think excessively about their disability.

Endogenous

Inordinate attention to pain, physical discomfort, and normal physiological processes of the body reaches a zenith during Stage III. Sickness becomes a

TABLE 6–3, continued

dominant theme and incurability a constant thought as patients concentrate on their bodily sensations. The presence of pain and physical discomfort reinforces the belief that something is terribly wrong with them. Shortcomings, failures, and inability to cope are blamed on the "trauma-produced physical injury." Patients have little appreciation of the ability of pathologic anxiety to initiate or intensify somatic symptoms. The Spiral Effect between endogenous and encephalic events contributes to increasing anxiety and is operative throughout the chronic stage of Post-Traumatic Stress Disorder.

Symptoms

Anxiety Symptoms
Any of the anxiety symptoms listed in Tables 6–1 and 6–2 can be found during Stage III; however, the intensity of anxiety is usually lower and less obvious. Patients are more likely to complain of generalized anxiety and irritability. Occasionally, surges of high anxiety occur in response to environmental stimuli, and patients may report a dissociative state with episodes of depersonalization or derealization.

Somatic Symptoms
Headaches
Musculoskeletal pain in almost any part of the body
Weakness
Epigastric pain
Chest pain
Pain in that part of the body injured during the traumatic incident

Encephalic symptoms (intrusive thoughts)
Thoughts about permanent disablement and incurability
Thoughts about pain
Thoughts about the carelessness and lack of concern of others
Thoughts about litigation
Thoughts about accidents and injury
Thoughts about the disruption of life caused by the trauma
Thoughts about financial problems
Thoughts about work
Thoughts about powerlessness

TABLE 6–3, continued

Depressive Symptoms
> Crying spells
> Low energy level
> Feelings of worthlessness
> Thoughts about death
> Thoughts about suicide
> Sleep disturbance
> Social withdrawal, isolation, loneliness
> Loss of interest in pleasurable activities
> Pessimistic attitude
> Psychomotor retardation
> Loss of appetite
> Feel "blue" or "down in the dumps"

Source: Compiled by author.

Sleep disturbance continues, but the frequency of nightmares usually diminishes during Stage III. Some patients resort to alcohol or other drugs as a form of self treatment to allay anxiety, but a Psychoactive Substance Use Disorder only camouflages PTSD and complicates treatment.

Pessimistic ruminations permeate the patient's outlook during Stage III, and depression is often a secondary manifestation. In the chronic stage of PTSD, patients look unhappy and relate that they are "down in the dumps." They may sardonically complain of the following dysthymic symptoms: feelings of worthlessness, crying spells, thoughts of despair, death, and suicide, low energy level, lack of enjoyment, sleep disturbance, indecision, and appetite disturbance. An emotional detachment and withdrawal from family and friends together with a lack of interest in activities formerly found to be pleasurable accentuate a depressed mood. Most patients in the chronic phase are somewhat depressed; however, in some, the symptoms are quite severe, and clinicians must be alerted to the possibility of a Major Depressive Episode and suicide. A depressed mood also interferes markedly with marital relations, especially interest in sex (Scrignar, 1987), and performance at work.

A retributive attitude toward those believed to be responsible for their trauma, and hence their disability, evolves into litigiousness. A monetary award for injuries sustained as a result of the trauma helps to salve the mind as litigation becomes a way for the patient to strike back. Although some patients involved in litigation tend to exaggerate their symptoms, outright deception or malingering occurs infrequently and is usually easy to detect. Treatment is retarded when patients begin to concentrate on forensic matters. The resolution of legal issues does not mean treatment should be terminated, for successful litigation does not lead to a cure.

Trauma victims normally do not seek consultation or treatment for PTSD, but are referred by their treating physician or lawyer. During initial sessions, suspiciousness causes the patient to be guarded, and some resent the referral as an implication of insanity. The clinician is likely to be confronted with a fearful and irritable patient who may exhibit abruptness of manner, ill temper, and occasional outbursts of anger. A paranoid attitude may be evident when patients relate their symptoms and blame all of their problems on the trauma and the carelessness of others. Hostility may mount as patients give examples of a lack of concern or an uncaring attitude on the part of their employers, relatives, friends, doctors, or lawyers. Occasionally during Stage III, the patient's choleric mood intensifies and erupts into overt violent behavior towards others, usually a family member. These aggressive episodes are more likely to occur when the patient is experiencing undue stress or is under the influence of alcohol or other drugs. Verbal confrontations with physicians or lawyers occasionally occur, but physical violence is rare.

To summarize, in Stage III the patient's preoccupation with the traumatic incident recedes, and an obsessive concern with the disability attributable to the trauma predominates. Although the patient's chief complaint at this stage may be pain or physical discomfort, anxiety and anger are evident upon examination. Anxiety symptoms are similar to those of a GAD, but the onset of symptoms coinciding with a trauma distinguishes PTSD from GAD. A phobia or phobic anxiety of places or situations identical or similar to the surroundings where the trauma took place may worsen. Sleep disturbance continues, but nightmares become less frequent. PTSD in the chronic phase is often associated with secondary depression, and in some cases the Mood Disorder may be quite severe and suicide is a possibility. The somatic manifestations of anxiety when misinterpreted by patients hinder treatment and lead to frustration and dudgeon. Anger and a desire to be compensated for the negligence of others motivate legal action and preoccupy patients during Stage III.

CHILDREN AND PTSD

In DSM-III-R specific reference is made for the first time to children and PTSD. Previously, a variety of emotional disturbances in children had been reported following natural disasters such as the tornado in Xenia, Ohio, the earthquake in San Fernando, California, and in the well-known Buffalo Creek calamity (Frederick, 1981). Following these disasters, a significant number of children experienced phobias, sleep disturbances, fears, loss of interest in school, and were less responsible. In DSM-III-R age-specific features include: a child's refusal to discuss the trauma, distressing dreams of the event involving threats to self or others, generalized nightmares of monsters or rescue, reliving the trauma through repetitive play, diminished interest in significant activities, constriction of affect, a marked change in orientation towards the future (pessimism, no expectation of marrying, having children, or a career), "omen formation" (belief in an ability to prophesy future untoward events), and general symptoms of increased arousal (stomach aches, headaches).

Some investigators feel that in children, no preexisting phenomenology or psychiatric symptomatology need be necessary for PTSD to develop (Benedek, 1985). Others conclude that the course, impairment, and complications in children are distinguishable from symptoms in adults. Areas which need further clarification include the impact of various types of trauma, the age and developmental level at which the trauma occurs, the level of family and community support, and the type of treatment best suited for children (Eth and Pynoos, 1985). One can be sure with the recognition that children can develop PTSD, more cases will be diagnosed and treated by mental health professionals and more children will become plaintiffs in personal injury cases.

SEVEN

DIFFERENTIAL DIAGNOSIS*

Diagnosis of PTSD is easy when the clinician is oriented to the concept that trauma, whether it produces physical injury or not, can precipitate a stress disorder. A history will reveal the quadriga of PTSD, drawn by the horses of a markedly distressing stressor, persistently reexperienced traumatic event, persistent avoidance of stimuli associated with the trauma, and persistent symptoms of increased arousal. Continuation of symptoms beyond one month indicates a pathologic reaction to trauma and the development of a PTSD. As time passes, the relationship between the trauma and symptomatic behavior becomes less obvious, and misdiagnoses can occur when the clinician or patient either overlooks or de- emphasizes the connection between the two.

Depending upon the stage of PTSD, a plethora of symptoms confront the clinician: anxiety, intrusive thoughts, depression, phobias, pain, vague somatic complaints, sleep disturbance, nightmares, sexual dysfunction, fatigue, and irritability. Further examination may reveal physical injury, marital discord, inability to work, lack of interest in life, financial problems, an unresolved personal injury lawsuit, and other problem behaviors. If the patient presents with alcohol or drug abuse, this may deflect the clinician's attention from PTSD to a Psychoactive Substance Use Disorder. At times, deep depression mutes some symptoms of PTSD, making diagnosis

*All tables of diagnostic criteria in this chapter from: *Diagnostic and Statistical Manual of Mental Disroders*, Third Edition, Revised, 1987. Reprinted with permission of American Psychiatric Association.

117

difficult. Panic Disorder, Somatoform Disorder, Organic Mental Syndrome, Adjustment Disorder, and Antisocial Personality Disorders as well as malingering and Factitious Disorders must be considered before a diagnosis of PTSD is finalized. As clinicians ferret through the maze of diagnostic possibilities, they must keep in mind that trauma initiates PTSD and anxiety lies at its core.

ORGANIC MENTAL SYNDROMES

Following head trauma, especially if a long period of unconsciousness has resulted, psychological or behavioral signs and symptoms may suggest damage to the brain. In Organic Personality Syndrome (Table 7-1), three patterns of behavior may emerge, depending upon the nature and location of the pathologic process within the brain. Affective instability and impairment in social judgment characterize one type. Irritability and temper outbursts that are inappropriate and out of proportion to a precipitating event may be observed, and persons may engage in socially inappropriate behavior, such as sexual indiscretions, with little concern for the consequences. A second pattern of Organic Personality Syndrome consists of marked apathy and indifference. These persons may minimize or deny symptoms and claim that they have not been affected by the trauma, even though relatives and friends report a marked change in personality. Lack of interest in usual activities or hobbies and an apparent unconcern with daily events has led some researchers to label this type as "frontal lobe syndrome." A third pattern, seen in some people with temporal lobe epilepsy, involves a marked tendency toward humorless verbosity. Religiosity coupled with exaggerated aggressiveness is a quizzical finding. When paranoid ideation (suspiciousness, distrustfulness, and outright feelings of persecution) and outbursts of rage are the predominant features, this is known as the "Explosive Type of Organic Personality Syndrome."

If trauma resulted in damage to the brain, Organic Personality Syndrome may be irreversible and lifelong in duration. A verified history of head trauma, unconsciousness, a personality change attested to by those familiar with the victim before the trauma and a mental status examination consistent with organic brain pathology is sufficient to make a diagnosis. Negative laboratory tests such as CAT scan, nuclear magnetic resonance, electroencephalogram, or other procedures do not necessarily nullify or exclude a diagnosis of organicity. Some neuropsychological tests can disclose cognitive deficits associated with Organic Mental Syndrome.

TABLE 7–1
Diagnostic criteria for Organic Personality Syndrome

A. A persistent personality disturbance, either lifelong or representing a change or accentuation of a previously characteristic trait, involving at least one of the following:

    (1) affective instability, e.g., marked shifts from normal mood to depression, irritability, or anxiety

    (2) recurrent outbursts of aggression or rage that are grossly out of proportion to any precipitating psychosocial stressors

    (3) markedly impaired social judgment, e.g., sexual indiscretions

    (4) marked apathy and indifference

    (5) suspiciousness or paranoid ideation

B. There is evidence from the history, physical examination, or laboratory tests of a specific organic factor (or factors) judged to be etiologically related to the disturbance.

C. This diagnosis is not given to a child or adolescent if the clinical picture is limited to the features that characterize Attention-deficit Hyperactivity Disorder.

D. Not occurring exclusively during the course of Delirium, and does not meet the criteria for Dementia.

Specify explosive type if outbutsts of aggression or rage are the predominant feature.

Following a head trauma resulting in an Organic Personality Syndrome, a person may also develop the signs and symptoms characteristic of PTSD. When this occurs, both diagnoses should be made.

> One patient, a 42-year-old married woman, was crossing a street when she was hit by an automobile and rendered unconscious. She was in a coma for ten days and upon regaining consciousness could not remember the accident. Her recuperation was slow, and initially she was in great pain owing to fractures of two ribs and the right upper arm. X-rays of the skull, CAT scan, and electroencephalogram were negative. The signs and symptoms of PTSD were not present, but the

patient experienced emotional lability, impairment in impulse control, mild apathy, indifference, and suspiciousness. The patient's mental symptoms were a result of trauma but caused by an Organic Personality Syndrome and not PTSD. Neuropsychological tests confirmed the diagnosis.

Another Organic Mental Syndrome, Organic Anxiety Syndrome, is characterized by recurrent panic attacks or generalized anxiety which may be confused with symptoms of PTSD. Organic Anxiety Syndrome (OAS) is generally caused by endocrine disorders or the use of psychoactive substances. Although uncommon, brain tumors and epilepsy involving the diencephalon are also associated with anxiety. DSM-III-R lists other possible etiologies of OAS: pulmonary embolus, chronic obstructive pulmonary disease, aspirin intolerance, collagen-vascular disease, brucellosis, vitamin B-12 deficiency, demyelinating disease, and heavy metal intoxication. Head trauma is an unlikely cause for OAS.

PSYCHOSIS AND PTSD

Sometimes a trauma is associated with the presence of a psychotic mental disorder such as Schizophrenia, Delusional (Paranoid) Disorder, or Mood Disorder. Although stress related to trauma may aggravate these major mental disorders, a careful history and mental status examination usually reveal that psychosis and poor reality testing preexisted the trauma. An environmentally-induced traumatic event may worsen but does not cause Schizophrenia or any of the psychotic disorders. In the absence of Organic Mental Syndromes, psychosis is widely believed to be a genetically determined biological mental disorder that may be made more manifest but not caused by environmental stress. There are some exceptions to this general rule, *e.g.,* Brief Reactive Psychosis, but this condition is relatively rare.

Questions may arise when there is an absence of any previous history of psychosis and the trauma seems to precipitate a mental disorder with symptoms of psychosis. Medical and legal experts may wish to debate the causal relationship between trauma and psychosis, but the link is, at best, tenuous. However, persons suffering from Schizophrenia, when exposed to an environmental trauma, may develop symptoms of stress and PTSD. In this case both mental disorders should be diagnosed—Schizophrenia as a preexisting disorder and the PTSD as a consequence of the trauma. During legal proceedings, mental health professionals may feel that they are trying to untie the Gordian knot as they attempt to explain to the court the relationship of trauma, Schizophrenia, and PTSD. No dilemma exists, however, if clinicians explain that Schizophrenia is a preexisting genetically-determined, biological mental disorder and PTSD is an environmentally-induced disorder.

PANIC DISORDER

As can be seen from Section C of Table 7-2, Panic Disorder (PD) and PTSD share many of the same symptoms. Typically in PD, panic attacks begin with the sudden onset of intense fear or terror and a feeling of impending doom; however, in most cases no realistic threat to life or limb exists. The junior executive mentioned at the beginning of Chapter 3 experienced a panic attack while temporarily trapped in a hotel bathroom. Avoidance behavior is common to both PD and PTSD, but in PD, some patients develop agoraphobia, the fear of being in places or situations from which escape would be difficult or help not forthcoming. In PTSD, avoidance behavior centers around the theme of the trauma; patients tend to avoid those things which arouse recollections of the trauma. PD and

TABLE 7–2
Diagnostic criteria for Panic Disorder

A. At some time during the disturbance, one or more panic attacks (discrete periods of intense fear or discomfort) have occurred that were (1) unexpected, i.e., did not occur immediately before or on exposure to a situation that almost always caused anxiety, and (2) not triggered by situations in which the person was the focus of others' attention.

B. Either four attacks, as defined in criterion A, have occurred within a four-week period, or one or more attacks have been followed by a period of at least a month of persistent fear of having another attack.

C. At least four of the following symptoms developed during at least one of the attacks:

　(1)　shortness of breath (dyspnea) or smothering sensations
　(2)　dizziness, unsteady feelings, or faintness

TABLE 7–2, continued

---

    (3) palpitations or accelerated heart rate (tachycardia)
    (4) trembling or shaking
    (5) sweating
    (6) choking
    (7) nausea or abdominal distress
    (8) depersonalization or derealization
    (9) numbness or tingling sensations (paresthesias)
    (10) flushes (hot flashes) or chills
    (11) chest pain or discomfort
    (12) fear of dying
    (13) fear of going crazy or of doing something uncontrolled

Note: Attacks involving four or more symptoms are panic attacks; attacks involving fewer than four symptoms are limited symptom attacks.

D. During at least some of the attacks, at least four of the C symptoms developed suddenly and increased in intensity within ten minutes of the beginning of the first C symptom noticed in the attack.

E. It cannot be established that an organic factor initiated and maintained the disturbance, e.g., Amphetamine or Caffeine Intoxication, hyperthyroidism.

Note: Mitral valve prolapse may be an associated condition, but does not preclude a diagnosis of Panic Disorder.

PTSD share symptoms of increased arousal but differ in respect to onset. PTSD is precipitated by an environmental event which poses a realistic threat to life or limb and afterwards patients persistently reexperience the traumatic event in the form of intrusive thoughts, flashbacks, and nightmares. No such sequence of events occurs in PD. The application of the Traumatic Principle and the Three E's quickly differentiates PD from PTSD during the diagnostic evaluation.

DEPRESSIVE DISORDERS

Major Depression or Dysthymia (Table 7-3) is often a psychological sequela to trauma. When trauma produces injury with physical disability, especially if recovery is protracted or not forthcoming, patients may develop a Mood Disorder. Depression following trauma is probably more common than PTSD, especially when lifestyle has been significantly altered by physical infirmity or disfigurement. Severe burn scars, dismemberment, loss of a sensory organ, paralysis, or severe chronic pain serve as constant reminders of a loss resulting in a change of body image and a Mood Disorder.

During Stage III of PTSD, sleep disturbance, chronic fatigue, poor concentration, lack of interest in work, impaired family relationships, social withdrawal, irritability and anger, concern with physical health, and a pessimistic attitude toward life are frequent complaints of a patient. As can been seen from Table 7-3, these characteristics fulfill many of the criteria for Dysthymia. Depression, as has been noted earlier, is a common secondary manifestation of trauma and may mask the signs and symptoms of PTSD. Sometimes the depressive symptoms are severe, as in a Major

TABLE 7–3
Diagnostic criteria for 300.40 Dysthymia

A. Depressed mood (or can be irritable mood in children and adolescents) for most of the day, more days than not, as indicated either by subjective account or observation by others, for at least two years (one year for children and adolescents)

B. Presence, while depressed, of at least two of the following:

   (1) poor appetite or overeating
   (2) insomnia or hypersomnia
   (3) low energy or fatigue
   (4) low self-esteem
   (5) poor concentration or difficulty making decisions
   (6) feelings of hopelessness

C. During a two-year period (one-year for children and adolescents) of the disturbance, never without the symptoms in A for more than two months at a time.

TABLE 7–3, continued

D. No evidence of an unequivocal Major Depressive Episode during the first two years (one year for children and adolescents) of the disturbance.

Note: There may have been a previous Major Depressive Episode, provided there was a full remission (no significant signs or symptoms for six months) before development of the Dysthymia. In addition, after these two years (one year in children or adolescents) or Dysthymia, there may be superimposed episodes of Major Depression, in which case both diagnoses are given.

E. Has never had a Manic Episode or an unequivocal Hypomanic Episode.

F. Not superimposed on a chronic psychotic disorder, such as Schizophrenia or Delusional Disorder.

G. It cannot be established that an organic factor initiated and maintained the disturbance, e.g., prolonged administration of an antihypertensive medication.

Depressive Episode, and suicide is a real possibility. At other times, the dysthymic symptoms are submerged beneath more obvious problems and clinicians, unless alert, can fail to make the proper diagnosis. The debilitating effects of a trauma together with a failure of medical treatment causes hopelessness which fuels depression. In those PTSD patients having severe depression which definitely interferes with the person's functioning, the additional diagnosis of a Major Depressive Episode or Dysthymia should also be made.

SOMATOFORM DISORDERS

Complaints of pain or physical discomfort dominate many trauma patients' verbalizations, therefore, mental disorders in which somatic symptoms play a prominent role should be ruled out before making a diagnosis of PTSD. Of course, organic pathology must be assessed by appropriate physical and laboratory examinations before any psychiatric disorder is considered. In the absence of a physical disorder, a Somatoform Disorder should be considered when patients continue to complain of physical symptoms. Since any of the following Somatoform Disorders—

Somatization, Conversion, Pain, and Hypochondriasis—can be mistaken for a PTSD, the important differences among all of these disorders will be highlighted.

Somatization Disorder

Table 7-4 illustrates the similarity of symptoms for Somatization Disorder and PTSD. Pain, cardiopulmonary, psychosexual, gastrointestinal, and pseudoneurological symptoms may be present in patients with PTSD who also appear to be quite sickly during the chronic stage of the disorder.

Important differences, however, exist between Somatization Disorder and PTSD. In PTSD, the onset of symptoms follows a specific environmental trauma and may occur at any age. During Stage II, the traumatic incident is a dominant and intrusive feature of PTSD. The patient's ruminations, fantasies, and dreams about the trauma also differentiate PTSD from Somatization Disorder. An exaggerated startle response, sleep disturbance, nightmares, a phobia or phobic anxiety related to the trauma, or a disinterest or withdrawal from significant activities beginning soon after the trauma further distinguish PTSD from Somatization Disorder. PTSD patients may exhibit a wide range of symptoms as they progress from Stage I to Stage III, but these do not reflect an almost lifelong, polysymptomatic disorder as is the case in Somatization Disorder.

TABLE 7–4
Diagnostic criteria for 300.81 Somatization Disorder

A. A history of many physical complaints or a belief that one is sickly, beginning before the age of 30 and persisting for several years.

B. At least 13 symptoms from the list below. To count a symptom as significant, the following criteria must be met:

  (1) no organic pathology or pathophysiologic mechanism (e.g., a physical disorder or the effects of injury, medication, drugs, or alcohol) to account for the symptom or, when there is related organic pathology, the complaint or resulting social or occupational impairment is grossly in excess of what would be expected from the physical findings

TABLE 7–4, continued

(2) has not occurred only during a panic attack
(3) has caused the person to take medicine (other than over-the-counter pain medication), see a doctor, or alter life-style

Symptom list:

Gastrointestinal symptoms:

(1) **vomiting (other than during pregnancy)**
(2) abdominal pain (other than when menstruating)
(3) nausea (other than motion sickness)
(4) bloating (gassy)
(5) diarrhea
(6) intolerance of (gets sick from) several different foods

Pain symptoms:

(7) **pain in extremities**
(8) back pain
(9) joint pain
(10) pain during urination
(11) other pain (excluding headaches)

Cardiopulmonary symptoms:

(12) **shortness of breath when not exerting oneself**
(13) palpitations
(14) chest pain
(15) dizziness

Conversion or pseudoneurologic symptoms:

(16) **amnesia**
(17) **difficulty swallowing**
(18) loss of voice
(19) deafness
(20) double vision
(21) blurred vision
(22) blindness
(23) fainting or loss of consciousness

TABLE 7–4, continued

(24)   seizure or convulsion
(25)   trouble walking
(26)   paralysis or muscle weakness
(27)   urinary retention or difficulty urinating

Sexual symptoms for the major part of the person's life after opportunities for sexual activity:

(28)   burning sensation in sexual organs or rectum (other than during intercourse)
(29)   sexual indifference
(30)   pain during intercourse
(31)   impotence

Female reproductive symptoms judged by the person to occur more frequently or severely than in most women:

(32)   **painful menstruation**
(33)   irregular menstrual periods
(34)   excessive menstrual bleeding
(35)   vomiting throughout pregnancy

Note: The seven items in boldface may be used to screen for the disorder. The presence of two or more of these items suggests a high likelihood of the disorder.

Conversion Disorder

As in a PTSD, there is a relationship between an environmental stimulus and the onset of a Conversion Disorder (Table 7-5). Unlike in PTSD, patients suffering from conversion reaction often exhibit "la belle indifference," an attitude of unconcern for their physical disability, which is discordant with the severity of the impairment. Issues of primary and secondary gain are of prime importance and are present from the onset in a Conversion Disorder, whereas in PTSD the onset is associated with a stressor, "that is outside the range of usual human experience and that would be markedly distressing to almost anyone" (DSM-III-R).

127

Acute anxiety symptoms are evident from the start in PTSD, and chronic anxiety is commonplace during the latter stages. Anxiety is absent or not prominent in a Conversion Disorder. If "la belle indifference" characterizes a Conversion Disorder, "la belle difference" marks PTSD patients, who are fearful, irritable, and ill-tempered, frequently exhibiting a belligerent attitude toward those believed to be responsible for their trauma. Litigious PTSD patients may have a "secondary gain" in mind when they file a lawsuit, but self-righteousness, a belief that they should be compensated for damages caused by another's negligence, motivates this action. The primary and secondary gain of those with a conversion disorder reflects more subtle needs based on a psychological conflict. The PTSD patient's somatic symptoms are usually anxiety related, whereas the physical disturbance of patients with a Conversion Disorder cannot be explained by any physical disorder or pathophysiological mechanism.

TABLE 7–5
Diagnostic criteria for 300.11 Conversion Disorder

A. A loss of, or alteration in, physical functioning suggesting a physical disorder.

B. Psychological factors are judged to be etiologically related to the symptom because of a temporal relationship between a psychosocial stressor that is apparently related to a psychological conflict or need and initiation or exacerbation of the symptom.

C. The person is not conscious of intentionally producing the symptom.

D. The symptom is not a culturally sanctioned response pattern and cannot, after appropriate investigation, be explained by a known physical disorder.

E. The symptom is not limited to pain or to a disturbance in sexual functioning.

Specify: single episode or **recurrent.**

Somatoform Pain Disorder

In both Somatoform Pain Disorder (SPD) and Conversion Disorder, psychological factors are judged to be etiologically important, and motivation for the maintenance of symptoms involves primary and secondary gain. Somatoform Pain Disorder, therefore, could be considered a Conversion Disorder with pain as the most prominent symptom. According to the DSM-III-R, owing to the different course and treatment implications, pain that can be conceptualized as a conversion symptom should instead be coded separately as a Somatoform Pain Disorder.

TABLE 7–6
Diagnostic criteria for 307.80 Somatoform Pain Disorder

A. Preoccupation with pain for at least six months.

B. Either (1) or (2):

  (1) appropriate evaluation uncovers no organic pathology or pathophysiologic mechanism (e.g., a physical disorder or the effects of injury) to account for the pain
  (2) when there is related organic pathology, the complaint of pain or resulting social or occupational impairment is grossly in excess of what would be expected from the physical findings

Pain following trauma can be common to both PTSD and SPD. In the absence of any organic cause, complaints of pain associated with PTSD are usually related to fluctuations in the level of anxiety. The source of the patient's pain can usually be traced to pathologic anxiety emanating from any combination of the Three E's, whereas in Somatoform Pain Disorder no pathophysiological mechanism can be found to account for the pain. Additionally, pain in PTSD, unlike in SPD, is not the primary disturbance. At times pain may be the most prominent symptom, but the onset, course, signs, and symptoms of PTSD clearly indicate an anxiety disorder with pain as one possible feature within a constellation of other symptoms.

Hypochondriasis

The common features shared by Hypochondriasis (Table 7-7) and some PTSD patients are "preoccupation with the fear of having, or the belief that

TABLE 7–7
Diagnostic criteria for 300.70 Hypochondriasis

A. Preoccupation with the fear of having, or the belief that one has, a serious disease, based on the person's interpretation of physical signs or sensations as evidence of physical illness.

B. Appropriate physical evaluation does not support the diagnosis of any physical disorder that can account for the physical signs or sensations or the person's unwarranted interpretation of them, **and** the symptoms in A are not just symptoms of panic attacks.

C. The fear of having, or belief that one has, a disease persists despite medical reassurance.

D. Duration of the disturbance is at least six months.

E. The belief in A is not of delusional intensity, as in Delusional Disorder, Somatic Type (i.e., the person can acknowledge the possibility that his or her fear of having, or belief that he or she has, a serious disease is unfounded).

one has, a serious disease, based on the person's interpretation of physical signs or sensations as evidence of physical illness." Onset following an identifiable trauma and obsessive preoccupation with the traumatic incident characterize PTSD and distinguish it from Hypochondriasis. Physical defect caused by the injurious effects of a trauma captures the concern of the PTSD patient, whereas fear of having a dreaded disease occupies the mind of a hypochondriacal patient. Complaints fluctuate with hypochondriacal patients, involving various organ systems and diseases, but in PTSD the somatic complaint, usually pain, is steadfast and focuses on the part of the body believed to have been damaged by the trauma. In many respects, symptoms of Hypochondriasis correspond to Stage III—the chronic stage of PTSD. The onset and markedly different clinical course, however, clearly separate PTSD from Hypochondriasis.

ADJUSTMENT DISORDERS

Adjustment Disorders (Table 7-8) are usually a mild, time-limited maladaptive reaction to a psychosocial stressor(s) manifested by an anxious or depressed mood or an inhibition or breakdown related to work, school, or conduct. Stressors are easily identifiable and may include divorce, business reversal, chronic illness, discordant intra-familial relationship, or a natural disaster. Symptoms usually occur within three months after the onset of the stressor and persist for no longer than six months. In Adjustment Disorder, an anxious or depressed mood may interfere with occupational (including school) functioning or interpersonal relationships, but within a short period of time symptoms abate as persons so affected reach a new level of adaptation.

Application of the Traumatic Principle distinguishes PTSD patients from those suffering from an Adjustment Disorder. No serious threat to life or limb usually exists, and flashbacks and recurrent and intrusive distressing recollections of the event are absent. Persons with an Adjustment Disorder may obsess about their current plight, but worrisome and pessimistic ruminations about the future should not be confused with intrusive thoughts related to a trauma. The nature of the stressor, the relatively mild

TABLE 7–8
Diagnostic criteria for Adjustment Disorder

A. A reaction to an identifiable psychosocial stressor (or multiple stressors) that occurs within three months of onset of the stressor(s).

B. The maladaptive nature of the reaction is indicated by either of the following:

(1) impairment in occupational (including school) functioning or in usual social activities or relationships with others
(2) symptoms that are in excess of a normal and expectable reaction to the stressor(s)

C. The disturbance is not merely one instance of a pattern of overreaction to stress or an exacerbation of one of the mental disorders previously described.

D. The maladaptive reaction has persisted for no longer than six months.

E. The disturbance does not meet the criteria for any specific mental disorder and does not represent Uncomplicated Bereavement.

and brief duration of symptoms, the absence of persistently recurrent intrusive thoughts, and limited or no avoidance behavior clearly differentiate an Adjustment Disorder from PTSD.

PHOBIC AND GENERALIZED ANXIETY DISORDERS

Clinicians unfamiliar with the concept of stress and avoidance behavior following a trauma might mistakenly conclude that the patient's complaints reflect a Generalized Anxiety or Phobic Disorder. Simple Phobia and GAD may be erroneously diagnosed when an unsuspecting clinician fails to trace the beginnings of symptoms to a trauma which may have been experienced months or even years before. The ubiquity of anxiety necessitates closer scrutiny and comparison between many clinical syndromes and criteria for PTSD.

Simple Phobia

At the time of the traumatic incident, patients may be conditioned adversely to the surroundings where the trauma took place. Depending upon the circumstances, patients subsequently can develop a phobia or avoidance of situations, surroundings, or objects identical or similar to those present at the time of the trauma. It is not uncommon for patients who have been involved in automobile accidents to avoid driving or riding in cars, or for workers who have been injured in industrial accidents to avoid the work place. Seamen who have been involved in a marine accident may avoid ships and the sea. The avoidance may not be limited to the site of the trauma, but may extend to the performance of activities related to the original trauma. For example, a young man who was seriously burned during an explosion in an oil refinery avoided lighting matches, cooking on an open gas burner, barbecuing steaks, and handling solvents or any potentially flammable materials.

PTSD patients experience pathologic anxiety while they are in surroundings which resemble those where the trauma took place. Any avoidance of such places is accompanied by anxiety reduction, which in turn reinforces avoidance behavior, as is true in all Phobic Disorders. In PTSD, the phobia that was precipitated by the acute trauma is symptomatically indistinguishable from a Simple Phobia (see Table 7-9). The post-traumatic onset of the phobia and the presence of the symptom cluster of PTSD place the phobia in the context of a broader disorder, thus distinguishing it from a Simple Phobia.

TABLE 7–9
Diagnostic criteria for 300.29 Simple Phobia

A. A persistent fear of a circumscribed stimulus (object or situation) other than fear of having a panic attack (as in Panic Disorder) or of humiliation or embarrassment in certain social situations (as in Social Phobia).

   Note: Do not include fears that are part of Panic Disorder with Agoraphobia or Agoraphobia without History of Panic Disorder.

B. During some phase of the disturbance, exposure to the specific phobic stimulus (or stimuli) almost invariably provokes an immediate anxiety response.

C. The object or situation is avoided, or endured with intense anxiety.

D. The fear or the avoidant behavior significantly interferes with the person's normal routine or with usual social activities or relationships with others, or there is marked distress about having the fear.

E. The person recognizes that his or her fear is excessive or unreasonable.

F. The phobic stimulus is unrelated to the content of the obsessions of Obsessive Compulsive Disorder or the trauma of Post-traumatic Stress Disorder.

Generalized Anxiety Disorder

Even a brief glance at Table 7-10 will reveal that the diagnostic criteria for a Generalized Anxiety Disorder (GAD) have striking similarities to symptoms found in PTSD. This is not strange, however, because during Stages II and III of PTSD, anxiety is a prominent feature. The onset, however, of the two disorders is markedly different. In GAD, the history reveals no clear-cut precipitant; rather, the onset is gradual and insidious, the course of the disorder fluctuates with psychosocial stressors. In contrast, the onset of PTSD is acute and well-defined, and during the acute stage, anxiety symptoms are intense. During Stage III, when anxiety becomes chronic and less obvious, PTSD and GAD share common characteristics.

In addition to obsessive concern and preoccupation with an identifiable traumatic event, PTSD patients frequently report a phobia or phobic anxiety and complain of pain or physical discomfort. Whereas worry and physical discomfort may also be complaints of GAD patients, the history reveals no relationship to a traumatic event. An absence of intrusive thoughts about a trauma and persistent avoidance of stimuli associated with a specific trauma also helps to differentiate GAD from PTSD. It is both interesting and puzzling to note that the section on differential diagnosis of PTSD in DSM-III-R states that if an Anxiety Disorder develops following the trauma, this diagnosis should also be made.

TABLE 7–10
Diagnostic criteria for 300.02 Generalized Anxiety Disorder

A. Unrealistic or excessive anxiety and worry (apprehensive expectation) about two or more life circumstances, e.g., worry about possible misfortune to one's child (who is in no danger) and worry about finances (for no good reason), for a period of six months or longer, during which the person has been bothered more days than not by these concerns. In children and adolescents, this may take the form of anxiety and worry about academic, athletic, and social performance.

B. If another Axis I disorder is present, the focus of the anxiety and worry in A is unrelated to it, e.g., the anxiety or worry is not about having a panic attack (as in Panic Disorder), being embarrassed in public (as in Social Phobia), being contaminated (as in Obsessive Compulsive Disorder), or gaining weight (as in Anorexia Nervosa).

C. The disturbance does not occur only during the course of a Mood Disorder or a psychotic disorder.

D. At least 6 of the following 18 symptoms are often present when anxious (do not include symptoms present only during panic attacks);

Motor tension

(1) trembling, twitching, or feeling shaky
(2) muscle tension, aches, or soreness

TABLE 7–10, continued

    (3)   restlessness
    (4)   easy fatigability

Autonomic hyperactivity

    (5)   shortness of breath or smothering sensations
    (6)   palpitations or accelerated heart rate (tachycardia)
    (7)   sweating, or cold clammy hands
    (8)   dry mouth
    (9)   dizziness or lightheadedness
  (10)   nausea, diarrhea, or other abdominal distress
  (11)   flushes (hot flashes) or chills
  (12)   frequent urination
  (13)   trouble swallowing or "lump in throat"

Vigilance and scanning

  (14)   feeling keyed up or on edge
  (15)   exaggerated startle response
  (16)   difficulty concentrating or "mind going blank" because of anxiety
  (17)   trouble falling or staying asleep
  (18)   irritability

E.   It cannot be established that an organic factor initiated and maintained the disturbance, e.g., hyperthyroidism, Caffeine Intoxication.

PSYCHOACTIVE SUBSTANCE USE DISORDERS

    Psychoactive substance abuse is characterized by a maladaptive pattern of one of the following behaviors: (1) continued use despite knowledge of having a persistent or recurrent social, occupational, psychological, or physical problem that is caused or exacerbated by use of the psychoactive substance, or (2) recurrent use of the substance in situations when use is particularly hazardous. Psychoactive substance dependence, a more severe condition, is defined by a cluster of cognitive, behavioral, and physiological symptoms that indicate an impaired control of psychoactive substance use with physiologic symptoms of tolerance and withdrawal. In dependence, persons continue the use of the substance despite adverse consequences. The DSM-III-R lists nine classes of psychoactive substances which are associated with both abuse and dependence: alcohol; amphetamine or similarly acting sympathomimetics; cannabis; cocaine; hallucinogens; inhalants; opioids; phencyclidine (PCP) or similarly acting arylcyclohexylamines; and sedatives, hypnotics, or anxiolytics. Following a trauma it is not unusual for patients to abuse or become dependent on psychoactive substances. Patients with PTSD may self treat their pathologic anxiety or mood disturbance with alcohol, cannabis, sedatives, hypnotics, or less commonly amphetamines. Occasionally, cocaine and less commonly heroin or other opioids also serve to lower anxiety and psychic discomfort.

When the history reveals a Psychoactive Substance Use disorder only following a traumatic incident, one should be alerted to abuse of dependence secondary to a PTSD. Clinicians who focus only on a patient's Psychoactive Substance Use Disorder may overlook the signs and symptoms of PTSD, which would then go untreated.

The issue of alcohol abuse and illicit drug use is particularly relevant for the estimated 500,000 to 1.5 million Vietnam-era veterans believed to suffer from PTSD (Mace et al., 1978; Wilson, 1980; Walker, 1981; Card, 1983). Although the relationship between Psychoactive Substance Use Disorder and PTSD in Vietnam-era veterans is unclear, at least two explanations can be advanced. The first is that substance abuse or dependence is related to the veteran's experience in Vietnam and is one of the manifestations secondary to the war and possibly PTSD. A second explanation is that psychoactive substance abuse antedated service in Vietnam and continued post-Vietnam, having no or only a marginal relationship to experiences in Southeast Asia. A corollary to this proposition is that even if a veteran has a preexisting Psychoactive Substance Use Disorder, a PTSD might coexist with it and be directly related to war experiences in Vietnam (Sierles et al., 1983). Lifelong abuse or dependence on substances, which is related to an Antisocial Personality Disorder, raises questions of a person's character and credibility. The correct conceptualization of a Vietnam-era veteran's or a civilian's substance use patterns preceding and following a trauma has an important bearing on diagnosis and treatment.

ANTISOCIAL PERSONALITY DISORDER

Persons with an Antisocial Personality Disorder have a lifelong history of irresponsible behavior, including deceit, and are more likely to malinger than are most people. The essential feature of an Antisocial Personality

Disorder is a history of continuous and chronic antisocial behavior that begins in childhood or early adolescence and continues into adulthood. As can be seen in Table 7-11, DSM-III-R indicates that before a diagnosis of Antisocial Personality Disorder is made, the person must be at least 18 years of age and have a history of Conduct Disorder before the age of 15. Lying, truancy, running away from home, assaultive behavior, physical cruelty to animals and people, coercive sexuality, stealing, and other forms of delinquency are typical childhood signs. Irresponsible behavior continues as a person matures and is evidenced by erratic and poor work performance, rejection of social norms, aggressiveness including fights, financial irresponsibility, prevarication, lack of goal-directedness, recklessness, nonacceptance of a parenting role, drunkenness, sexual promiscuity, and drug abuse.

In addition to a lifestyle that includes habitual lying, involvement in illegal activities, and periodic incarceration in a penal institution, antisocial persons have difficulties maintaining personal relationships. As stated in the DSM-III-R, "has never sustained a totally monogamous relationship for more than one year." This observation is very important, since persons with an Antisocial Personality Disorder display no loyalties to anyone, except perhaps to themselves, a crucial point when differentiating an antisocial personality from a person who is only intermittently involved in antisocial behavior.

Veracity is a question of prime importance when persons who have a history of criminal conduct claim a PTSD and later sue for damages. Antisocial persons may fabricate a PTSD for financial advantage or to avoid criminal sanctions. If a veteran fakes PTSD and convinces others that it is service connected, disability payments from the government can be collected. Following a trauma, antisocial civilians may malinger a PTSD in order to collect workers' compensation payments or during a personal injury suit to collect a monetary award (Chapter 11). In criminal cases, defendants who are antisocial can claim PTSD to avoid prosecution or to support a plea of not guilty because of insanity (Chapter 12).

Before establishing a diagnosis of PTSD, a detailed chronological history of any antisocial behavior must be taken and, most importantly, verified. Interviews with members of the patient's family and friends along with a review of all pertinent records help to identify falsehoods. The absence or presence of preexisting patterns of antisocial behavior, beginning as a child and continuing into adulthood, has great significance in interpreting post-traumatic behavior. Outside sources of information are

TABLE 7–11
Diagnostic criteria for 301.70 Antisocial Personality Disorder

A. Current age at least 18.

B. Evidence of Conduct Disorder with onset before age 15, as indicated by a history of *three* or more of the following:

   (1) was often truant
   (2) ran away from home overnight at least twice while living in parental or parental surrogate home (or once without returning)
   (3) often initiated physical fights
   (4) used a weapon in more than one fight
   (5) forced someone into sexual activity with him or her
   (6) was physically cruel to animals
   (7) was physically cruel to other people
   (8) deliberately destroyed others' property (other than by fire-setting)
   (9) deliberately engaged in fire-setting
  (10) often lied (other than to avoid physical or sexual abuse)
  (11) has stolen without confrontation of a victim on more than one occasion (including forgery)
  (12) has stolen with confrontation of a victim (e.g., mugging, purse-snatching, extortion, armed robbery)

C. A pattern of irresponsible and antisocial behavior since the age of 15, as indicated by at least *four* of the following:

   (1) is unable to sustain consistent work behavior, as indicated by any of the following (including similar behavior in academic settings if the person is a student):

      (a) significant unemployment for six months or more within five years when expected to work and work was available
      (b) repeated absences from work unexplained by illness in self or family
      (c) abandonment of several jobs without realistic plans for others

   (2) fails to conform to social norms with respect to lawful behavior, as indicated by repeatedly performing antisocial acts that are grounds for arrest (whether arrested or not), e.g., destroying property, harassing others, stealing, pursuing an illegal occupation

TABLE 7–11, continued

(3) is irritable and aggressive, as indicated by repeated physical fights or assaults (not required by one's job or to defend someone or oneself), including spouse- or child-beating

(4) repeatedly fails to honor financial obligations, as indicated by defaulting on debts or failing to provide child support or support for other dependents on a regular basis

(5) fails to plan ahead, or is impulsive, as indicated by one or both of the following:

    (a) traveling from place to place without a prearranged job or clear goal for the period of travel or clear idea about when the travel will terminate

    (b) lack of a fixed address for a month or more

(6) has no regard for the truth, as indicated by repeated lying, use of aliases, of "conning" others for personal profit or pleasure

(7) is reckless regarding his or her own or others' personal safety, as indicated by driving while intoxicated, or recurrent speeding

(8) if a parent or guardian, lacks ability to function as a responsible parent, as indicated by one or more of the following:

    (a) malnutrition of child

    (b) child's illness resulting from lack of minimal hygiene

    (c) failure to obtain medical care for a seriously ill child

    (d) child's dependence on neighbors or nonresident relatives for food or shelter

    (e) failure to arrange for a caretaker for young child when parent is away from home

    (f) repeated squandering, on personal items, of money required for household necessities

(9) has never sustained a totally monogamous relationship for more than one year

(10) lacks remorse (feels justified in having hurt, mistreated, or stolen from another)

D. Occurrence of antisocial behavior not exclusively during the course of Schizophrenia or Manic Episodes.

important and can confirm or negate a diagnosis of Antisocial Personality Disorder. The quality and duration of interpersonal relationships, employment, marriage, as well as responsible financial management, and regard for the truth must be determined to support a diagnosis of either Antisocial personality Disorder with malingering or PTSD.

Information concerning three different time periods must be gathered in order to establish with reasonable certainty a diagnosis of PTSD as contrasted with Antisocial Personality Disorder and malingering. First, the pre-traumatic personality and behavior of the individual should disclose no or minimal antisocial characteristics. Second, the trauma should be documented in detail and the person's presence at the time of the trauma verified; the signs and symptoms shortly following impact should be consistent with the acute stage of PTSD. Finally, post-traumatically the symptoms of Stage II or III of PTSD must be present. It is risky to lie about personal past history, which can be substantiated; however, current symptoms can be more easily falsified with less likelihood of detection. If Antisocial Personality Disorder is suspected, inconsistencies in the history should alert the clinician to collect data concerning the patient's pre-traumatic, traumatic, and post-traumatic behavior which can then be verified, compared, and evaluated.

FACTITIOUS DISORDERS AND MALINGERING

The voluntary feigning, pretending, and malingering of illness constitute an intriguing problem, perhaps more suited for a detective or police officer than a clinician. Assessment of the credibility of statements by patients runs contrary to a physician's usual role of supplying succor and solace to suffering patients. Detection and correct diagnosis of a Factitious Disorder, however, ensure that inappropriate treatment will not be rendered. Uncovering malingering also precludes unnecessary therapy and prevents a criminal act if the deception was designed to extort or finagle money from unsuspecting persons or insurance companies. Both Factitious Disorder and malingering involve conscious deception, although the motivation for each condition differs.

Factitious Disorder

Factitious Disorder falls into two categories depending upon whether a psychological or physical symptom is simulated (Tables 7-12, 7-13). Factitious means produced artificially or by special effort, in essence a sham. According to DSM-III-R, the feigning of symptoms is apparently under the person's volitional control and is motivated by the desire for the patient to assume a "sick role." Although the simulation of symptoms is under voluntary control, there is a compulsive quality to the disorder which results in repeated trips to doctors' offices and multiple hospitalizations.

In a Factitious Disorder with psychological symptoms, patients may present with a pan-symptomatic complex including depression, suicidal ideation, memory loss, hallucinations, dissociative episodes, and conversion reactions. The patient may give approximate answers to questions asked during the history, a condition known as "vorbeireden." Factitious Disorder with psychological symptoms is also known as Ganser's Syn-

TABLE 7–12
Diagnostic criteria for 301.51 Factitious Disorder with Physical Symptoms

A. Intentional production or feigning of physical (but not psychological) symptoms.

B. A psychological need to assume the sick role, as evidenced by the absence of external incentives for the behavior, such as economic gain, better care, or physical well-being.

C. Occurrence not exclusively during the course of another Axis I disorder, such as Schizophrenia.

TABLE 7–13
Diagnostic criteria for 300.16 Factitious Disorder with Psychological Symptoms

A. Intentional production or feigning of psychological (but not physical) symptoms.

B. A psychological need to assume the sick role, as evidenced by the absence of external incentives for the behavior, such as economic gain, better care, or physical well-being.

C. Occurrence not exclusively during the course of another Axis I disorder, such as Schizophrenia.

drome (Ganser, 1898; Golden and MacDonald, 1955; Auerbach, 1982; Ford, 1982), Pseudopsychosis, or Pseudodementia. It is characterized by a voluntary production of severe symptoms, sometimes of psychotic proportions, suggesting a mental disorder. Factitious Disorder with psychological symptoms is almost always superimposed upon a severe personality disorder and is rarely confused with PTSD.

Over the years, chronic Factitious Disorder with physical symptoms, also called Munchhausen's Syndrome, has captured the imagination of medical practitioners (Asher, 1951; Spiro, 1968). This syndrome was named after Munchhausen, a German baron who lived in the eighteenth century and was reputed to have traveled from tavern to tavern telling tall tales about fantastic travels and adventures (Zusman and Simon, 1983). Fabrication of physical illness by persons who are well, understandably fascinates and confounds clinicians as well as the public. A dramatic self presentation with vague and inconsistent complaints characterize these patients. Complaints center around the abdomen, but symptoms are limited only by the person's medical knowledge and imagination. The reason for feigning physical symptoms tends to be obscure, but many visits to doctors and numerous requests for hospitalization seem to indicate that these patients desire to assume the "sick role." Some patients become experts in their masquerade, often presenting elaborate and well-rehearsed medical histories gleaned from textbooks. If persons with a Factitious Disorder claim physical symptoms following trauma, the clinician may confuse the condition with PTSD. Factitious Disorder must also be differentiated from malingering, which, as will be described later, is motivated by the more understandable goal of achieving a definite objective that is of value, e.g., money or property.

PTSD is distinctly different from a Factitious Disorder (Sparr and Pankratz, 1983). Whereas PTSD patients may elaborate or exaggerate symptoms, fabrication is uncommon. In addition, the onset following a specific trauma, predictable clinical symptoms, and the course of the disorder, together with the absence of a bizarre pre-traumatic medical history further distinguish PTSD from Factitious Disorders.

Malingering

The conscious, voluntary fabrication of an injury, illness, or mental disorder for the purpose of achieving a definite goal characterizes the malingerer (Robitscher, 1966; Cohen, 1970; Slovenko, 1973; Rosner,

1982). The goal may vary, but it is usually something of value (Bromberg, 1979; Trimble, 1981), a tangible asset such as money, property, or some concrete advantage. Falsification of facts and lack of veracity when relating the history of injury or illness may be done cleverly or naively, making a clinician's task more or less difficult (Holland and Ward, 1966).

In differentiating between the pretender and a genuinely traumatized person, interviews with malingerers will usually reveal an inconsistent history of the present illness and a lack of conformity to the usual symptom cluster of known physical or mental disorders. Clinicians should also be alerted to the possibility of malingering when any of the following antedate the trauma: antisocial behavior, litigation, poor work history, Psychoactive Substance Use Disorder, arrest or conviction for a serious misdemeanor or felony, and a chaotic lifestyle. If malingering is suspected, it is wise to verify the history from other sources. Objective data from medical records, police reports, military service file, payroll records from previous employers, and even income tax returns give some indication of a person's coping behavior and lifestyle. Mental health professionals cannot be expected to obtain information from all of these sources, but if litigation is involved it can be expected that lawyers have made appropriate inquiries and can furnish the clinician with some information from outside sources. With the patient's permission, interviews with relatives, friends, former employers, and other acquaintances may illuminate the character and veracity of the patient. Since the appellation of "malingering" means no treatment will be administered, utmost care must be taken to avoid error. It is not the physician's responsibility to report malingerers to authorities, but only to refrain from treating patients who fake a medical or mental disorder. When physicians are subpoenaed into the courtroom for expert testimony, it then becomes appropriate for them to render an opinion regarding the authenticity of the patient's complaints.

In a section of DSM-III-R (Table 7-14) titled "For Conditions Not Attributable to a Mental Disorder That Are a Focus of Attention or Treatment," it is noted that a high degree of suspicion of malingering should be aroused if any of the four items listed are present. Items 1 and 3 are to be found in many PTSD patients and, contrary to the manual, should not in themselves necessarily raise a high index of suspicion for malingering. It is true that some clinicians may suspect malingering when patients fail to respond to treatment following a trauma and file a lawsuit. A certain amount of self-interest seems to be served when patients maintain symptoms despite vigorous treatment, but it is rash to assume that all such patients are

Table 7–14
V65.20 Malingering

Malingering should be strongly suspected if any combination of the following is noted:

(1) medicolegal context of presentation, e.g., the person's being referred by his or her attorney to the physician for examination;
(2) marked discrepancy between the person's claimed stress or disability and the objective findings;
(3) lack of cooperation during the diagnostic evaluation and in complying with the prescribed treatment regimen;
(4) the presence of Antisocial Personality Disorder.

malingerers. Patients with PTSD may not consider their conditions to be mental, therefore do not seek the services of psychiatrist or psychologist. Furthermore, those who sustain injuries in accidents often consult lawyers to obtain advice concerning avenues of redress and treatment. Lawyers conversant with the concept of PTSD are, therefore, a natural conduit for the referral of patients, though their motivations may not be entirely altruistic. The self-interest of the patient and lawyer is of course served by litigation, but the medicolegal context of presentation should not in itself indicate a high level of suspiciousness for malingering.

Contrariness and contentiousness are qualities found in many persons who are chronically ill. Physicians with little appreciation or toleration for traumatized patients with chronic mental disorders may mistake anger and ill temper as a sign of uncooperativeness. Instead, the ill humor and hostility frequently found in Stage III of PTSD emanate from the chronic course of the disorder and the failure of previous treatment. Because chronic patients have usually consulted many physicians, they are familiar with and often disdainful of medical practitioners. After their anger has subsided, discontented patients can usually be persuaded to cooperate with a diagnostic evaluation and treatment. Malingerers, if they are fearful that diagnostic tests may uncover their pretense and thwart their objective of material gain, may steadfastly refuse to cooperate with any diagnostic evaluation.

Item 2 in Table 7-14, "marked discrepancy between the person's claimed stress or disability and the objective findings" must be considered in light of a documented trauma. Many complaints referable to PTSD cannot be substantiated by objective tests (*e.g.,* x-rays, CAT scans, blood tests, etc.), and the clinician must make a diagnosis based on history of a trauma, self-report of symptoms by patient, psychological tests, interviews with relatives or friends, review of records, and a mental status examination. By definition, criterion 2 eliminates Somatoform Disorders such as a Conversion Disorder or Somatoform Pain Disorder where symptoms cannot be explained by a known physical disorder or pathophysiological mechanism.

The presence of Antisocial Personality Disorder, Item 4, does correlate with malingering. The character of a person with an Antisocial Personality Disorder is at question, and veracity may be correctly challenged. Persons with a life-long history of antisocial behavior, including incarceration as a youth and imprisonment as an adult following conviction for a felony, have little chance for obtaining damages in a civil lawsuit in the absence of objective tests substantiating injury. Although not common, the author has examined several patients with an extensive antisocial history who have "reformed" and evinced no antisocial history for over a decade. After years of a chaotic lifestyle, these individuals found employment to their liking and a stable love relationship. When they were involved in a well-documented traumatic incident, disablement followed the usual path of those with no antisocial history. When evaluating patients, the clinician must be aware of the difference between Antisocial Personality Disorder and intermittent antisocial behavior; one must be suspicious of malingering in the former, while in the latter, the interpretation is not necessarily that of an unreliable scoundrel.

CONCLUSION

Disagreement among mental health professionals concerning the presence or absence of a mental disorder following trauma can represent legitimate differences based on an honest assessment of the patient. Differences of opinion can also be attributed to the following: (1) lack of knowledge or insight relating to the possible psychological effects of trauma upon a person, especially patients who continue to complain of symptoms long after the expected time of healing. Malingering is mistakenly chosen as the best explanation to describe this behavior; (2) a deep moralistic belief of the clinician based on the Protestant work ethic that all persons, even those who have been involved in a severe trauma, should make a genuine and determined effort to return to a productive life, however limited, within a reasonable time following the trauma. Some physicians get impatient, irritated, and reject traumatized patients who fail to comply with this expectation. Although these clinicians may be quite knowledgeable about the signs and symptoms of PTSD, they are likely to state that, "I don't believe in the disorder," as if the clinical entity required faith and not good clinical judgment for diagnosis, and (3) less commonly, the "Charlie Mc-Carthy" or "Howdy Doody" phenomenon, in which some expert witnesses will state in court or in writing anything that those who pull the monetary strings want to hear.

This chapter begins and ends with the statement that diagnosis of PTSD is easy when the clinician is oriented to the concept that trauma can precipitate a PTSD. As an addendum, trauma can be associated with a wide variety of mental disorders or none at all. To preserve objectivity and enhance accuracy, clinicians must abandon bias toward trauma, chronic illness, and litigation. Numerous persons who have been traumatized still await a proper diagnosis and treatment.

EIGHT

TREATMENT

PTSD has drawn adherents from many specialties, and clinicians scramble to advance theories and propose treatment based on a variety of approaches including biologic, behavioral, cognitive, and psychoanalytic (van der Kolk et al., 1985; Scrignar, 1984; Horowitz, 1974). Thus far, enthusiasm has far exceeded scientific rigor, and talented therapists of different theoretic orientations report good results with some PTSD patients, but no controlled study currently exists which demonstrates superiority of one method. As will be seen later, data are accumulating to support a cognitive-behavioral approach in the treatment of PTSD (Keane, Zimering, and Caddell, 1985; Fairbank and Brown, 1987).

Psychodynamic Treatment

In early psychodynamic formulations of PTSD, theorists postulated an energy overload. After a trauma, the ego attempted to restore homeostasis by "binding, discharging, or abreacting" the excess energy (Horowitz, 1974). More recently, psychodynamic formulations have emphasized information overload rather than energy overload. The task confronting patients is seen as one of reconciling the occurrence of the traumatic event, including its various meanings, with the individuals enduring schemata, such as his concept of himself and the world around him. Within this framework, emotions are viewed as reactions to discrepancies between external and internal information and also serve as motives for defense and control (Horowitz and Kaltreider, 1980). The fundamental problem of patients with PTSD has been variously described as ideational incongruity (Horowitz, 1974), "split-off experience" (Brende and McCann, 1984), emotional blocking and "unfinished business" (Crump, 1984), or disruption of the normal course of psychosocial and personality development (Blackburn et al., 1984). The optimal goal of psychodynamic treatment of PTSD is the integration of the traumatic experience, usually by means of therapeutic "revivification" (Brende, 1981). The particular psychodynamic techniques used to accomplish this end will vary as a function of the phase of PTSD (Horowitz and Kaltreider, 1980), the stage of therapy (Brende and McCann, 1984), and the personality style of the patient (Horowitz, 1974).

Two studies have systematically investigated the efficacy of psychodynamically-oriented psychotherapy for stress response syndromes (Horowitz et al., 1984; Lindy et al., 1983). These studies, however, were uncontrolled and did not deal exclusively with PTSD. Although these studies represent an important first step in the evaluation of dynamic psychotherapy in the treatment of stress response syndromes, Fairbank and Nicholson (1987) have pointed out that the diagnostic heterogeneity of the treated groups and the absence of untreated controlled groups were serious limitations, and their analysis indicated that there were no differences between treated and untreated groups. Caution was urged in interpreting the finding of significant before-after change in these studies, and the need for controlled outcome research was also underscored (Fairbank and Nicholson, 1987).

One must also be cautious about applying psychodynamic concepts in the treatment of patients with PTSD. Unlike classically neurotic patients who have developed problems over a lifetime, PTSD patients become symptomatic later in life following an environmentally induced event. Therapy based on psychodynamic formulations related to psychopathologic conflicts earlier in life is, therefore, inappropriate. Traumatized patients see little relevance between neurotic conflicts and post-traumatic symptoms, and research does not indicate a clear-cut relationship between pre-traumatic personality and the development of a PTSD. Psychodynamically-oriented therapy, which focuses on psychopathology rather than on stratagems which help patients cope with post-traumatic symptoms and behavior, can adversely influence outcome by heightening anxiety and reinforcing negative symptoms. Traumatized patients require information to correct misconceptions, encouragement to employ therapeutic interventions, and support from the therapist, and not a personality overhaul.

Psychodynamic insight involving knowledge about human motivation is important in assessing therapy, but this information is best possessed by the therapist to guide treatment. Psychodynamic interpretations of the patient's pre-traumatic personality may have value if they enhance the patient's ability to cope with the aftermaths of trauma. The therapist functions as part of a social support system to help patients overcome traumatic sequelae. Psychodynamic interventions which lend support and comfort can contribute to the patient's welfare.

Cognitive-Behavioral Approaches

A cognitive-behavioral approach to the treatment of PTSD impacts the hallmark symptoms: persistent, distressing, and intrusive recollections of aspects involving the traumatic event (cognitive); disturbed affect (emotional); conditioned autonomic reactivity to cues associated with the trauma (physiological); and avoidance of various stimuli that remind one of the traumatic event (behavioral) (Fairbank and Nicholson, 1987). While there is a paucity of controlled and comparative outcome research regarding the treatment of PTSD, more data on the efficacy of behavioral interventions exist than do for all other theoretical orientations. Three controlled studies regarding the treatment of Vietnam-era veterans suffering from PTSD are currently in progress at the Boston Veterans Administration Medical Center; at the Augusta, Georgia, Veterans Administration Medical Center, and at the Eastern Pennsylvania Psychiatric Institute, a treatment-research study regarding sexual assault victims is being conducted (Fairbank and Nicholson, 1987; Fairbank and Brown, 1987).

The effectiveness of stress inoculation training (SIT) (Pearson et al. 1983) for sexual assault victims has been examined by a comparison of three types of group therapy for rape victims (Resnick et al., 1985): SIT (n=12), assertion training (n=13), and supportive psychotherapy (n=12). The SIT package included Jacobsonian relaxation, diaphragmatic breathing, role-playing, covert modeling, thought stopping, and guided self-dialogue (Pearson et al., 1983). Group treatment consisted of six two-hour sessions led by male-female co-therapists. All three groups were given a cognitive-behavioral explanation of the development of rape-induced fear and depression during the first session. The wait-list control group remained unchanged, while the three treatment groups evidenced significant improvement on a standardized and self-monitored measure of fear and anxiety, interpersonal sensitivity, assertiveness, and to a lesser extent depression. The majority of these gains were maintained at a three and six month follow up. Although none of the three types of group therapy appear

TABLE 8–1
Self-Assessment Form

Name _____
Date _____

Time	Sources of Anxiety			Antianxiety Intervention			
	Environmental	*Endogenous*	*Encephalic*	*Environmental*	*Endogenous*	*Encephalic*	*Comment*
Selected Behavior							

Global Rating 0-1-2-3-4-5-6-7-8-9-10

Source: Reprinted from *Stress Strategies: The Treatment of the Anxiety Disorder* (Scrignar, 1983). Reproduced with permission.

to be a superior mode of treatment, the authors speculated that the group format or the educational component (*i.e.*, cognitive-behavioral model) may have accounted for similar results in all three groups.

Although most research is related to Vietnam-era veterans and sexual assault victims, cognitive-behavioral approaches to treatment may ultimately prove to be important in the treatment of all types of PTSD. The author (Scrignar, 1983) has advocated a number of therapeutic interventions for anxiety disorders, including PTSD, which include: explanation-education, training in relaxation, cognitive restructuring, medication, exposure treatment (systematic desensitization-flooding), assertive training for anger reduction, family participation, and problem- solving. All the symptom themes of PTSD mentioned earlier in DSM- III-R are impacted by one or more of these therapeutic interventions. Future research involving controlled studies will shed more light on the cognitive-behavioral approach to the treatment of PTSD.

Biological and Pharmacologic Approaches

Since Cannon (1929) and Selye (1946), it has been known that stress produces neuroendocrine alterations affecting the nervous system. A more recent review (Anisman, 1978) of the literature on stress-induced neurochemical transmitter activity indicates that there is a norepinephrine depletion under conditions of acute stress. Stress is also known to precipitate peripheral endorphin release and to induce a centrally mediated analgesia response (Kreiger, 1983). Utilizing these concepts, van der Kolk et al., (1984) proposed an animal model for PTSD involving "inescapable shock." This biological hypothesis states that animals exposed to inescapable shock had depletions in norepinephrine, brain dopamine, and serotonin with an increase in acetylcholine. Animal experiments seem to demonstrate a "chronic and exaggerated neurochemical change in response to subsequent stressors which interfere with response initiation and maintenance" (Anisman, 1978). Because some PTSD patients present with a "lifelong preoccupation with repetition of the trauma," van der Kolk proposes an "addiction" hypothesis, supporting this contention by referring to the central nervous system opioid response seen in animals in response to inescapable shock. The release of endogenous opioid peptides in animals exposed to inescapable shock reinforces behavior leading to more shocks. Extrapolating these results to humans, van der Kolk postulates that both the central noradrenergic system and central nervous system opioid peptides play an active and reciprocal role in the initiation and maintenance of post-traumatic stress states. This intriguing hypothesis requires verification by experiments with humans. Based on this model, psychopharmacologic agents, supportive interventions, and systematic desensitization are promising areas of treatment (van der Kolk et al,. 1984).

A variety of psychotropic agents has been used in the treatment of PTSD. Efficacy utilizing phenelzine sulfate, a monoamine oxidase inhibitor, has been reported in the treatment of PTSD patients by several investigators (Hogben and Cornfield, 1981; Levenson, Lanman, and Rankin, 1982; Milanes, Mack, Dennson, and Slater, 1984; Shen and Park, 1983). Chronic PTSD in combat veterans has been treated with some success by propanolol, a beta adrenergic blocking agent, and clonazepam, a benzodiazepine with anticonvulsive properties (Burris, 1983; Kolb and Mutalipassi, 1982). Various antianxiety agents and trycyclic antidepressants have been useful in the treatment of PTSD, but reports are either anecdotal or based on uncontrolled studies. To date, there have been no published reports of controlled studies involving psychotropic agents on PTSD patients. Fairbank and Nicholson (1987) suggest that studies are needed that employ accepted standards of design for research on drug therapy, including the use of relevant comparison groups (*e.g.*, placebo control groups) and blind outcome evaluation procedures. They suggest important research questions include the following: (1) What is the comparative utility of different pharmacologic therapies in the treatment of PTSD? (2) What are the consequences of combining drug therapies with various psychotherapies? and (3) Can drug therapy be said to be more or less effective than specific psychotherapeutic interventions? The answers to these questions await future research.

THERAPEUTIC INTERVENTIONS

Successful treatment of PTSD depends upon a correct conceptualization of the disorder and an accurate analysis of the impact and continuance of certain stimuli from environmental, encephalic, and endogenous sources—the Three E's—which maintain the pathologic features of the disorder. The objective of treatment, therefore, consists of modifying selective stimuli from the external world, physiological processes of the body, and cognitive activities of the brain. Successful treatment depends upon the selection of appropriate therapeutic interventions and the patient's personal resources, ability to cope, and social support system.

During the first phase of treatment, four therapeutic interventions are recommended to lower the patient's current discomfort. Explanation-education, training in relaxation, encephalic reconditioning (cognitive restructuring), and medication afford the patient immediate relief from stress and pathologic anxiety. Thereafter, the prescription of additional treatment depends upon the needs and progress of the patient.

When PTSD becomes chronic, a complex array of psychosocial factors lowers the probability of a quick resolution of the disorder. PTSD is a multifaceted disorder involving not only post-traumatic stress, but also depression, disordered family relationships, problems of physical disability, inability to work, disruption of social and recreational life, workers' compensation claims, personal injury litigation, impaired interpersonal relationships, Psychoactive Substance Use Disorder (Gallant, 1987), and, at times, criminal conduct. Since personal, interpersonal, and social factors interact pathologically in PTSD, the formulation of a comprehensive treatment regimen must be based on a broad spectrum of approaches. In addition, patient attitudes reflecting pessimism, demoralization, hostility, anxiousness, and disablement demand and require the special skills and sensitivity of a trained therapist.

Perhaps the clinician's attitude towards chronic illness presents the largest obstacle to a successful outcome. Unattractive characteristics of patients who complain constantly, show slow progress in treatment, and seem unappreciative of their therapist's best efforts, generate negative attitudes in the clinician. If hostility is reciprocated, effective treatment cannot take place. Forbearance and tolerance for slow progress become necessary attributes for clinicians. Ultimately, however, the barometer that indicates success is the diminishment or disappearance of symptoms and problem behaviors with the restoration of the patient to a useful, productive, and satisfying life.

Explanation-Education

Patients, before they are referred to psychiatrists or other mental health professionals, usually have undergone a barrage of tests and diagnostic procedures. Orthopedic surgeons and neurosurgeons have exhaustively examined the bony and neural structures of traumatized patients who may continue to complain of pain or physical discomfort. In addition, other physicians are likely to have been consulted concerning an assortment of complaints, and the patient has usually been subjected to numerous diagnostic tests and examinations. Unfortunately, many patients do not receive a complete or clear-cut explanation regarding their physical condition, but instead physicians relate vague opinions that can easily be misinterpreted. Visits to doctors, therefore, confuse patients, especially when treatment is unsatisfactory.

Referral to a psychiatrist usually takes place when patients continue to complain of incapacitating symptoms in the absence of objective findings or exhibit eccentric and quarrelsome behavior. Frequently, patients confront their physicians with the embarrassing question, "If all of the tests are negative, why do I still have symptoms?" To gain patients' confidence so that they will comply with treatment after a diagnosis of PTSD, the most important step is explanation-education.

At the onset it is imperative that prior medical records be obtained and patiently explained to the patient. Sometimes reference to an anatomy atlas or the utilization of other visual aids helps clear up a patient's misconceptions about his body. Consultation with physicians, especially those doctors who continue to see the patient, mitigates contradiction, allays patients' concerns of organic etiology for their disorder, and facilitates cooperation.

The development of a stress disorder can best be explained by a reiteration of the patient's history in a logical, chronological sequence. To respond with anxiety following exposure to a traumatic event is a normal reaction, the patient is told, and one need not be ashamed of nervousness, trembling and shaking sensations, nausea, or vomiting. Palpitations, tachycardia, hyperventilation, and a variety of other symptoms may occur normally following exposure to a traumatic event, the explanation continues. These symptoms result from an activation of the autonomic nervous system when the environmental trauma impacts on one or a combination of the five senses; however, the patient is emphatically told, prolongation of symptoms beyond one month represents a pathologic emotional reaction called a PTSD.

The patient's symptoms are enumerated and explanations are given to account for their presence and continuation. The Symptom Inventory Checklist or DSM-III-R diagnostic criteria can be used as a guide when explaining the significance of each symptom. The most troublesome symptoms are usually intrusive thoughts, flashbacks, sleep disturbance, nightmares, phobic behavior, and a feeling of fearfulness. Patients are told that obsessive preoccupation with the trauma generates pathologic anxiety, but they will be taught how to manage this cognitive symptom. Flashbacks are usually precipitated by exposure to environmental stimuli reminiscent

of the trauma, but they will diminish with time and therapy. Sleep disturbance, usually problems in falling asleep or interrupted sleep, is caused by
hyper-attentiveness to the trauma. To fall asleep is difficult when one
ruminates about a life-threatening event. Dreams can be so realistic and
disturbing that patients awaken in the middle of the night, panic-stricken
with night clothes damp from perspiration. Repeated episodes of nightmares cause patients to dread sleep, further aggravating insomnia. Patients
are told that as a general rule the continuing occurrence of nightmares
means excessive preoccupation with the trauma during the day. Patients are
reassured that if insomnia is a serious problem, medication will be prescribed until they learn alternative methods to induce somnolence, such as
progressive muscle relaxation or self-hypnosis. When avoidance behavior
exists, mechanisms of a phobia or phobic anxiety are explained to the
patient in terms of a conditioned process directly related to the original
trauma. Situations closely resembling the trauma trigger pathologic anxiety, often followed by phobic avoidance, but the patient is reassured that
systematic desensitization or exposure treatment reverses this process.
Fearfulness is unbridled anxiety caused by a hyperactive nervous system,
the patient is told. Anxiety-related symptoms are enumerated and an
explanation of the Three E's—the sources of pathological anxiety—is
given. An anxious state is also characterized by increased motor tension and
an apprehensive expectation, with ruminations about the trauma, irritability, and sometimes a sense of unreality, the explanation continues. Whenever possible, therapeutic tactic and technique is tied to symptomatic
behavior in order that patients become oriented to the concepts of change
and coping.

When the clinician encounters chronic patients who have developed
fixed opinions concerning disablement, glib explanations of PTSD and
disability must be avoided. The patient should be taken slowly through the
various stages of PTSD with a detailed explanation concerning the reasons
for symptoms. The idea of permanent disability must be dispelled by a
reiteration of medical reports indicating that no evidence of a serious
physical defect exists. Paradoxically some patients, especially if they are
seriously depressed, become suspicious when the physician proffers an
optimistic prognosis. The seemingly unrelenting course of chronic PTSD,
unaffected by previous therapeutic attempts, provides patients with ample
reason for pessimism. Chronic PTSD patients tend to take a global view of
disability and an all-or-nothing attitude concerning illness and wellness.
Patients during the educative phase of treatment must be dissuaded from

these extreme and rigid negative positions in favor of a positive approach involving a gradual return to normal activities. Over the course of treatment, the patient is resolutely told, symptoms will become less intense and less frequent, and the disability will be minimal. Initially patients may be unmoved by pronouncements from physicians that they will overcome their disorder. An adroitness in explaining, instructing, interpreting, persuading, and even exhorting facilitates the acceptance of the idea that a positive change in behavior is not only possible, but probably (Frank, 1961, 1978).

Patients often fail to grasp the significance of therapeutic interventions, as other issues obfuscate the importance of treatment. They continue to ruminate about the traumatic incident and obsess about disability. Patients may insist that they want to be the way they were before the traumatic incident without exerting any effort. This expectation can frustrate treatment, since one cannot turn the clock backward and a spontaneous cure seldom occurs. A trauma disrupts lives, the patient must be told, and wanting to turn the clock back and make things the way they were suggests an unrealistic magical wish. A more fruitful goal that can be pursued during the course of treatment consists of understanding the concepts of retraumatization, the Three E's, and the Spiral Effect. Throughout the course of therapy, whenever the patient complains of symptoms, the relationship of symptomatic behavior to these concepts must be explained and emphasized. A Self-Assessment Form (Table 8-1) helps patients to organize behavioral information in a form that contributes to the educative process. Unless patients become knowledgeable about the cause of PTSD, they are likely to conjure a more exotic explanation for their symptoms, usually a vague and mysterious physical ailment. When theoretical constructs are translated into real-life experiences, the exercise becomes more meaningful and therapeutically useful.

The rationale for treatment is based upon the premise that PTSD psychopathology is largely learned and conditioned. Relearning and deconditioning form the main therapeutic thrust. As each element of the treatment program is added, the patient must be instructed on its significance and reason for employment. Explanation-education continues throughout treatment and must be done repeatedly in order for patients to thoroughly assimilate the salient points of theory and therapy preparatory to altering symptomatic behavior.

Training in Relaxation

All relaxation techniques (Schultz and Luther, 1969; Wallace, 1970; Jacobsen, 1974; Shapiro, 1977) produce the beneficial physiological result of reducing motor tension and lowering the activity of the autonomic nervous system. A quiet environment, the use of pleasant visual images, and a focus on pleasant internal sensations of the body facilitate the effectiveness of various relaxation methods. The observation that many of these principles have been incorporated into yoga, transcendental meditation, and prayer attests to the universality and agelessness of these empirically derived procedures. Although many relaxation methods exist and may be equally efficacious, progressive muscle relaxation (PMR) (Jacobsen, 1974) and hypnosis (Cheek and LaCron, 1968; Kroger and Fezler, 1976) are recommended for clinical use in the treatment of PTSD, because both are easy to learn and apply.

Progressive Muscle Relaxation

Jacobsen's technique (1974) of PMR is probably the most widely used method of muscle relaxation and is preferred by the author. Before beginning the procedure, an explanation is given to patients regarding the relationship between relaxation and stress. The patient is then asked to sit, preferably in a comfortable reclining chair, close the eyes, listen, and follow instructions. After several deep breaths, the patient is asked to breathe normally and in sequence contract then relax the various muscles of the body. At the conclusion of the exercise, which takes about 30 minutes, most patients report a subjective feeling of tranquility and deep relaxation. Some patients report residual tension in certain muscle groups, which requires additional time and more practice. Like the learning of any skill, "Practice makes perfect," and ten to fifteen hours of training leads to proficiency. When progressive muscle relaxation has been mastered, patients should also be familiar with the technique of passive relaxation, which can be done unobtrusively, in any position, with the eyes open and without actively contracting the muscles. By first noting the presence of existing tension in the muscles, the patient takes several slow, deep breaths, and during exhalation systematically reduces the tension in selected muscle groups. Passive relaxation affords the patient a means of controlling stress while walking, driving, standing, and sitting and is of particular benefit when overcoming phobias during in vivo desensitization. Controlling symptoms of PTSD is a strange but exhilarating experience for patients who have long been victims of stress.

The key to the successful utilization of PMR lies in the recognition of symptoms as a manifestation of a stress disorder and not due to a vague and undiagnosable physical ailment. Muscle aches, pain, nausea, excessive sweating, headaches, diarrhea, dizziness, tachycardia, dyspnea, and other stress-related symptoms can serve as cues for the employment of PMR. Even insomnia can be alleviated when PMR is practiced while attempting sleep. To gain proficiency and achieve maximal advantage from PMR, patients must practice the technique at least once daily for several weeks.

A prerecorded instructional audio-cassette for use at home assists patients in mastering PMR. Many relaxation tapes and records are currently on the market, but clinicians should consider recording their own. While the voice of the narrator of professionally prepared tapes may be more mellifluous, most patients prefer to hear the voice of their own therapist. The hours of practice required to master muscle relaxation are made less arduous and less costly by the use of an audio cassette. As time passes, relaxation eventually becomes an almost automatic response to stress.

Hypnosis and Self-Hypnosis

To help pierce the shroud of mysticism, patients should be told that all hypnosis is self-hypnosis, since subjects place themselves in the hypnotic state and the clinician or hypnotist functions as a teacher. Self-hypnosis is a skill that can be acquired quickly by some people and with practice by others. In the state of mind called hypnosis, there is enhancement of bodily relaxation, concentration, and receptivity to suggestions.

Hypnotic relaxation begins with suggestions to recumbent patients to close their eyes and concentrate on the voice of the therapist. Further instructions go something like this: "If you should hear any sounds other than the sound of my voice, let them go in one ear and out the other. Similarly, if you should have thoughts going through your mind, thoughts not related to what I am talking about, try to push those thoughts out of your mind when and if they should occur." The patient is then asked to take three consecutive deep breaths and at the conclusion of the third to breathe normally. Next the patient is told to concentrate on any feelings or sensations that may be present in the feet. The patient is requested to note the tingling sensations in the toes and on the bottom, top, and heels of the feet. These sensations are labeled as "your own personal relaxation feelings." In a slow and repetitious fashion, the patient is directed to notice these "personal relaxation feelings" moving slowly up the body from the feet to the legs, hips, stomach, chest, back, shoulders, arms, hands, fingers, neck, head, and face. A counting sequence of ten to zero with interspersed suggestions of relaxation deepens the hypnotic state. An intensification of the relaxation results when patients are asked to visualize—clearly and vividly—pleasant scenes such as lying on a beach, walking through a flower-laden garden, or perhaps a prearranged scene that elicits pleasant and peaceful feelings. At this point the patient may be given positive suggestions or cognitive corrections, which will be discussed in more detail in the section on encephalic reconditioning.

For patients who complain of pain, hypnosis can act as a powerful anodyne. The relaxed state of hypnosis, in itself, reduces the awareness of pain, but a visual technique sometimes is superior. The patient is asked to visualize a "pain gauge" with the number zero (no pain) on the left and ten (maximal pain) on the right. The patient is then requested to evaluate his or her current perception of pain by visualizing the gauge needle on the appropriate number. Suggestions are given to the patient to move the needle of the gauge to the left as much as possible by concentration and willful effort. Time is allotted to accomplish this, and although zero may not be reached, as the needle moves to the left the patient begins to notice a subjective reduction of pain. This simple mental device affords the patient a means of changing the perception and memory of pain, thereby reducing physical discomfort.

All hypnotic sessions can be individually recorded on an audio-cassette and given to the patient for use at home. Audio- cassettes permit patients to experience hypnotic phenomena outside the clinician's office, thereby saving time and money. Occasionally, patients exhibit concern or even alarm about using tapes with hypnotic suggestions, fearing some adverse consequence. Such apprehension is needless and can be quickly quelled by the simple statement that the worst thing that can happen is that the positive suggestions concerning relaxation and amelioration of discomfort will not be effective. Most patients, however, derive benefits from audio-cassettes and sharpen their skills of self- hypnosis.

Some clinicians argue that there is no difference between PMR and hypnosis. Undeniably, the two techniques are similar and exert influence on the same psychophysiological systems. Hypnosis, however, has the added advantage of utilizing a broader range of visual and verbal suggestions and the disadvantage of being cloaked in mysticism and myth that may frighten certain patients. PMR and hypnosis both can serve as a nonmedicinal means of controlling stress symptoms, pain, and physical discomfort. Both should become part of the patient's coping repertoire.

Encephalic Reconditioning (Cognitive Restructuring)

Encephalic events are of paramount importance in the continuance of PTSD. In fact, without the essential ingredients of retraumatization and the Spiral Effect, it is doubtful whether pathologic symptoms would be maintained. The repetitious replaying of the "videotapes of the mind" portraying the traumatic incident with grisly elaborations involving more serious injury or death sensitizes the patient, thus aggravating the disorder. The "videotapes of the mind" contain inaccuracies, distortions, and fictions, often omitting the fact that the patient survived the trauma and is still alive. Similarly, innocuous physical sensations elicit thoughts of grave physical disturbance, thus initiating the Spiral Effect. As a general rule, the more time a patient spends envisaging the trauma and misinterpreting somatic sensations, the more frequent and intense become pathologic symptoms and the degree of disability. Unquestionably, obsessive preoccupation with the trauma and its consequences is the most pernicious aspect of PTSD and to a large extent perpetuates the disorder.

In the context of this book, the term "encephalic reconditioning" refers to clinical procedures that alter negative encephalic activity by changing verbal or visual images for the purpose of lowering stress. Modifying the emotional impact of certain beliefs, perceptions, visual images, and thoughts is not a new idea. Guided affective imagery (Kosbad, 1974), fantasy evocation (Klinger, 1970; Gottschalk, 1974), imagery conditioning (Kroger and Fezler, 1976), and cognitive restructuring (Beck, 1976; Meichenbaum, 1977) are all similar and have a wide range of clinical applications in psychotherapy, clinical hypnosis, and behavior therapy (Meichenbaum and Cameron, 1983). Encephalic reconditioning for PTSD patients includes the following clinical techniques: thought stopping, positive encephalic practice (thought substitution), and the four positive reinforcing statements. Hypnosis can be used in encephalic reconditioning to alter negative self-statements and to promote positive visual images.

Thought Stopping

A simple and effective way to reduce thoughts and images that evoke stress is through a stopping procedure (Bain, 1928; Taylor, 1963; Yamagami, 1971). While in the consulting room, the patient is asked to close his eyes and to produce stressful thoughts and images related to the trauma. After about one minute, the clinician shouts, "Stop! Get out of there!" or "Stop the action!" The patient is momentarily shaken but will invariably report that the thought processes were interrupted. The procedure is repeated, but now the patient is instructed to silently but emphatically repeat the phrases "Stop! Get out of there!" or "Stop the action!" each time that the therapist signals by a light tap on the hand. The patient is then requested to employ the stopping procedure independently as often as necessary to control and reduce the anxiety generating encephalic events. A rubber band can be worn around the wrist and snapped simultaneously when the patient silently commands, "Stop! Get out of there" (Mahoney, 1971). The combination of momentary pain and the simultaneous phrase is often more effective in stopping unwanted mental activity. Most patients are amazed and pleased with the results.

Positive Encephalic Practice

Positive encephalic practice consists of substituting new "videotapes" that have a happy and pleasant ending in place of old ones with a traumatic theme. It is salutary for patients to visualize themselves coping with their symptoms and problems, for it builds confidence and assuages anxiety. Visualizing the completion of productive tasks not only serves as impetus to change but also provides patients with personal pleasure and satisfaction. Other scenes of a relaxing nature can evolve from fantasy or by a retrieval of former pleasant memories of happy events. Patients are instructed to utilize positive encephalic practice twice daily for ten to fifteen minutes. When patients begin to ruminate or obsess about their trauma, it is important that relaxing scenes be substituted immediately. Positive encephalic practice sessions conducted by the clinician in the consulting room can be recorded on an audio-cassette and given to the patient for use at home. The use of recordings regularizes and structures home practice, thus minimizing procrastination. When successful, positive encephalic practice, a form of thought substitution, reduces pathologic anxiety and contributes to the reversal of PTSD.

The Four Positive Reinforcing Statements

Somatic sensations, whether physical residuals of the traumatic incident or anxiety induced, remind patients of their trauma, increase anxiety, and trigger the Spiral Effect. Despite repeated reassurance and normal physical examinations, PTSD patients incorrectly interpret normal physiological sensations or minor muscular spasms as evidence of some serious physical defect. Erroneous self statements concerning somatic sensations serve to heighten pathologic anxiety and increase motor tension, thus making the physical sensation more evident. The Spiral Effect can be reinterrupted by the utilization of the four positive reinforcing statements. Whenever patients first notice any physical sensations that might be misinterpreted, they are instructed to repeat, silently but with conviction, the following statements:

1. "I feel uncomfortable." (This confirms that the feeling is not imaginary and that they are experiencing uncomfortable physical sensations.)
2. "I have had these feelings before and nothing really bad has ever happened." (This is a true statement, for no dire or irreversible consequences have ever resulted from these feelings.)
3. "There is nothing seriously wrong with me." (This is also a true statement. The patient's physical examinations and various laboratory procedures have disclosed no serious abnormalities.)
4. "I am experiencing the effects of stress." (This is a correct assessment.) "I shall employ anti-anxiety interventions and these uncomfortable feelings will pass more quickly." (The patient then practices PMR or self-hypnosis.)

The four positive reinforcing statements are all true. Patients must be convinced of this and encouraged to recite them whenever any of the somatic manifestations of PTSD are felt.

Hypnosis and Encephalic Reconditioning

Hypnosis is a natural adjuvant to encephalic reconditioning, since both involve the modification of visual and verbal images to achieve a therapeutic goal. Following a formal hypnotic induction as described earlier, patients are more attentive and become better listeners. The clinician's statements therefore impact more profoundly, which allows for easier correction of patient misconceptions. Specific suggestions, given under hypnosis, can also reinforce the influence of the four positive reinforcing statements and serve to develop pleasant scenarios during positive encephalic practice. Post-hypnotic suggestions can cue patients to visualize pleasant scenes whenever they focus on physical sensations or think about the bad effects of the trauma. In addition, hypnosis can aid in the treatment of depression by assisting in cognitive restructuring (Beck et al., 1979). Age-regression allows patients to relive the trauma to permit abreaction, catharsis, and cognitive correction.

Abreaction

A reenactment of the past traumatic experience can produce dramatic results with good hypnotic subjects, especially if the trauma is of recent origin. Following a formal hypnotic induction, care must be taken to secure permission from the patient, in the form of a finger signal or verbal assent, to go back to the time of the trauma and to reexperience it. The clinician then encourages the subject to relate and relive the traumatic experience. As catharsis occurs, fearful emotions emerge and patients may begin to cry, tremble, and exhibit other signs of extreme anguish and agitation, invariably including the fear of dying. Following revivification of the trauma and abreaction, patients must be reassured that everything is all right. Encephalic corrections include specific statements such as, "You have gone through a terrible trauma, but you have survived. You were not killed or seriously injured. You are okay." Direct suggestions should also include statements encouraging the patient to disassociate the fearful emotions from the memory of the trauma and to discourage future ruminations.

In acute cases of PTSD, abreaction under hypnosis affords the patient an opportunity for a quick and dramatic cure. In chronic cases patients are less likely to derive salutary benefits from abreaction; however, suggestions correcting misconceptions about their original trauma may be beneficial (Spiegel, 1981). Abreaction utilizing the intravenous administration of sodium pentathol or sodium amytal (narcosynthesis) has been used with some success with Vietnam-era combat veterans who have developed PTSD (Kolb and Mutalipassi, 1982). In chronic cases, however, abreaction alone, whether induced by hypnosis or barbiturate drugs, does not resolve PTSD, but in conjunction with a comprehensive approach it can be helpful.

Depression

Positive suggestions given to patients under hypnosis can allay the dispirited, demoralized, pessimistic, and depressed mood that is often a secondary manifestation of PTSD. Depressed patients have a tendency to overgeneralize, making a dismal mood pervasive and disproportionate to reality (Beck, et al., 1979). Positive events and experiences get lost in a mental morass of gloom and doom. Extrication from melancholy can be assisted with the use of positive suggestions given under hypnosis. Typical suggestions include: "Your frame of mind and general attitude will become more and more optimistic and positive as time goes on. You will begin to think more and more optimistically and positively about yourself, your relationship with people who are important to you, and things that you will be doing today, tomorrow, and in the near future and...You will feel better...and...You will begin to act and behave in a more positive manner." To allow the patient to practice positive thinking, while still under hypnosis, the clinician states, "I am going to be quiet in a minute and during that silent period I want you to give yourself some positive suggestions about issues important to you." The session is concluded with the suggestion that, with time and practice, thinking optimistically and positively about one's life will become easier. When the sessions are recorded and the audio-cassette given to patients, learning is facilitated and treatment enhanced.

Medication

Many PTSD patients who complain of anxiety, depression, insomnia, and pain may have taken a wide range of medicinal agents. Their previous response to medication can assist the physician in the selection and prescription of a therapeutic agent. If the patient has been subjected to polypharmacy, it is desirable at the beginning of treatment to discontinue or limit the use of all medications so that a baseline of symptomatic behavior may be obtained. In this way, the patient's complaints are more accurately measured and future psychopharmacologic therapy can be more objectively evaluated. Three classes of medications are generally prescribed for PTSD patients: anti-anxiety agents and sedatives, anti-depressants, and analgesics.

When patients present with high levels of anxiety that markedly interferes with daily living, one of the benzodiazepines can be prescribed during the initial stages of treatment. Diazepam (Valium), lorazepam

(Ativan), and alprazolam (Xanax) (Dunner, 1983) are safe, predictable, effective, and can complement other anti-anxiety interventions (Hollister et al., 1980; Shader et al., 1981). Anti-anxiety agents should be prescribed for short periods of time or if a crisis arises and anxiety severely impairs the patient. Long-term usage of a benzodiazepine or other anti-anxiety agent causes patients to neglect nonpharmacologic means (progressive muscle relaxation, self-hypnosis, and cognitive restructuring) of controlling anxiety. Swallowing a pill is easy, while it requires effort and persistence to master other anti-anxiety interventions. Learning how to cope with pathologic anxiety adds an element of control and is a skill which strengthens character.

Sleep disturbance merits the clinician's special attention. During periods of insomnia, patients are likely to obsess about their trauma, increasing anxiety and further decreasing the likelihood of sleep. While awake at night, retraumatization often takes place, as the "videotapes of the mind" continuously replay the traumatic event and its aftermath. On the following morning, the sensitizing effect of distressing mental activity and fatigue undermine treatment. Patients should be told to regularize their life as if they were going to work or engage in some productive activity and to avoid naps. The sleep cycle, meals, and activities should be similar to pre-traumatic schedules. Before taking any sedatives for insomnia, patients are advised to attempt sleep by listening to a PMR or self-hypnosis tape. Suggestions regarding the treatment of insomnia (Table 8-2) can be given to promote sleep. If these methods fail, flurazepam (Dalmane), temazepam (Restoril), or triazolam (Halcion) can be prescribed thirty minutes before bedtime. Sedatives to promote sleep can be used most effectively during the initial stages of treatment;to prevent psychological dependence, long-term usage is discouraged. Adequate sleep is essential, because a rested patient responds more readily to the total treatment regimen.

In the event that depressive symptoms are prominent, one of the anti-depressants can be prescribed. Anti-depressants can elevate mood, lessen agitation, diminish somatic symptoms, and curb insomnia. The choice of a specific anti-depressant depends upon the clinician's experience and the effect desired. When insomnia is a prominent feature, a more sedating anti-depressant, amitriptyline (Elavil), can be given in one evening dose. The starting dosage of anti-depressants should be low, with a gradual increase until a therapeutic level is reached. Even after the patient's depressive symptoms have diminished or disappeared, the anti-depressant should be maintained until there is a definite improvement in the life of the patient.

TABLE 8–2
Treatment of Insomnia or Difficulty Falling Asleep

1. Lie down intending to go to sleep *only* when you are sleepy.

2. Do not use your bed for anything except sleep; that is, do not read, smoke, listen to radio, or talk to roommate once you intend to go to sleep.

3. If you find yourself unable to fall asleep, get up and go to another room or sit up. Stay as long as you wish and then return to the bedroom to sleep.

   Although you should not watch the clock, you should get out of bed if you do not fall asleep after 10 minutes. *Remember, the goal is to associate your bed with falling asleep quickly.* If you are in bed more than 10 minutes without falling asleep and have not gotten up, you are not following these instructions.

   If you still cannot fall asleep, repeat previous steps. Do this as often as necessary throughout the night.

4. Get up at the same time every morning, no matter how little sleep you got during the night. This will help your body acquire consistent sleep rhythm.

5. Do not nap during the daytime or lie in the bed for any other reason such as reading.

   Our goal is to have you associate your bed with falling asleep quickly.

Source: Bloom, W. A., and Gallant, D. M., Southeast Louisiana State Hospital, Mandeville, Louisiana. Reproduced with permission.

When the patient discloses positive changes in mood, better sleep, diminished somatic symptoms, involvement in sexual and social/recreational activities, and a general improvement in life circumstances, including a resumption of work, the dosage of the anti-depressant can be slowly reduced over a period of two to three months and eventually discontinued.

Some investigators (Hogben and Cornfield, 1981; Levenson, Lanman, and Rankin, 1982; Milanes, Mack, Dennison, and Slater, 1984; Shen and Park, 1983) report that the monoamine oxidase inhibitor, phenalzine sulfate (Nardil), has specific therapeutic effects for the symptom complex presented by the PTSD patient. While these studies report that phenalzine has produced good results with PTSD patients, they represent uncontrolled studies contaminated by other forms of treatment such as psychotherapy. To date there have been no carefully controlled studies involving phenalzine or any other psychotropic agent in the treatment of PTSD.

PTSD patients who complain of chronic pain and report daily usage of prescribed narcotic analgesics usually do poorly in treatment. The presence of pain interferes with the ability to concentrate on nonmedicinal modes of therapy and the frequent use of narcotic analgesics temporarily numbs the mind, nullifying patient's motivation to implement other treatment methods. Sometimes, control of pain can be achieved by teaching patients the technique of self-hypnosis in an attempt to raise the patient's tolerance for physical discomfort. Generally, chronic pain portends a poor prognosis and it may become necessary to hospitalize the patient in a pain unit where a multidisciplinary approach to the problem of pain and PTSD can be more realistically approached.

It is always the therapeutic objective to teach patients techniques of coping with stress, depression, and pain nonpharmacologically. Treatment gains can then be attributed to the patient and not wholly to the medication. Personal independence, not dependence on drugs, is the ultimate goal.

Systematic Desensitization

The site, situation, or surroundings where the trauma took place has the potential, by the process of classical conditioning, of being a phobic stimulus. Even when patients do not avoid situational aspects of their trauma, phobic anxiety is almost always present. Persons involved in automobile, airplane, or boat accidents frequently develop phobias (avoidance) or phobic anxiety (no avoidance but high levels of anxiety) related to traveling in those conveyances. Although all phobias impose limitations causing personal inconvenience, some affect a person's vocation and livelihood. Teamsters who have been involved in a truck accident may avoid driving, and workers who are injured in an industrial plant may develop a phobia of the premises, resulting in an avoidance of work, unemployment, and financial difficulties.

> A 46-year-old oil refinery worker was checking gauges and valves of a catalytic converter when suddenly, without warning, one of the valves burst. Following a loud explosive sound, "like a cannon," a blast of pressurized, superheated steam erupted from the

fragmented valve, missing the oil refinery worker by inches. He staggered away from the column of superheated steam, towards the railing, and looked down ten stories below. The worker collapsed, clutching the railing, paralyzed with fear, as he excitedly thought how close he had come to death. Feeling nauseated and trembling violently, the worker was assisted to the infirmary where an examination disclosed a slight bruise, some muscle spasms, but no evidence of serious injury. He was given a mild tranquilizer, sent home, and told to return to work the next day. That night during fitful sleep, the worker dreamed about the accident, but in his nightmare, the column of steam perforated his abdomen, propelling him over the railing into space. Awakening in terror, the worker could not return to sleep. Subsequently intrusive thoughts and flashbacks about the accident focused on the image of his body being bisected by the blast of steam and hurled off the tenth level. Thoughts about being killed and symptoms of increased arousal were accompanied by a strong and persistent desire to avoid the oil refinery. The worker developed a PTSD with a phobia of the work premises, which resulted in unemployment after twenty-three years of service.

When a phobia or phobic anxiety is associated with PTSD, systematic desensitization or graded exposure is the treatment of choice. Happily, when done properly, desensitization is successful in eighty to ninety percent of the cases (Wolpe, 1958, 1982; Paul, 1968; Mavissakalian and Barlow, 1981; Marks, 1981). This therapeutic technique is based on the principle that when patients are gradually exposed under specified conditions to a phobic or anxiety-evoking stimulus, they will eventually become habituated or deconditioned. Systematic desensitization may be employed in the consulting room by using imaginal techniques or, if practical, by gradually exposing the patient to phobic situations in real life (in vivo desensitization). Prolonged exposure (flooding), if tolerated by patients, can be extremely useful and has been reported to be successful in the treatment of Vietnam-era veterans (Fairbank and Keane, 1982; Keane and Kaloupek, 1983).

Construction of Hierarchy

The first step in desensitizing phobic PTSD patients consists of developing a hierarchy of anxiety-evoking situations related to the traumatic incident. Depending upon the circumstances of the trauma, patients may have become so anxious that they avoid driving automobiles, flying in airplanes, operating a truck or heavy machinery, climbing into high places, or being around fire or combustible materials. Scenarios based upon the appropriate theme are developed and hierarchically arranged according to the intensity of anxiety that would be evoked if the patient were in that situation (Scrignar, 1974; Scrignar, Swanson, and Bloom, 1973). When constructing hierarchies, precise measures such as distance, time, quantity, or temporal sequence give the best results. For example, the oil refinery worker who was involved in the accident atop the tenth level of a tower adjacent to a catalytic converter developed acrophobia as well as a fear of the work premises. He could no longer go to work checking gauges and valves located at each of the ten levels of the tower. Prior to desensitization, a hierarchy from low to high anxiety was constructed utilizing vertical distance or height and a temporal sequence as follows:

1. You are at home thinking about returning to work.
2. You have made a decision to return to work. It is morning and you are at home, preparing to leave.
3. You are driving to work.
4. You drive through the entrance gate of the refinery and park your car.
5. You go to the employees' locker room, change clothes, punch the time clock, and walk to the work area.
6. You stand at the base of the ten-level tower and look at the catalytic converter with the gauges and valves at each level.
7. You walk up to the first level and touch the various valves.
8. In turn and in sequence, you climb from the first to the tenth level, pausing at each level until your anxiety diminishes.

For patients who have been involved in an automobile accident and have subsequently developed a phobia of driving, the distance driven from home can be the hierarchical variable along with traffic conditions (light to heavy traffic, daylight to nighttime, dry to rainy weather). Proximity to or time spent at the traumatic site can be the variable used in the construction of a hierarchy for patients who have experienced industrial accidents involving explosions, fires, or malfunctions of machinery. In these cases, low anxiety is correlated with greater distance and less time spent at the scene of the accident. As distance is shortened and time lengthened, the hierarchy progresses to more anxiety-evoking situations.

Imaginal Desensitization

Imaginal desensitization (Wolpe, 1958, 1982) begins after the patient has become proficient in the technique of PMR and a hierarchy has been developed. The procedure is simple and begins as follows:

The patient is asked to sit in a comfortable chair, preferably one that reclines, close his or her eyes, and spend several minutes getting completely relaxed.

The least anxiety-evoking item on the hierarchy is read to the patient. The patient is asked to visualize that scene as clearly and as realistically as possible.

As patients are visualizing the selected scene on the hierarchy, they are asked to imagine that they are coping satisfactorily with their anxiety. Sometimes patients visualize the devastating consequences of the trauma or an equivalent disaster rather than the selected scene. It is important that patients experience a reduction of anxiety as they are visualizing the scene.

After fifteen to twenty seconds, the therapist says, "Erase that scene from your mind and relax." This is a signal for the patient to take a deep breath, hold it, count to five, then slowly breathe out, and relax. The counting sequence helps erase the scene from the patient's mind and facilitates relaxation.

When the patient is reasonably relaxed, the anxiety experienced while visualizing the scene is rated on a scale from 0 to 10.

The procedure is repeated until the patient reports little or no anxiety while visualizing the scene. Then the next lowest item on the hierarchy is presented as above.

The anxiety reduction experienced during imaginal desensitization transfers to situations in real life.

In Vivo Desensitization

Some clinicians feel that in vivo desensitization or exposure is preferable to imaginal techniques (Marks, 1981; Mavissakalian and Barlow, 1981), and if no logistical impediments preclude an in vivo approach, it is the method of choice. As in imaginal desensitization, exposure to the lower items of the hierarchy takes place first, followed in a graduated sequence by the more anxiety evoking ones. In vivo desensitization can be facilitated when the patient is accompanied by the clinician or an assistant who serves as a nonanxious model (Rosenthal and Bandura, 1978) and also gives praise and precise feedback on the amount of improvement (Agras et al., 1969). Care must be taken neither to bring patients along too quickly nor to push them into phobic situations without their consent, because they may experience an anxiety or panic attack. When this happens, the unexpected anxiety retards treatment and the patient may refuse to cooperate in the future. During desensitization or exposure treatment, patients must experience a definite lowering of anxiety while they are in the phobic situation if treatment is to be successful (Mavissakalian and Barlow, 1981). It is good practice to end each in vivo desensitization session with positive gains, because this diminishes anticipatory anxiety and encourages a positive anticipatory attitude.

The key to success in desensitization, whether done in imagination or in the environment, is persistence. When treating PTSD patients, systematic desensitization is held in abeyance until other anti-anxiety interventions have been implemented, for phobic anxiety and phobias may abate or disappear when the patient's generalized anxiety level diminishes.

Family Conferences

The patient's social support system plays in important role in treatment; therefore, sound practice argues for arranging a meeting with the patient and significant others—father, mother, spouse, lover, or close friend. The objectives of a family conference include: enlisting the family members' cooperation; gathering additional information about the patient; and determining the family members' role in the reinforcement of symptoms. Teaching concepts regarding the reinforcement of positive behavior also add another dimension to treatment.

The family conference begins with an explanation, in nontechnical terms, of the patient's PTSD. The significance of symptoms is explained to the family member(s), and any fixed opinion concerning permanent disability should be purposely dislodged. Since family members have been closest to the problem, they should be asked about their observations of the patient's behavior. Useful information can be obtained concerning the patient's coping patterns, degree of emotional detachment from the family, involvement in recreational/social activities, and use or abuse of alcohol and other drugs. Sleep disturbance, nightmares, a "personality change," hypersensitivity to sudden environmental stimuli, preoccupation with bodily sensations, and symptoms of depression can be verified during family conferences. A spouse or lover can confirm a lack of sexual desire or other psychosexual dysfunction.

The family member can be invited to comment and to furnish additional information that augments the treatment program. "How has family life been affected by the patient's illness?" "What changes do you think will be necessary to improve family life?" These questions immediately involve the family members who add extra pairs of eyes and ears to treatment, provide information concerning outcome, and thereby increase the patient's compliance with treatment recommendations. It is the clinician's responsibility to titrate and moderate the role of relatives, since arguments and acrimony may emerge if spouses are perceived as spies who will snitch on all failures to comply with treatment. To counter this perception, family members must to taught to verbally reinforce positive gains made by the patient and discuss this progress during family conferences. As treatment proceeds it becomes obvious to all that the entire family benefits from success.

Marital conflicts frequently arise as a direct result of the altered relationship between spouses caused by the PTSD. Frequent arguments, decrease in sexual activity, diminished frequency of shared pleasures, and difficulties in communication indicate marital disharmony necessitating therapy. Conjugal conferences can become an arena for vituperation and hate unless certain precautions are taken. The couple must be instructed that the first rule of successful marital therapy consists in setting aside past grievances and concentrating on the current marital relationship. This nonhistoric approach, emphasizing changes in current marital interaction and deemphasizing past conflicts, affords a couple the best means of improving their marriage (Stuart, 1980). Positive interaction is encouraged and verbally reinforced by the therapist. As problem areas arise, they are identified and commitments are obtained from the couple to change specific behaviors. Compromises can be negotiated and behavioral contracts signed to promote positive changes in the areas of child management, housekeeping chores, money management, love-making, social and recreational pursuits, and talking together harmoniously (Stuart, 1975). A continual failure to adhere to the terms of the agreement portends protracted unhappiness or divorce; however, when a couple faithfully pursues a path of positive interaction, quick progress invariably results. People who please each other maintain a good relationship.

Assertive Training

Not all patients with PTSD have problems with assertion, but those who do must be identified. The consequences of anger, unpleasantness, lack of consideration, and sarcasm, as well as an inability to express gratitude or appreciation contribute to symptomatic behavior. PTSD patients frequently have a retributive attitude toward those believed to be responsible for their trauma and ensuant disability. Anger, engendered by the belief of negligence on the part of others, fuels memories of the trauma and symptomatic behavior. Patients frequently rail about the stupidity and carelessness of those people perceived to be responsible for the trauma. Absence of appreciation for the efforts of clinicians or other helping persons is an assertive deficiency that influences the quality of care the patient receives. Disagreeable and unappreciative patients frequently are rejected by clinicians and friends alike; owing to lack of insight, PTSD patients interpret such action as proof of the uncaring nature of people.

Outbursts of temper, aggressive acts, or just thinking angrily activate the autonomic nervous system and produces uncomfortable sensations that contribute to the patient's sense of unwellness. Although anger is appropriate at times, patients should be taught when it is not. Popular psychiatric parlance pronounces that open expression of anger should be promoted because of its therapeutic effect. This is unsound advice; although a patient may experience momentary relief, the long-range effects of expressing hostility and acrimony are always damaging.

PTSD patients often confuse anger and aggression with assertion (Dawley and Wenrich, 1976; Alberti and Emmons, 1978). Aggression is a militant act which is motivated by the willful intent of harming someone, either verbally or physically. Assertion, on the other hand, is primarily an affirmation of one's personal rights, including expressions of affection or opinions, and is an action that enhances self-esteem and mitigates pathologic anxiety. Understanding the difference is important, especially for patients who confuse the two. For example, if a patient feels aggrieved because of a perception that his PTSD has resulted from the negligence of others, the appropriate course to follow is to hire an attorney and file a civil suit. The redress of wrongs can be negotiated or adjudicated calmly and it is hoped, objectively in a legal setting. Patients need not distress themselves or others by castigating their perceived antagonist. Aggression in a civilized society almost always proves to be a self-injurious action, whereas assertion more frequently leads to the attainment of desired goals.

Thinking angrily, a less obvious aggressive action, contributes to feelings of dis-ease. During periods of disability involving inactivity, patients have time to think about unpleasant things. Like the old adage, "An idle mind is the devil's workshop," idle patients have ample opportunity to think angry thoughts and become very impatient and irritable. Teaching patients techniques of self-control based on behavioral principles reduces the tendency for aggressive outbursts (Feindler and Fremouw, 1983).

One might assume that most patients with a PTSD always act or think angrily and interact aggressively with people, but of course this is not true. Many patients exhibit passive, nonassertive behavior and are quiet and withdrawn. Nonassertiveness directly influences treatment when there is an inhibition of self-action leading to patterns of indecisiveness and procrastination. Since a successful outcome of treatment depends upon the implementation of various therapeutic techniques, failure to act decisively when performing muscle relaxation, encephalic reconditioning, beginning exercise programs, seeking work, or initiating social/recreational activities thwarts progress. When procrastination patterns extend to other areas of life and become extreme, owing to pathologic anxiety, the unfinished business can become a burden and a source of additional anxiety.

Assertive training consists of a varied combination of behavioral rehearsal, modeling, instruction, feedback (Marks, 1981), and encephalic reconditioning. Encephalic reconditioning, especially thought stopping and positive encephalic practice, can reduce the flow of hostile thoughts. When the patient begins to act assertively, angry thoughts, in turn, will usually diminish and disappear. Learning how to act assertively with others and initiating self action can best be achieved by behavioral rehearsal and graded task assignments (Wolpe, 1982). Before behavioral rehearsal begins, the patient identifies the nonassertive situations and the people who are involved. The situations are discussed and several assertive "scripts" are created and ranked in accordance with the degree of difficulty and the amount of anxiety associated with each. The "easier," less anxiety-evoking "scripts" are chosen first and enacted in the consulting room with the clinician playing the role of the other person. These behavioral rehearsal sessions may be recorded on a video or audio-cassette and played back for analysis and critique (Server, 1972). The same situation is rehearsed again, and a comparison between the first and second attempt usually facilitates learning because the patient invariably does better the second time. Homework includes assignments for patients to practice assertion in real-life settings, starting with the easier situations and then moving to the more difficult ones. Acting assertively is an interpersonal skill and, like other skills, improves with practice and time.

Procrastination patterns respond to the successful completion of graded task assignments (Curren and Gilbert, 1975). Patients begin by compiling a hierarchical procrastination list that starts with the simpler tasks and progresses to the more difficult and anxiety-evoking ones (Scrignar, 1983). It must be kept in mind that patients procrastinate not only on onerous tasks, such as filling out reports, writing letters, and paying bills, but also in such matters as deciding to take a vacation, visit a friend, or engage in some new pleasurable social activity. Failure to act on these issues can result in a future source of anxiety and eliminate a potential source of enjoyment. Information concerning self-assertiveness as it applies to each item on the hierarchy assists patients in decision making and eventually in assertive action. Following instruction, homework assignments begin with one or two of the less difficult items on the list, which are to be completed before the patient returns for the next session. As patients reap the rewards of assertion, procrastination diminishes. Change is slow, but adherence to the principles of assertive training yields results, and behavioral rehearsal assignments become pleasurable exercises.

Problem Solving

Unresolved problems are a source of anxiety which aggravates a PTSD. During family conferences and assertive training sessions, many common problems involving family life, interpersonal issues, and decision making are addressed and resolved. Of the remaining problems, all that may be required is sound counsel from the clinician. PTSD patients often develop tunnel vision and are unable to see alternatives to their dilemmas. Through discussion the clinician presents information and opinions that widen the patient's vision and make it easier to envisage and decide upon solutions.

Often when patients file a civil lawsuit, it creates conflict, which tends to intensify anxiety. Some patients become obsessed with their tort action and constantly complain of court delays and real or imagined injustices, which contribute to stress. When the clinician is familiar with the legal process, information concerning depositions and courtroom procedures allays the patient's apprehension. To place litigation in perspective, sometimes it is helpful to express the opinion that civil litigation is impersonal and revolves around monetary issues. Advice to solicit a trustworthy, competent attorney who can attend to all aspects of legal matters also mitigates anxiety.

A problem that causes considerable distress in unemployed patients is lack of money. A state of poverty alters the living standard and imposes hardships on all members of a family. If the patient had been the breadwinner, the burden of insolvency adds more stress. No solution is perfect, but temporary remedies include: assistance from governmental agencies, instructions on money management and budgeting, loans, and employment of the well spouse. Impecuniousness can also serve as an impetus to motivate a patient to work in a limited capacity or to obtain a different job.

Occasionally, solutions to problems may have been delayed simply because the patient did not possess the requisite information upon which to base a plan of action. Governmental bureaucracies at the federal, state, and local levels often offer seemingly insurmountable obstacles to the solution of simple problems, and the clinician can serve as a cicerone, guiding the patient through the maze of administrative procedures. Letters, phone calls, or advice from the clinician often remove bureaucratic barriers and break the impasse to a viable remedy. Solutions to problems reduce or eliminate a source of anxiety which, after all, is one goal of treatment.

In some circles advice giving by clinicians, especially psychiatrists, is viewed with skepticism, yet a mental health professional as a respected authority figure can have a profound positive influence upon a patient by giving sound advice. Successful people in all walks of life consult experts for guidance and counsel, and the clinician can provide this service or direct the patient to an appropriate resource. Advice giving under these circumstances should not be discouraged, but promoted as of value to the patient.

Exercise and Nutrition

It is axiomatic to state that people function best when they exercise regularly and eat properly. This maxim, however, has specific significance for patients with chronic PTSD who may avoid physical activity and neglect nutrition. The body, like a machine, requires proper maintenance and fueling. Proper exercise and good nutrition contribute to successful treatment of PTSD.

Exercise

The benefits of exercise cannot be stored; rather, physical fitness requires regular involvement in some physical activity. Fitness flags quickly when idleness ensues, especially if injury causes physical inactivity. In cases of chronic PTSD, physical discomfort can persist long after the expected time of healing and can nurture the idea of an unsound body. There is some evidence for this idea, because prolonged physical inactivity causes muscles to become flabby, strength to ebb, and the body to become easily fatigued. Verification of physical infirmity and defect seems to occur when patients engage in minor acts of physical exertion or short spurts of arduous activity and later complain of muscular aches and pains. After a while patients honestly believe they cannot perform certain physical actions and attribute failure to some pathologic process within the body. In reality, poor physical conditioning caused by lack of exercise is the culprit. Despite repeated physical examinations and various laboratory procedures that disclose no organic pathology, some patients are loath to accept this conclusion. This may lead to an impasse in treatment, since patients may obstinately refuse to comply with recommendations to return to work, to assume more responsibility at home, to engage in more social/recreational activities, and, of course, to embark upon an exercise program.

To dissuade patients from erroneous ideas concerning their physical status and to persuade them of the value of exercise, an explanation for the presence of any current physical discomfort or pain is mandatory. The sources of the patient's pain and discomfort can usually be traced to: (1) chronic anxiety and increased motor tension; (2) residual injury related to the original trauma; and (3) muscular aches and pains owing to poor muscle tone. As anxiety is alleviated by self-hypnosis and muscle relaxation during treatment, the patient is told motor tension will be greatly reduced. Minor aches and pains caused by poor muscle tone can be corrected by physiotherapy and exercise.

Brief instruction in anatomy, utilizing an atlas to illustrate the affected anatomical areas, augments the educational process and is usually enthusiastically received by patients who formerly harbored ignorance concerning the functioning of their body. Although patients may be experiencing some pain and physical discomfort, the main message, "There is nothing seriously wrong with you," must be conveyed along with the recommendation that a sensible, well-designed exercise program would be of great value. Confirmation of this opinion by an orthopedic surgeon reduces the patient's apprehension and increases compliance.

Many medical centers and hospitals have physical fitness clinics or health centers where an individual's physical state of health can be evaluated. Trained personnel in these centers utilizing special instruments and equipment can measure cardiopulmonary functioning, percentage of total body fat, and muscular strength prior to the preparation of individualized exercise programs. In the absence of human performance centers in the community, well-staffed and organized health clubs, spas, and similar groups devoted to physical health are acceptable alternatives. Some patients prefer unsupervised exercise, but this must be avoided or carefully controlled, lest overexertion lead to pain, thereby discouraging future exercise. To ensure compliance with the prescription of regular exercise, part of each therapy session with the patients should include a discussion of physical progress. When a medical center or health club conducts the program, ongoing communication with the agency maximizes compliance and successful outcome.

The recommendation to engage in regular exercise carries with it the implicit message that "you are capable of improving your physical health." When patients begin to derive the benefits from exercise, enhanced strength and endurance also reinforce the idea of physical soundness. Some pain may still be present, but as patients learn to cope, discomfort becomes subordinated to a more active lifestyle. Fatigue and listlessness caused by chronic anxiety also respond favorably to a program of graduated exercise. More energy, sounder sleep, increased interest in sex, improved appetite, and a physical and psychological feeling of well-being all accrue as a result of regular exercise.

Nutrition

An inquiry into the dietary habits of the PTSD patient should always include the quantities of alcohol, coffee, tea, other caffeine-containing products, and proprietary medications that are consumed. Caffeine and sympathomimetic substances directly affect the nervous system and abet anxiety (Goldstein, et al., 1969; Greden, 1979; Rapoport, et al., 1981).With the use of a log, the eating habits of the patients are surveyed. If diets are not adequate, information concerning the daily minimum requirements of essential foodstuffs (proteins, carbohydrates, fats, vitamins, and minerals) is provided. Overweight patients should be placed on an appropriate diet based on behavior modification (Scrignar, 1980; Stuart and Davis, 1982). If the clinician does not feel competent in this area, consultation with a nutritionist or dietician assists in the analysis and formulation of a good nutritional program.

Related Issues—Work and Social/Recreational Activities

Work

Work is defined as any productive activity that regularly utilizes a person's mental and physical energy and consumes a significant amount of time each day, for which an individual receives a reward, usually money. The manifestations of PTSD—chronic anxiety, fatigue, phobic anxiety, pain, physical discomfort, and depression—interfere with work performance. The consequences of unemployment are all bad, but generally lack of money places the most stress on the patient. Insolvency is not only demoralizing, but also affects the living standard of the family. The patient's time, normally spent working, is not spent on leisure but wasted on worry, an encephalic activity that generates more anxiety, further encumbering the patient.

When a physical injury is associated with the development of a PTSD, somatic symptoms sometimes persist long after the expected time of healing, and patients feel physically incapable of performing even minor tasks. They also avoid more arduous activity, fearing an aggravation of the injury. Patients who cling to the belief of an organic defect seem bereft of psychological insight and choose to concentrate, in vain, on a physical cause and surgical cure for their condition. Wisdom dictates that clinicians communicate with the patient's surgeon in order to avoid mixed messages concerning physical impairment and fitness for work. Moreover, physiotherapy and other medical treatments can complement the psychological treatment of PTSD, so that patients can return to work as soon as possible. A quick return to work is always desirable, but without the patient's consent, this recommendation meets with resistance. Often, patients become truculent if they feel that their doctor is insensitive or in cahoots with the company. Recommendations to return to work, therefore, must be delicately handled.

Initially, patients are persuaded that work will not aggravate their condition, but rather will be part of a return to normal life. A resumption of limited or light duty with the goal of a gradual resumption of regular tasks almost always hastens a patient's recovery. When work requires hard labor or employers are uncooperative, reemployment under these circumstances may not be possible. When a change in occupation and vocational rehabilitation becomes necessary, a longer road to recovery is prognosticated.

Reports, letters, and phone calls from the clinician can expedite an unemployed patient's return to work. Personal attention helps remove administrative red tape that may have blocked reemployment. For example, the oil refinery worker mentioned on page 167 who was involved in the accident in which he received minor physical injuries developed PTSD with a phobia of heights and the work premises, specifically related to reading gauges and adjusting valves at various levels of a ten-story tower. Following imaginal desensitization for his phobia, a phone call was made to his company physician. The principles underlying PTSD, particularly the worker's phobia, were explained to the company doctor who made arrangements for the patient to visit the oil refinery, especially his immediate work area, for the purpose of in vivo desensitization. The patient was desensitized of his phobia, returned to work, and successfully resumed his job.

Although work has a high priority in treatment, the symptoms of PTSD must have abated to a large extent before this goal is addressed. To be successful, the recommendation of a return to work must be titrated with symptomatic improvement. Pending personal injury litigation or workers' compensation payments complicate efforts regarding employment.

Social/Recreational Activities

When patients experience chronic anxiety, physical discomfort, or depression, they derive little delight from social/recreational activities. Concentration on the trauma and its consequences causes a self-centeredness that draws attention away from enjoyable activities. PTSD is a desocializing condition, and patients soon become withdrawn and isolated from family and friends, thus diminishing potentially pleasing interactions. During the later stages of treatment, patients frequently need guidelines to reestablish old pleasures and discover new ones. It is during family conferences that discussions concerning social/recreational activities are best conducted. At this time, it is imperative to secure a commitment from the patient and spouse to engage in one or more mutually satisfying activities during the coming week. The involvement of the spouse facilitates the patient's compliance, and the pleasure derived from the activity reinforces a repeat performance. Patients are well on their way to recovery when the environment provides enjoyment, the physiological sensations of the body feel good, and the cognitive apparatus of the mind begins to presage pleasure. The patient's improvement measured by enjoyment in social/recreational activities is a good index of progress.

Self-Assessment

Recording the occurrence and frequency of selected symptoms helps to control and regulate targeted behavior and is a way of assessing outcome of treatment (Fisher et al., 1982; Mahoney and Arnoff, 1979). Too often, PTSD patients complain of symptoms as if they were occurring throughout the entire day. Additionally, patients may disparage therapeutic recommendations as if they have absolutely no effect on altering symptoms or pathologic behaviors. For example, patients will complain of insomnia or physical discomfort, suggesting that they never sleep and are in constant pain. Similarly, patients may report that PMR or self-hypnosis had absolutely no effect in inducing somnolence or ameliorating pain. Neither patients nor clinicians receive encouragement from these nihilistic reports, but fortunately these assessments are usually in error. When patients are asked to record the total number of hours spent napping or sleeping during the day and night, or if pain is a problem, to record hourly on a scale from zero to ten, the intensity of physical discomfort that they experience, the symptomatic profile discloses significant variation. The all-or-nothing reports—"I have the symptoms all the time and nothing seems to work to alleviate them" are not only untrue but hinder treatment. Unknowingly, the patient makes these inaccurate estimates of pathology and response to treatment because "that's the way it seems." Unless there is a dramatic and profound change in symptoms, patients will report no change. The small but steady positive alterations in behavior, the usual response to treatment, must be verbally reinforced by the therapist in order to promote continuing therapeutic gains.

Patients must be persuaded that accurate self-assessment is one way to control and regulate selected behaviors. By the use of a Self-Assessment Form (Table 8-1), patients record the occurrence and source of pathologic anxiety, as well as selected target behaviors. Since pathologic anxiety is a crucial element in PTSD, the Three E's, which stimulate and alleviate anxiety, must be identified and recorded. On the left side of the Self-Assessment Form, the patient records the source of pathologic anxiety, and on the right side the interventions employed to reduce anxiety. Space is also included for comments related to outcome. An example of a typical entry for a PTSD patient who was involved in an automobile accident and had phobic anxiety while riding in a car was as follows:

Sources of Anxiety

Environment   -   Riding in a car driven by a friend.

Endogenous   -   Heart beginning to beat rapidly; I feel tightness in my chest and have a dizzy feeling.

Encephalic   -   I think I am going to faint or maybe lose control of myself.

Anti-anxiety Interventions

Environment   -   Stayed in the car, conversed with my friend as a distraction.

Endogenous   -   Initiated muscle relaxation, especially slow deep breathing.

Encephalic   -   Repeated the four positive reinforcing statements and told myself everything would be all right.

Comment   -   After several minutes, the anxiety symptoms went away, my heart slowed, and the tightness in my chest and dizziness were alleviated. Soon I began to feel better and more in control.

Other items that the patient may record are: participation in exercise (specify in detail), participation in social/recreational activities (specify in detail), time spent in a phobic situation, presence and duration of any somatic symptoms, amount of alcohol consumed, quantity and type of medication taken, and the intensity (low, moderate, severe) and place where anxiety is experienced. The record should include an assessment of positive coping behaviors and other signs of improvement. At the conclusion of each day, the patient is asked to make a global rating of progress based on a scale of zero (no progress) to 10 (excellent progress).

Recording events facilitates self-analysis and self-management of pathologic behavior and associated symptoms. The information also furnishes the clinician with data concerning the patient's progress, upon which an adjustment of the therapeutic regimen depends. When patients are doing well, they should be praised. If they founder, however, appropriate adjustment in treatment must be initiated. The goal of treatment is not complete tranquility, for patients must learn to differentiate between anxiety and pathologic anxiety but, more importantly, learning how to cope with the consequences of trauma.

TERMINATION

Treatment for chronic PTSD, like any other chronic illness, is imperfect, and criteria for termination lack precision. There is no dramatic reduction of symptoms, except in those exceptional cases responding to hypnosis and abreaction. Rather, a slow and sometimes tedious return to normal functioning occurs. Pending litigation may retard treatment, but it is questionable whether successful litigation hastens recovery. More often than not, dogged adherence to the treatment described in this chapter and the passage of time are the important ingredients of recovery. Treatment is successful when patients report a significant reduction or elimination of symptoms as determined on the SIC, including improvement in work performance, family life, social/recreational activities, and coping skills. As patients make progress, the frequency of sessions diminishes from weekly to twice monthly, then to monthly until termination. To ensure a stable improvement during the first year, the patient should be seen in the office every three months for a current status review. Thereafter, a mental status examination is conducted annually, similar to an annual physical examination. Studies have shown that PTSD patients are susceptible to Generalized Anxiety Disorder, Psychoactive Substance Use Disorders, and Mood Disorders, and the clinician must be alert to the likelihood of these psychiatric disorders in the patient (Kluznik, et al., 1986). Continued contact with patients, without fostering undue dependency, prevents exacerbation of symptoms and minimizes the occurrence of other mental disorders. When patients learn to cope with the everyday stresses of life by utilizing appropriate therapeutic techniques, treatment is considered to be successful.

NINE

GROUP TREATMENT*

A homogeneity of symptoms exists among persons who develop PTSD, and a subdivision of patients into groups according to the commonality of stressors occurs naturally. Women suffering from a rape trauma syndrome (Burgess, 1983) gather for group treatment in rape crisis centers. Group therapy is an important treatment modality for Vietnam-era veterans who are treated in Veterans Administration facilities or Vet Centers (Walker and Nash, 1981; Parson, 1984). Many of the five to six million children, spouses, and elderly individuals who are neglected, battered, and abused in the United States each year develop PTSD and can benefit from group therapy (Rosenbaum, 1986). The alarming increase of crime statistics parallels the growing number of criminal assault victims, many of whom develop a PTSD and could benefit from group treatment. Group therapy is useful for victims of terrorism, many of whom have been subjected to torture (Ochberg and Soskis, 1982). Trauma centers which cater mainly to a victim's physical injuries following an industrial or vehicular accident should routinely evaluate the psychological status of patients in order to identify PTSD sufferers; group therapy would be the ideal vehicle for treating large numbers of these patients (Rosenheim and Elizur, 1977). There is no doubt that treatment conducted in groups has the advantage of economy in terms of time, effort, and money (Marks, 1981).

---

*This chapter is reprinted in part from Scrignar, C. B., Group Therapy with Victims of Post-Traumatic Stress Disorder. In M. Seligman and L. A. Marsak (Eds.), *A Practitioner's Guide to Interventions with Special Populations*. Orlando, Grune & Stratton (in press).

Selecting Group Members

Selecting appropriate patients, an important decision for all group therapists, is no less important when forming PTSD groups. The therapist must decide whether to mix patients suffering from heterogeneous trauma or to limit the group to individuals who have experienced a similar trauma. Circumstances and availability of patients usually determine the types of groups which are assembled. Veterans suffering from PTSD flock for treatment to Veterans Administration hospitals or Vet Centers where groups are formed. Sexual assault victims filter through law enforcement agencies who refer prospective patients to rape crisis centers or to sex therapy clinics, and groups evolve from these centers. Mental health professionals rush to the site of natural or man-made disasters where group therapy is administered, "in situ," to victims of a mass tragedy. At the conclusion of a hostage incident, survivors are herded into groups where they receive debriefing and therapy. Shelters for battered women provide crisis intervention and an opportunity to implement group therapy. Trauma centers, which are beginning to emerge throughout the United States, deal primarily with accident victims' broken bones and battered bodies; liaison with these centers would certainly disclose emotionally traumatized patients who could form the nucleus of a group. As a natural consequence of their function, community institutions and administrative agencies separate persons who are involved in a trauma into unified groups ready for professional consideration and placement into therapy groups.

When organizing a group of PTSD patients, common sense indicates the selection of a homogeneously traumatized group. Combining Vietnam veterans, rape victims, and recently-released hostages into one therapy group does not seem wise. Group members with similar traumatic experiences can empathize with each other and in a collegial fashion, learn from one another. It is a good rule to select patients for group therapy based on a commonality or similarity of a trauma.

Whether to mix acute cases of PTSD with patients who have become chronic is another decision which must be made. Chronic patients, especially those who have become despondent and hopeless, project a sense of futility and would seem to be poor role models for acute PTSD cases. On the other hand, mixing acute and chronic PTSD patients allows for the discussion of a broader range of issues during group therapy. The distinction between acute and chronic may not be as important as an assessment of motivation. Prior to placement in a group, patients who complain of chronic pain, obsess about physical symptoms, exhibit symptoms of a major depression, require daily use of a narcotic analgesic, or exaggerate symptoms must be carefully screened and evaluated regarding a desire to change. Often secondary issues take precedence over therapy, and patients who have a different agenda may contaminate the group process. Patients displaying any of the following characteristics should be carefully screened: Psychoactive Substance Use Disorder, Somatoform Disorders, Antisocial Personality Disorder, Factitious Disorder, and malingering. By and large, in regard to mixing acute and chronic cases when forming a PTSD group, the fewer restrictions the better. The group process creates an impetus which can overcome most obstacles brought forth by acute and chronic patients.

Starting a Group

Group treatment for PTSD is not complicated, but it keeps the therapist busy. Preliminary diagnostic interviews identify PTSD from other disorders that patients may experience post-traumatically. Dysthymia, Major Depressive Disorder, Panic Disorder, Organic Personality Syndrome, and Somatoform Disorders must be ruled out by a mental status examination. If the trauma resulted in head injury and unconsciousness, a neurosurgeon must be consulted to determine the extent of Organic Mental Syndrome. When physical injury coexists with PTSD, liaison with the treating physician(s) allows for an exchange of information related to ongoing medical treatment and prognosis. For those patients who are selected and offered an opportunity to enter group therapy, the introductory interview consists of a thorough explanation of PTSD, emphasizing the need and rationale for group treatment. An outline of therapy, consisting of PTSD themes, group therapy interventions, objectives, goals, and duration of treatment is developed. Prior to the start of group therapy, it is a good idea to furnish each patient with a copy of the agenda, briefly summarizing the ten-session package that will be discussed shortly. A syllabus stating the objectives and goals of each session allows patients time for preparation and serves to maintain continuity. Patients' questions are answered, fees for professional services are settled, and a date is set for the first session.

The group leader(s) is an active participant and fulfills the role of empathic therapist, compassionate teacher, and pragmatic professor. The therapist, like the director of a new play, has a flexible script, the details of which may be modified as therapy progresses. The fundamental elements of group treatment consist of education, encephalic reconditioning (cognitive restructuring), training in relaxation, and exposure treatment. Assertive training (anger reduction), family interventions, and problem-solving constitute a second phalanx of stratagems. Homework assignments glue the sessions together and are an essential component of therapy. Throughout therapy, patients apply therapeutic interventions, assess progress, and reset goals. Because of the numerous tasks, inexperienced therapists are advised initially to limit the number of patients in a group to three or four. When the treatment process has been mastered, subsequent groups can include a maximum of eight to ten patients.

TEN SESSION OUTLINE

Session 1: Explanation-Education — At the beginning of each session, the group leader sets the stage for therapy by delivering a lecturette (Yost, et al., 1986). During the first session, group members receive information concerning the various themes of PTSD. Many patients are unaware that their response to trauma is pathological, even as symptoms become protracted. Acceptance of a stress disorder as "normal" or "justifiable" contravenes the necessity for change. The "bad news-good news" message of the brief lecture emphasizes: you are suffering from a PTSD, but it is treatable. The rationale for each treatment intervention is explained, with the imperative that a good outcome depends upon cooperation and completion of all homework assignments.

Correcting misconceptions about the emotional sequelae of trauma allows patients to proceed in therapy, unencumbered by a false belief. Some common misconceptions include:

1. **I cannot control my thoughts about the trauma.** Although intrusive thoughts seem guided by unseen forces, the truth is that all thoughts can be altered or modified to some extent by cognitive restructuring. Patients are reassured that if they follow instructions and consciously reduce thoughts about their trauma by twenty to thirty percent, significant positive changes will result.
2. **I cannot influence what I dream.** While nightmares occur spontaneously during a sleeping state, what one dreams usually reflects what one thinks during the day(s) preceding sleep. When patients continue to report frequent nightmares, it indicates obsessional thinking about the trauma during the day. Persistent bad dreams, therefore, can signify the

necessity for more assiduous attention to techniques of cognitive restructuring.

3. **I can never return to the scene of the trauma or any place which resembles it.** This misconception may prevent patients from working, driving automobiles, flying in airplanes, or engaging in any activity related to the trauma. Systematic desensitization or exposure treatment allows patients to overcome fears related to the traumatic event. Results from numerous studies involving exposure treatment (systematic desensitization or flooding) help to rid patients of a pessimistic attitude and point the way to an effective treatment intervention (Marks, 1981).

4. **I'll never forget the trauma.** While it is true that the traumatic event will remain embedded in memory, the emotions associated with it will diminish and recede with therapy and time. The traumatic event will be removed from the front-center stage of the mind by appropriate therapy and will be allowed to recede into the "attic of the mind", a place similar to the attic in a house where things are stored and remain unseen, sometimes forever.

5. **My personality has been irreversibly changed by the trauma.** Everyone experiences unpleasant events during life; although the personality may become nicked and scarred, it does not basically change following a trauma. All human beings have the capacity of adapting to adversity, and group treatment will facilitate this process.

6. **I am dead sexually.** Anxiety, anger, pain, or physical discomfort cause sexual dysfunction, but as these dysphoric emotions abate, pleasurable sexual feelings will return and a resumption of normal sexual activity can be expected.

7. **My spouse doesn't love me anymore.** At times chronically dependent PTSD patients may not be so lovable, and disability certainly places a strain on a marriage, but in the author's experience divorce seldom occurs. Spouses of patients may resent the child-like dependent behavior exhibited by some PTSD patients, but treatment promotes independence and improves marital relations.

8. **I can't do anything.** Even for severely injured PTSD patients, this generalization is not true. Normal life activities may have been disrupted and patients may have to make adjustments, however, a repertoire of useful behaviors stills exist or can be developed. When patients make a comparison between pre and post- traumatic life style, dissatisfaction invariably results; patience is an attribute patients must acquire because a resumption of pre-trauma activities is slow and

gradual. The pattern of establishing a regular routine of eating, sleeping, and exercising "normalizes" life and precedes major changes.

After the introductory remarks and the question and answer period, patients are asked to give an account of their trauma. To ensure against repetition, patients are informed that they will be allowed to relate the trauma in detail only once. This admonition is consistent with the therapeutic philosophy of the group: concentrate on coping rather than on the trauma. Catharsis and abreaction may occur as patients recall their trauma, and this is empathetically accepted, however, the group leader must emphasize the fact of survival. At the conclusion of each recitation, group members are encouraged to comment; the therapist assists by pointing out salient aspects of the history which can be impacted by therapeutic interventions.

During the first session, an atmosphere which encourages a positive expectation must be created in concert with the necessity of self-help. Information will be provided, therapeutic techniques taught, but success or failure depends upon the patient's ability to carry out recommendations. Throughout treatment, the modality of explanation-education occupies a prominent position. Brief lectures furnish information and are the vehicle for instruction, but informal discussions supplement didactic presentations at each group session.

Sessions 2 and 3: Encephalic Reconditioning (Cognitive Restructuring) — During the lecturette, the therapist presents the basic constructs of cognitive theory, explaining the relationship between intrusive thoughts and subsequent symptoms. How positive or negative thoughts influence feelings and ultimately behavior can be illustrated by examples common to everyone. Thoughts about one's achievements leads to feelings of well-being and predisposes a person to further accomplishment. Sexual thoughts lead to sexual arousal and a desire for sexual fulfillment. Thoughts about a gourmet meal, especially if one has not eaten for awhile, stimulates the gastrointestinal tract, causing a feeling of hunger and a strong urge to eat. Similarly, negative emotions and behavior can be stimulated and influenced by distressing thoughts. Frightening thoughts lead to a feeling of fear, which to a varying extent, immobilizes a person. Angry feelings are always preceded by angry thoughts and followed by verbal or physical manifestations of rage which is expressed directly or obliquely. For example, thinking about being wronged by a boss, friend, or relative leads to feelings of indignation, irritation, and anger, followed by a strong desire to retaliate with words or deeds. Recurrent and intrusive distressing thoughts about a trauma are associated with feelings of fear, anxiety, despair, anger, or guilt, depending upon which aspect of the trauma comes to mind. These dysphoric emotions or feelings, in turn, stimulate negative behaviors which are usually maladaptive.

Once patients understand and accept cognitive theory, they are asked to become more introspective; recognition of one's thoughts precedes the application of cognitive restructuring. Next, patients record the frequency and duration of traumatic thoughts in a log or diary. These data direct the patient to unwanted thoughts and can serve as a baseline from which to measure progress.

Changing or modifying a distressing thought is achieved by thought-stopping and thought-substitution techniques (Bain, 1928; Yamagami, 1971). The stopping and substitution method, as described in Chapter 8, can be adapted for use in groups. Once proficiency has been achieved, patients are asked to practice the techniques outside the group whenever intrusive thoughts enter their mind. Some patients may report that they cannot control their thoughts or think of any happy or pleasant situations. This resistance usually dissolves as other group members report success with stopping procedures and give illustrations of pleasant thoughts and memories that they used during thought-substitution exercises.

At the third session, group members discuss homework assignments by referring to logs or diaries. Successes are verbally reinforced, failures are analyzed, suggestions are given, and patients are encouraged to keep trying. As patients report good results with cognitive restructuring, the group process not only serves as an elixir for all, but also creates a positive attitudinal change which promotes coping.

Session 4: Relaxation Training — Fear and anxiety, symptoms of increased arousal, are ameliorated by training patients in the technique of muscle relaxation (Jacobsen, 1974). During the lecturette preceding group instruction in relaxation, patients are told that progressive muscle relaxation, hypnosis and self- hypnosis, autogenic training, transcendental meditation, and even prayer are all similar. When practiced successfully, all methods produce the same beneficial physiologic result, lowering the activity of the autonomic nervous system and decreasing motor tension. After this preamble, the entire group is taught progressive muscle relaxation. The technique of tensing and then relaxing various muscle groups is simple (Chapter 8), but proficiency depends upon daily practice. Coping with symptoms of increased arousal by a relaxation procedure gives patients control over symptoms, and this leads to a positive expectation related to treatment, as well as feelings of self-confidence. At the conclusion of the session, all group members invariably report a feeling of relaxation and well-being, something that they have not experienced in a long time.

Session 5: Exposure Treatment — PTSD patients tend to avoid activities, situations, or places reminiscent of the trauma because exposure to various elements of the trauma elicits uncomfortable feelings of anxiety. Behavior theorists postulate that the traumatic event, the unconditioned stimulus, elicits feelings of fear and anxiety which became conditioned to stimuli associated with the trauma. Following the trauma, these cues or conditioned stimuli stimulate fear and anxiety. To reduce or eliminate these uncomfortable feelings, patients tend to avoid situations which produce them. If avoidance or phobic behavior persists, it can be terribly debilitating.

Information about learning, conditioning, avoidance behavior, and the rationale underlying exposure treatment (systematic desensitization or flooding) is integrated during the lecture. Afterwards, patients are asked to list all situations or activities which they currently avoid. Often the place where the trauma occurred becomes a phobic stimulus. If a sexual assault took place in their apartment, rape victims may abandon autonomous living, even though it is their personal preference (Chapter 14, Case Two). For a factory worker who is traumatized in an industrial accident, avoidance of the work place means unemployment. In this instance, exposure treatment should be coordinated with the plant physician and supervisor or foreman who must understand the principles of desensitization. Time spent in the factory and proximity to the accident site are the main variables which correlate with increasing anxiety. Time is lengthened and distance shortened as exposure therapy proceeds. Following successful treatment, the factory worker experiences minimal discomfort at the accident site and can spend the full working day in the plant.

During the procedure of exposure treatment, patients are encouraged to utilize cognitive restructuring and progressive muscle relaxation to diminish fear and anxiety. Progression to a more anxiety-evoking step of the hierarchy should not take place unless the patient feels reasonably calm in the preceding step. At the end of the group session, patients are given homework assignments and asked to assess and record the results of exposure treatment which will be discussed at the next session. Any difficulties are analyzed and remedied and, of course, progress is verbally reinforced by the group leader and usually applauded by the group members.

Session 6: Assertive Training (Anger Reduction) — PTSD patients have a tendency, especially if the trauma is of human design, to engage in periodic outbursts of anger directed towards anyone believed responsible for the trauma. Even if overt expressions of anger do not occur, resentment smolders as patients ruminate about the negligence of others. After provocation has passed, anger, a disruptive emotion, is maladaptive, patients are told. Overt anger or covert resentment revivifies the trauma, causing a resurgence of symptoms.

The lecture at the beginning of the sixth session outlines the difference between aggression and assertion (Chapter 8). Nonassertive or passive behavior, another characteristic of PTSD patients, is also discussed. The group leader gives several examples of each type of behavior, pointing out that assertive actions make a person feel good and maximize the achievement of objectives.

Group members are asked to air their grievances, then to engage in appropriate assertive responses by behavioral rehearsal or role-playing exercises, first with the group leader and later with other group members. Any irrational outburst of anger or inappropriate passive acceptance becomes evident to all. Following a discussion and analysis of the interaction, behavioral rehearsal is repeated using principles of assertion mentioned in Chapter 8. Patients are told that it is useless to berate employers or those believed responsible for the trauma; if negligence occurred, it usually was not intentional. However, the rightful avenue for redress is in the courts. In civilized society, retribution occurs as a result of civil legal action and is not based on the code of Hammurabi: "an eye for an eye and a tooth for a tooth." Civil litigation offers victims an opportunity to receive monetary compensation for damages, both physical and emotional. If legal action is not possible, traumatized patients must assume a philosophical attitude because harboring resentment interferes with treatment and a return to normal living.

Session 7: Family Relationships — Family life goes out of kilter when one member develops a PTSD. This is especially true when disability leads to unemployment and a role reversal occurs within the marital unit. Dysfunctional dependent behavior may be tolerated by a spouse for a short period of time, but eventually increased marital tension results in disputes and sexual dysfunction (Scrignar, 1987).

The lecturette which begins session seven presents information about the duties, responsibilities, and roles of the various members of a family unit. When one member becomes ill, the balance and burden of responsibility shifts to healthy members of the family. Unless one is seriously incapacitated, the lecture continues, a disabled person can usually make some contribution to the welfare of the family. Group members may protest that they can't do anything, but these complaints are countered with stories illustrating how others have overcome adversity. The therapist, from his own experiences or from newspaper accounts, can relate stories about the tenacity and courage of disabled persons who learned how to cope with illness and handicaps.

Patients, hopefully motivated by inspirational stories, are asked how they can contribute more to the functioning of their family. Group process and the therapist can deal benevolently with any negative reaction, and patients are persuaded to look beyond themselves to the needs of the family. Following a trauma, it is natural for the mind's eye to turn inward, causing patients to become self-centered and oblivious to the needs of others. This tendency can be reversed by gentle non-accusatory, but firm persuasion, directing patients toward the acquisition of behaviors to remedy damaged family relationships. Whining and complaining, social isolation, and outbursts of anger are some negative behaviors which diminish pleasurable interaction with family members. Conversely, the addition of positive behaviors such as sharing household duties, helping manage children, increasing intimate interaction (conversation as well as sexual activity), and engaging more frequently in social and recreational activities helps to restore the family equilibrium.

Patients are asked to construct two lists. The first consists of previously enjoyed activities and tasks. General terms such as work, exercise, or recreational activities are to be avoided in favor of specific time-limited activities. Work might include clean out garage, take out the garbage, or mow the lawn, while exercise would consist of walking around the block, lifting light weights for five minutes, and jogging one-quarter mile; recreational activities would include watching a baseball game, going to a party, bowling, etc. The second list includes the names of all significant family members. The patient is then asked how an increase in activities compiled in the first list would affect the people in the second list. As group members come to grip with the answer, they begin to realize the reciprocal nature of relationships; you get what you give.

Homework assignments consist of a commitment to engage in three helping behaviors which impact directly upon family members. The result, including the response of the family member, becomes grist for group discussion during the next session. Group members are generally surprised as they begin to reap the benefits of improved family relationships produced by seemingly small changes in their behavior. Success reported by one patient has a motivating impact on all members of the group, especially when the group leader verbally rewards positive change. Occasionally a conjoint session with patient and spouse must be arranged outside of the group in order to resolve intense marital conflicts (Stuart, 1980).

Session 8: Problem-Solving — Unresolved problems are a source of stress, and PTSD patients often develop mental myopia and are unable to see alternatives to dilemmas. Problem-solving sessions, like a visit to an optometrist, gives patients the opportunity to improve their vision by group discussion which clarifies problems and offers alternative solutions. The introductory lecture reviews the principles of cognitive theory mentioned during sessions two and three. Thinking or worrying about unresolved problems does increase stress and anxiety, even if the thoughts are not directly related to the trauma. Patients are instructed to record in a notebook the amount of time they think about specific problems each day. By the end of one week, data concerning worrisome subjects accumulate, and the time spent thinking about specific problems reflects the relative importance of that problem. The list is subdivided into problems which have a long-range solution and ones which can be acted upon immediately. Those problems which have a long-range solution are set aside, while the second list becomes the subject for sessions. The group then grapples with the most expeditious way to manage each problem. Family conferences and assertive training sessions resolve most problems; the remainder may only require sound counsel from the group, making it easier for the patient to decide upon solutions.

The therapist and group members can help redefine the problem so that it is specific. Problems should not include symptoms of the stress disorder which have been addressed earlier. Inability to work, financial problems, legal difficulties, diminished involvement in social and recreational activities, and lack of exercise can be addressed and discussed by the patient and the group. Advice about budgeting, debt consolidation, or bankruptcy can resolve many problems dealing with money. When patients have legal difficulties, the names and addresses of several competent and respected lawyers may be all that is necessary to alleviate this problem.

The therapist records, as a reminder, the acceptance of the solution by the patient so that the outcome can be reported during the next session. Action, no matter what the outcome, is applauded and patients are reminded that in life, perfect solutions occur infrequently. Partial resolution of problems, however, diminishes stress and provides the impetus for further change. Some clinicians may disparage advice-giving, but successful people in all walks of life consult outside sources for guidance and counsel as they decide upon a course of action.

Problems which have no immediate solution must be placed in the "attic of the mind" to await future consideration. Placing a problem in proper perspective reduces urgency; all problems eventually are resolved or forgotten, and life moves on.

Sessions 9 and 10: Consolidation-Termination — In many ways, the termination of group treatment is the most difficult part of therapy. Time grows short for the implementation of the various therapeutic interventions. The therapist sorts out and concentrates on those patients who have made insufficient progress with their problems. A few members of the group may say, "I still don't understand why I have problems." "I can't relax." "I don't understand how I can change what I think." "Exposing myself to the traumatic situation only makes me feel worse." "I'm still mad as hell at those people who hurt me." "My spouse doesn't understand me." Rather than confront patients with the obvious retort, "Where have you been for the last eight weeks?", the therapist solicits the help of group members who have done well (usually the majority) to serve as models and "trouble-shooters" for those having difficulty. Thus, the group leader avoids a nonproductive confrontation with a resisting patient and can still function to facilitate the flow of information from the "doing good" group members to the others. The benefits derived from cognitive restructuring, muscle relaxation, exposure treatment, and other therapeutic interventions are reviewed by the "doing good" group. Those patients who have had difficulties applying these therapeutic concepts and have reached an impasse are encouraged to keep trying as the principles of therapy are reviewed. The therapist's expertise and knowledge about group process and dynamics help to overcome resistance. The maintenance of an optimistic atmosphere within the group fosters a positive expectation which effects motivation and outcome.

All group members prepare for termination by setting post-therapy goals and assigning priorities for future action. Termination from therapy does not mean the cessation of treatment. The necessity for the continued application of the therapeutic interventions learned during group treatment becomes a major issue during the last two group sessions. To keep patients motivated, plans for a three and six-month follow up are finalized, and patients are asked to keep notes and record all post-therapy progress. Setting a specific date for follow up not only indicates the therapist's interest in the welfare of the patients, but also reminds patients to continue working on their problems. Two weeks before the follow-up date, a letter or phone call alerts each group member of the impending follow-up session.

CONCLUSIONS

Data from uncontrolled studies and single case designs involving group and individual cognitive-behavioral approaches for the treatment of PTSD are proliferating, mainly with Vietnam-era combat veterans and sexual assault victims. Existing evidence points to a conceptual model for PTSD which involves learning and conditioning. Classical and instrumental conditioning explain the genesis and sustainment of PTSD symptoms, while behavioral techniques currently exist for the treatment of the classes of symptoms found in a PTSD: cognitive restructuring for intrusive and distressing thoughts, exposure treatment for avoidance behavior, and relaxation training for symptoms of increased arousal. This chapter enlarges the range of possible therapeutic interventions to include assertive training, family intervention, and problem solving. Related issues involving work, social and recreational activities, exercise and nutrition are interwoven during the later stages of group therapy into a comprehensive treatment program.

TEN

THE FORENSIC EVALUATION

Similar to any psychiatric or psychological assessment, the forensic evaluation requires systematic observation, the collection of data in a logical fashion, and sound judgment on the part of the clinician. Dissimilarities emerge, however, as chronic disability and poor response to treatment are evaluated in the light of litigation. An analysis of personality and an evaluation of credibility are important when clinicians evaluate forensic patients who continuously complain of symptoms, blame others for their problems, exaggerate or lie during the mental status examination, sue for damages, or expect a mental disorder to excuse criminal behavior. These patients tend to evoke little sympathy from most people. To maintain objectivity, the clinician must be aware of his own personal proclivities about chronic patients who are involved in civil litigation or criminal proceedings.

In civil cases, the clinician's attitude about a patient who slips and falls to the floor and afterward claims incapacitating and intractable emotional distress can distort the forensic evaluation. Skepticism is understandable, but any tendency towards prejudgment and immediate dismissal of such patients without a thorough evaluation is unwarranted. A judgmental attitude towards criminal defendants who commit heinous crimes must also be avoided by forensic clinicians. A sadistic rapist, child molester, or ruthless murderer brings forth a reflexive response of loathing in most people.

Tangential issues may also influence judgment. Clinicians who have been sued for malpractice may harbor resentment towards the plaintiff's bar. Problems with insurance companies who refuse to pay fees for professional services may sour the professional's attitude towards the defense. Whatever bias that the examiner possesses, it must be identified and resolved. Prejudice or, as it is called in psychological jargon, countertransference, must not mar clinical judgment or influence expert opinion.

When examining a patient, it is useful to bifurcate the psychiatric evaluation into clinical and forensic sections. The first leads to a diagnosis and the second concludes with an expert opinion related to the legal issue under consideration. During the clinical phase, the mental health professional interviews the patient, performs the mental status examination, administers appropriate tests, interviews the spouse or significant relatives or friends, reviews relevant records including medical or psychiatric reports, and concludes with a diagnosis of the mental disorder. Upon completion of the clinical-diagnostic portion, the legal issue is addressed. In personal injury suits (Chapter 11), certain questions must be asked: Did the trauma precipitate a mental disorder? In workers' compensation cases, two issues must be considered: Did the mental disorder develop as a result of a work-related accident? Does the mental disorder prevent the employee from returning to work? A correlary to the second question relates to prognosis. How much psychiatric treatment is necessary before the employee can return to work? In criminal cases, mental competency to stand trial and criminal responsibility lie at the core of the forensic evaluation (Chapter 12). At the conclusion of the forensic evaluation, the clinician integrates the diagnostic-clinical conclusion with the legal issues and formulates an expert opinion based on reasonable medical probability.

A fundamental difference between a forensic evaluation and a routine psychiatric/psychological examination is utilization. Routine psychiatric evaluations lead to a diagnosis and the formulation of a treatment plan and seldom need to be defended, except politely in the dignified halls of academe during Grand Rounds or in a conference room during a hospital staff meeting. Expert opinions rendered during a forensic proceeding have monetary significance, or in criminal cases involve issues of probation or punishment. Decorum but not necessarily politeness greets the forensic clinician who participates in adversarial proceedings. Regardless of the correctness of clinical conclusions, expert opinions will be challenged. For some clinicians, confrontation with lawyers is acutely uncomfortable; however, a thorough forensic evaluation and proper preparation prior to testimony will fortify the clinician against embarrassment, and participation in adversarial proceedings may then become enjoyable.

Although trauma centers, insurance companies, workers' compensation boards or judicial commissions may refer patients for evaluation, attorneys are the ones who most frequently request a psychiatric evaluation. Prior to a commitment to undertake a forensic examination, a brief telephone consultation with the lawyer helps to sort out inappropriate referrals. The mental health professional should insist that the lawyer forward all previous medical and psychiatric reports. Following a review of records, the clinician should discuss the case with the referring attorney who decides whether to continue the consultation. When a plaintiff's attorney requests a forensic evaluation and it becomes apparent that no mental disorder was associated with the trauma, a telephone call apprising the lawyer of that conclusion usually ends the consultation, and a written report ordinarily is not requested. After reviewing medical and psychiatric records for a defense attorney, the clinician may decide that the plaintiff probably does have a significant mental disorder and this opinion may terminate the consultation because it favors the plaintiff. In these cases, the clinician bows out of official forensic proceedings; however, important information has been conveyed to the attorney which may assist in negotiations. In criminal cases the issues are more complex, but an off-the-record, face-to-face consultation with either the prosecutor or defense attorney to discuss the merits or demerits of an insanity defense determines the clinician's further involvement. Finally, during the referral process, professional fees are discussed and agreements are formalized in writing.

THE FORENSIC EVALUATION

The following is a suggested guideline for organizing observations and data during a forensic evaluation. The elements constituting an examination are basic, and most clinicians have learned the rudiments during their training. The following information, therefore, will not be new but perhaps the manner of organization into a comprehensive forensic report may be helpful. With some exceptions the author constructs his reports as indicated on the following pages.

Identifying Data

Icebreaker questions concerning name, address, telephone number, age, marital status, number of children, occupation, education, religious background, and referral source not only serve to put the patient at ease but offer the clinician a "thumbnail sketch" of the patient's adaptive functioning in important areas of life and a "peek" at character. An ability to sustain an emotional commitment to another person is reflected by the answer to marital status. Whether the patient is married, single or has had multiple marriages, tells the clinician something about the patient's judgment in picking a mate and the ability to successfully resolve conjugal problems. Vocational choice and achievement indicate to some extent intellectual level, perspicacity, ability to get along with others, and goal setting. Length of employment, job changes, and periods of unemployment give insight concerning the patient's physical and emotional stability. Educational attainment not only reflects intelligence but also tenacity, ambition, and an attitude towards systematic learning in an educational institution. Attendance as an adult in a vocational training facility or night school to advance formal education indicates good motivation for self-improvement. Since the abolition of selective service, fewer patients have served in the military; however, for those who have volunteered, questions regarding length of service, highest rank achieved, type of discharge received, and current status in the Reserve or National Guard reveal much about a person's character, intelligence, and ability to cope with the vicissitudes of military life. Questions relating to religious preference and practice during childhood and at the present time give the clinician insight into the value system and moral fibre of the patient. The presence of strong religious beliefs and practices has more significance than their absence. The referral source and purpose of the examination are related and focus the clinician's attention on the legal question(s) to be addressed. Data upon which the report is based include dates of the forensic evaluation, persons interviewed, tests which were administered, and past records and reports which were reviewed. Patients seldom lie or greatly distort information gathered during the identifying data stage of the examination, probably because the questions may seem relatively innocuous and the answers can be easily verified.

Chief Complaint - Chronologic History

After rapport has been established during the identifying data stage of the evaluation, the patient is asked questions about the reason for the referral. In a criminal case, it is the clinician's responsibility to tell the defendant-patient who requested the examination, that confidentiality is not protected, and in fact, the forensic report might be used against him in a court of law. After completing the chief complaint, the patient is asked to relate, in a chronologic fashion, a detailed account of the trauma or alleged crime. It is especially important to determine the patient's perception moments before, during, and immediately after the trauma or alleged crime and to precisely quote the patient's response. For example, "I was certain I was going to be killed"; "I could see myself in heaven"; "I didn't know what I was doing"; or "It seemed as if someone else pulled the trigger." Any physiological reactions occurring at the time of the trauma should also be noted. Shaking, trembling, nausea, in some instances vomiting, a dissociative state, or any signs or symptoms indicative of an intense sympathetic nervous system discharge suggest a severe emotional reaction and the possibility of a PTSD. Sometimes a state of shock or numbness and lack of responsiveness follows the trauma. Frequently patients gloss over the trauma, skipping important details because recalling them produces uncomfortable feelings. Repeating the history is unpleasant and anxiety-evoking, however, reassurance that the emotional reaction will be short-lived facilitates history taking. Patients are told that an accurate recitation is necessary for the evaluation and are asked to relate the history of the trauma as if it were occurring in slow motion. The patient's perceptions, thoughts, and feelings are recorded in detail, again using the patient's own words whenever possible. During the retelling of the trauma or alleged crime, the patient relives the experience and the clinician should be alert to any signs or symptoms of agitation and anxiety. Abreaction sometimes occurs and patients will break down, sobbing in relief or sorrow, lamenting the loss of loved ones if that were the case, or marveling that they are not dead.

After the history of the acute phase of the trauma or circumstances of the alleged crime has been gathered, questions are asked concerning the presence or absence of other symptoms in much the same way as a routine examination (Burnside and McGlynn, 1987; McGarry, 1986). Good clinical technique involves the ruling in or out of various mental disorders by asking a series of questions to pinpoint the specific diagnosis. Lawyers trained in the adversarial system of fact finding tend to be suspicious when leading questions are asked of patients, but in clinical practice, this is standard procedure. Judgments concerning the credibility of the patient and whether the symptoms fit into a logical pattern suggesting a specific mental disorder are made throughout the forensic evaluation. All medical or psychological treatment received since the trauma or alleged crime is reviewed. Patients are asked to give information including the names of doctors, results of examinations, and outcome of treatment. The patient's current physical and psychological status concludes the history of the present illness. Whenever possible, it is extremely important to verify the patient's account with information from other sources.

Symptom Inventory Checklist

After the first session, the author always gives the patient a fifty-item Symptom Inventory Checklist (SIC) to complete by the next session (Table 10-1). Patients are asked to read the instructions carefully and to fill out the form as accurately and honestly as possible. The SIC allows the clinician to analyze the patient's self-report of symptoms before and after the traumatic incident or alleged crime. Clarification of the patient's responses is obtained by direct questioning after the SIC has been completed. Since the patient rates the frequency of symptoms, an assessment of the degree of disability can also be determined by an analysis of the SIC so any tendency toward underrating or overrating symptoms also becomes apparent. The outcome of treatment can be assessed by the periodic administration of the SIC. The validity of the SIC increases when the clinician re- administers the test so that patients can respond to the current frequency of the symptom without reference to a previous response. Reference to the SIC during

TABLE 10–1
Symptom Inventory Checklist

In the following list, please mark an O to show the degree to which you have experienced each item *before* the accident or traumatic incident. Next please mark with an X to show to what degree you experienced that item *after* the accident or traumatic incident.

	1. *Not at All*	*2.* *Sometimes*	*3.* *Often*	*4.* *Very Often*	*5.* *Practically All of the Time*
1. Heart beating fast					
2. Difficulties in breathing					
3. Trembling or shaking of the hands or body					
4. Nausea or vomiting					
5. Poor appetite					
6. Diarrhea					

TABLE 10–1, continued

		1.	*2.*	*3.*	*4.*	*5.*
						Practically
		Not at			*Very*	*All of the*
		All	*Sometimes*	*Often*	*Often*	*Time*

7.	Dizziness, light-headedness, feeling faint					
8.	Feelings of terror or panic					
9.	Hot flashes or flushing					
10.	Tingling sensations in the arms or legs					
11.	Headaches					
12.	Physical pain					
13.	Nervousness (stress, anxiety)					
14.	Blurred vision					
15.	Ringing in the ears					
16.	Problems sleeping					
17.	Nightmares					
18.	Extreme sensitivity to noise					
19.	Irritability					
20.	Outbursts of anger					
21.	Lack of interest in sex					
22.	Excessive sweating					
23.	Feeling that my personality has changed					
24.	Marriage problems					
25.	Lack of interest in life (family, social/recreational activities)					
26.	Feeling detached from others					
27.	Depression, feeling "blue" or "down in the dumps"					
28.	Feelings that familiar things seem strange or unreal					
29.	Being told by others that I have changed					
30.	Crying spells					
31.	Not able to express or show my feelings					
32.	Unable to remember recent events					

TABLE 10–1, continued

		1. Not at All	2. Sometimes	3. Often	4. Very Often	5. Practically All of the Time
33.	Thoughts of death					
34.	Thoughts of suicide					
35.	Thoughts about accidents					
36.	Thoughts about injury					
37.	Feelings of worthlessness					
38.	Low energy level					
39.	Slowness in thought or movements					
40.	Difficulties in concentrating					
41.	Tiredness, fatigue, weakness					
42.	Problems at work (school)					
43.	Difficulties in making decisions					
44.	Feeling unreal or like another person					
45.	Avoidance of places that are not related to but remind me of the accident place					
46.	Avoidance of places related to the accident or traumatic incident					
47.	Thinking about the accident					
48.	Anger toward self or others for their part in the accident					
49.	Guilt feelings for or about the accident					
50.	Having such feelings as if the accident were happening again (flashbacks)					

Source: Compiled by author.

testimony in court helps to explain the progression or remission of symptoms to the judge and jury.

Medical History

A chronologic listing of all illnesses, diseases, and injuries requiring treatment by a physician gives some indication of the patient's past physical health. Hospitalizations, surgical procedures, and outpatient visits should be listed with a brief statement of outcome. Any history of accidents should be explored, along with the response to treatment and length of incapacity. Questions related to head trauma should always be asked. This section is concluded by a statement from the patient describing his general state of physical health prior to the trauma or alleged crime.

Psychiatric History

If the question, "Have you ever had any nervous or mental disease or disorder?" is answered negatively, follow-up questions should be asked: "Have you ever seen a psychiatrist? A psychologist? A social worker? A counselor? Have you ever had a nervous breakdown? Have you ever gone out of your mind? Have you ever heard voices talking to you when no one was around? Have you ever thought that you were someone you were not?" All treatment for nervous or mental illness should be documented when possible with dates, names of therapists, and diagnoses. It is also important to determine whether the patient has ever been committed to a mental hospital, or treated in an outpatient psychiatric setting, drug or alcohol abuse clinic, or by a counselor in a public school. Any psychiatric/psychological treatment following the traumatic incident should also be listed.

Medication

All current medication and psychotropic agents taken following the trauma should be listed by name and dosage. Any history of the usage of psychotropic drugs, whether prescribed by a physician or not, should be included. Often, the use of a specific medication gives clues to the type of mental disorder for which the patient was treated. For example, if an antipsychotic agent such a phenothiazine was prescribed, a major mental disorder is suspected. The prescription of lithium carbonate suggests a Mood Disorder, while anticonvulsants indicate epilepsy. Current use of illicit drugs such as cocaine, marijuana, or any other street drug should be listed. Whether illicit drug use as an adolescent should be recorded in a forensic evaluation is questionable. Information not relevant to the issue at hand may obfuscate rather than cast light on the current legal issue. As Modlin (1980) has stated, "Facts as that the patient was of illegitimate birth, has had an abortion, or smokes marijuana may have no bearing on matters relevant in his civil suit. Moreover," Modlin continues, "certain of the psychiatrist's speculations or educated hunches about the patient are better conveyed to the attorney orally, if at all, rather than in writing. Such imprudently dropped phrases such as 'latent homosexuality,' 'seductive hysterical character,' or 'sadistic fantasies' can be pursued in court by an astute cross-examining attorney to the point that their author regrets his conjectural excursion from clinical exactness."

Social History

This section of the history elaborates on material in the identifying data section. Educational background, financial status, employment record, marital status, social and recreational activities, and environmental milieu gives some indication of the patient's daily routine. Notes are made of habits including cigarette smoking, alcohol consumption, drug use, and exposure to potential toxins. By assessing various aspects of the social history, the clinician gains insight into the patient's lifestyle and possible psychosocial stressors.

Antisocial Behavior

Credibility overshadows almost all aspects of a forensic evaluation. The truthfulness of a patient's statements must be accurately assessed by the clinician when preparing a report. The absence or presence of antisocial behavior is one facet of honesty or the lack of it. Disposition following apprehension for an antisocial act must be noted. Probation, a prison sentence, or commitment to a maximum security mental hospital have different implications and reflect how the antisocial act was perceived by law enforcement officials and the court. Arrests and convictions for a serious misdemeanor or felony, especially if multiple, suggests antisocial traits and possibly an Antisocial Personality Disorder. Of the four characteristics mentioned in DSM-III-R which should arouse suspicion of malingering, Antisocial Personality Disorder is the most important. The patient's previous arrests and convictions should be documented, and repeated offenses certainly cast suspicion on the patient's character. Care must be taken when evaluating antisocial behavior and diagnosing a personality disorder because antisocial behavior is not tantamount to Antisocial Personality Disorder. A long and persistent pattern of antisocial acts beginning in childhood and extending into adult life characterizes an Antisocial Personality Disorder (Chapter 7). The author has evaluated several patients with extensive antisocial behavior beginning in childhood and extending into adulthood but ceasing abruptly at a critical juncture in life. For example, one patient, upon marriage and the securing of a highly desirable job, had no history of antisocial behavior for the succeeding ten years. In this case, past antisocial history is interpreted differently than of a person with a continuous chaotic lifestyle of law-breaking. One must be careful not to tarnish a patient's reputation by wielding a tar brush too freely, especially if the patient is young and antisocial patterns have not solidified. Even if the patient is a complete reprobate, care, courtesy, and consideration must be accorded him during a forensic evaluation.

History of Previous Litigation

This section of the psychiatric evaluation is designed to uncover those persons who are unlucky, accident-prone, quick to sue, or malingering. Although it is true that most people go through life without filing a lawsuit, litigiousness seems to be a part of modern life, making it difficult to interpret previous legal action. "Nuisance" lawsuits or cases involving minor accidents are usually settled out of court for relatively small sums.One must be suspicious of patients who have a history of filing several lawsuits in quick succession, especially if the trauma is insignificant and coupled with disproportionate emotional sequelae. The credibility of those with a severe personality disorder, especially antisocial personality, is questionable. The dates, circumstances, and outcome of all previous lawsuits should be listed. Persons who file spurious lawsuits should be weeded out because they cheapen the legal process for those who are genuinely traumatized.

Family History

A brief description of the patient's father, mother, and siblings is recounted. The name, age, marital status, occupation, and current state of physical and mental health gives some indication of family dynamics. If family members have died, the reason for death is listed. Some mental disorders have a genetic component; therefore, any history of nervous or mental illness in the family should be documented, if possible, with a diagnosis, treatment received, and degree of disability. Any antisocial behavior on the part of a family member should be evaluated in light of the family milieu. The structure of the family has some relationship to the patient's developmental history, but does not necessarily have any connection to a mental disorder following trauma or to the motivation for an alleged crime.

Personal History

Mental health professionals, by training and custom, gather a detailed history of a patient's life. This information may be interesting, but a minute account of a patient's life history, emphasizing past conflicts and psychopathology, may have little relevance to the reason for referral and in fact may lend confusion rather than clarity to the forensic issue under question. In lieu of objective data, speculations concerning past conflicts and psychopathology may be frivolous and misleading. Focusing on unrelated psychopathology deflects attention from the forensic issue at hand and may be detrimental to the patient and confusing to the court. Mental health professionals unschooled in forensic matters must resist the temptation to display their knowledge by dissecting out from the patient's history inconsequential or unmeaningful personality quirks or long-buried conflicts.

Salient information concerning a history of medical or psychiatric disorder, criminal behavior, Psychoactive Substance Use Disorder, involvement in previous litigation, educational background, vocational achievements, marital adjustment, and family stability has been obtained in other parts of the forensic evaluation and need not be repeated under the heading "personal history". Patients can be asked various questions concerning adaptation during various stages of life: preschool (up to age five), grade school (ages six to thirteen), high school (ages thirteen to seventeen), post-high school or college (ages seventeen to twenty-five), and to the present. Any major life events including previous accidents or criminal conduct will require a detailed analysis. In general, an extensive and detailed account of a patient's personal history may be justified in the context of research but has limited value in clinical practice.

MENTAL STATUS EXAMINATION

Throughout the history taking, the clinician observes the patient's general mannerisms, speech patterns, thought processes, and mood, recording the verbal and nonverbal behavior. During the dictation of the report, these observations are expanded and placed under the headings: General Appearance, Stream of Speech, and Content of Thought. Judgments concerning reality testing and the presence or absence of psychotic symptoms are recorded along with any signs of anxiety, depression, or other significant symptoms suggesting a mental disorder. Questions relating to sensorium (orientation to time, place, and person) are always asked and an estimate of intelligence, judgment, and insight is made. The patient's fund of general information and knowledge of current events as it correlates with intelligence and socioeconomic background are assessed by asking relevant questions. Intactness of recent and remote memory can be estimated by direct questioning of past events or by a three item recall test. When intactness of memory is critical to the evaluation (e.g., Organic Mental Syndromes), more sophisticated psychological tests provide refined data. In another part of the mental status examination, interpretation of similarities and proverbs gives the clinician some indication regarding the patient's ability to abstract concepts.

The mental status examination is an important tool for psychiatrists/ psychologists and in many ways is comparable to the physical examination of a general practitioner or internist. Based on the mental status examination and observations made throughout the entire forensic evaluation, some estimate of the patient's character can be made. Observations concerning credibility, tendency to exaggerate symptoms, incongruities and inconsistencies in the history, or characteristics which bear on the patient's veracity should be mentioned and fully described.

Diagnosis

Although it is not essential, DSM-III-R suggests a diagnosis based on the use of a multi-axial evaluation which refers to five different classes of information:

Axis	I	Clinical Syndromes
Axis	II	Personality Disorders
Axis	III	Physical Disorders and Conditions
Axis	IV	Severity of Psychosocial Stressors
Axis	V	Global Assessment of Functioning Past Year

The Axis I diagnosis designates the clinical syndrome such as PTSD, Somatoform Disorder, Major Depression, Organic Mental Disorder, etc., and is the principal diagnosis. Axis II, personality disorders (Paranoid, Schizoid, Schizotypal, Histrionic, Narcissistic, Antisocial, Borderline, Avoidant, Dependent, Compulsive, Passive-Aggressive, and Atypical) are developmental disorders which reflect a lifelong learned pattern of behaving. Coping styles may, to some extent, be determined by one's personality, but personality disorders are not precipitated by a trauma or changed by involvement in a criminal act. The basic personality structure becomes established early in life and usually remains unaltered during adulthood. Anecdotal proof for this thesis occurs at class reunions - the body may age, but personalities of classmates remain untouched by time.

Axis III reflects any physical disorder or condition that may be relevant to the principal mental disorder. Injuries including concussions, fractures, burns, strained muscles, or any other physical sequelae of trauma which are related to a PTSD should be recorded on Axis III. Diseases that may affect mental functioning (Multi-Infarct Dementia, endocrine disturbances, metabolic diseases, intracranial lesions, and other neurologic disorders) should also be listed on Axis III. Whenever possible, Axis III diagnoses should be substantiated by medical reports from the treating physician.

Whether formalized in the multi-axial system, psychosocial stressors (Axis IV) have usually been uncovered and discussed while taking the patient's history. Family problems, interpersonal problems with friends, occupational difficulties, financial or legal problems, involvement in a natural or man-made disaster, pregnancy out of wedlock, or rape are examples of psychosocial stressors. Some of the situations listed in DSM-III-R for inclusion under Axis IV can be considered environmental trauma sufficient to precipitate a PTSD. Ordinarily, however, psychosocial factors exacerbate a preexisting mental disorder or increase the level of stress within an individual, and in this case is usually, though not always, time limited.

Axis V, Global Assessment of Functioning, permits the clinician to make a judgment of the patient's highest level of adaptive functioning (for at least a few months) during the past year regarding psychological, social, and occupational functioning. Axis V has prognostic significance, since current functioning is contrasted with past functioning, and any differences between the two represent disability. In personal injury cases, disability and prognosis has monetary significance, while in criminal cases at the post-trial stage, it may be relevant to disposition. In DSM-III-R, the Global Assessment of Functioning Scale ranges from one (persistent danger of severely hurting ones self or others) to ninety (absent or minimal symptoms). Although unwieldy and difficult to use, this system of determining the level of functioning has merit.

Summary and Conclusions

When reading a report, all eyes quickly seek out this section, for it is the quintessence of the entire forensic evaluation. In personal injury cases, a brief summary of the evaluation, leading to a diagnosis and concluding with the statement that the trauma did or did not precipitate a mental disorder, helps to resolve legal issues. If an active mental disorder has been diagnosed, an opinion concerning the necessity for present psychiatric treatment and prognosis should also include the patient's ability to work. In criminal cases, depending on the issue an opinion should focus on the defendant's current mental competency to stand trial or his state of mind at the time of the commission of an alleged criminal act. If requested at the post-trial stage of a criminal procedure, the clinician may give an opinion regarding present and future dangerousness; recommendations for treatment may also be pertinent.

CONCLUSIONS

Clinicians, as they gain experience defending their psychiatric evaluations during depositions or in court, will modify and shape their words to fit the forensic issue at hand. Superficial speculations which may be amusing during a case conference in a medical school are irrelevant and potentially damaging to plaintiffs or defendants in a court of law. A clinician's ego may be bruised as he attempts to defend highly speculative comments or inappropriate conclusions during cross-examination. It is suggested in this chapter that the clinician initially disregard the legal status of the patient and conduct a thorough mental status examination, obtain a history, review documents from outside sources, and interview persons knowledgeable about the patient. After a diagnosis has been established, the clinician can then put the pieces of the forensic puzzle into place and render an expert opinion regarding the legal issue. Familiarity with the rudiments of civil and criminal law allows the clinician to make a meaningful contribution. Concise and well-written reports focusing on the relevant legal issues are used during negotiations or plea-bargaining and frequently obviate the presence of the expert in court. Clinicians will also find that the preparation of forensic evaluations sharpens clinical skills, which in turn benefits all of their patients.

Table 10-2
Organization of the Forensic Evaluation

    I.   Identifying Data
        A.   Name
        B.   Address
        C.   Telephone Number
        D.   Sex
        E.   Age
        F.   Marital Status
        G.   Number of Children
        H.   Occupation
        I.   Education
        J.   Service in the Military
        K.   Religion
        L.   Referral Source and Purpose of Examination
        M.   Data Upon Which This Report is Based

    II.   Chief Complaint - Chronologic History of the Present Problem

    III.   The Symptom Inventory Checklist

    IV.   Medical History

    V.   Psychiatric History

    VI.   Medication (Past and Present)

    VII.   Social History

    VIII.   Antisocial Behavior

    IX.   History of Previous Litigation

    X.   Family History

    XI.   Personal History

    XII.   Mental Status Examination

    XIII.   Diagnostic Impression

    XIV.   Summary and Conclusions (Opinion)

Table 10-3
Summary Outline of the Mental Status Examination

I. General Appearance
    A. Posture and gait
    B. Dress and grooming
    C. Facial expression
    D. Physical characteristics (include description of scars or tattoos)
    E. Motor activity (include any bizarre motor movements)

II. Stream of Speech
    A. Spontaneity and coherency
    B. Rate, volume, clarity
    C. Affect (mood)
    D. Flow of ideas, appropriateness of thinking processes

III. Content of Thought
    A. Dominant themes
    B. Distortions (delusions, ideas of reference, dissociative reactions)
    C. Preoccupations (obsessions, phobias, somatic concerns)
    D. Suicidal of homicidal ideation
    E. Perception (illusions, hallucinations)

IV. Sensorium and Intellectual Functions
    A. Orientation
    B. Estimate of intelligence
    C. Knowledge of current events
    D. Fund of general information
    E. Memory (recent and remote)
    F. Concentration
    G. Judgment
    H. Insight
    I. Abstraction

V. Diagnostic Impression

ELEVEN

LEGAL ISSUES — CIVIL

PTSD is of interest to lawyers and mental health professionals in civil cases involving personal injury suits and workers' compensation disputes. The type and severity of mental suffering or degree of incapacity imposed by the stress disorder become a matter for negotiation or trial. Lawyers need to know the basis upon which mental health professionals formulate conclusions and should also become familiar with the elements that constitute a complete forensic evaluation. Additionally, when the theoretical and practical aspects of PTSD are blended by psychiatrists or psychologists during depositions or trials, lawyers should become conversant with specialized vocabulary, psychiatric constructs, diagnostic criteria of mental disorders, treatment methods, and their application to a client's case. Mental health professionals who participate in forensic proceedings should also be familiar with the legal concepts underlying tort and workers' compensation as they relate to the evaluation of a patient and testimony in court. In this way, judges and jury who make the final decision in civil cases may have access to clear and concise thinking and lucid testimony upon which to base judgment.

The purpose of this chapter is to provide information for mental health professionals and attorneys who participate in civil matters involving PTSD. Recommendations concerning the preparation of expert testimony and guidelines for direct and cross- examination emerge from the author's experience. Examples of typical questions and answers from the plaintiff's and defendant's perspective give lawyers and clinicians a compass point to chart a course for the most accurate and effective display of facts and clinical observations.

TORT AND PTSD

Tort stems from the root word "torquere" (to twist), as does the word "torture," and in a sense, that is what is alleged by plaintiffs in personal injury cases. Everyone understands that torture consists not only of the infliction of intense physical pain but also includes anguish of the mind. In fact, the most effective forms of torture involve subtleties requiring little or no infliction of physical pain (Zunaunegui, 1982). In a personal injury suit, the plaintiff generally claims that a trauma has caused injury resulting from the negligence, intentional action, or omission by the defendant. If the injury was physical and can be objectively evaluated, few problems arise in elaborating its extent and the resultant disability. Part of the claim may also include pain and mental suffering, a legal principle that is firmly established and time-honored. At the conclusion of the legal proceeding, if the defendant is found to be at fault, damages are awarded to the plaintiff and unless the verdict is appealed to a higher court, the case is closed.

For many years in tort actions, only physical defect related to a trauma commanded the attention of judges and lawyers because physical injury was observable and could be objectively measured. The less tangible emotional accompaniment of a trauma was difficult to describe and quantify, so in the past the judiciary was unwilling to accept mental consequences of an accident as a compensable entity. As knowledge in the behavioral sciences accrued, the resistance to the concept of trauma and mental disorder lessened. "Traumatic Neurosis" emerged and became widely recognized, so that by the late 1940's, testimony relevant to this psychiatric syndrome was accepted by many courts. Since that time, experience has shown that traumatic events may bring about a disabling mental disorder that can be either a combination of physical and mental disorders, a residual mental incapacity continuing after the physical injury has healed (Malone and Johnson, 1980), or solely a mental disorder without physical injury. With the inclusion of the term "Post-Traumatic Stress Disorder" in the official nomenclature of the American Psychiatric Association's *Diagnostic and Statistical Manual of Mental Disorders* (1980, 1987), PTSD has now become the language of many tort actions.

WORKERS' COMPENSATION

Unlike tort litigation which may be viewed as an adversarial contest to right a wrong between contestants, workers' compensation is an insurance system to supply security to injured workers to meet their marginal needs during a period of disability. Workers' compensation differs from the conventional damage suit in two important aspects: (1) fault on the part of either employer or employee is eliminated, and (2) compensation is substituted for damages and payable according to a definite schedule based on the type of injury sustained by the worker (Malone, 1951). Workers' compensation is a mechanism for providing cash wage benefits and medical care to employees involved in work-related accidents that produce injury. The cost is ultimately placed on the consumer through the medium of insurance premiums, which are passed on in the cost of the product when possible (Larson, 1972).

Five major objective of a modern workers' compensation program, as identified by the National Committee on State Workers' Compensation Laws, are: provision for sufficient medical care, accessibility to rehabilitation services, encouragement of safety, prompt and effective system for delivery of benefits, and prompt and effective system for delivery of services (Supplemental Studies, 1973). Although initially intended for physical disablement, workers who are suffering from PTSD and other mental disorders are entitled to such benefits. Physicians, including psychiatrists, are involved in four of the five objectives when they provide medical care and educational programs during primary, secondary, and tertiary prevention (Chapter 13).

PREPARING FOR TESTIMONY

Clinicians, ordinarily accustomed to diagnosing and treating patients in the privacy of their office, may have difficulties "shifting gears" to a more public forum where their views are contested. In civil cases as emphasis changes from therapy to tort, clinical attention alters from prognosis to pecuniary issues. Questions asked during direct and cross- examination reflect the concern for blame and the monetary significance of an injury. What is the relationship, if any, between the trauma and the plaintiff's mental disorder if present? Can the patient work? What is the type and length of treatment required and how much will it cost? What part does litigation play in the plaintiff's mental illness? How do you know that the plaintiff is not faking in order to collect financial compensation? Will the patient's mental illness disappear after receiving a monetary award?

On cross examination, questions sometimes seem to impugn the motivation and integrity of the expert witness. How much are you getting paid for your testimony? How often do you appear as an expert witness? Do you testify for this lawyer very often? What percent of your income is derived from appearances in court as an expert witness? The mental health professional should never forget that the main purpose of the legal proceeding is to determine whether or not money is awarded, either in the form of workers' compensation or, following a personal injury suit, a lump sum payment. Expert witnesses in a sense are agents to facilitate or inhibit the transfer of money; as such, they incur the enmity or goodwill of plaintiff or defense lawyers, depending upon which side their testimony benefits. To some mental health professionals this may seem monetaristic and unprofessional, but it is the way the law works. The legal process during civil suits attempts to resolve human issues by the use of money to right wrongs and redress grievances of traumatized persons. Ultimately, money compensates victims for injuries, both physical and psychological, and is the vehicle for obtaining future medical and psychiatric treatment, vocational rehabilitation, and the purchase of any rehabilitative service. Understanding the relationship between clinical issues and monetary compensation places expert testimony into proper perspective. The mental health professional is only one visitor to the forensic forum where others also participate and ultimately still others decide the outcome.

The adversarial nature of the law demands confrontation and conflicting opinions. Opposing lawyers invariably choose professionals who are philosophically compatible with their point of view, thus setting up the stage for the "battle of the experts." The plaintiff's expert witness highlights the psychological sequelae of trauma, while the defense's expert minimizes, ignores, or denigrates it. If an attorney wishes to know "the truth," it has been suggested that consultation with an independent mental health professional, not wedded to a plaintiff or defense position, can clear the air of bias. This may be so, but if an expert makes the claim that he testifies 50% for the plaintiff and 50% for the defense, one can raise eyebrows in amazement or incredulity. Ordinarily, all of the truth does not lie on one side and most differences between opposing testimony can be explained by emphasis. Therefore, lawyers will always seek and find experts who are sympathetic to their position.

The essential characteristic of an ideal expert is probity mixed with forthrightness. The expert who contributes most to a legal proceeding is an experienced clinician with impeccable credentials who enjoys the verbal jousting of cross-examination. Although expert testimony and the "battle of the experts" has received much public comment and criticism, no better system exists for the presentation of specialized knowledge during a trial. Despite outcries (Imwinkelried and Giannelli, 1986) about the growing misuse of expert testimony, the adversarial system is a great leveler and the judge and jury, in most cases, can sort through conflicting psychiatric testimony and reach a just decision.

PRETRIAL PREPARATION

Prior to trial, it is mandatory for the clinician and lawyer to meet and discuss testimony. During the pretrial meeting, the mental health professional explains the results of the forensic evaluation and analyzes all data leading to an expert opinion and conclusion. Like a professor teaching a medical student, the clinician educates the lawyer about the onset, clinical course, signs and symptoms, treatment, and prognosis of a PTSD or other mental disorder. A copy of DSM-III-R diagnostic criteria for PTSD should be supplied to the attorney, then compared to the patient's history and mental status examination. The presence or absence of each diagnostic criterion is discussed and analyzed in terms of the final diagnosis. The reports of other psychiatrists or psychologists are reviewed with the lawyer, and conflicting opinions and discrepancies are explained. Suggestions for the cross-examination of opposing experts stem from an analysis of depositions and psychiatric/psychological reports. Finally, the clinician discusses with the lawyer all weaknesses in his case. History of antisocial behavior, previous psychiatric treatment, Psychoactive Substance Use Disorder, involvement in previous litigation, and tendencies toward hyperbole usually weaken a plaintiff's case.

The expert and attorney must agree upon the manner of presentation of testimony. Some attorneys prefer an outline of questions and answers, but a strict adherence to a script often results in stilted testimony. A narrative spontaneous style covering all of the basic elements of the case, transmits information more effectively. The utilization of visual aids (charts, diagrams, a blackboard, or models of the brain) is discussed and arrangements are made and finalized for their presence in court. During jury trials, the author prefers that a blackboard or easel with paper and felt pens be placed directly in front of the jury box. At an appropriate time, permission is asked of the court to leave the witness stand to illustrate on the blackboard the Three E's concept of PTSD to the jury. Any objection is often overruled by the judge, and the "chalk talk" is an excellent vehicle to draw the jurors' attention. Some opposing counsel object to a free flow of information with minimal questions by the attorney conducting direct examination. If this occurs, the attorney must ask more related questions and any future objections are usually overruled.

At the pretrial meeting, the lawyer provides information concerning the legal issues which will be presented at trial. All weaknesses of the case should be thoroughly explored, and the clinician should ask the lawyer what questions can be anticipated from the opposing attorney on cross-examination. When unanticipated facts emerge during cross-examination, most lawyers will object and this gives the expert time to clear his mind and think about an appropriate answer. Lawyers usually instruct experts to pause and ponder unexpected questions so that they have time to put forth an objection. It is important to discuss trial strategies, especially if the clinician is unfamiliar with the lawyer who is conducting direct examination. An experienced forensic clinician can usually alert attorneys to possible pitfalls in psychiatric testimony.

Lastly, the place and time of the trial must be verified and recorded in the chart. Sometimes subpoenas are not served or the time and place of the trial has been changed without notification, and the clinician may not be aware of it until the date of the trial, or worse when he arrives at the wrong court. The clinician should always remember that pallid and ambiguous testimony does little to assist in the legal process, and he should be prepared to state, based on all of the data available, a specific opinion regarding the relationship of the trauma to a mental disorder, and the diagnosis, treatment, and prognosis. A motto which should be emblazoned on a forensic clinician's mind is: "Proper and thorough preparation minimizes mistakes and is the best protection for mishaps."

THE TRIAL

In most personal injury cases, no battle of the experts takes place because in over ninety percent of the cases opposing attorneys negotiate differences before trial. The forensic clinician contributes to the process by furnishing reports and testifying during depositions. Insurance companies frequently agree to settle on the basis of an expert's report. That is why an attorney values an expert—and experts knowing that, charge appropriately. If negotiations break down because legitimate differences exist between experts or, more commonly, when opposing sides cannot agree upon a monetary settlement, the case goes to trial. Even though a trial date has been set and the expert has been subpoenaed, negotiations continue up to the trial date and it is not uncommon for a settlement to be reached after a jury is selected. Opposing attorneys, sometimes in chambers with the judge as facilitator, may reach a compromise at any time, thus obviating the need for expert testimony.

Because of the uncertainty of a trial and the necessity for expert testimony, clinicians are placed in an awkward position concerning the scheduling of their time for a court appearance. To avoid a wastage of time and money, the clinician must remember that most cases do not come to trial and no action is required even though a trial date may have been set and subpoenas issued. A phone call one week before the trial to the attorney who has issued the subpoena can give some indication of the probability of a courtroom appearance. The time for testimony and the fees are discussed. The attorney must assume financial responsibility for the segment of time that the clinician has allotted for expert testimony. In cases occurring within the city where he resides, the author makes no special arrangements to set aside any time for the courtroom appearance until the attorney, on the day of the trial, telephones and informs him that the trial is proceeding. Testimony is not usually required until one or two days after the trial has begun, and it is usually easy to adjust one's schedule by cancelling and rescheduling other patients. If testimony is scheduled around the noon hour, this allows the clinician time for travel and a minimal disruption of his office practice. As has been mentioned, in most cases a settlement is negotiated and expert testimony is not required. When the case does go to trial, the following discussion of the plaintiff's and defense's position may prove helpful to the clinician and lawyer.

THE PLAINTIFF'S POSITION

During a trial, the attorney for the plaintiff will attempt to prove that, by negligence, or deliberate intent on the part of the defendant, his client sustained injury, either physical, psychological, or both. Secondly, by the testimony of experts the attorney will attempt to demonstrate the extent of injury and a causal nexus between the harm and the defendant's actions. In the case of a PTSD, psychiatrists or psychologists who have examined the plaintiff will testify regarding the diagnosis, treatment, prognosis, and relationship between the trauma and the mental disorder. Throughout the testimony, the mental health professional is not only rendering an expert opinion, but is also educating the judge and jury about mental disorders. The concept of PTSD can be explained simply, utilizing nontechnical vocabulary that is easily understood by lay persons. The degree of disability imposed by the PTSD and requirements for future treatment are also issues of vital importance. During direct examination, the dialogue between lawyer and expert has been discussed during a pretrial meeting and agreements have been reached regarding the best way to convey essential information to the judge and jury.

Direct Examination

The following is an outline of typical questions likely to be asked by a plaintiff's attorney of an expert witness during direct examination. For the purpose of this exercise, it is assumed that the expert has concluded that the plaintiff is suffering from PTSD.

1. Qualification as an expert witness: "Please state your name, educational background, professional experience, specialty, board certification, academic appointments, publications, and memberships in professional organizations. Also indicate whether you have ever been qualified as an expert witness in a court of law."

2. Basis of opinion: "Have you ever had an occasion to examine the plaintiff? Please state the dates of all examinations or treatment. Please indicate all sources of information upon which you have based your expert opinion, including interviews of all persons, other than the plaintiff, as well as all records and reports that you have reviewed."

3. Findings: "Please state the results of your examinations." The history is related in a chronologic sequence. As the traumatic event is described, special emphasis is placed on the patient's psychophysiological reactions moments before, during, and immediately after impact. Reference to the Symptom Inventory Checklist (Chapter 10) expedites testimony, and all symptoms present before and after the trauma are mentioned and their significance explained. The results of all pertinent examinations, tests, and laboratory findings are summarized. An analysis of interviews and a

summary of reports and records that have been reviewed are presented. A simple declarative sentence, concluding that the trauma did precipitate a mental disorder, specifically a PTSD, ends this part of the testimony.

4. Explanation: "What is a PTSD?" During the explanation, the plaintiff's history is utilized to illustrate the DSM-III-R criteria for PTSD. In this manner the judge and jury can be educated about PTSD as it relates directly to the plaintiff. Concepts of the Three E's, retraumatization, and the Spiral Effect (Chapter 2) can best be explained by utilizing visual aids or a blackboard. The question of how symptoms of PTSD are maintained long after the acute phase of the trauma has passed is easily answered by using a chart similar to that in Chapter 2. An environmental event initiates the stress disorder, the judge and jury are told, but encephalic events, "the videotapes of the mind," result in future retraumatization, thereby sustaining the disorder. The trauma is recorded in the mind like an image on a videotape, which can be replayed time and time again, eliciting similar or sometimes more intense emotional reactions than those which occurred at the time of the trauma, an expert explains. A judge and jury easily understand this analogy, which can be further compared to those thoughts of a malingerer who has no mental videotape of a trauma, but instead dreams of acquiring wealth, property, or personal advantage. When physical symptoms are present, it is explained that somatic symptoms, especially pain, activate mental images of the trauma, thus stimulating more pathologic anxiety, which in turn intensifies physical symptoms or pain, producing the self-perpetuating cycle of the Spiral Effect. The Spiral Effect chart (page 23) explains how environmental events similar or identical to those present at the time of the trauma can also stimulate encephalic activity, causing retraumatization and a sustainment of the disorder.

5. Causation: "What is the relationship of the trauma to the plaintiff's current emotional or mental state?" A framework for presenting and explaining the diagnosis of PTSD requires close attention to three well-defined time periods: (1) the time preceding the traumatic event, (2) the traumatic event itself, and (3) the time following the traumatic event. Questions related to these time periods would include: "Please describe the plaintiff's lifestyle and personality before the trauma? Please describe any changes in the

plaintiff's life and personality after the trauma?" In the absence of any significant intervening events, any change in the plaintiff's pre- and post-traumatic personality and behavior must be attributed to the trauma. Interviews with those who were acquainted with the plaintiff before and after the trauma help to substantiate behavioral changes and lend weight to expert testimony. Academic achievement, work performance, and treatment by physicians or other therapists before and after the trauma can be compared by securing report cards, work evaluations, and medical records. Deficiencies in performance at school or work and medical treatment which occurred only after the trauma can reasonably be attributed to the stress disorder. It is important to document, if possible, all symptoms and deficiencies in behavior which occurred after the trauma.

6. Treatment: "How is PTSD treated?" A brief summary of the treatment principles and methods mentioned in Chapter 8 is usually more than a judge or jury would like to hear.

7. Length of Treatment: "How long will the plaintiff require treatment?" This is a difficult question to answer. A forty-year follow-up study (Kluznik et al., 1986) of 188 World War II veterans who were former prisoners of war indicated that seventy-eight percent had PTSD. Of those affected, twenty-nine percent had fully recovered, thirty-nine percent still reported mild symptoms, twenty-four percent improved but had moderate residual symptoms, and eight percent did not recover or had deteriorated. The authors concluded, "While the symptoms of PTSD diminished in intensity with time, the exposure to catastrophic trauma may increase morbidity in general, including an increased likelihood of developing other psychiatric disorders." Most of the veterans in the study were satisfied with their compensation status and did not expect an increase in benefits. This study has had important implications for the long-term outcome of patients with PTSD. Less than one-third fully recovered, while over two-thirds of the patients still reported psychiatric symptoms. In addition, the veterans had an increased likelihood of developing Generalized Anxiety Disorder, alcohol dependence or abuse, or a Mood Disorder.

If the plaintiff is still symptomatic at the time of the trial, outpatient psychiatric treatment is definitely indicated. The duration of therapy is difficult to determine and depends upon the patient's strengths and weaknesses as well as social support systems. The VA report of World War II POW's and other studies (Gleser, Green, and Winget, 1981; Sprehe, 1984) dispel the notion of the "greenback poultice," that the balm of money causes the plaintiff's symptoms to subside or disappear after the trial is over. The question concerning length of treatment has monetary significance, since this fact will be taken into consideration if damages are awarded to the plaintiff. The expert witness, therefore, must state a definite length of time and translate this into a sum of money. In the experience of the author, it is best to state a minimum and maximum time required for treatment and a range of medical costs. As mentioned, persons who develop a stress disorder are peculiarly sensitive to future stressors and may require intermittent treatment during the course of their life.

8. Work Impairment: "Does the plaintiff's PTSD prevent him or her from working?" The plaintiff's occupation together with the severity of symptoms determines the answer to this question. If the accident was work-related, the plaintiff may have developed a phobia of the work premises and, therefore, cannot return to work until proper treatment has been rendered. Even if a phobia is not present, generalized anxiety may impair work performance. In blue collar work settings which are inherently dangerous, workers suffering from PTSD may endanger not only themselves but co-workers. Inattentiveness or lack of concentration, characteristics of a PTSD, may also impair a worker's efficiency in other occupations. When physical injury and PTSD coexist, chronic pain or physical incapacity may interfere with reemployment. The issue of work is paramount in workers' compensation cases but is also an important issue in personal injury suits, as it relates to prognosis.

9. Life Impairment: "How has the trauma and the PTSD affected the plaintiff's life? To what extent is the plaintiff currently impaired?" These questions can be answered by pointing out any deficiencies or difficulties in the patient's life which followed the trauma and can be reasonably attributed to it. PTSD interferes with one's productivity and enjoyment of life. Any problems involving the family, marital life (including sexual functioning), interpersonal relationships, social/recreational activities, financial matters, and work must be uncovered, documented, and presented in court. This question addresses any impairment that the plaintiff may have suffered as a result of the trauma and, hence, has importance in the awarding of damages.

10. Malingering: "Do you feel that the plaintiff is malingering?" The question of malingering is always an issue whenever a diagnosis of a mental disorder is made, especially if there is no objective evidence of physical injury. Most plaintiffs' attorneys feel that the question of malingering is best brought up during direct examination, anticipating questions concerning the veracity of the plaintiff during cross-examination. The character and credibility of the plaintiff is always assessed during the mental status examination and the question of malingering must be answered forthrightly with a simple yes or no. Hyperbole or exaggeration of symptoms, a characteristic of some plaintiffs, must be distinguished from overt fabrication. A person with an Antisocial Personality Disorder is most likely to feign illness for monetary gain. Malingerers are usually sorted out long before trial, and it is rare when a pretender is unmasked in court.

11. Summing Up: "Again, will you please tell the jury what the relationship is between the trauma and the plaintiff's mental disorder—the PTSD?" At the end of direct examination, most plaintiff's attorneys ask the expert witness to reiterate his or her conclusions regarding the relationship between the trauma and PTSD.

Cross-Examination

The objective of the defense attorney is to portray the plaintiff as a malingerer or to demonstrate that if a mental disorder exists, it was present before the traumatic incident. From the standpoint of the defense, the veracity of the plaintiff and the competence and objectivity of the expert witness are at issue. When attempts to negotiate fail and a tort action comes to trial, there are usually legitimate differences between the opposing sides. Later, the defense has an opportunity to present its own expert witness to counter the plaintiff's psychiatrist or psychologist, and the stage is set for the "battle of the experts." During cross-examination of the plaintiff's expert witness, the following questions are likely to be asked:

1. Assault of credentials: The defense attorney probes into the background of the plaintiff's expert witness, attempting to erode the confidence of the mental health professional. Expert witnesses who have limited experience in the courtroom and are

unaccustomed to being challenged may become angry, defensive or intimidated, thereby weakening the effect of their testimony. If the direct examination has gone smoothly and was effective, sometimes defense attorneys will open cross-examination with a remark edged with sarcasm, "Doctor, you and the plaintiff's attorney seem to work well together," or "You certainly communicate very well to the jury with your modulations of voice and your hand gestures," or "Doctor, you are well-practiced in the courtroom." The author, who has been confronted with these comments, ignores the obloquy, and thanks the defense attorney. He acknowledges pretrial meetings with the plaintiff's attorney, pointing out that a failure to do so is inexcusable and represents professional dereliction. Although attempts to impugn one's character and professional competence may sting a bit during cross-examination, imperturbability is the best response.

2. Upon what do you base your diagnosis? This is a good question, especially if the expert witness has based his opinion only on information provided by the plaintiff. A prepared expert witness will answer this question by stating the number of hours spent interviewing and evaluating the plaintiff, the spouse, and other relatives or friends, and by reviewing all reports and records that have been used to formulate an opinion. When the expert witness is not sufficiently prepared and has not based his testimony on a broad base of data, another question has already formed in the defense attorney's mind.

3. Isn't it true, Doctor, that much of your testimony merely restates what the plaintiff has told you? On one occasion, the author answered this question in mock indignation with another question, "What do you think I am, a Xerox machine?" The question can be better answered by restating all of the elements that went into the conclusion and opinion. To a psychiatrist or psychologist, a mental status examination is equivalent to the physical examination of an internist. Experience and judgment, as in a good physical examination, are required to evaluate a patient's history and mental processes. No objective tests are available at present to conclusively support a diagnosis of PTSD. However, behavior can be observed, and the self-report of the patient is a valid source of information. PTSD, unlike many mental disorders, is precipitated by an observable environmental event, and many of the signs and symptoms can

be observed and validated (Erlinger, 1983). Sometimes defense attorneys attempting to demonstrate that psychiatric testimony is non-scientific and a lot of "guesswork" will ask several questions about subjectivity. The best policy is to answer all of these questions politely and calmly. Whenever possible the clinician should state that PTSD is a mental disorder recognized by the APA, first in 1980 in DSM-III and affirmed in 1987 in DSM-III-R, and that the plaintiff fulfills the essential criteria for the disorder.

4. What is malingering? Familiarity with the characteristics of malingering, Antisocial Personality Disorder, and Factitious Disorder is required when answering this question (Chapter 7).

5. How do you know that the plaintiff is not a malingerer? In all honesty one can never be a hundred percent certain that a patient is or is not malingering. However, based upon the expert's clinical experience and reasonable medical probability, a definite opinion can be rendered regarding the plaintiff's character and credibility. Many plaintiffs will have a tendency to exaggerate symptoms, but such hyperbole is not tantamount to malingering. When the patient has a past history of antisocial behavior, though not necessarily an Antisocial Personality Disorder, this unquestionably weakens the plaintiff's case. Depending upon the proclivities of the defense attorney, a series of questions may be asked about malingering, all designed to cast doubt upon the honesty of the plaintiff as well as the testimony of the expert witness.

6. Are some persons predisposed to a PTSD? Although most clinicians who are involved in psychotraumatology feel that this is so, no carefully controlled scientific study has ever been conducted to firmly establish a predisposition to PTSD. It is a moot point as far as the law is concerned, because the defense "takes the victim as he finds him." The defense attorney, however, may attempt to demonstrate that the plaintiff's mental disorder was a preexisting condition and has little or nothing to do with the alleged trauma.

7. When the plaintiff has a past history of treatment for a mental disorder, the following questions are likely to be asked: "What is the relationship between the patient's previous mental disorder and current mental status?" "Is the plaintiff's current mental status an extension of a previously diagnosed mental disorder?" "If the plaintiff did not have a previous mental disorder, would PTSD have developed?" When issues of predisposition or prior mental disor-

der are raised and the plaintiff has developed PTSD after a trauma, the appearance of the characteristic signs and symptoms of PTSD post-traumatically, with no evidence of these symptoms pretraumatically, clearly defines the relationship between trauma and subsequent symptoms. The absence of the nuclear symptoms of PTSD (intrusive cognitions, avoidance behavior, numbing of general responsiveness, increased arousal) pretraumatically and their appearance only after exposure to a well-defined trauma nullifies the argument that the disorder predated the trauma.

8. What is a "normal" person's response to trauma? Reference to Stage 1 (Response to Trauma) as described in Chapters 5 and 6 answers this question.

9. Tangential information: The defense attorney may ask a series of short, precise questions relating to irrelevant findings in the mental status examination. "Is the plaintiff in good contact with reality?" "Is the plaintiff psychotic?" "Is the plaintiff delusional?" "Has the plaintiff ever hallucinated?" "Is the plaintiff well-oriented?" "Is the plaintiff's intelligence within normal limits?" "Does the plaintiff have any objective evidence of brain damage?" These questions are answered briefly, usually with a "yes" or "no."

10. Bias of the expert: The defense may ask questions aimed at uncovering any bias of the expert witness. "When testifying as an expert witness in the past, what percentage of the time did you testify in favor of the plaintiff; what percentage in favor of the defense?" "During the last several years, how many clients have you examined for the plaintiff's attorney?" "What is your fee for testifying as an expert witness and who is paying your fee?" These questions should be answered dispassionately and briefly. In regard to fees, the best response is: "I'm not paid for my testimony but for my time."

11. Detracting tactics: The defense may ask a series of questions related to psychiatry, psychology, mental disorders, and PTSD which are intended to demonstrate to the judge and jury that psychiatry is unscientific, imprecise, and just short of "witchcraft." This tactic can backfire if the defense attorney is not well versed in concepts, nomenclature, and technology of psychiatry, psychology, and the behavioral sciences.

THE DEFENSE'S POSITION

To use or not to use an expert to counter the plaintiff's expert is a question that the defense attorney must answer during the preparation of his case. Merely pitting experts in opposition to one another for the sake of an adversarial contest seems unwise. The defense attorney should arrange a consultation with a mental health professional if any of the following are present: (1) the trauma (stressor) seems insignificant, (2) preexisting history of mental disorder, (3) prior history of antisocial behavior, (4) evidence of malingering, (5) marked discrepancies in existing medical records, or (6) suspicion of untruthfulness following the plaintiff's deposition. Before deciding upon a psychiatric evaluation of the plaintiff, a telephone consultation with a mental health professional who has reviewed all medical and psychological reports will provide information regarding any possible relationship between the trauma and a mental disorder. Depending upon the results of this consultation, an appointment may be arranged between the plaintiff and the defense's expert. The defense always has the option of presenting its own expert or on cross-examination, to discredit and dispute critical portions of the plaintiff's expert. Alternatively, negotiation can conclude the case prior to trial.

When legitimate differences of opinion exist, the defense's expert can highlight and analyze points favorable to the defense. In order to be effective and persuasive, an opposing opinion must stand alone and reflect a logical and well-reasoned explanation of known facts. Conclusions must be based on data from multiple sources and formulated in language consistent with DSM-III-R criteria. A point-by-point refutation of the plaintiff's expert only serves to confuse a jury so that all expert testimony may be ignored, or the most persuasive expert will be believed, regardless of evidence.

The defense's expert is always at a disadvantage, especially in those cases where the trauma is clear-cut and indisputable. Usually the clinician for the defense must formulate an opinion following only one interview with the patient. This may prove insufficient when compared to the plaintiff's expert who usually has interviewed or treated the plaintiff over a longer period of time. To be believable, conclusions drawn by the defense's expert must pass the "reasonable man test". Is it reasonable to conclude that following exposure to the documented trauma that the plaintiff suffered no emotional sequelae? An expert who testifies eloquently that the plaintiff experienced no significant emotional sequelae or PTSD following exposure to an obviously severe trauma, e.g., a fire causing severe burns, may lose all credibility when the jury views the victim's scarred face. Explanations which reflect "common sense" are more likely to influence juries. The interpretation of the facts and the emphasis placed on the mental status examination in regard to severity of symptoms, differentiate the conclusions drawn by the defense from those of the plaintiff's expert.

Direct Examination

During the selection of an expert witness, the defense attorney must consider credentials, clinical experience, previous forensic experience, academic appointments, publications, honors, and other activities which lend credibility to the witness. Most, but not all, defense-oriented experts have a philosophical orientation which can best be described as conservative. Injured individuals, according to this orientation, should pick themselves up by their own bootstraps and get on with it. Little sympathy is accorded to those who suffer emotional symptoms post- traumatically, but instead conservative-minded defense experts tend to minimize emotional symptoms and are quick to suspect malingering. The philosophical orientation and attitude of many defense experts represent real beliefs and are reflected in written reports and during testimony. Experts with a conservative proclivity make excellent witnesses for the defense and cannot be accused of bias more than the opposing plaintiff expert witness. Both can advance their opinions without compromising basic integrity.

Questioning of the defense expert during direct examination proceeds in the same manner as for the plaintiff's expert. Following qualification and examination of credentials, questions are asked regarding the type of examination conducted, persons interviewed, the review of medical and psychiatric records, and other sources of information upon which the expert's opinions rest. The following are a list of questions which might be asked of a defense expert witness on direct examination:

1. What are the results of your findings? Usual answers to this question include one of the following: (a) the plaintiff is malingering or has a Factitious Disorder, (b) the plaintiff has no mental disorder as codified in DSM-III-R, (c) the plaintiff had a preexisting mental disorder which has little or no relationship to the trauma, (d) the plaintiff did have psychiatric symptoms following

the trauma but they were minor and have subsided or are not sufficiently severe to warrant a DSM-III-R diagnosis, or (e) the patient did have PTSD (or other mental disorder) but through treatment and time it has resolved, and more treatment is not required.

2. What is a PTSD? The answer to this question allows the defense's expert to explain his concept of PTSD. This question is only asked when the plaintiff's expert has testified that the trauma precipitated a PTSD. The answer lays the groundwork for the refutation of the plaintiff's expert witness. The expert acknowledges the existence of PTSD, but in subsequent testimony he will dispute the presence of this stress disorder in the plaintiff.

3. Do you think that the plaintiff has a PTSD? After answering "no," questions regarding each diagnostic criterion of PTSD are asked, allowing the expert to fully explain the basis for the opposing opinion. A scholarly, dispassionate presentation pointing out the differences between the patient's symptoms and PTSD usually impresses a judge and jury. Technical jargon should be avoided, but if used, must be translated into everyday language. A lucid exposition of the clinical findings followed by an analysis of all data, concludes with a definite opinion regarding the current mental status of the plaintiff.

4. Does the plaintiff require treatment? Obviously this question is only asked when the answer is "no" and should be consistent with previous testimony. The expert must be prepared to explain his answer, especially if there is acknowledgement that the trauma did produce some mental symptoms. When appropriate, the issue of prognosis should be addressed.

5. Can the plaintiff work? The expert must differentiate between psychiatric and physical disability and defer in the latter instance to medical specialists or vocational rehabilitation experts. Psychological fitness to work, however, lies within the domain of the mental health professional and represents an appropriate avenue for inquiry. In most cases, activity, including work, benefits those with mental disorders. From the defense's perspective the issue of work needs comment only if the opposing expert concludes that the plaintiff cannot work. When work impairment is claimed, it can be expected that the plaintiff's attorney and expert will raise this issue.

6. In your opinion, does the plaintiff have a mental disorder which seriously affects his life? The answer to this question depends upon the defense expert's evaluation of the plaintiff's social support system. Ability to cope with problems of living, together with the capacity to enjoy family, marriage, social and recreational activities, is appraised. Ability, not disability, is the key word. Data gathered from clinical interviews and a review of pertinent records and investigations must support any conclusion.

7. After this lawsuit is resolved, do you think that the plaintiff will be less symptomatic? The answer to this question is usually "yes." Once the stress of the trial is over, anxiety related to the lawsuit usually diminishes. Care must be taken when answering this question because the plaintiff's expert will state that the core symptoms related to PTSD remain after trial. Symptoms feigned by malingerers, of course, disappear completely following litigation.

8. Again, Doctor, do you think that the plaintiff has suffered from any serious mental disorder as a result of his trauma? The answer simply stated is "No."

Cross-Examination

The purpose of cross-examination is to discredit testimony by showing the witness to be a fool, a liar, and a nitwit (Resnick, 1986), or just honestly mistaken. Drama in the courtroom is heightened by the anticipated confrontation. The defense's expert challenges the claim of the plaintiff, the contention of opposing counsel, and the testimony of the plaintiff's experts. Rather than act defensively, the best policy for a defense's expert witness is to stay composed, answer all questions calmly, and reiterate the basis for the opposing opinion.

During qualification, it is vital for the plaintiff's attorney to determine the extent of involvement of the defense's expert with traumatized patients. When an expert examines patients only for forensic purposes and not for treatment or research, it may indicate a lack of empathy for patients with psychological problems following trauma. Some defense-oriented experts may believe that money motivates all patients who claim psychiatric distress following trauma, and if present, this bias must be unearthed during cross-examination. Insensitive experts who display suspiciousness and investigative zeal, characteristics more associated with a private detective than a physician, must be suspected of prejudice. Is the expert a clinician who is truly involved in the field of psychotraumatology? This question underlies all others, for it separates the clinician who is an expert in trauma from those who are an expert in court.

The following is a list of questions which might be asked during cross-examination of an expert who is testifying for the defense:

1. Do you have any academic appointments and do you teach students or write papers about PTSD and psychological trauma? This is an obvious question designed to measure the degree of expertise and the personal involvement of the expert in PTSD. Defense-minded experts are likely to expose any bias in their lectures or writings about PTSD, emphasizing malingering or Factitious Disorders and decrying patients who sue for damages.

2. What percentage of the time do you testify for the defense? Unless the expert is young and has testified infrequently, the answer to this question should be "the majority of the time for the defense." To answer otherwise usually means that the expert is taking some latitude with the truth. Although most forensic psychiatrists have testified for the plaintiff and defense at various times during their careers, the author has never met a colleague who testifies equally for the plaintiff and the defense. As time passes, the personal and professional proclivities of the expert translate into a reputation which is generally appealing to either a plaintiff or defense attorney. A mutual educational process fosters a professional relationship between a lawyer and expert witness, and as a result, referral patterns develop. As it is with lawyers, expert witnesses usually become identified as a clinician oriented either toward the plaintiff or defense.

3. Do you treat patients with PTSD? If so, how many? The defense's expert is not likely to have treated many patients with PTSD or other psychiatric disorders associated with trauma. If the expert states to the contrary, a follow-up question should be, "Who referred these patients to you?" A defense attorney is unlikely to refer patients for treatment. Defense-oriented clinicians are usually not identified as therapists for PTSD patients, therefore, receive few referrals for treatment from any source. The degree of personal discomfort that this question raises, perhaps tells more than words.

4. Do you feel that people can be affected psychologically by a

trauma? If so, how? As the defense's expert answers, the plaintiff's attorney should carefully record all of the symptoms mentioned, especially those which have relevance to his client. A follow-up question would refer to other psychiatric and psychological reports which state that the plaintiff does have many of those symptoms, and the defense's expert is asked if he specifically inquired about each symptom.

5. What is the Traumatic Principle? If the expert does not know the answer to this question, the plaintiff's attorney should read it (Chapter 2), and then ask whether the trauma and its impact on the plaintiff fit the definition. A negative response should be followed by another question, "You mean that the trauma posed no realistic threat to life or limb?" This is a poignant question when physical injury accompanies PTSD or if the circumstances of the trauma were especially horrific.

6. How many times have you seen the plaintiff? In most instances the answer to this question is "once." A follow-up question, "Is this sufficient time to make a diagnosis of PTSD?" This question serves to compare the time spent by the opposing experts to arrive at an opinion and is intended to disclose any inadequacy in the examination of the plaintiff by the defense.

7. When the issue of malingering or a past history of antisocial behavior has been raised during direct examination, the plaintiff's attorney on cross-examination may decide to avoid any further tarnishing of his client. However, if the labeling is undeserved, clarification is in order. The credibility of plaintiffs who have an Antisocial Personality Disorder is problematic; however, isolated antisocial behavior is not synonymous with Antisocial Personality Disorder. Some defense experts dredge up past behavior such as truancy or behavior disturbances in primary school and offer this as proof of an Antisocial Personality Disorder. At other times, speculations involving past psychopathologic conflicts are offered as evidence of an Antisocial Personality Disorder, when indeed, no arrests, convictions, or psychiatric treatment had resulted from the hypothesized conflict. Psychoactive Substance Use such as smoking marijuana must be placed in a societal context, and abuse patterns must be differentiated from "normative" behavior. Also, some traumatized plaintiffs have no history of antisocial behavior for a decade or more prior to the trauma, and interpretations of

current behavior must reflect this fact. To counter testimony that his client is malingering or has an Antisocial Personality Disorder, the plaintiff's attorney may pursue the following line of questions: "Is an Antisocial Personality Disorder an important aspect of malingering?" The answer to this question is "Yes." Antisocial Personality Disorder is a lifelong pattern of antisocial behavior beginning in childhood and continuing to adulthood as indicated in DSM-III-R (Chapter 7). Using the diagnostic criteria as a guideline, the plaintiff's attorney then asks a series of questions designed to demonstrate that his client does not fulfill the criteria for an Antisocial Personality Disorder. The plaintiff's attorney may decide that the best way to explain any antisocial behavior exhibited by his client in the past would be during direct examination of his expert and may decide not to cross-examine the defense's expert on this point. One can be sure, however, that any evidence of antisocial behavior occurring at any time during the plaintiff's life will be brought forth by the defense to cast doubt on the character and veracity of the plaintiff.

8. If the defense's expert tenaciously clings to the conclusion that no significant emotional symptoms have resulted and the trauma would reasonably, in most people's minds, be expected to produce some emotional reaction, the plaintiff's attorney can formulate a hypothetical question which would encompass all elements of the trauma sustained by the plaintiff. The final question should be, "Would you expect a person subjected to that trauma to have any emotional symptoms?"

CONCLUSIONS

No matter whether the mental health professional evaluates patients for the plaintiff or defense, there is no substitute for good clinical judgment and knowledge about mental disorders following trauma. During the initial stage of the forensic examination, it is best to dissociate the plaintiff from the patient and focus the evaluation on diagnosis—the presence or absence of a mental disorder. The late Sir William Osler, a world-renown physician, advised students, "Listen to the patient. He will tell you the diagnosis." Forensic clinicians should heed Osler's sage advice; patients, regardless of their legal status, will furnish clues to diagnosis. Once a diagnosis has been established, the legal issue is addressed and an expert opinion formulated.

Fitting the forensic facts into a comprehensive mosaic which makes good clinical sense requires skill and sensitivity. Experts with integrity evaluate all available data and in court, "tell it like it is."

An ideal expert witness is a good teacher who, during the course of testimony, takes the jury through the various steps of a mental status examination, logically pointing out the progression of ideas which led to the final conclusion. An expert opinion represents the best possible explanation of the relationship between the trauma and the plaintiff's current mental state. It must be remembered that expert opinions are based on reasonable medical probability and do not represent absolute certainty.

Some writers denounce psychiatric testimony (Ziskin, 1981; Imwinkelried and Giannelli, 1986) and recommend against the use of mental health professionals in the adversarial process. Whether these commentators are timid and do not wish to participate in an adversarial proceeding, contemptuous of the mental health profession, or simply pompous professionals not accustomed to having their views challenged is not for the author to say. The use of experts in the courtroom is well-established and, like it or not, is here to stay. For mental health profession-als who are interested in the field of psychotraumatology and enjoy the repartee of verbal confrontation and an opportunity to match wits with an adversary, the courtroom offers an arena for such an engagement. Somehow the truth usually emerges and justice is served, as the judge and jury sort through the facts and conflicting testimony and arrive at a decision. When all is done, plaintiffs return to patient status and experts return to doctoring.

TWELVE

LEGAL ISSUES—CRIMINAL

Charles Heads, a Marine Corps combat veteran who was estranged from his wife, broke into his sister-in-law's house, brandishing and firing a pistol. After running out of ammunition, Heads got a rifle from his car and resumed firing. One shot struck and killed his sister-in-law's husband. Heads was arrested, tried, and found guilty of murder in 1978 and was sentenced to life imprisonment. Through a series of appeals not related to PTSD, Heads was retried in October, 1981. By this time, the APA officially recognized PTSD as a diagnostic category, and Heads' attorney, Wellborn Jack, Jr.(1980), explained his client's behavior on the basis of a stress disorder related to his combat experience in Vietnam. The jury found Mr. Heads not guilty of murder because of temporary insanity stemming from his war experiences—the first time Post-Traumatic Stress Disorder had been used successfully in a capital case (State v. Heads, 1981).

The *Heads* decision was not a fluke but a new dimension of the insanity defense. In 1982 four juries found Vietnam-era combat veterans who were accused of various violent offenses, "not guilty by reason of insanity because of PTSD" (Slovenko, 1984). Thereafter, combat-induced PTSD became a factor in other criminal cases, and a number of veterans have had their charges reduced or were released on early parole. The utilization of PTSD in the courtroom ushered in a new chapter in an age-old debate concerning the insanity defense. The viability of PTSD in mitigating criminal responsibility, especially with defendants who are not combat veterans of Vietnam, remains uncertain.

CRIMINAL RESPONSIBILITY

The laws governing criminal responsibility have evolved from philosophical, theological, psychiatric, and legal theory and represent a merging of moral, religious, medical, and judicial beliefs. It has long been recognized that children, idiots, and lunatics lack *mens rea*, a guilty mind, and were incapable of forming a criminal intent because of a basic inability to discern good from evil and right from wrong. The frame of mind and motivational state of a defendant is also important when assessing blame and meting out punishment. It did make a difference if a person killed in the heat of passion, after cool deliberation, accidentally, in self-defense, or while dazed from a blow, intoxicated, or insane (Maeder, 1985). A sequence of English cases beginning in 1724 and culminating in 1843 with the trial of Daniel M'Naughten firmly established the "insanity test" into criminal law.

The M'Naughten Rule

The M'Naughten rule also known as the right and wrong test remains the law governing the insanity defense in the federal system and is the mainstay of the law in 45 states. In 1843 Daniel M'Naughten, a deluded Scotsman, believed that he was being persecuted by the Tories, and acting on this belief, he attempted to assassinate the Tory prime minister, Sir Robert Peel, but by mistake killed Peel's personal secretary, Edward Drummond. M'Naughten's trial and subsequent acquittal by reason of insanity aroused Queen Victoria's attention. A few years earlier in 1840, the Queen and Prince Albert were almost victims of an assassination by Edward Oxford, who also was acquitted on the grounds of insanity. The two attempted assassinations of important personages of the realm impelled the House of Lords to submit certain questions to the judges of England for clarification and an authoritative statement of the existing law (Glueck, 1962). After deliberation, Chief Justice Tindal, speaking for 14 of the 15 judges, enunciated the now-famous M'Naughten Rule (Bromberg, 1979):

> "To establish a defense on the grounds of insanity, it must
> be clearly proven that at the time of committing the act, the

party accused was laboring under such a defect of reason, from disease of the mind, as not to know the nature and quality of the act he was doing, or if he did know it...he did not know he was doing what was wrong" (Guttmacher and Weihofen, 1952; Davidson, 1965).

The insanity defense saved Daniel M'Naughten from the gallows and resulted in the rule that bears his name, but he was never again to see freedom. Following his trial, M'Naughten was committed to the Bethlehem Hospital and later was transferred to the Broadmoor Asylum where he died in 1865, spending the last 22 years of his life in confinement (Diamond, 1956). Clearly M'Naughten was suffering from a psychosis with delusions, and the right and wrong test was intended for those defendants who had a break with reality. Cognitive impairment or not knowing the difference between right and wrong is not only present in major mental disorders, but also in mental retardation, Organic Mental Syndromes, and as described later, in PTSD during a dissociative episode.

The Irresistible Impulse Test

Criticism of the M'Naughten Rule focused around the narrowness of the concept regarding legal insanity. Cognition, "knowing the difference between right and wrong at the time of committing the act," was the essential element determining criminal responsibility in the M'Naughten Rule (Glueck, 1962; Silving, 1967). In the 19th century proponents for reform, mainly from the United States, advocated a broader definition of insanity to include other facets of mental functioning. Isaac Ray, the leading forensic psychiatrist at the time, in his famous book A Treatise of *the Medical Jurisprudence of Insanity* (1962) was an outspoken proponent of including the "irresistible impulse" and the concept of moral insanity into rules determining criminal responsibility. In 1886, when Alabama adopted an irresistible impulse rule, it was the first time in the United States that volitional impairment joined the cognitive defect of M'Naughten as a defense in the test on criminal responsibility. "When the will was dominated by uncontrollable impulses and emotions resulting in a criminal act, the defendant was not responsible for his actions" (Robitscher, 1966). An irresistible impulse is not to be confused with "unresisted impulse," where reason is temporarily blinded by anger, jealousy, or other overwhelming passions not the result of a mental condition (Robitscher, 1966). The irresistible impulse test expands the M'Naughten Rule, for "the defendant may have known what he was doing and known that it was wrong, but nevertheless may have been unable to resist an overwhelming impulse to commit the crime" (Glueck, 1962).

Defendants suffering from a variety of mental disorders—Organic Mental Syndromes, epilepsy, Schizophrenia, Delusional Disorders, Brief Reactive Psychosis, Schizophreniform Disorder, Schizoaffective Disorder, Induced Psychotic Disorder, Mood Disorders, Dissociative Disorders, and Impulse Control Disorders under certain conditions could meet the test under the irresistible impulse rule. Many defendants suffering from the preceding mental disorders would also qualify under the M'Naughten test. There is no question that the irresistible impulse rule broadens the base and would include more mentally-disordered defendants who could legitimately claim "insanity" or diminished criminal responsibility.

The ALI Test

The American Law Institute (ALI) test for criminal responsibility is a combination of the right-wrong rule and an update of the irresistible impulse test. The elements of cognition, volition, and capacity to control behavior comprise the ALI Standard (Slovenko, 1973):

> "A person is not responsible for criminal conduct if at the time of such conduct, as a result of mental disease or defect, he lacks substantial capacity either to appreciate the criminality of his conduct or to conform his conduct to the requirements of law."

It is noted that the term "mental disease" or "defect" does not include abnormalities of behavior manifested only by repeated criminal or otherwise antisocial conduct. The ALI's model penal code, which was prepared during the years 1952 to 1962, allows improved opportunity for the inclusion of psychiatric testimony while excluding habitual criminals (Silving, 1967).

The ALI test, considered generally satisfactory as a test for criminal responsibility, is the law in almost one-half of the states and was the accepted standard in the federal system until 1984. Following the attempted assassination of President Reagan and the acquittal on the grounds of insanity of Hinckley, the insanity defense has come under fire. Cries for its abolishment or restricted use led to a change in federal law. The Congress in 1984 struck the volitional test from federal law and adopted an insanity test that requires a defendant to prove that he was unable to appreciate the nature and wrongfulness of his acts. The new law also limits psychiatric testimony to presenting and explaining a diagnosis of mental disease or defect. Additionally, this new law provides for the confinement to a mental hospital or other facility of anyone found not guilty by reason of insanity (NGRI). Release from an institution of a NGRI acquittee would not occur until the court determined the issue of future dangerousness.

CRIMINAL RESPONSIBILITY AND PTSD

Ordinarily, persons with PTSD are in contact with reality and do not display any symptoms of psychosis such as hallucinations or delusions. PTSD is essentially an anxiety disorder. However, some patients, especially those who are subsequently subjected to extreme stress, develop a transient dissociative reaction with episodes of depersonalization or derealization. Most of the time, these feelings of unreality pass without incident, but occasionally criminal behavior may erupt. The question of criminal responsibility, therefore, is pertinent since a person's cognitive or volitional state may be impaired during a dissociative reaction.

Dissociative Reaction — Depersonalization/Derealization

According to DSM-III-R, "The symptoms of depersonalization involve an alteration in the perception or experience of the self so that the usual sense of one's own reality is temporarily lost or changed." During periods of depersonalization, patients often report that they feel like spectators and look at various parts of their body as if they belong to someone else. The sensation of self estrangement makes patients feel "mechanical" and not in complete control of their actions. During periods of derealization, which may occur independently of or be associated with depersonalization, patients relate that their external environment looks strange, different, unusual, and unreal. Sensory awareness can be heightened or dimmed, and there may be a perceived change in the size or shapes of objects in the surroundings. People in the immediate environment look different and may be perceived as dead or mechanical. In Depersonalization Disorder, the customary feeling of one's own reality is lost and is replaced by a feeling of unreality. During these periods of unreality, the onset of which is rapid and the subsidence more gradual, persons can become extremely fearful and agitated. In addition, patients often report a disturbance of the subjective sense of time and difficulties or slowness in recall.

Whenever stress intensifies, especially if the heightened anxiety is prolonged, persons may have a dissociative reaction and experience feelings of unreality (depersonalization/derealization). Those with a PTSD may experience "flashbacks" (dissociative reaction) at any time but more commonly during periods of increased psychosocial stress. Victims may feel they are going insane or out of control and begin to act strangely or bizarrely. The onset occurs quickly, frightening the patient; however, gradually the feelings of unreality diminish in intensity and eventually disappear altogether. The entire experience may linger in the mind of the PTSD patient who wonders about its significance and the possibility of a recurrence. Generally, patients report that they were "stunned" or "in shock" and may or may not attribute the altered feeling state to the original trauma.

The level of stress that a person experiences in Stages II and III of a PTSD depends upon psychosocial factors as reflected by the Three E's, the sources of anxiety (Scrignar, 1983). When pathologic anxiety is high, patients are extremely vulnerable to stressors related or unrelated to the original trauma, and it is at these times that a dissociative episode may develop.

A search for the sources of anxiety—the Three E's—will reveal the stimuli responsible for the dissociative state. At times, obsessive concern about the trauma and preoccupation with its sequelae are sufficient explanations for heightened anxiety. More often, however, environmental events play a significant role in raising anxiety to the point that the patient experiences a dissociative reaction. Family disputes, interpersonal conflicts, unemployment, financial worries, and a host of other problems mentioned in Chapters 5 and 6 can increase pathologic anxiety, predisposing a person to the development of a dissociative reaction.

In the chronic stage of PTSD, patients are vulnerable to episodes of depersonalization/derealization because they are continuously anxious and depressed. In DSM-III-R the predisposing factors for depersonalization, a form of Dissociative Disorder are "severe stress, such as military combat or an automobile accident." Those PTSD patients who are suffering from severe stress are prone to the development of a dissociative reaction.

A dissociative reaction with feelings of unreality may also be present in Schizophrenia, Mood Disorders, Organic Mental Disorders, anxiety disorders, personality disorders, and epilepsy. The differential diagnosis also includes a Depersonalization Disorder, a form of Dissociative Disorder not associated with PTSD. It is possible for PTSD to coexist with another mental (Sierles et al., 1983) or neurologic disorder; in these cases the more severe psychiatric disorder or epilepsy is more likely to be the primary cause of the dissociative reaction.

During a dissociative reaction, a person suffering from PTSD may feel unrestrained by reality and unable to control his behavior. Lawyers representing Vietnam-era veterans accused of committing criminal acts attempt to prove that the defendant was reliving traumatic war experiences during a flashback (dissociative reaction) and uncontrollably engaged in violent and aggressive behavior typical of a combat soldier. Motivated by memories from the past, the legal argument contends, that the defendant under considerable stress and experiencing a dissociative reaction, did not appreciate the criminality of his conduct and could not control his conduct to the requirements of law, therefore should not be criminally responsible for his actions.

THE CRIMINAL PROCESS AND PTSD

From the time of arrest and indictment, a mentally disordered defendant passes through various stages of the criminal process. Beginning with the pretrial stage, hearings are conducted to determine the defendant's mental competency to stand trial. An assessment of criminal responsibility takes place during the trial, the most dramatic stage during which the "battle between the experts" receives much attention. The post-trial phase, involving disposition of the defendant, is anticlimactic and relatively invisible, although it is the most important step of the legal process. When insanity is raised as a criminal defense, the law provides different procedures for the pretrial, trial, and post-trial stages of criminal procedure, and different issues confront lawyers, mental health professionals, and the court (Slovenko, 1963).

The Pretrial Stage

The issue of triability is separate from that of criminal responsibility but often when the plea of not guilty by reason of insanity (NGRI) is raised by the defendant's attorney, a sanity commission consisting of two or more physicians (usually psychiatrists) is convened to determine the accused's present mental capacity to proceed. The mental status examination focuses on two questions: Does the defendant understand the proceedings against him? Can the defendant cooperate and communicate with the attorney during the preparation of the case? (Scrignar, 1967a). The determination of a defendant's mental competency to stand trial thus depends upon cognitive intactness and communicative ability. This is appropriate because defendants certainly cannot properly defend themselves if they do not understand the proceedings against them or cannot communicate and cooperate with legal counsel in the preparation of their case.

When it is pleaded that a defendant was suffering from PTSD and was experiencing a dissociative reaction at the time the criminal act was committed, a sanity commission usually concludes that the accused is mentally competent to stand trial. Unless the defendant is experiencing a dissociative reaction—episode of depersonalization or derealization—at the time of the mental status examination, no cognitive impairment or loss of ability to cooperate and communicate with an attorney will be discovered. Defendants will look "near-normal." However, a mental status examination will reveal symptoms of pathologic anxiety together with depression and other signs and symptoms of PTSD mentioned in Chapter 6. After a judicial hearing, it can be expected that most defendants with the diagnosis of PTSD will be remanded for trial.

The Trial Stage

For the purpose of this discussion, the ALI test will serve as the standard for criminal responsibility because it includes components of the cognitive (right and wrong) and volitional (irresistible impulse) tests. In 1984, as noted the federal law has gone back to a cognitive standard—"At the time of the commission of the acts constituting the offense, the defendant, as a result of a severe mental disease or defect, was unable to appreciate the nature and quality or the wrongfulness of his acts." Despite the change in federal law, a survey published in 1985 (Wettstein, Rogers and Mulvey, 1986) disclosed that in the U.S., 23 states use the M'Naughten test, 22 use ALI, and three have no insanity defense, while the situation in the other two was unclear.

The question to be addressed during the trial stage is: At the time of the alleged criminal conduct, as a result of mental disease or defect, did the defendant lack substantial capacity either to appreciate the criminality of his conduct (cognitive test) or to conform his conduct to the requirements of law (volitional test). PTSD is certainly a mental disorder (disease or defect) and during a dissociative reaction, persons may lack substantial capacity to appreciate the criminality of their conduct. Blurring of reality occurs during flashbacks, best exemplified by Vietnam combat veterans who, during a dissociative reaction related to traumatic war experiences, exhibit aggressive or assaultive behavior appropriate for wartime but criminal during peacetime. Individuals may know it is wrong to hurt or kill people; however, during a dissociative episode, cognitive awareness becomes blurred and the ability to appreciate the criminality of conduct is impaired. Concerning the volitional prong of the ALI test, "the ability to conform conduct to the requirements of law," the case is clearer. Under the influence of a flashback, a PTSD patient may react automatically as if under the control of an irresistible impulse. Thus, cognition and volition are impaired during the dissociative episode involving a temporary loss of the defendant's capacity to appreciate (know, understand) the criminality of his conduct and to conform his conduct (control impulses) to the requirements of law. It would, therefore, seem evident that PTSD would be an acceptable defense in a criminal trial, utilizing either the ALI standard or just the M'Naughten test. Furthermore, PTSD is a clinical entity that ordinarily does not include abnormalities of behavior manifested by repeated criminal or otherwise antisocial conduct.

During the trial, the defense attorney must first establish that prior to the alleged criminal act, the defendant manifested signs or symptoms characteristic of a PTSD and, ideally, demonstrated evidence of dissociative episodes. The trauma and its effects, which predate the alleged criminal act, should be elaborated in detail so that the jury understands the defendant's mental disorder. For example, if the defendant is a Vietnam-era combat veteran, an analysis of his military record documenting specific instances of war trauma helps to explain the development of PTSD. It must be emphasized that PTSD patients are vulnerable to dissociative reactions which interfere with the perception of reality. Next, and most importantly, a connection must be established between the defendant's PTSD and mental state at the time of the "alleged" criminal act. Any similarity between the trauma and the surroundings at the scene of the crime helps to explain a flashback (dissociative episode) during which the defendant may not have been criminally responsible for his actions. Finally, at the trial the expert witness offers an opinion of the defendant's mental state at the time of the alleged criminal conduct in accordance with the court's rules relating to criminal responsibility.

The Defendant's Position

When a PTSD is used in the insanity defense, the defendant's attorney proceeds much in the same fashion as a plaintiff's lawyer in a personal injury suit. The emphasis and objective are, of course, different—awarding of damages in a personal injury suit and acquittal by reason of insanity in a criminal proceeding. The task facing the defendant's attorney is to demonstrate that at the time of the crime an obviously culpable client was suffering from a dissociative reaction within the context of a PTSD.

First, the attorney for the defendant must prove that prior to the alleged crime a trauma took place and was responsible for the production in the client of an officially recognized mental disorder—PTSD. Furthermore, it must be established that persons with a PTSD are sensitive to stress and can develop a dissociative reaction. Finally, evidence must demonstrate that at the time of the alleged criminal act, the defendant was suffering from a great deal of stress and experienced a dissociative reaction which rendered him not criminally responsible. The tactics and strategy for the utilization of PTSD in the insanity defense vary, but extensive preparation on the part of the defense attorney and mental health professional is essential. The following outline may be helpful in organizing testimony.

> **Data Upon Which Testimony Is Based:** Psychiatry and the other behavioral sciences are suspect during a criminal trial. Many people believe that the insanity defense is a "gimmick" designed to free obviously guilty defendants and turn them loose on the streets. Mental illness is viewed as a myth conjured up by men who wear beards and speak in a strange accent. To counter this caricature, the defense attorney and the expert witness must take pains to educate the jury and to substantiate as much of the testimony as possible. Relatives, friends, colleagues, and others knowledgeable about the defendant's personality and behavior can provide valuable information concerning the mental state of the defendant. Mental health professionals must also have access to reports and records which can be used to document personality changes in the defendant. It has been said that we all leave a legacy of letters beginning with our birth certificate and ending with our death notice, and the defense attorney can retrieve relevant records and make them available to the expert witness for evaluation. School reports, military records, written appraisals of work performance, medical and psychiatric records, and

police reports furnish information concerning the defendant's proficiency or maladjustment. For the defendant who claims he was a combat veteran, all branches of the military keep careful records of military engagements which can factually validate the nature of the war trauma. A chronologic sequence of events utilizing charts and diagrams is an effective device to imprint salient facts upon a juror's mind during testimony. Juries are more likely to accept a well-reasoned explanation of events based on a wide body of data which are distilled into an opinion by the expert witness.

A Detailed and Documented History of the Defendant's Life Before, During, and After the Trauma: Ideally, the patient's life before the trauma was relatively normal with no evidence of mental disorder or antisocial behavior. School performance, service in the armed forces, work history, and marital relationship should reflect a good adjustment indicative of a normal person living life without any major difficulties. When discussing the stressor which precipitated PTSD, the expert witness should describe the traumatic event in detail. When answering the question, "What is a PTSD?" the expert responds in much the same way as in a civil case. In criminal cases, however, a further explanation is required to compare the similarities of stressors which were present at the time of the trauma with those which may have been present at the time of the commission of the "alleged" crime. When the circumstances of the crime are described, comparisons should be made to demonstrate that a flashback or a dissociative reaction occurred at the time of the crime. For example, in People v. Wood (1982), the attorney for Wood, a Vietnam-combat veteran, demonstrated to the jury that the auto assembly plant where Wood worked was painted in a camouflage-like pattern similar to Army installations. In addition, the hand grip of tools was similar to the pistol grip of weapons. The contention was that the environs of the factory were similar to military surroundings in Vietnam, where Wood first experienced a dissociative reaction. A jury, understanding the comparison, returned a verdict of not guilty by reason of insanity.

During testimony involving post-traumatic behavior, the expert draws upon the Traumatic Principle (Chapter 2) and also demonstrates that the defendant meets the diagnostic criteria for PTSD, as defined in DSM-III-R. Signs, symptoms, and changes in behavior occurring post-traumatically are attributed to PTSD. Personality changes, whenever possible, should be verified by sources other than the defendant, and any evidence of dissociative episodes occurring before the alleged criminal conduct, but after the trauma, should be fully documented and described. Expert testimony must establish that prior to the alleged commission of the crime, the defendant was suffering from a mental disorder—specifically a PTSD.

The Defendant's State of Mind at the Time of the Alleged Crime: In order to qualify within the cognitive or volitional tests of legal insanity, the defendant must have been experiencing a dissociative reaction with feelings of unreality at the time of the alleged criminal act. A retrospective reconstruction of events leading to criminal behavior must focus on any similarity between the crime and the circumstances of the original trauma (combat experiences, accident, rape, etc.). The concept of a flashback or automatism occurring at the time of the crime must be explained and linked to the PTSD. The defense must prove: (1) the defendant was suffering from PTSD prior to the criminal act; (2) persons with PTSD can subsequently develop a dissociative episode; (3) at the time of the alleged criminal act, the defendant was suffering from a dissociative reaction and was not responsible, in the legal sense, for any criminal behavior; and (4) if the defendant did not suffer from PTSD, it is more likely than not he would not have committed the criminal act.

The Prosecutor's Position

The prosecutor will attempt to denigrate the testimony of the defense's expert as "intellectual balderdash" designed to excuse an obviously guilty defendant from the penalty usually imposed on all lawbreakers. Whenever possible, the prosecutor will introduce and emphasize inflammatory information detrimental to the defendant. For example, prior antisocial history, abuse of alcohol or other substances, as well as equally unflattering evidence indicating that the defendant is a reprobate deserving punishment, not acquittal on the grounds of insanity. Part of the prosecutor's strategy during the trial is to describe the crime in the most heinous manner possible and to picture the perpetrator, the defendant, as an evil person totally in control of all mental faculties.

The ultimate issue during the trial is the defendant's state of mind at the time of the commission of the alleged criminal act. Since it is unlikely that the mental health professional was present at that time, the prosecutor will ask, during cross- examination, how the expert can be so certain about the defendant's state of mind at a specific point in time. The best answer is to reiterate all of the data upon which a conclusion was reached and end with the statement that the opinion is based on "reasonable medical probability."

Prosecutors are on the alert for any inconsistencies or inaccuracies, however small or unimportant, in the testimony of the defendant's expert. Seemingly inconsequential statements or lapses of memory, although not directly related to the major issue at hand, may be seized by the prosecutor to undermine other aspects of the expert's testimony. If a mistake has been made, it is better for the mental health professional to admit it, apologize, and calmly correct it. Another tactic of the prosecutor is to facetiously challenge certain conclusions of the expert in the hope that this will anger the mental health professional and nullify the impact of his testimony. Clever prosecutors will make the most out of unflattering characteristics of the expert such as pomposity, grandiosity, dogmatism, and an unwilling- ness to concede even small or inconsequential points and will attempt to portray the defendant's expert as an instrument to subvert the dispensing of justice—a guilty verdict. Despite any attempts on the part of the prosecutor, the defense's expert must maintain composure and repeat, whenever necessary, his findings and conclusions. The spotlight of public attention exaggerates the importance of the expert who must always remember that he is but one player in the courtroom drama, and others render the final verdict.

The prosecutor will put forth an expert who will usually testify in one of two ways: (1) the defendant is not suffering from PTSD or any other mental disorder, or (2) the defendant does have PTSD but this mental disorder is not "severe", therefore, the defendant was criminally respon- sible for his acts. The following typifies the strategy of the prosecutor and his expert.

> **The Defendant Does Not Have PTSD:** To contest a claim of PTSD suffered by the defendant at the time of the offense, the prosecutor asks his expert many of the same questions which would be raised in a civil suit by the attorney for the defense (Chapter 11). After disposing of the PTSD diagnosis, the prosecutor's expert may decide that the defendant is malingering

to avoid criminal penalties. Alternatively, the prosecutor's expert may conclude that the defendant does display some psychological symptoms, but they are consistent with a person who has been charged with committing a criminal offense and are not "abnormal" or sufficiently severe to impair the cognitive or volitional aspects of the mind.

As with all expert testimony, the basis for opinion must be supported by in depth interviews of the defendant, a thorough mental status examination, as well as data from sources external to the defendant including, if possible, interviews with those who may have witnessed the crime. The prosecutor asks questions aimed at demonstrating the defendant's cognitive intactness and ability to control behavior. Is the defendant in good contact with reality? Has the defendant ever suffered from psychosis? Is the defendant delusional? Has the defendant ever experienced auditory or visual hallucinations? Would the defendant be able to control his behavior if a policeman were at his elbow? The prosecutor's expert will attempt to portray the defendant as a relatively "normal" individual who understood the wrongfulness of any act and possessed the ability to control his behavior.

The Defendant Does Have a PTSD: When there is indisputable evidence from past psychiatric records that indeed the defendant was exposed to a traumatic event (military combat, accident, rape, etc.) and did develop a PTSD, the expert for the prosecution should acknowledge this but may conclude that the defendant had a PTSD in the past but was successfully treated. If the mental status examination indicates that the defendant still suffers from some symptoms of PTSD, the expert may conclude that PTSD is not a serious or severe disorder. In psychiatry the severe mental disorders include: Organic Mental Disorders, Schizophrenia, Mood Disorders, or other mental disorders of a psychotic type. PTSD is an anxiety disorder, and in this group of mental disorders reality testing is generally intact. The prosecutor's expert can contrast differences in cognitive functioning and impulse control between major mental disorders and anxiety disorders.

Dissociative Reaction: The prosecutor's expert witness must refute the opinion of the defense's expert that the defendant was experiencing a dissociative reaction at the time of the alleged crime. Dissociative episodes are not peculiar to PTSD and can be manifested by patients with Schizophrenia, Mood Disorders, Organic Mental Disorders, personality disorders, and epilepsy. Malingering must be considered because defendants may feign a dissociative reaction for the purpose of avoiding conviction and punishment. Persons prone to dissociative episodes usually will have exhibited this phenomenon prior to any criminal proceedings, and when this cannot be documented in the past, this tends to favor the proposition that none occurred at the time of the alleged criminal act.

A tactic of the prosecutor which is designed to instill fear in the minds of the jurors is to portray the defendant as a ticking time bomb and a dissociative reaction as an explosion of uncontrolled fury. Jurors may then disregard the rules governing criminal responsibility and return a verdict of guilty to protect society (and themselves) from future harm by the alleged miscreant. Questions concerning the transient and unpredictable nature of a dissociative reaction are analogized to Dr. Jekyll and Mr. Hyde. The likelihood of "future outbursts" of antisocial behavior, although not relevant to the trial issue of criminal responsibility, may be introduced by the prosecutor in the form of a hypothetical question to buttress the ticking time bomb hypothesis. This conjecture is a risky gambit for the prosecutor because it supports the contention of the defense that the defendant did not know what he was doing at the time of the commission of the alleged criminal act because of a dissociative episode.

During the final phase of direct examination, the prosecution will attempt to refute, point by point, any damaging testimony of the defense's expert. Whether contesting the presence of a PTSD or minimizing the seriousness of anxiety disorders, the prosecutor's expert witness always assumes the attitude of the reasonable man. Answers to all questions should be stated simply and logically in language unfettered by professional jargon or complicated psychiatric concepts. Professional testimony translated into "common sense" makes "good sense" in the courtroom.

The Post-Trial Stage

The undercurrent that covertly permeates all aspects of a trial is the disposition of defendants who are adjudicated not guilty by reason of insanity. After a verdict of NGRI, the public has visions of a maniacal ogre being released from custody to feed on hapless citizens. In most cases following an adjudication of NGRI, the acquitted person is committed to a mental hospital for further evaluation and treatment (Scrignar, 1971). Incarceration may last for a lifetime, as in the case of Daniel M'Naughten, or until hospital physicians and the court are convinced that the NGRI acquittee has recovered and is not a danger to self or society. The determination of dangerousness is difficult, and NGRI acquittees involved in acts of violence pose a special problem for the predictive powers of mental health professionals. Presaging dangerousness becomes more complicated when NGRI acquittees require ongoing psychopharmacologic treatment (Scrignar, 1967b). The question of who is going to take responsibility for the future behavior of NGRI acquittees assumes great importance. Certainly not the prosecutor, defense attorney, or even the "expert witnesses," all of whom usually bow out after the trial has been concluded. Judges have legal authority to commit the NGRI acquittee to a maximum security hospital or a comparable facility, but once this is done, they retire to their chambers. During the post-trial stage, the burden falls on the physicians and staff of hospitals designated to accept such acquittees. Interestingly, recidivism among conditionally-released NGRI's is lower than among paroled convicts or unconditionally-released NGRI's Conditionally- released NGRI's show a good rate of compliance with the medical terms of their release, and in those cases where rehospitalization has been necessary, it was achieved with relative ease and rapidity (Maeder, 1985).

The American Psychiatric Association (APA) in its statement on the insanity defense (1983) recognizes the importance of the post-trial stage, especially in reference to violent NGRI acquittees. The APA has recommended that special legislation should constitute a board to include psychiatrists and other professionals representing the criminal justice system with the authority to confine, release, and reconfine NGRI acquittees. Not mentioned in the APA report, but implied, is that the legislature should also appropriate funds for the administration and implementation of such a system. Certainly, the best interests of the individual and society are served when the law and the behavioral sciences work together during the post-trial stage of the legal process.

A challenge confronts the court and mental health professionals who have the responsibility for serving and treating NGRI acquittees with PTSD. These acquittees are not as seriously ill as persons suffering from psychosis. Pathologic anxiety and dissociative episodes can usually be treated in a relatively short period of time. Hospital treatment may not be required; however, in lieu of alternative treatment systems, it can be expected that most NGRI acquittees with PTSD will be committed to a maximum security hospital for further evaluation. Even though PTSD is not a severe psychiatric disorder, certain precautions regarding confinement, release, supervision, and treatment should be taken, especially in the case of NGRI acquittees who have committed violent acts. As patients move from the hospital to the outpatient phase, the coordination of supervision and treatment is absolutely essential. Periodic reports to the court regarding the NGRI acquittee's progress and compliance with treatment should be mandatory. The involvement of a multidisciplinary board to review all cases at designated intervals ensures that the best interest of the individual and society are served. Such a system can provide better supervision than most probation and parole agencies and better ongoing treatment than most public mental health clinics. Ironically, PTSD may serve as the impetus for reform within the criminal justice system for a long-neglected group, the NGRI acquittees.

PTSD IN CRIMINAL TRIALS

The use of PTSD in the insanity defense is relatively new, and the "case law" is limited. Defenses based on PTSD have been advanced in cases ranging from murder, attempted murder, assault including rape, and weapon offenses to nonviolent crimes such as burglary, robbery, drug conspiracies, and tax fraud (Erlinger, 1983).

Murder, Attempted Murder, and PTSD

As has been mentioned, a Louisiana case involving a defendant charged with murder (State v. Heads, 1981) was the first in which PTSD and the insanity defense was used successfully during a jury trial. The following year, another case (People v. Wood, 1982) also successfully utilized PTSD and the insanity defense.

>Jearl Wood, a Vietnam-era veteran, attempted to murder his foreman following a dispute at work. In an ingenious and meticulously prepared presentation, Wood's attorney demonstrated to a jury that his client's conduct was related to combat experiences in Vietnam and was the result of a delayed PTSD. After an adjudication of not guilty by reason of insanity, it was determined at a post-trial commitment hearing that Wood was not dangerous at the time of the hearing and would not be dangerous in the future. He was released to receive outpatient treatment supervised by the court.

The Heads and Wood cases shared the following characteristics: (1) both defendants were Vietnam-era combat veterans; (2) except for the conduct that led to the criminal charges, both had little or no history of antisocial behavior; (3) PTSD and the insanity defense were argued before a jury; and (4) both men were found not guilty by reason of insanity. Unlike Heads, Wood did not testify at the trial, and he was released following trial with the proviso of court-supervised outpatient psychiatric treatment. In 1982, several juries found veterans accused of various violent crimes not guilty by reason of insanity because of PTSD. PTSD has also been a factor in other cases when charges have been reduced or veterans have received lighter sentences or were released on early parole. In each case, the veteran had served in heavy combat, was suffering from PTSD, and the attorney was able to demonstrate a link between combat experience and criminal conduct. The viability of the insanity defense and PTSD not related to war trauma remains to be seen.

Rape and PTSD

The presence of PTSD in a victim claiming sexual assault has been used by prosecuting attorneys to bolster their cases. In a Kansas case (State v. Marks, 1982), the defense asserted that sexual relations were consensual, whereas the woman contended that she was raped. There were no eyewitnesses, and evidence rested on the credibility of the complainant and defendant. During the trial a mental health professional testified that the woman suffered from a rape trauma syndrome (PTSD), thus indicating that a forcible assault had indeed taken place. The judge allowed the testimony, stating that it was relevant when the defendant argued that the victim consented to sexual intercourse, and as such the expert witness' opinion did not invade the providence of the jury. On appeal the State Supreme Court upheld the lower court's ruling that allowed the expert to testify.

In a case with the opposite outcome (Minnesota v. Saldana, 1982), the State Supreme Court overturned the conviction of a defendant accused of rape because an expert witness testified that the complainant suffered from a rape trauma syndrome (PTSD). The expert testimony was rejected because it "does not assist a jury in its fact-finding function," and "may not be introduced until further evidence of the scientific accuracy and reliability of the syndrome can be established." A new trial in which the expert would not be allowed to testify was ordered.

In a more recent case (People v. Pullins, 1985) where the defendant was convicted of first degree criminal sexual assault, the appellate court reversed and remanded with instructions, "The trial court erred in admitting evidence that the complainant suffered from rape trauma syndrome for the purpose of proving that a sexual assault occurred."

There is no doubt that in the future expert testimony and rape trauma syndrome will become more common (Burgess, 1983) and acceptable by the court. It would not be surprising if some women who have been raped in the past and have subsequently been charged with committing a criminal act will plead insanity related to a rape trauma syndrome.

Assault, Self-Defense, and PTSD

Battered women who kill abusing spouses may attempt to plead insanity, diminished responsibility, or self-defense utilizing PTSD to explain their actions (Raifman, 1983). It is possible for any person who has been traumatized and later develop a PTSD to claim a connection between altered mental functioning and criminal conduct. In an ironic twist, PTSD patients may be viewed as potentially violent and dangerous; hence self-defense against the PTSD sufferer would be seen as justifiable homicide. The vicissitudes of PTSD and the law seem bound only by the imagination of attorneys, but common sense and the restraint of a judge and jury usually prevail and will determine the limits of PTSD and the insanity defense.

THE FUTURE

The clamor and current criticism concerning the insanity defense continues, periodically incited by the appeals of Hinkley, the would-be assassin of President Reagan, for release from St. Elizabeth's Hospital. The

Hinckley case no doubt spurs sentiment against the insanity defense and, in part, contributed to changes in the federal law regarding insanity and resulted in the abolition of the insanity defense in a few states. The application and acceptance of the insanity defense, however, appears little changed. A recent study (Wettstein, Rogers, and Mulvey, 1986) disclosed the results of a survey which involved four full-time forensic psychiatrists working in a large mid-western city court clinic. Of the 203 consecutive defendants examined during 1984 and 1985, the psychiatrists concluded that 200 of the 203 met the criteria for the ALI test; sixty-seven percent met the M'Naughten test criteria and sixty-seven percent met the criteria for the ALI cognitive test. The investigators concluded that elimination of the volitional test for insanity reduces the psychiatrists' recommendations of insanity acquittals by twenty-eight percent. Interestingly, the outcome of trials which was available in eighty-eight cases disclosed no rejection of the insanity defense; ninty-three percent of the defendants were found not guilty by reason of insanity, three and one half percent were convicted, two and one half percent were found guilty but mentally ill, and one and one half percent were acquitted of charges. The polemics are protracted, but the praxis of psychiatry and the judicial result remain unchanged. This study supports the alarm of an outspoken critic of the insanity defense who ironically stated, "The Hinckley verdict served as a stimulus for organizations and individuals involving retention of the defense to conjoin the concept to state and federal laws more firmly than ever before" (Halpern, 1986).

Disagreements abound among pundits, politicians, and professional societies regarding the merits of the insanity defense. However, as Professor Ralph Slovenko of Wayne State Law School has aptly put it, "It is textbook learning that the insanity defense is essential to the moral integrity of the criminal law" (Slovenko, 1984). Maeder (1985) agrees and points out that the choice is between a draconian policy which would abolish the insanity defense and a compassionate law regarding criminal responsibility which recognizes mental illness. He cautions that there is no justice that is not tempered with mercy and that mercy run wild and untempered by justice is neither just nor merciful.

In the case of PTSD, there can be no question that objective tests will be developed to quantify pathologic anxiety and identify brain structures associated with anxiety and dissociative reactions. As evolving psychiatric concepts become based on more concrete criteria, treatment will become more predictable and effective. Disagreements will still occur, but arguments will involve the interpretation and analysis of more objective data. At the present time, the emergence of PTSD in the courtroom has forced mental health professionals to broaden and sharpen their clinical skills, benefiting both the law and the behavioral sciences.

THIRTEEN

PREVENTION

The prevention of disease, illness, or mental disorder has always been the goal of a health provider; however, like the patient who avoids doctors until illness strikes, mental health professionals give only lip service to prevention while concentrating on the treatment of manifest mental disorders. Cowen (1986) delineates two programmatic approaches to prevention: systems-centered and persons-centered. System approaches concentrate on changing social policy and injustices to forestall the sequelae of stressful life events. System-centered strategies focus on social action to reduce sources of stress and increase life opportunities for people. In prevention, the professionals who are system-oriented are specialists in the fields of epidemiology, communication and education, sociology, and public health. Person-centered strategies emphasize the development of skills and competencies in people to strengthen adaptive capacities. Person-centered professionals are patient-centered clinicians trained in psychiatry and psychology. Community and social psychiatrists and psychologists have attempted to bridge the gap between system and person oriented approaches to maximize the effectiveness of prevention programs.

Traditionally under a public health classification, there are three types of prevention: primary, secondary, and tertiary (Weston, 1975). Primary prevention refers to the elimination of those factors that cause or contribute to the development of disease. Early detection of pathology and the implementation of treatment as soon as possible is the task of secondary prevention. Tertiary prevention has been defined as the elimination or reduction of residual disability after illness. Although some investigators disagree with this classification and point out that prevention and treatment must be clearly differentiated (Munoz, 1986), no problem arises if one keeps in mind that primary prevention attempts to intervene before a disease or mental disorder is manifest, while secondary and tertiary prevention represent time periods after a disorder is recognized and treatment is proposed to prevent future disability.

In the field of psychiatry, prevention has been described (Caplan, 1964) as that body of professional knowledge both theoretical and practical that may be utilized to plan and carry out programs for reducing: the incidence of mental health disorders of all types in the population (primary prevention), the duration of a significant number of those mental disorders that do occur (secondary prevention), and the impairment that may result from these mental disorders (tertiary prevention). Caplan adapted traditional public health theories and practices for use in the mental health field and focused on two issues: (1) developing a list of past biopsychosocial stressful events and processes that were thought to increase the risk of future mental disorder in an exposed population; and (2) studying life crises which involved limited time periods of upset in the psychosocial functioning of individuals, precipitated by current exposure to environmental stressors, which appeared to be turning points in the development of mental disorder. More recently, Caplan (1986) has supplemented his original model by postulating: (1) competence as an internal constitutional and acquired quality of individuals that enables them to withstand the harmful effects of hazardous circumstances; and (2) social supports as an external mechanism that protects individuals against the damage that might be caused by environmental stressors.

PREVENTION AND PTSD

Programs and interventions designed to reduce the risk, and hence the incidence of PTSD constitute primary prevention. After a PTSD has developed, the identification and prompt treatment of the disorder reduce risks to health and shorten the duration of the mental disorder—secondary prevention. Programs of tertiary prevention decrease the prevalence of chronic PTSD and reduce morbidity and impairment.

Primary Prevention of PTSD

Although stress following trauma has been described and noted over the years, its codification, as mentioned, has occurred only recently (DSM-

III, 1980; DSM-III-R, 1987). However, outside professional circles, there is still a lack of awareness of the relationship between a mental disorder and trauma. News programs and documentaries occasionally report human emotional suffering caused by natural catastrophes or human-caused disasters, and these reports often mention that emotional reactions following a trauma may exist long after the physical wounds have healed. The idea that accidents or industrial trauma may precipitate or be associated with a psychiatric disorder is slowly being disseminated, but public awareness of this concept, a form of primary prevention, needs bolstering.

Places where industrial organization exists offer the best opportunity for implementing programs of primary prevention (McLean, 1975). Most large companies employ safety experts who conduct meetings on a regular basis to reduce or eliminate the occurrence of accidents that cause physical injury. However, information related to mental health and mental disorders is usually excluded, when its addition would require little extra effort. The theme that all accidents, regardless of the extent of physical injury, are stressful should be highlighted. There is no mind-body dichotomy, rather the brain and body together respond to a trauma. An understanding of this fact by workers could maximize acceptance of psychiatric consultation or treatment if an accident were to occur in the future. Too often, workers equate mental disorders with "craziness" or feel that an emotional response to trauma indicates weakness or a "lack of manliness." These myths can be erased during safety meetings. There are a wide range of emotional reactions to trauma, the employees can be told, and most mental symptoms dissipate and eventually disappear with time. Industrial psychiatrists or psychologists can elaborate on treatment interventions that are available when mental symptoms persist beyond four to six weeks. During primary prevention educational programs are aimed at improving the competency of workers to adapt to any future trauma.

Case histories or videotaped interviews with persons who have developed a PTSD can augment primary prevention by explaining the psychiatric signs and symptoms following an accident as well as concepts of treatment, coping skills, and the importance of a good social support system. Once workers are acquainted with the syndrome of PTSD, no surprises await them if they are involved in an accident and experience symptoms of a stress disorder. Knowledge that effective treatment is available also decreases stress. Cries of faker or malingerer by fellow workers and supervisors can be quelled when the relationship between trauma and stress is understood by all.

Programs of primary prevention in an industrial setting are easy to implement if management supports the concept. However, in small or poorly administered companies, primary prevention becomes a more difficult goal to attain. Outside of private industry, primary prevention becomes a public health responsibility. Here, persons at risk must depend upon information available through governmental health and safety agencies and the public media. Television and radio programs on public broadcasting systems and articles in popular periodicals can be of great assistance in the dissemination of information concerning trauma and stress. Unfortunately, as has been discovered in the "wellness movement," persons seem unmotivated to act in their own behalf until after the fact and circumstances necessitate action. Often management seems unmoved to change hazardous working conditions until a lawsuit exposes negligence. Non-mandatory programs emphasizing principles of primary prevention as it relates to trauma and stress might be difficult to put in place, but their implementation is not an impossible task.

In primary prevention circles, "empowerment" is considered to be a key factor and its lack a source of psychological stress (Rappaport, 1984). Although lack of empowerment may be a system- level problem, it impacts adversely on workers who feel they have little control over unsafe work conditions. Moreover, if an accident and injury does occur and management displays a lack of interest or little sympathy for the disabled worker, a feeling of powerlessness contributes to stress and further emotional disability. A lack of empowerment extends to the consulting room when workers, who after their physical injury has healed, continue to experience symptoms and encounter a physician who has little insight or understanding about the psychological sequelae of trauma. Perhaps a lack of empowerment leads many injured workers to a lawyer; the mechanism of a lawsuit "empowers" the victim. Unfortunately, power achieved in this manner dissipates after the lawsuit has been resolved, leaving the victim unempowered, still symptomatic, and unemployed.

Secondary Prevention

People who develop PTSD know that something is wrong with them but tend to attribute symptoms to some physical process. Likewise, relatives and friends notice changes in the patient's demeanor following a trauma, but unless previously instructed, feel helpless to intervene. Quick identification and detection of emotionally upset persons following exposure to a trauma depends upon the observer's familiarity with key signs and symptoms of PTSD. When physical injury is present, ministration to fractures, lacerations, or bruises understandably supersedes attention to the emotional consequences of the trauma, but mental reactions must not be ignored. Any trauma which poses a realistic threat to life or limb is capable of precipitating PTSD. When persons display or complain of the cardinal characteristics of PTSD (Chapter 6), prompt intervention is warranted.

One need not have the clinical skills of a psychiatrist or psychologist to make a determination that a traumatized person has changed. In fact, those who have been closest to the patient before the accident may be in a better position to note the reaction to trauma and subsequent alterations in behavior. In work-related trauma, supervisors and fellow employees will certainly notice differences in overt behavior. Such observations can be the impetus for referral of the traumatized person to an appropriate mental health professional.

In industrial settings, a nurse, paramedic, or industrial physician usually has first contact with a traumatized worker. After the injury has been assessed, it is wise to engage patients in a discussion concerning their emotional response to the trauma. Relating the details of the accident to the company nurse or doctor allows for catharsis and attests to management's interest in the worker's welfare. Both can be extremely therapeutic and are a part of secondary prevention. Injured individuals who are near retirement age are particularly sensitive to the psychological effects of trauma because injury seems to magnify the perception of waning power due to aging. Therefore, older workers should receive more emotional support from supervisors and professionals. Persons who have been involved in previous accidents or have a past history of mental illness should also be targeted for more intensive psychiatric evaluation and intervention. To ensure compliance, sensitivity and good judgment must be mixed when injured persons are referred to psychiatrists for evaluation and treatment following trauma. Family members should be involved as quickly as possible and an atmosphere of hope, encouragement, and positive expectation should be fostered.

For many persons involved in a traumatic incident, professional assistance may first be encountered in a trauma center or the emergency room of a hospital. Commonly, if the injury is not severe as confirmed by examinations and x-rays, emergency room physicians send the patient home with instructions to contact the family doctor if symptoms persist. Quick dismissal by the emergency room physician without adequate explanation and emotional support plants in the mind of the patient the idea of an incomplete examination with the possibility of an undetected physical defect. Victims may awaken the next day racked with pain caused by sprained muscles and a belief that they are seriously injured. Family doctors or specialists are then consulted and examinations including x-rays repeated. If no serious physical abnormalities are diagnosed, patients are usually sent home with prescriptions for muscle relaxants and analgesics. Failure to respond to this regimen often leads physicians to the sardonic conclusion that the patients have a high serum porcelain level and are crocks. Unenthusiastic treatment, referral, or dismissal of the patient can result when the clinician misses the diagnosis of PTSD. The opportunity for secondary prevention is lost, and the patient proceeds to the chronic stage of the stress disorder. In the experience of the author, the preceding sequence of events is too common. When the trauma has resulted in observable physical injury, including fractures or muscle sprains, physicians are frequently perplexed when symptoms persist long after the expected time of healing. In many instances the psychological response to trauma is ignored or minimized and a diagnosis of PTSD is never considered.

Whether they be experts in traumatology (orthopedic surgeons, neurosurgeons, forensic psychiatrists) or family doctors, physicians must be alert to the signs and symptoms of PTSD in those patients who report for examination and treatment following a trauma. In addition, physicians and other clinicians should be on guard to the likelihood of PTSD when patients remain symptomatic despite vigorous medical treatment. The normal physical and psychological response to trauma involves a gradual diminution of symptoms, so when symptoms continue or intensify, a stress disorder should be suspected and a psychiatric consultation ordered. Clinicians should always secure information from relatives or friends to expand the patient's history and substantiate symptomatic behavior. Early detection and intervention mean prophylaxis and secondary prevention, for when a PTSD becomes chronic, treatment and resolution of the disorder are more difficult.

Caplan (1986) has proposed the following interventions which help to repair cognitive erosion, reduce and contain negative emotional arousal, and extend material assistance in mastering the predicament:

1. Repeated short contacts during crisis to satisfy increased dependency needs.
2. Support strategic withdrawal at height of crisis.

3. Then support active confrontation of problems.
4. Help family members communicate with each other.
5. Help plan activities to solve crisis problems.
6. Help them bear the frustration of unknown outcome and urge perseverance despite confusion.
7. Warn them about danger of expectable fatigue.
8. Maintain hope.
9. Encourage invoking outside help and counteract shame that this means weakness.
10. Remind them of their pre-crisis identity. Do not validate crisis-eroded identity of weak helplessness.
11. Use family members to express negative feelings and help each other master them.
12. Counteract blaming of self or others to relieve tension.

The author has described many of these therapeutic interventions previously (Scrignar, 1983, 1984) and they are to be found in Chapters 8 and 9 of this volume.

Tertiary Prevention

Tertiary prevention becomes an issue when primary and secondary prevention have failed because they were not implemented or were ineffective. Tertiary is equivalent to the chronic third stage of PTSD, when the stress disorder goes unrecognized, undiagnosed, and untreated. Disability, which may lead to lifelong invalidism, is the hallmark of Stage III and leaves people demoralized and despondent. Untreated chronic PTSD can lead to unemployment, insolvency, disruption of family life, Psychoactive Substance Use Disorder, depression, alienation from others, suicide, and a possible lifetime of nonproductivity. Tertiary prevention attempts to reduce or eliminate these chronic aftermaths of PTSD.

Frequently, chronic PTSD patients are grouped and labeled as suffering from Disproportionate Disability Syndrome, Catastrophic Disability Syndrome, or some other catchall classification. Such appellations focus attention on chronic, unrelenting, end-stage disablement and fail to place in perspective the onset and course leading to disability. As in secondary prevention, tertiary prevention depends upon the correct identification of those suffering from PTSD. However, chronicity often obscures the basic stress disorder, making diagnosis difficult. If the constellation of symptoms

TABLE 13–1
Persons in Contact with Patient following Trauma

Relatives or friends

Employer (supervisor)

Industrial nurse, paramedic, physician (if available and trauma occurred at
    workplace)

Emergency room physician

Family doctor

Medical specialist
    Orthopedic surgeon
    Neurosurgeon
    Other

Physiotherapist

Vocational rehabilitation specialist, occupational therapist

Lawyer

Pain unit/rehabilitatin center personnel

    Surgeon (neuro or orthopedic)
    Psychiatrist
    Psychologist
    Nurse
    Social worker
    Support personnel (aides, rehabilitation experts, etc.)

Psychiatrist, psychologist, social worker

Mental health clinic, psychiatric hospital personnel

Forensic psychiatrist

Source: Compiled by author.

peculiar to PTSD persist in a patient following a well-documented trauma, this should alert the clinician to the possibility of a chronic stress disorder. In addition, the continuance of symptoms in lieu of objective physical findings and lack of response to usual medical treatment should be reason enough for psychiatric consultation.

Practical considerations involving tertiary prevention arise when certain questions are asked: Who will identify and refer chronic PTSD patients? To whom should such patients be referred? Any of the professionals listed in Table 13-1 could recognize, refer, or treat Stage III patients. In many instances, however, the mental health profession participates in neither the identification nor the treatment of such patients. Psychiatrists, psychologists, and social workers are often not consulted unless litigation is pending and lawyers request a forensic evaluation, not treatment. How, then, can the chronic PTSD patient be identified and helped?

System-level approaches and strategies can help to identify potential PTSD patients. Legislation passed by the federal government funded outreach programs in vet centers for Vietnam veterans in an attempt to curtail the chronic effects of PTSD (Walker and Nash, 1981). Women who have been sexually assaulted are identified and treated when rape crisis centers establish a liaison with law enforcement agencies. The publicity attendant to natural or man-made disasters quickly attracts mental health professions who can consult with governmental agencies to coordinate psychological assistance to victims. Not as well- publicized are the psychological needs of crime victims or the estimated five to six million children, spouses, and elderly individuals who are neglected, battered, and abused in the United States each year. System-level strategies involving the police, public health agencies, human service organizations, and agencies for children and the elderly are fertile areas for the implementation of prevention programs and the identification of potential PTSD patients. Trauma centers deal primarily with the physical needs of injured patients; however, its network offers an opportunity for referrals and the implementation of prevention programs. The environment's potential for producing a serious injury to an individual is almost limitless, as are the opportunities for innovating programs of prevention.

Once victims of trauma are identified, programs involving person-centered strategies can be put in place. Cowen (1985) has suggested that linkages between certain life situations or stressful events and psychological programs tend to forestall predictable negative emotional sequelae and that the development of relevant skills and competencies (competence-enrichment) strengthen adaptive capacities. The goal is to short-circuit otherwise predictable psychological problems and to bolster well- being.

Caplan's (1986) person-centered strategies are useful in tertiary prevention, either individually or in groups. These guidelines and emotional interventions, originally intended for use during a crisis, can be modified for chronic PTSD patients:

1. Intervene close in time and place to crisis.
2. Arouse anticipatory distress by describing expectable stress in evocative detail.
3. Predict boundaries of intensity and duration of likely pain and discomfort.
4. Urge active self-help and help from others to reduce discomfort.
5. Arouse hope that such activity will lead to mastery.
6. Guide family members in helping each other.
7. Emphasize normality of expectable cognitive and emotional disorganization and counteract fear of psychological illness.

For ongoing research, consultation, and treatment, trauma centers especially designed to meet the psychological needs of potential patients could easily be established. A residential center, a day hospital, or clinic could serve as the base for services and the development of outreach programs. A comprehensive, multidisciplinary approach would include individual sessions, group treatment, educational programs, family conferences, as well as consultation with community agencies and the legal profession. The programs should be aimed at increasing an individual's competence to master stressful situations and to strengthen social support systems. Outreach programs would focus on system-level approaches to impact governmental policy, private industry, law enforcement agencies, and existing health maintenance organizations in the private and public sectors. Prevention and treatment occur at different points on a continuous time line, but share the same goal—the alleviation of human suffering.

CONCLUSION

In workers' compensation claims and personal injury suits, the recognition of psychic trauma or psychic stress has been increasing. An important trend was noted by Larsen (1986) in his review of 266 applicants for workers' compensation. The majority of his cases (fifty-eight percent) involved an alleged work related psychiatric injury, while in about one-third of the cases, the initial injury was said to be physical. Less than ten percent involved a mixed physical/psychic trauma leading to an emotional disability. Sixty-seven percent of the cases were from service-oriented jobs and the remainder consisted of labor and trade occupations. As the service industry expands, the number of service workers who are involved in stress-at-work will also climb, as will the claims for workers' compensation and personal injury suits. Larsen urges more employee assistance programs and more rational management approaches to meet the need of this growing patient population. A more fundamental recommendation would involve the implementation of programs of primary prevention.

The therapeutic concepts and strategies mentioned in Chapters 8 and 9 are applicable to primary, secondary, and tertiary prevention of PTSD and can be employed in almost any setting. Whether these interventions are used to educate persons to prevent or lessen the emotional impact of a trauma (primary prevention), to intervene promptly following a trauma (secondary prevention), or to eliminate or reduce chronicity (terti y prevention), morbidity is reduced and patients can be returned to a useful and productive life. Prevention can also be translated into a saving of time and money, a fact which is appealing to private enterprise.

Prevention, given only lip service in medical and graduate schools, is almost completely ignored in the behavioral sciences. Even in this book this chapter comes at the end, almost as an afterthought, and probably will be skipped or skimmed by most readers. This does not contravene the importance of preventive interventions in the management of PTSD.

FOURTEEN

CASE HISTORIES

CASE ONE: AUTOMOBILE ACCIDENT

Mrs. C, a widow in her late forties, tearfully related that six months previously she was involved in an automobile accident that resulted in the death of her husband. Since that time she had had crying spells, lost 15 pounds, felt fatigued, and had difficulties sleeping. In addition to symptoms of depression, the patient complained of anxiety and agitation, frequent nightmares in which she relived the accident, headaches, hot flashes associated with sweating, heavy feelings in her chest with periodic palpitations, nausea ("I have a tight knot in my stomach all of the time"), dizzy spells, difficulties in concentration, irritability, and fears of going crazy and of being alone, especially at night. She also had a phobia of driving on expressways or bridges and experienced phobic anxiety whenever she was in an automobile. She also stated that her adolescent son was becoming a behavioral problem.

History of the Present Illness

One Saturday afternoon about six months ago, the patient's husband was driving her to a suburban shopping center. They were traveling on an expressway, and the traffic had backed up, forcing her husband to slow, then stop the car. While waiting for the traffic to clear, her husband suddenly hollered, "Watch out!" His warning was cut short by a terrible collision with a fully-loaded dump truck traveling at high speed. The truck hit the rear of the car very hard and propelled it forward into the air. The door of the car burst open, and Mrs. C and her husband were hurled out of the vehicle onto the pavement. She got to her feet shakily and went to her husband's assistance. She looked down at him and saw that he was bleeding profusely from the head and was unconscious. Taking his head in her hands to comfort him, she noticed that his skull was cracked and brains seemed to be oozing out. Screaming hysterically, she begged onlookers to come to her aid. No help was forthcoming for almost an hour until the police cleared the traffic jam, allowing the passage of an ambulance. Inside the ambulance she was aghast at the pale gray coloring of her husband's face and collapsed when ambulance attendants told her he had multiple fractures, was critically injured, and "probably would not make it." At the hospital Mrs. C was revived and treated for minor bruises of her legs and one hand. Her husband had been pronounced dead on arrival, and afterward she felt guilty because she had survived and her husband had not.

At home Mrs. C felt terrible. Sleep was interrupted by nightmares of the accident that depicted the bloodied and crushed head of her husband. Fatigue followed insomnia, and her mood fluctuated from irritability to despair. She was plagued with thoughts about the accident, which she relived again and again in her imagination. At times she experienced intense anxiety, severe headaches, and dizzy spells, and believed she was going crazy. Heavy feelings in her chest were punctuated by palpitations. Nausea and stomach pains led to anorexia and weight loss. Her phobia of driving on elevated expressways, bridges, and in unfamiliar places limited her mobility. Elsewhere when driving alone she was tense and nervous, especially in heavy traffic. She became obsessed about the accident and the death of her husband. In a ritualistic manner she visited the cemetery two or three times a week to place flowers and to pray.

Additional stress emerged when the patient's adolescent son became unruly. After her physical symptoms intensified, mystifying her physicians, she was hospitalized for a "thorough physical examination." A myriad of examinations and tests revealed no organic base for her symptoms. She was discharged from the hospital and told that although she had not yet gotten over the death of her husband, in time she would. Time did not heal and she was referred for psychiatric treatment.

Past History

The patient's memories of her childhood were basically happy ones. As the youngest of four children, she admitted that she was the center of attention and probably "a bit spoiled." Her preschool years passed pleasantly as did grade school. She had many friends and was an excellent student and the "teacher's pet." Academic excellence continued in high school, where she was involved in many extracurricular activities. She also had an active social life and a "steady" boyfriend whom she married upon graduation. College was interrupted by pregnancy, and her husband got a job to support the developing family. The years passed comfortably, centered around family life. She had three children and spent the major part of the next 10 years tending to the responsibilities of wife and mother. She and her husband were well-matched. Although they had many friends, the family was close-knit and did not require much outside social interaction. At the time of the accident, her daughter and older son were married, while the younger son, in his late teens, was still living at home. In a year, when their younger son had completed high school, she and her husband planned to retire and had purchased a camper in order to leisurely tour the United States. These plans were tragically ended by the accident.

Family History

Both of the patient's parents were deceased. She remembers her father as a stern but kindly man who doted upon her when she was young. Her mother, the disciplinarian of the family, was recalled less fondly but respectfully. "Mother was a hard worker who made many demands upon herself and her family," the patient reminisced. Her family was very religious and she was inculcated with a puritan work ethic. She managed good relationships with her parents until their death, even though they were geographically separated by over 500 miles. Her father died of heart disease and her mother of cancer. Her two older sisters and a brother live in different states, and she maintains regular contact with them.

Treatment

The patient's ordeal—the shouts of warning from her husband, collision with the speeding dump truck, being hurled into the air and onto the pavement, the sight of her seriously injured husband, the announcement of his death—was a severe trauma. It was clear that her life would never be the same. The sequence of events leading to her husband's death impacted upon her nervous system and produced high levels of autonomic activity that culminated with her fainting in the ambulance. Subsequently, scenes of the accident and its aftermath dominated her mind and prolonged anxiety, which deepened her depression. In an agitated state, prior to psychiatric treatment, she could not piece her life together and lamented her deceased husband while pitying herself and excoriating the careless truck driver. Litigation eventually ensued.

During the explanation-education stage of treatment, the mental mechanisms underlying PTSD and depression were discussed. Concepts of retraumatization and cognitive causes of depression were related to the patient, emphasizing that rumination ruins recovery. Techniques of encephalic reconditioning can counter these obsessional proclivities, the patient was told. Time spent thinking about the accident and its consequences, particularly the death of her husband, was reduced when the patient learned the techniques of thought stopping and positive encephalic practice. She was also urged to engage in attention-capturing activities whenever she thought about the accident and to avoid protracted periods of solitude. The patient received training in relaxation, including both PMR and self-hypnosis. She was an adept pupil and was able to utilize these techniques to reduce anxiety and later to initiate sleep. Self-hypnosis was also used as an adjuvant in encephalic reconditioning to change anxiety-evoking or pessimistic and gloomy thoughts. Audio tapes containing instructions regarding PMR and self-hypnosis were prepared for her, and it was recommended that she listen to these tapes daily. At the onset of treatment, medication was prescribed for depression and sleep disturbance. The tricyclic antidepressant, trazodone HCl (Desyrel) was prescribed, and the patient responded well to a dose of 100 milligrams before bedtime. Insomnia was treated by flurazepam 30 milligrams before bedtime. The patient remained on trazodone for several months, but regular use of a sedative was required for only a few weeks.

Although possessing excellent secretarial skills, Mrs. C was not working and spent most of the day at home alone. Under these conditions she was vulnerable to anxiety and depression, because she had ample time and opportunity to think and morbidly obsess about the accident and its consequences. Frequent trips to the cemetery each week to pray and to place flowers at her husband's grave were exercises in self-torment and extended beyond the bounds of propriety and normal grief. During problem-solving sessions, she was encouraged to cease her funereal pilgrimage and to visit the grave site only at appropriate occasions, such as birthday, anniversary, or All Saints' Day. Discussions during problem-solving centered on reinvolving her in the outside world. She expressed an interest in returning to work as a secretary and taking some college courses. It was decided initially to concentrate on work, since that activity would regularize her life. From eight to five each day, her time would be occupied and she would have an opportunity to meet and talk with other people. Although her husband's life insurance left her comfortably situated, money earned as a result of work added to her security. She quickly procured a secretarial position and also enrolled in a night course at a community college.

The patient quickly improved—her anxiety lessened and her mood elevated. However, during the evening and especially on weekends, she experienced intense headaches and gastrointestinal upsets. Her self-assessment form revealed that symptomatic behavior was associated with thoughts about the accident, the death of her husband, loneliness, and the future. She was encouraged to continue the use of thought stopping and positive encephalic practice and to consider involvement in social/recreational activities. It was recommended that she join a community social organization devoted to the needs of those who have been separated from their spouses by divorce or death. She began attending lectures, parties, dances, and other events at the community organization, and her interest in people picked up. Even though she was a pleasant woman and a good conversationalist, Mrs. C was ill at ease and awkward with men. She had been married for over 25 years and had never dated a man other than her late husband. She felt guilty and acted cautiously when talking casually to men, thinking that she was being disloyal to her deceased husband. She had to be disabused of that idea and persuaded that guilt was inappropriate. Gradually her discomfort subsided and she began enjoying herself socially. Work, school, and social engagements filled her time in a pleasing and pleasurable way. However, she reported that her younger son was becoming hostile. A family conference was convened to discuss the son's negativistic attitude and belligerent behavior. The boy disclosed that he was angry because his mother was involved in too many activities. He also felt that his deceased father would not approve of his mother dating other men. It soon became apparent that the son was depressed, and his complaints reflected the need for support and reassurance from his mother. These issues were discussed and resolved during family conferences in combination with several individual sessions with the boy.

After six months of treatment, Mrs. C was still phobic about driving across elevated expressways and bridges and in unfamiliar places. Even when driving elsewhere, she became wary and anxious when the weather was bad or the traffic heavy, fearing a rear end collision. She still could not drive or be driven near the area where the original accident took place. A program of in vivo systematic desensitization was developed. Desensitization began with the least anxiety-evoking driving situation in the hierarchy. The first assignment was driving on an elevated expressway in good weather with little or no traffic, until the first exit was reached. When the patient drove her car in that situation without experiencing appreciable anxiety, she was instructed to move up to a more difficult and anxiety-evoking one. The patient then began to drive longer distances in heavier traffic, which eventually included inclement weather. Bridges were added next, and the patient was advised to bring a friend during initial in vivo driving sessions. As the patient became desensitized of her fear of driving across small bridges, longer bridges were added. Finally she was able to drive across all bridges by herself. She was advised to keep a log of her driving experiences, which was discussed at each therapy session. Eventually, she was able to drive on the section of the expressway where her husband was killed.

The patient was terminated following 58 sessions of treatment extending over a 14-month period. Anxiety symptoms abated as did headaches and gastrointestinal upsets. Her phobia of driving on expressways and bridges and in unfamiliar places was successfully treated, but occasionally she was apprehensive in heavy traffic. She no longer obsessed about the accident but at times gets tearful when she thinks about the loss of her husband. Her nightmares have ceased, and her sleep patterns have returned to normal. Her depression was alleviated and the antidepressant discontinued. Her appetite returned, and she gained the weight she had lost. The patient's youngest son settled down and now attends college. Mrs. C's social life is good. She has a steady male friend and is contemplating marriage. Three years following termination, the patient reported that her lawsuit was settled favorably and she maintained her improvement.

CASE TWO: RAPE*

Miss D, a young elementary school teacher, had been raped and complained of an extreme fear of being alone at night. She ruminated about the possibility of someone breaking into her house, and this interfered with sleep. She was hypersensitive to night noises and exhibited a startle

---

*Reprinted from C.B. Scrignar (1983), *Stress Strategies: The Treatment of the Anxiety Disorders*, Basel, S. Karger.

response whenever she heard a quick, sharp noise. The school teacher's anxiety symptoms were so intense and unbearable that she moved from her apartment into her parent's house where she felt more comfortable. Her phobia of being alone at night conflicted with her desire to be independent.

History of Present Illness

One and a half years prior to treatment, the patient was raped late one night in her apartment. The odious incident began when she was awakened by noises in her apartment. She opened her eyes and saw an indistinct form in her bedroom. Her scream was cut short by a powerful hand held over her mouth. At the same instant, she felt the prick of a knife point on her neck and heard a deep voice admonishing her to be quiet or she would be dead. A few minutes later, the hand left her mouth and began tearing off her nightclothes. The sharp point of the knife was still at her throat as the man raped her. The patient felt physically numb, but her mind was racing wildly. Death or mutilation was inevitable, she thought, and her body responded with severe palpitations, dyspnea, and trembling. After he had finished, the rapist said he would not kill her. Momentary relief turned to terror when the rapist said he would murder her if she told anyone about the incident. The masked miscreant bound and gagged the young school teacher and left. For an hour she remained still, her body racked with fear, thinking that the rapist might return. Finally, with great difficulty, she freed herself and telephoned her parents. Her father rushed to the apartment and took his sobbing daughter home. Miss D refused to call the police, suspecting that the rapist was the janitor of the building and feared further abuse and possible retaliation. Her parents reluctantly agreed, but insisted that she move out of the apartment into their home.

The young woman was still shaken after the incident and experienced nightmares, insomnia, extreme anxiety, and a hypersensitivity to night noises. She ruminated about the trauma and had vivid recollections of the rape, openly expressing the sentiment that she was lucky to be alive. While symptoms gradually subsided as time passed, she remained fearful of the dark, especially when she was alone. One year passed and Miss D, desirous of autonomous living, told her parents she would like to move into her own place. Her father purchased a small house for her located in a good neighborhood. Before the patient moved into the house, the father hired a home security specialist to make the home intruder-proof. Dead-bolt locks, burglar bars, an alarm system, and outdoor lights were installed to safeguard the patient from interlopers. At the patient's request, her mother stayed with her during the first week, but on the first night alone she was restless and could not sleep. The young woman presaged a repetition of the rape and was startled and alerted by normal nocturnal noises. On the second night, the patient, now fatigued and frantic, phoned her father and asked to be taken home. Shortly thereafter the patient sought treatment.

Past History

The patient described her childhood as happy. Until college she attended an all-girl parochial school. Miss D was an excellent student and, although shy and reserved, had many friends. She did not date until her university years and even then did so sporadically, never having a steady boyfriend. During this time she attended a university in the community and lived with her parents. Following graduation she began teaching elementary school, and two years later, against her parents' wishes, began living by herself. She lived in her apartment successfully and happily for almost two years before the rape incident.

Family History

Miss D was the oldest of five children. Her parents, staunch Catholics, were hard-working people who were overly involved in the lives of their children. They tended to be overprotective, the mother especially, making unsolicited decisions for the patient. As a reaction to this control by her parents, she desired independence and got her own apartment.

Treatment

Although the violence of the rape had occurred a year and a half earlier, the patient kept the sexual assault alive by imagining a recurrence. The concept of encephalic retraumatization was related to the young school teacher during the explanation- education phase of treatment in the context of a PTSD. For over an hour during and after the rape, she suffered from the effects of high levels of autonomic nervous system activity. While in this state of autonomic arousal, she became conditioned to various elements associated with her trauma. Being alone, darkness, and night noises continued to serve as conditioned stimuli for anxiety. Over the course of a year and a half, the acute symptoms of PTSD had subsided. Anxiety, nightmares, insomnia, and ruminations were reduced in intensity and frequency. A recrudescence of symptoms occurred when she moved into her own house and was alone at night. Being alone, darkness, and night noises vivified memories of the rape, and this encephalic activity increased anxiety. The resurgence of symptoms was frightening and caused the patient to move back into her parents' home. A reduction in anxiety and a feeling of relief reinforced this pattern of phobic avoidance. Her confidence was shaken when she unsuccessfully coped with her anxiety. Nightmares and ruminations about being raped, together with anxiety and insomnia fostered dependency upon her parents and interfered with the school teacher's desire to be independent. Coercion, the forceful subjugation and violation of individual will, is terrible, the patient was told during explanation-education, but once a vile act is over, it must be put aside and forgotten. Concepts of conditioning, phobic avoidance, and phobic anxiety were explained in the context of a PTSD (Burgess, 1983). Furthermore, the patient was reassured, that anxiety-reducing interventions, including systematic desensitization were methods that would be utilized to successfully treat her disorder.

The patient's anxiety had become chronic. Therefore, she received training in relaxation consisting of PMR and self- hypnosis. The patient was to practice these techniques daily and to utilize relaxation methods whenever she felt anxious. In addition, PMR or self-hypnosis could curtail insomnia and serve as a substitute for a sedative.

Understandably, the patient was preoccupied with the circumstances of the rape, but ruminations and faulty interpretations served only to perpetuate her PTSD. Miss D had to believe that she was in a safe environment at night, and that proper precautions (dead-bolt locks, burglar bars, alarm system, outside lights) would prevent a repetition of the rape. Although this is not 100 percent true, these precautions are the best defense against assault, along with prudent judgment and common sense. Although security may be imperfect, rapists do not lurk behind every bush, and one cannot live in a state of constant fear. Miss D, while lying in bed at night, misinterpreted normal night noises as signs of forced entry by a sadistic rapist, and these encephalic activities prophesying constant danger of an assault generated and maintained high anxiety. The condition of darkness and being alone also stimulated thoughts and images about a sexual assault, death, and mutilation, which in turn stimulated anxiety. To counter encephalically produced anxiety, she was taught techniques of encephalic reconditioning. It was suggested that thought-and image-stopping procedures as well as positive encephalic practice would reduce the flow of encephalic stimuli and diminish anxiety. The patient was encouraged to practice these procedures as often as necessary and to insert appropriate self-statements correcting fallacious thinking, such as "I have taken the necessary precautions and my home is safe. Those noises I hear are the normal sounds of a slumbering city. I have experienced a terrible assault but I have survived." Encephalic reconditioning was facilitated when she filled out a self-assessment form daily and discussed it during sessions.

Since Miss D was extremely apprehensive and her symptoms were beginning to interfere with her work, medication (diazepam 5 milligrams) was prescribed three times daily for two weeks. Insomnia prevented proper rest and fatigue interfered with her functioning as a school teacher, so flurazepam hydrochloride 30 milligrams was temporarily prescribed before bedtime until she mastered techniques of muscle relaxation and self-hypnosis.

The patient's phobia was now addressed, and imaginal systematic desensitization proceeded with the hierarchical theme of being alone at home. The variables associated with this theme were time and illumination. Desensitization began with scenes of being alone for periods of short duration and high levels of illumination. For example, the first scene was: You are in your house alone for 10 minutes and it is broad daylight. Time spent in the house was increased and the level of illumination decreased as the hierarchy progressed. Subsequent scenes were: (1) You are in your house alone for one hour and it is twilight. (2) You are in your house alone for two hours. It is dark outside, but your house is fully lighted. (3) You are in your bedroom alone and resting with the nightlight on. (4) You are in your own bedroom alone, attempting sleep, and the room is dark.

During in vivo desensitization, the presence of the mother for a predetermined time each night and the luminosity of the bedroom were variables. As desensitization progressed, the mother's time each night was limited, and the light in the bedroom was lessened by the use of a rheostat. Undue anxiety during in vivo desensitization was to be managed by muscle relaxation, self- hypnosis, and encephalic reconditioning. Diazepam was to be used only if necessary.

With the patient's permission, a family conference was held and the mother was included as a member of the treatment team. Techniques of in vivo desensitization were explained to the mother as they related to the phobic portion of her daughter's PTSD. The mother was a worrier and had to be persuaded that her daughter was a grown woman who could take care of herself. The mother also had to be convinced that the security precautions to safeguard the house were adequate. With some hesitancy the mother and daughter agreed to follow the proposed treatment plan. At times, this proved to be difficult because the mother was reluctant to leave at night if her daughter displayed any anxiety. This issue was mediated and desensitization progressed satisfactorily.

Treatment terminated after 11 sessions extending over a four- month period. Miss D was able to sleep in her own house with minimal discomfort and eventually with ease. Her nightmares and insomnia ceased. Her anxiety diminished significantly, and her ruminations about the trauma gradually subsided over time. Two years following termination, the patient was experiencing no difficulty sleeping and was able to stay in her house alone whenever she desired. Occasionally, thoughts about the rape intruded upon her mind, but she was able to use thought stopping and relaxation techniques successfully to eliminate them. She was enjoying her work as a school teacher and had a steady boyfriend.

CASE THREE: AIRPLANE CRASH

Mr. A, a married businessman in his early thirties, was in a commercial jet liner crash, following which he developed insomnia, nightmares of airplanes crashing, severe headaches, generalized anxiety, problems in concentration, and marital conflicts with a diminished interest in sex. He also felt anxious when he heard or saw a jet aircraft. A phobia of flying in airplanes restricted his travel and interfered with his business enterprises.

History of Present Illness

Three months after the crash Mr. A sought treatment. He recalled that his airplane had landed at an intermediate city and, following transfer of passengers and baggage, was beginning its takeoff. It was nighttime and he was in his seat dozing, having concluded a long day of business. Suddenly, the undercarriage collapsed, and the airplane skidded down the runway on its belly. The sound of metal scraping, rending, and tearing filled his ears, and when he looked out of the windows, both wings appeared to be on fire. The lights inside the airplane went out, and as the plane came to a stop, the interior of the aircraft was dimly illuminated by flames issuing from both wings. Confusion grew into pandemonium as passengers began to scream in fear and scramble for the exits. The almost complete darkness was pierced by dim emergency lights, and he hurried behind a flight attendant to one of the emergency exits. The flight attendant struggled with the latch, but it would not budge and the exit could not be opened. Other passengers pressed behind him, shoving and shouting before they were led away to another emergency exit. Mr. A felt trapped and feared for his life believing that the airplane would explode burning him to death. His heart began to pound wildly and he was gasping for breath when a flight attendant grabbed his arm and led him to another exit. He slid down an escape chute, landing heavily on his right ankle, spraining it severely. As he limped away from the burning aircraft to a safe area, he paused and watched the conflagration. He marveled at his escape from death or serious injury and began to feel nauseated as his body trembled and shook uncontrollably. Mr. A and the rest of the passengers were bussed to the airport terminal, a fitting term he later mused, where they were taken to a VIP lounge and given free spirits. He accepted the free liquor but refused tickets for the next flight home and instead took a train.

Upon returning home Mr. A had difficulty sleeping and experienced vivid nightmares about airplane crashes. Anxiety was evoked when he heard the sound of jet engines or saw an airplane. He refused to fly, although this resulted in great inconvenience and seriously affected his business. He began to obsess about accidents, injury, and death, frequently complaining of headaches and a feeling of nausea. Irritability replaced a calm and friendly demeanor, and marital problems emerged. Lovemaking became less frequent, and he experienced problems getting and maintaining an erection during sexual intercourse. He was cross with his children and caustic with his business customers. Finally, with the encouragement and insistence of his wife, he decided to seek treatment.

Past History

Mr. A's memories about his early life were scant, but he distinctly remembered being poor. As a child he felt different because he always seemed to be dressed in ill-fitting, hand-me-down clothing and had less money and possessions than other children. Academic problems and poor grades led to psychological testing and placement in a special education class where he felt further alienated. Nevertheless, he struggled with his schoolwork and his academic performance improved. He was industrious even as a young boy, working at various odd jobs to help support his family. Following graduation from high school, he entered a trade school where he learned auto mechanics. His sedulousness led to success, and several years later he opened up his own automotive business, which grew and prospered. He married his childhood sweetheart and they had four children. Prior to the airplane accident, his life was in reasonable order and he was having no major difficulties.

Family History

Mr. A came from a large family. His father, a chronic alcoholic, was disabled and could not work regularly. His mother, whom he described as a hard-working and loving person, was the breadwinner in her employment as a maid. The patient was the oldest of eight siblings and, as the eldest, assumed much responsibility for household affairs early in his life. Although his family was poor, he stated they were never hungry and felt loyal to each other. He did not like or respect his father, a dissolute man who existed around the fringes of the family.

Treatment

During the explanation-education stage of treatment, an elaboration of the onset and course of PTSD was presented. As the plane was speeding down the runway, Mr. A became aware of the increased noise of the jet engines, followed by a feeling of sudden descent, and then a tremendous jolt. He was jarred to full consciousness by the screeching sound of metal rending and fragmenting as the bottom of the airplane scraped along the concrete runway. These stimuli, along with the sight of the plane's wings on fire and the shouts of confusion and alarm of other passengers, combined to activate the patient's autonomic nervous system. Anxiety reached a zenith when the patient was at the emergency exit that would not open and he was momentarily pinned to that door by frantically pressing passengers. Mr. A felt trapped and was certain that he could not escape and would die. Palpitations and dyspnea seemed to confirm this notion, but the patient was quickly hustled out of the airplane by the efficient flight attendants who propelled him toward the escape chute at another door. As he hit the ground, spraining his ankle, the patient's autonomic nervous system was working wildly: he felt extreme nausea and a severe shaking of his body as he staggered off to safety, away from the burning jet liner.

During this frightening sequence of events, the patient experienced the effects of intense autonomic activity, thus conditioning him adversely to various situational aspects of flying. Subsequently, whenever he saw airplanes or considered flying, he encephalically overexaggerated the dangers of air travel by visualizing airplane crashes and his certain demise. Anxiety was generated by this encephalic activity, but was reduced when the patient decided not to fly. Mechanisms of phobic behavior were explained, and it was emphasized that approach behavior (any activity that leads to a flight) increased anxiety, whereas avoidance behavior (any activity that led to a decision or action not to fly) reduced anxiety. Unfortunately, the anxiety decrement reinforced the phobic avoidance behavior.

A PTSD, the explanation continued, is sustained encephalically when a patient thinks, visualizes, or talks excessively about the traumatic incident, because this serves to maintain high levels of pathologic anxiety. Dreams reflect to a large extent the concerns of the waking state, so nightmares accompany an agitated mind overly concerned with the traumatic incident. When patients frequently dream about trauma, they often quit the struggle for sleep because somnolence is associated with upsetting nightmares, not rest. Patients yearn for sleep, yet dread it at the same time. Headaches and gastrointestinal upsets are somatic manifestations of pathologic anxiety, and these and other symptoms not present before the airplane crash would diminish as treatment proceeded, the patient was reassured.

Control and diminishment of pathologic anxiety and the induction of sleep can be achieved by learning relaxation techniques, the patient was told. He proved to be especially adept at self-hypnosis but also learned the technique of PMR. Both methods were recorded on an audio-cassette for home use. It was important, he was informed, to master relaxation procedures since they would be part of the desensitization process when addressing his flying phobia.

Preoccupation with thoughts of mortality may be intellectually beneficial for theologians and philosophers but it is not beneficial for patients with a PTSD. Morbid ruminations about death or injury serve only to heighten anxiety and maintain the disorder. Reliving the trauma in imagination retraumatizes patients, thus sensitizing them to various aspects of it. Obsessive preoccupation with trauma, the patient is warned, is the most important reason for enduring anxiety and the sustentation of the disorder. He was taught methods of encephalic reconditioning. Whenever envisaging unpleasant ideas related to his trauma, he was instructed to use a stopping technique. To dispel the distressing thoughts, he was to repeat to himself as often as was necessary, "Stop! Get out of there!" When the thought or scene was expurgated from his mind, he was urged to employ positive encephalic practice or to utilize a distraction technique involving conversation with another person or the pursuit of an engaging activity.

Rather than dwell on the uncomfortable sensations of headache or nausea and speculate about the possible presence of some pernicious process within the body, Mr. A was advised to state emphatically to himself the four positive reinforcing statements: (1) I feel uncomfortable. (2) I have had these feelings before and they always pass. (3) There is nothing seriously wrong with me. (4) My discomfort is caused or aggravated by pathologic anxiety, and if I utilize anti-anxiety interventions, these uncomfortable feelings will pass more quickly. The patient was then asked to practice self-hypnosis or PMR. Listening to audio tapes with instructions related to self-hypnosis and PMR can facilitate encephalic reconditioning, Mr. A was informed. Adherence to a policy of limiting, reducing, and ultimately stopping ruminations about the trauma would pay dividends of symptomatic improvement, he was told, and was an important factor in the resolution of his PTSD.

The patient's phobia of flying was treated by systematic desensitization. A hierarchy was constructed according to principles found in Chapter 8, and imaginal desensitization was conducted in the office. Initially, desensitization proceeded with difficulty because the patient visualized scenes that included an airplane crashing. For example, when he was asked to visualize that he was at home packing and preparing prior to driving to the airport, he simultaneously recollected his awful experience inside the disabled jet liner. The patient had to be repeatedly warned not to include as part of the desensitization any scenes depicting his traumatic experience. He was also advised not to anticipate, but merely to visualize the stated scene. When this was sorted out, desensitization proceeded normally. Following imaginal desensitization the patient was encouraged to go to the airport and observe airplanes taking off and landing. This in vivo desensitization experience exposed him to the hustle and bustle of airport activity as well as to the sights and sounds of airplanes landing and taking off. Finally, Mr. A scheduled a short flight. Prior to his flight, however, he saw a news report of an airplane crash on television. He postponed his trip, and his fears about flying and thoughts about the airplane crashing were rekindled. After a short delay, desensitization was reinstituted as before. The patient's confidence was somewhat shaken by the resurgence of symptoms, but soon another flight was scheduled. It was decided that prior to his initial flight, medication would be prescribed. The patient was instructed to take diazepam 5 milligrams the morning of his flight and to take another 5 milligrams while he was at the airport waiting to board his plane. Additional diazepam could be taken as needed during the flight. The patient, as are most flight phobic patients, was impervious to declarations that flying was the safest form of travel, but to demonstrate that desensitization had indeed lowered his anxiety, he agreed to take a short flight from New Orleans to Houston. He was accompanied on the flight by the author, and he was delighted with the outcome. Anticipatory anxiety made him feel a bit uncomfortable prior to the flight, but during the flight he was at ease most of the time. He experienced a surge of anxiety on takeoff when he heard the roar of accelerating jet engines and during landing when he felt a noticeable "bump" on descent, but his discomfort quickly subsided. Following this initial successful flight, longer flights in which he was unaccompanied were scheduled. In vivo exposure to flying led to further decreases in anxiety, and eventually Mr. A discontinued the use of diazepam. Five years following termination of treatment, he reported that he now flies with ease and no vestige of a phobia of flying remains.

A family conference was convened because the patient complained of marital problems, especially difficulties in getting and maintaining an erection. Mrs. A, a woman who was obviously in love with her husband, was very concerned about his welfare. She stated that since the airplane accident, her husband did not sleep well and frequently woke up in the middle of the night screaming and sweating profusely. Upon questioning, he related nightmares that involved burning airplanes and imminent death. During the conjoint conference, Mrs. A reported that her husband was irritable, on edge, tense, and would "fly off the handle" easily, which was contrary to his usual easy-going, pleasant personality. She also exclaimed that her husband seemed preoccupied with death and lamented that his inability to fly impeded his growing business and affected his profits. Mrs. A was told that her husband was suffering from PTSD and that most of his symptoms and behavior could be attributed to this disorder. It was important for the couple to restore harmonious interaction, and this would be made easier by conjoint therapy sessions, Mrs. A was reassured. Initially, sexual disinterest and dysfunction, a common component of PTSD since anxiety and pleasurable sexual relationships are incompatible, were addressed during the family conference. The couple was placed on a modified Masters and Johnson (1970) program designed to reduce performance anxiety and overcome the problem of impotence. Both cooperated with this regimen, and within five sessions their sexual relationship was mutually satisfying.

Mr. A had just expanded his business, an automotive parts agency, and it was necessary for him to meet regularly with other dealers in various parts of the country. His phobia of flying prevented him from attending these meetings during the initial phase of treatment. Problem-solving sessions were conducted around this issue, and the patient made alternative arrangements to minimize any disruption to his business. At times he sent one of his employees or, if possible, drove or took the train to these meetings. Financial problems ensuant to expanding his business were not serious, but his symptoms of anxiety interfered with decisive action. Discussions helped clarify his options, rendering decision making easier. The patient had good business sense and needed only peace of mind to reflect calmly on a problem in order to arrive at a sound decision. As the patient's preoccupation with his trauma diminished, so did his anxiety and difficulties in problem solving.

The patient's exercise and nutritional status was discussed. Mr. A was obese and exercised little. Toward the end of treatment he was placed on a diet based on behavior modification principles (Scrignar, 1980; Stuart and Davis, 1982). Since he was a good hypnotic subject, a special hypnosis audio-cassette tape was prepared that contained positive suggestions designed to help him adhere to his diet. In addition, Mr. A was encouraged to join an exercise club and to work out regularly. He complied with both of these requests, lost weight, and began to feel the beneficial effects of self-control related to eating and physical activity. Periodic follow-ups after termination revealed that the patient was still struggling with his weight, but had managed to maintain a weight loss of 40 pounds. He exercised erratically but remains committed to the principle "sound mind—sound body."

At the end of 29 sessions extending over a seven-month period, treatment terminated. Quarterly follow-ups for the first year after termination disclosed that he had maintained his improvement. A personal injury suit that he had filed was negociated out of court. A telephone follow-up five years later revealed that he was doing quite well. All of the patient's pathologic anxiety symptoms had subsided and he was flying freely. His sleep was sound and nightmares were very infrequent. His relationship with his wife was excellent, and he was prospering financially. The airplane accident that he was involved in is now a dim memory in his mind.

CASE FOUR: ACCIDENT ON AN OIL RIG

Mr. B, a married oil field worker in his early forties, stated that following an accident on an oil rig in the Gulf of Mexico, "my whole life has changed." He explained that he was in constant pain, which was relieved to some extent when he wore a back brace or took various analgesics. Nervousness, a fear of possible paralysis, headaches, difficulty in concentrating, insomnia, disturbing dreams, irritability, marital conflicts, diminished sexual desire, and gastrointestinal upsets interfered with his ability to enjoy life. He admitted that he thought a great deal about the accident and its consequences and wondered whether he would ever get well. Displaying despondency, the patient cried as he related that friends had noticed a personality change and told him that he was moody, withdrawn, and distant. With regret, he stated that he had instituted a lawsuit against his former employers who he believed were unsympathetic and uncaring about his injuries. Litigation, he felt, had placed additional pressures upon him.

Mr. B was working on the drilling platform of an oil rig in the Gulf of Mexico, assisting in the removal of drilling pipe "out of the hole." A "wet string" (large amount of drilling mud) poured out onto the drilling platform, making it very slippery. In the performance of his duties, he slipped and fell backward, landing very hard on his buttocks. Although he was in pain, he got up and continued working. Shortly thereafter, he slipped again falling on his lower back and buttocks. At the time, although in great pain, he thought he was not injured seriously. He continued working but when his foreman asked him to get some test equipment, he could not lift it, although ordinarily he could have done so without difficulty. The thought that he might have injured his back passed quickly through his mind, but he asked another man to get the equipment and returned to work. At the end of his shift he went to the bunkhouse and slept. Several hours later he awakened and tried to get out of bed but severe pain prevented this. Instantly, he thought that he was paralyzed. Reasoning that the two falls he had endured must have seriously injured his spine making it impossible for him to pick up the test equipment. Unable now to get out of his bunk, he became panic stricken. He was alone in the bunkhouse, and the noise of the drilling rig drowned out his shouts for help. His chest tightened, he thought he would suffocate, and his heart was beating so fast he feared it would burst. These acute symptoms subsided somewhat, and with great effort he crawled out of his bunk and desperately called for help. The driller (foreman), alarmed at Mr. B's condition, called for a helicopter to evacuate him to a hospital.

During the 30-minute wait for the helicopter, Mr. B was in severe pain and believed that he was seriously injured and might never walk again. "My back felt like a nerve or muscle was pulled out and I was very scared."

In the hospital after receiving a complete physical examination including x-rays, Mr. B was treated with pain medication and bed rest. After seven days of hospitalization, he was surprised when doctors discharged him with recommendations to go home and rest. Two days later, Mr. B, greatly agitated and in severe pain, returned to the emergency room of the hospital, was readmitted, and was placed in traction for three days. Traction relieved his pain and he was again discharged with the recommendation to take analgesic medication and get some rest. He reacted to this prescription with disbelief, and when symptoms persisted was again admitted to the hospital. Examinations, laboratory procedures, and various tests were repeated and followed with the same recommendation—discharge, medication for pain, and bed rest. Still symptomatic, Mr. B became convinced that his condition was serious, undiagnosable, and untreatable. Over the course of the next several months, thoughts that he might become paralyzed led to many visits with various doctors. In an attempt to treat his symptoms, doctors prescribed muscle relaxants, analgesics, antipsychotic agents, antianxiety agents, antidepressants, beta-blockers, antacids, antispasmodics, vitamins, and a variety of drug-combination medications. In spite of this pharmacologic assault on the patient's body, his symptoms persisted.

Surgical consultation led to rehospitalization and a laminectomy and diskectomy were performed. Postoperatively the patient did well, but eventually complained of back pain radiating down his right leg. Pain was relieved by bed rest, and during ambulation a lumbar corset eased his discomfort. Four months later Mr. B was admitted to a university hospital where a diagnosis of degenerative disc disease with segmental instability was made. Another operative procedure, a lumbosacral fusion, was performed and his condition on discharge was good. Upon returning home, however, the patient became symptomatic. Psychiatric consultation was advised.

A mental status examination revealed a man who was extremely anxious and quite depressed. Pain was a prominent symptom, but he also suffered from generalized anxiety, sleep disturbance, frightening dreams, headaches, trembling, irritability, difficulties in concentration, fatigue, and marital problems. He was obsessed with his accident and had thoughts that he would become panic stricken and lose control. He had a long history of gastrointestinal disturbance, and two weeks prior to the psychiatric consultation had vomited blood, which led to a short hospitalization. His preaccident medical history included treatment for gastric ulcers and surgery to remove a gallbladder. The patient had never been evaluated nor treated for a nervous or mental disorder. There was no evidence of psychosis, and he was in good contact with reality. The patient's personal habits were good; he did not drink alcoholic beverages or smoke. There was no evidence of an antisocial personality. Previously, he had never been involved in personal injury litigation.

Past History

The patient was reared by a stepmother and father in a rural southern town. As a child he was sickly and frequently absent from school. Following the ninth grade, he quit school and worked on a farm for his father. Mr. B stated that his childhood and adolescence were not remarkable, but admitted that he was shy and preferred his own company. When he was 18 he joined the U.S. Army, served two years including one year in Europe, reached the rank of corporal and received an honorable discharge. His first marriage, which lasted four years, was a disaster and ended when his wife ran off with another man. Two children have resulted from his current marriage of eight years, and he felt that he and his wife were getting along quite well until his accident. Ten years ago he was involved in another accident while working as a roustabout on an oil rig. Drill pipe was being pulled out of the hole, he related, when suddenly one of the pipes broke loose, hitting him on the head. Unconscious, he was taken to the hospital where he remained for about three weeks after regaining consciousness. He was unable to work for one year and marginally subsisted on workers' compensation. No lawsuit evolved from this accident, and he returned to work for the same company that had employed him at the time of the accident. Although he stated that he had been in good health most of his life, medical history prior to his recent trauma indicated treatment for gastric ulcers and a cholecystectomy.

Family History

The patient's mother died in childbirth, and within a year his father remarried a widow with four children. He remembered that his stepmother was very critical of him and did not like him. He felt that his two stepbrothers and two stepsisters were favored by his stepmother. He described his father as a quiet, somber man who always acceded to his wife's wishes. His reasons for joining the Army were to escape from the tedium of farm work and his stepmother's temper.

Treatment

Pain and subsequent operative procedures obscured the signs and symptoms of PTSD, the patient was told during the explanation-education step of treatment. As physicians searched for a structural cause for his symptoms, the emotional aspects of his trauma were overlooked. Unlike in most patients who develop PTSD, the onset of Mr. B's disorder occurred several hours after the initial impact. Lying on a bed alone in a bunkhouse on an oil rig several miles offshore in the Gulf of Mexico, he awakened and discovered that he could not move. Vivid recollections of his two falls on the oil rig coupled with intense pain, lent credence to the conclusion that he was paralyzed. Two E's—encephalic and endogenous—combined to produce a sudden stimulation of his autonomic nervous system. Palpitations, dyspnea, and other acute anxiety symptoms surged as his shouts for help were drowned out by the roar of machinery. Feeling helpless, panic stricken, and in great pain, Mr. B struggled to get on his feet and, finding that he could still move, thoughts of paralysis were supplanted by equally frightening ideas of impending paralysis. Laboriously, half-crawling and half-walking, he got out of bed, left the bunkhouse, and attracted the attention of his foreman, who immediately radioed for a helicopter to take him ashore to a hospital. While awaiting transportation, Mr. B suffered from severe anxiety and pain. Nausea and fear also racked his body and he began to shake violently. For almost an hour, high levels of autonomic nervous system activity, an essential element in producing a PTSD, were experienced by the patient before he arrived at the hospital.

Examination and an assortment of laboratory procedures were inconclusive and revealed no gross abnormalities. To his surprise and confusion, Mr. B was discharged from the hospital and advised to rest and take pain medication when needed. At home he experienced intense back pain and envisaged impending paralysis, which set in motion the Spiral Effect, intensifying both anxiety and pain. Panic stricken and suffering from intense back pain, he went to the emergency room and was readmitted to the hospital. Conservative, nonsurgical treatment failed, so finally a laminectomy and diskectomy were performed, which only temporarily ameliorated pain. Symptoms of stress were present but largely overlooked or deemphasized by surgeons who concentrated instead on finding physical reasons for Mr. B's continuing discomfort. Four months later a diagnosis of mechanical back pain was made, and another surgical procedure, a lumbosacral fusion, was performed. Although the operation was judged to be successful, Mr. B remained symptomatic. Finally, attention focused on the patient's psychological status and a psychiatric consultation was requested.

With certitude, the patient was told during explanation- education that further surgery was neither indicated nor necessary. Existing pain and anxiety could be explained by postoperative soft tissue damage and anxiety. A further search for a physical cause obfuscated the real source of his discomfort. Mechanisms underlying PTSD were explained, emphasizing that obsessions about the trauma and the possibility of paralysis served only to perpetuate the disorder. Lowering of pathologic anxiety and control of pain could be achieved by training in relaxation and encephalic reconditioning. Dubiety greeted these suggestions, and Mr. B's anger rose as he queried, "If this is all in my imagination, why have I had two operations?" The patient's query was momentarily quieted by the explanation that his symptoms were not imaginary, but physiologically induced. He was wearing a lumbar corset, and it was difficult for him to believe that his spine had not been irreparably damaged by the original trauma. His dissatisfaction led to a discontinuance of treatment.

A month later the patient's wife, highly upset, telephoned and stated that her husband was not doing well. Mr. B had been hospitalized for several days because of bleeding gastric ulcer, and following his discharge was very depressed and talked about suicide. A family conference was immediately convened, during which Mrs. B said that she was at her wit's end and felt emotionally and physically spent, incapable of helping her husband. In a gloomy mood, Mr. B complained of low back pain, stomach cramps, insomnia, disturbing dreams, nervousness, irritability, restlessness, difficulties in concentration, and fatigue. He spent much of his time each day in bed, thinking about himself and the future. He obsessed about the dangerousness of working on oil rigs, reliving in imagination both of his accidents. "Even if I get over my back pain," he speculated, "I doubt whether I shall ever be able to work on an oil rig again." Untrained for any other work and in a depressed state of mind, he contemplated suicide as the best solution for his dilemma. Hospitalization in a psychiatric unit was a more responsible solution.

Upon entering the psychiatric unit, the patient was frightened but relieved as he confided that he believed he was going crazy. Bizarre nightmares, in which he was slipping and sliding on the muddied platform of an oil rig with drilling pipes and dangerous machinery imperiling him from all sides, roused him from sleep. Afterwards, sweat drenched and agitated, he found further sleep impossible. Instead he lay awake, wide eyed, pondering the significance of his dreams and fantasizing dangers associated with oil rigs. During the day back pain reminded him of his accidents and reinforced the idea that oil rigs were dangerous places in which to work. Disability lasted over a year and pessimism regarding the future fueled feelings of hopelessness and depression. In the hospital during the explanation-education phase of treatment, the mechanisms underlying PTSD were reexplained, emphasizing the importance of the Three E's in the production and maintenance of his disorder. Retraumatization occurred encephalically whenever the patient visualized or thought about the accidents, thereby exposing him to the trauma in imagination many times each day. The patient's attention to back pain initiated the Spiral Effect, which intensified his pain and increased anxiety. Depression, a secondary manifestation of PTSD, was due in large part to chronic disablement and was abetted by pessimistic self-statements portending permanent invalidism.

Control of pain and lowering of anxiety can be achieved by engaging in training in relaxation, which must be practiced, the patient was told. This time, he mastered the techniques of self- hypnosis and PMR, which were used to advantage when he experienced pain or anxiety. Control and reduction of thoughts and mental images related to the trauma are absolutely essential and can be achieved by encephalic reconditioning, he was advised. Thought stopping, positive encephalic practice, and the four positive reinforcing statements were discussed and taught to the patient. He was asked to fill out a daily self-assessment form to help him identify the stimuli inducing pathologic anxiety and pain in order to counter them with therapeutic interventions. Pessimistic and negative self-statements, which correlate with depression (Beck, 1976), were also to be recorded on the form, and he was urged to correct these. For example, the patient tended to overgeneralize and say to himself, "My life is ruined. I am no good to anyone." He was urged to substitute for these erroneous self-statements: "My life has changed but I will cope with my new circumstance. I have many positive attributes. My wife and children need me. Each day in my own way I shall get better and better." The self- assessment form provided data upon which revisions in the treatment program were based.

Because the patient was frightened and fatigued, on admission to the hospital, temazepam (Restoril) 30 milligrams was prescribed for sleep during the first week. The patient had taken many psychotropic agents and other drugs in the past with no marked clinical improvement. For this reason it was decided that no additional medication would be prescribed and, as it happened, no other medication was required during the course of treatment. The patient's nutritional needs were assessed by a dietician, and he was placed on a diet commensurate with his gastrointestinal status. An exercise program was developed and adapted to his physical condition. Mr. B was kept busy, and he was told that it was important for him to engage in all of the activities available on the unit. Ward personnel were assigned to monitor and encourage his participation. Weekly family conferences were convened and marital roles were redefined as he took more responsibility for housekeeping chores and the care of the children.

After two weeks Mr. B was given a weekend pass to go home with his wife. The couple was asked to engage in social/recreational activities that included the children. All progress was to be recorded in a log, which would form the basis of future discussions during family conferences. The first weekend was a huge success for the entire family. Mr. B was able to control symptoms of pathologic anxiety and pain while participating in many pleasurable activities. As he emerged from his cocoon of depression, his family was overjoyed. During subsequent weeks he continued his improvement, and on discharge, in an ebullient state, was making plans to seek work outside the oil field in a less strenuous occupation.

As an outpatient Mr. B continued to use relaxation techniques to lower anxiety and diminish pain. In addition, anxiety-evoking and pessimistic thoughts were reduced by techniques of encephalic reconditioning. His wife felt rejuvenated and her delight became infectious when, for the first time in a year, the couple went to movie theatres, to restaurants, and to the homes of friends. Mr. B began light repairs on his car and kept busy working in his yard. He bought bicycles for his daughter and himself, and together they cycled on progressively longer outings each day. To the surprise of everyone, he took his family on a week's vacation to Disneyworld, the first real vacation they had had in a long time.

Mr. B consulted his orthopedic surgeon who was satisfied with his progress and suggested that it was no longer necessary to wear a lumbar corset. Ambulation without the brace was now possible with only minimal discomfort. The patient's sleep patterns returned to normal and he no longer had nightmares. Anxiety, irritability, ruminations about the trauma, inability to concentrate, epigastric discomfort, and fatigue all diminished, and a pleasant, almost jubilant mood replaced dysphoria. His marital relationship improved, and pleasurable sexual interaction was restored. Mr. B's easy-going ways returned, his physical status improved, and reinvolvement with his family led to a happier, more optimistic outlook on life. Other people noticed his improvement and their comments reinforced positive changes in his behavior.

After six weeks of hospitalization and four months of once-weekly outpatient treatment, Mr. B was discharged. Follow-ups over a period of two years disclosed that the patient maintained his improvement. His lawsuit was settled out of court, and he used part of the financial settlement to establish a small business that he has operated successfully to this day.

CASE FIVE: THE VIETNAM-ERA VETERAN AND CRIMINAL CONDUCT

The following is a case history of a Vietnam-era combat veteran (Mr. E) who was charged with kidnapping and assault with a dangerous weapon at a VA Hospital and tried in a federal court. This case involved medical, legal, and moral issues. The information upon which this case report is based was obtained from interviews with the veteran and his mother, wife, and attorney. The following records were also reviewed: military service records from the U.S. Marine Corps, medical records from the VA Hospital, reports from the Vet Center, psychiatric reports from a court-appointed psychiatrist, and a report from the U.S. Department of Justice Bureau of Prison's Medical Center for Federal Prisoners at Springfield, Missouri. In addition, an audio cassette recording of negotiations between the veteran and authorities, which took place at a VA Hospital, was available for study. An analysis was also made of the veteran's journal (diary), which he had maintained following his discharge from the U.S. Marine Corps until the time of arrest.

Developmental History

The veteran's family was poor, living in a government project in a section of the city that could best be characterized as a ghetto. His father, a dissolute man, was absent from the home a great deal, so his mother bore the brunt of responsibility for the maintenance of the family. The veteran was undersized for his age, and his small stature caused others to call him "runt," "peewee," "gnat," and "small stuff." He was sickly as a youth. When he was eight years old, his mother gave him a severe beating for what she considered to be his incorrigible behavior. Following this punishment a purplish discoloration remained on his skin. His mother became alarmed and took him to see a doctor who made a diagnosis of idiopathic thrombocytopenia purpura. Many visits to Charity Hospital clinics ensued over the next two years, requiring his absence from school. The boy's grades dropped and he flunked the second grade. Already sensitive about his size, he felt awkward and embarrassed because the demotion placed him in a class with younger boys, many of whom were of superior size. Embarrassment in school led to truancy, which added to absences for medical reasons and resulted in poor academic performance and further flunking. At age 10 his idiopathic thrombocytopenia purpura "spontaneously cleared." He did not regularly attend school, and when he did, he was inattentive. School counselors labeled him as "learning disabled," and he was placed in a special education class. Teachers failed to awaken his intellectual curiosity, and he stagnated, sleeping or mischievously disrupting the class. His formal education came to an end at age 15 (he was still in the fourth grade) when he adamantly refused to continue in school. His mother acquiesced with this decision. Over the next two years, he ran the streets and occasionally got odd jobs. Idleness allowed opportunity for delinquency, and he began to associate with older boys who acquainted him with the practice of drinking wine, popping pills, and smoking marijuana. He and his peers were arrested on three occasions for assault and battery, disturbing the peace, and theft. The charges were eventually dropped, but on one occasion he had to appear in juvenile court with his mother. At age 17 he decided to join the armed services.

The Vietnam Experience

Mr. E attempted to join the Army, but was rejected and told he was illiterate. Later, at the height of the Vietnam conflict, he applied for the U.S. Marine Corps, and the Marines, apparently less discriminating than the Army, accepted him. He successfully completed the Marine's rigorous basic training and was immediately sent to Vietnam. After arriving in Vietnam, he was given a one-week orientation course and then sent into combat. Mr. E admitted that he was scared and for the first time in his life came into close contact with dead people. Following a combat action, it was part of his duty to find, count, and stack "like cord wood" dead bodies of North Vietnamese soldiers. He vividly remembers a woman with a baby in her arms who was burned by a white phosphorus shell and looked like a "black blob." He was given the nickname of "mini-man" and was assigned the duties of a tunnel rat. It was his responsibility to crawl into tunnels with a hand grenade and a 45-caliber pistol to ferret out Vietcong and locate caches of weapons and food. He traded his M-16 rifle for a more versatile sawed-off 12-gauge shotgun. While on patrol one day, he saw a head bob up from behind a wall and he reflexively fired at the profile. After crawling over the wall, he peered down at the first human being he had ever killed—an old, withered Vietnamese peasant whose face was "blown away." He became nauseated and vomited. Over the course of the next few months, he witnessed extensive death and carnage and was in an almost constant state of fear. Anxiety was attenuated by alcohol, and sleeplessness was soothed with soporific drugs. Although Mr. E insisted that alcohol, hashish, and heroin did not interfere with his duties, he became increasingly agitated, anxious, and fearful. Danger was everywhere, as evidenced by the sound of mortars, gunshots from snipers and the explosion of booby traps. Even though he was frightened, the veteran continued to perform his duties as a soldier. One morning he woke up with a fever, and a medical corpsman suspected Mr. E was suffering from heat stroke or malaria. He was sent to the rear for medical attention. He was not seriously ill, and after several days insisted that he be transferred back to his unit. Upon returning to his squad, he discovered that only four men were still alive. Eight of his buddies were killed by the Vietcong in an ambush. Mr. E was certain that his time was up and that he would never leave Vietnam alive. His premonition almost proved to be correct. While on night patrol a few days later, he saw a hand grenade, heard an explosion, and was knocked on his back, lapsing into unconsciousness. Later, when he awoke in the hospital, he was swathed in bandages. Thinking that he was mutilated, he became panic stricken and shouted for the nurse, who arrived shortly and calmly assured him that he was intact. He had shrapnel wounds involving his left and right upper legs, left testicle, and left forearm and hand. He was told that if he had not covered his face with his left arm, he might have been blinded. He was sent back to the United States where he spent several months in a military hospital. He signed a waiver and was given an honorable discharge, received a purple heart commendation, and was placed on 50 percent disability.

After Vietnam

Immediately after his discharge from the Marine Corps, Mr. E lived with his mother. She reported that her son was not the same person and seemed to have undergone a personality change. Before Vietnam her son had laughed and joked, but now he was sober, "held things in," and liked to stay to himself. Nervousness accompanied his withdrawn state, and nightmares about Vietnam frequently interrupted his sleep. He began to drink because alcohol "soothed his nerves," induced sleep, and stopped his mind from thinking about Vietnam. He received training in auto mechanics, but found it difficult to keep a steady job. Mr. E was likable, but his employers could not tolerate his absenteeism. Fortunately, his disability check from the U.S. Government met his minimal needs. Two years after he was discharged from the Marine Corps, Mr. E married. His wife did not know him before the war, but she related that he was quite nervous, had frequent headaches, and talked a great deal about Vietnam. She added that he had difficulties sleeping and frequently woke up terror stricken and sweating profusely. Upon becoming calm he would mutter, "It's Vietnam again." During the 10 years of their marriage, the wife said he was a good father to their three children and was a nonviolent person. "He would not hurt a fly," his wife emphatically stated. "In fact, he doesn't hunt like his friends because he dislikes killing animals." His wife insisted that even though they had tough times, their marriage had basically been a good one. She admitted that her husband drank, smoked marijuana, and used other drugs, especially when he associated with old friends who were veterans of Vietnam. During the time she has known him, the wife stated, her husband had never been arrested nor put in jail for any reason. His wife worked and together with the veteran's disability check, they had been able to meet the family's financial needs.

Three years after his discharge from the Marines, Mr. E was admitted to the VA Hospital drug abuse program. Dissatisfied with treatment, he abruptly quit. A year later he was hospitalized and treated at the VA Hospital for acute hepatitis. Shortly afterward, he had a minor surgical operation at the VA and several admissions for alcoholism and gastritis. On one occasion he was hospitalized after experiencing severe stomach cramps and vomiting coffee-ground material. Six years after discharge from the Marines, he was put on a methadone maintenance program, but after a few months was discharged from the program. Over the course of 10 years, Mr. E was hospitalized at the VA Hospital on 14 occasions. Although he complained of stress symptoms, sleep disturbance, nightmares, and became visibly upset when talking about Vietnam or viewing scenes of the conflict on television, a diagnosis of PTSD was never made. Substance Use Disorder was the only diagnosis rendered.

Discontentment with the VA Hospital led Mr. E to seek assistance at the Vet Center, an organization devoted to meeting the needs of veterans, primarily of the Vietnam era. Whenever he became agitated and obsessed with memories of Vietnam, he sought solace and received relief from counselors at the Vet Center. For the first time he heard the term "Post-Traumatic Stress Disorder" as applied to Vietnam-era veterans. During rap sessions Mr. E queried, "Why hasn't the VA diagnosed and treated me for this disorder?" His tirades during these sessions included a denunciation of the U.S. Government, and his angry cries were applauded by other veterans. He believed that an ungrateful government was trying to sweep the memory of Vietnam under the rug along with the men who answered the call to duty. During rap sessions, self-righteous proclamations resulted only in a temporary catharsis, for the ranting ultimately led to an intensification of dysphoric feelings. Ten days before the hostage incident, Mr. E, very upset and angry, went to the Vet Center and told his counselor that he was denied admission to the VA Hospital. The counselor attempted vainly to intercede for him.

The Diary

Since his discharge from the Marine Corps, he had the habit of secluding himself and writing in his diary whenever he got upset. His writing began in earnest in 1977, seven years after his discharge and five years before the hostage incident. The following are some selected quotes:

> "I came back from Vietnam filled with hate and nightmares that keep me on drugs to sleep at night. I would like to know if I am sick but I can't make myself go see the doctor. I have a feeling of sadness and death. I am a man filled with fears, like a boy. I don't sleep at night. This makes me into what my father is, an alcoholic. I tried to get help from the VA, but they never seemed to have the time. I think what makes a man go mad is if he can't sit and say what he feels about things. My fear, at first, when I came home was the want to kill still inside of me and the hate in me is still strong. Knowing the unhappiness inside of me has made me think of doing many things, even to take my own life but my will to live and find what I want in life is keeping me going."

The diary reflected his fears while he was in Vietnam and contained questions about the war after he was discharged. Depressing words of sadness and unhappiness permeated its pages. In January, 1980, he wrote:

"How do we tell our mothers and fathers we feel proud when we know what it was really like there in Vietnam...I remember one time I went to the VA Hospital because I was using too many drugs and was flipping out and went to ask for help with my life, just to have the nurse call a big red neck guard to tell me what I was doing was a no-no. If we Nam vets can't go to the hospital for help, where in the hell do they want us to go?...God, I would just like people to know the hell and nightmares of sleeping, but yet never being able to stop thinking. Knowing if you don't drink or use drugs you will not sleep. How many walking time bombs like me are walking around and so damn lost? They do not know if they are coming or going."

Two months prior to the hostage incident, he wrote:

"God, why does the pain hurt me so bad? To keep living is to fear every day of my life. I only know one way and that is death...My madness keeps going on and on. The hate and pain of death still walks within me...The nightmares of Vietnam still stay inside of me...Every day I ask myself, 'Why don't the people in government reach out and help us in our fight to overcome the things they had us do for them?'...I do not know myself how long I can keep fighting this madness I have inside of me...I just hope that what I feel never gets out of me...At times these things get so bad I feel like I could take my life but I just keep fighting back. I guess what this is coming to one day is I still have to win or lose...I feel, even in death, I can put the hate and pain to rest. I would then close my eyes with happiness in my heart...When I die, Vietnam will have a lot to do with it."

Mr. E continued to agonize over and lament about Vietnam.

"I am 30 years old and I have been home 11 years now, but yet I can still hear the screams of death. The faces of the innocent men, women, and kids that we killed. We killed many we did not have to...I find myself asking God to forgive me...God, how it hurts...Just thinking of sleep brings on fears that you are going to see all of those faces again...As I write this, the smell of death is well within me...How can I be sure that I am or have just gone mad? To keep going on is a fight in itself...My mind and me still don't get along with each other...Most people fear death or being killed but yet my biggest fear is life itself."

One month prior to the hostage incident, he addressed his youngest daughter in his diary:

"You are the purest, honesty of my life—putting the fire back in my heart. You have showed me how to love again and how to smile when I felt I didn't know how. You have made me want to wake up every day, just so I will see your happy face. My child, you have shown me how it feels just to think of someone and to feel all good inside. How can someone be so little and yet bring so much joy to everyone? You have been life for me. Without you, I would be so empty inside. You are a gift from God. With you, he sent love, life, and happiness and for this I will always love you within my heart."

The Hostage Incident

One Saturday morning Mr. E arose at 6:30, fixed himself a cup of coffee and began to read the newspaper. A story titled "Vietnam Suicide: I Was Never Given Any Help" caught his attention. The news story, datelined Miami, opened with a description of a Vietnam-era veteran who threw himself off an expressway bridge. "When he hit the pavement," the news story went on, "the body count from the Vietnam war went up by one." As he read and reread the account of the veteran's death by suicide, he became anxious, agitated, and angry. Very upset, he left his house to buy some Percodan, which he "shot up." The drug pacified him and he went home and slept all day. Upon awakening, he cut out the newspaper article about the suicide and pasted it into a scrapbook along with similar stories about Vietnam-era veterans. As he began scrutinizing other stories in his scrapbook, anxiety and anger mounted, and Mr. E began drinking wine to sooth his jitters. His wife, having viewed similar scenes on many occasions, quietly slipped off to bed with the expectation that he would be okay by the next day. Wine did not mollify him, so he left home at about 10:30 p.m. and went to a neighborhood bar. At the tavern he met another Vietnam-era veteran and they talked about the suicide, swapped stories about their Vietnam experiences, and commiserated about their mutual misfortune. The veterans celebrated their relationship by smoking hashish, and as time passed, Mr. E became dazed by the drug. "The hash hit me good," he remembered before he went into a state of not remembering.

305

At dawn of the following day, the veteran dimly recalled going to a friend's house where he borrowed a 12-gauge shotgun. Whenever he got upset, he liked to borrow his friend's gun and head out into the marshes to get away from it all. No shot was ever fired because he did not believe in hunting and killing living things. The peace and solitude of the swamp and the feeling of the shotgun cradled in his arms made him curiously calm and reposeful; these feelings were similar to those that he had first noticed in Vietnam following a battle. Later, on Sunday morning, he recalled driving his car into the emergency entrance of the VA Hospital. "Everything appeared to be extra bright, like a lot of lights were on," he stated. Mr. E walked up the stairs to the hospital entrance and then he went back to the car to get the shotgun. He related that he did not feel drunk or drugged, but that he felt different, a new experience. Everything seemed to be extra bright, in slow motion, and unreal. He walked into the hospital and down the corridor and turned into a room full of people. A patient was lying on a litter and Mr. E told an attendant to wheel him out of the room. A male nurse said, "Let everyone go and I'll stay." All of the people in the room left, except the nurse. The enormity of his action suddenly dawned upon Mr. E and he became distraught and began to cry. He put the shotgun barrel in his mouth but could not reach the trigger to fire it. Over the next several hours there were telephone conversations with police negotiators, a counselor at the Vet Center, and friends and relatives. Finally, the nurse asked if he could leave, and Mr. E assented. In response to requests from the police, Mr. E pushed the shotgun out of the room and walked out. He was quickly apprehended by two Federal Bureau of Investigation agents and taken to a room with a priest, his wife, and some friends. After a tearful reunion, he was formally arrested and taken to prison.

Discussion

An unstable family background, chronic childhood illness, and poverty during Mr. E's developmental years certainly contributed to feelings of insecurity and nervousness. His diminutive size and continued failure in school contributed to feelings of inadequacy. Although he was involved in delinquent activities as a juvenile, he was not truly antisocial. Occasional fights, petty thievery, and drug experimentation could be considered "normal" for his socioeconomic group. It is curious that at the height of the Vietnam conflict, the Army rejected him whereas the Marine Corps accepted him. Many years later Mr. E would focus on this "happenstance" and recall the slogan of antiwar hecklers that he was "cannon fodder." As a recruit he did well during boot camp, a considerable achievement considering the spartan quality of Marine Corps basic training. While in Vietnam he was exposed to many traumatic events including the death and maiming of women, children, and buddies. Frequently, he envisioned with abhorrence the faceless form of the old Vietnamese peasant whom he had killed. Alcohol and drugs assuaged his guilt and anxiety, and allowed him to continue to function as a soldier. His final trauma in Vietnam was twofold. The first occurred with the grenade explosion that wounded him. The second trauma occurred upon awakening in the hospital when he looked at his arms and legs swathed in bandages and thought that he might be armless, legless, or devoid of his genitals. His physical wounds healed and he was discharged from the Marines with a purple heart and a monthly 50 percent disability check.

Mr. E floundered in his attempt to cope with civilian life. Symptoms of stress interfered with his adjustment. Intrusive memories and vivid visual impressions of war in Vietnam generated pathologic anxiety, impaired sleep, and erupted violently in the form of flashbacks and nightmares. Clearly, he was suffering from a PTSD. Unfortunately, neither he nor his physicians at the VA Hospital recognized this. He discovered that respite from his tortuous thoughts could be achieved by drinking alcohol and using drugs. This form of self-treatment for his PTSD was not satisfactory since substance abuse created additional problems. The clinicians at the VA Hospital focused on the important but peripheral problem of drug abuse, neglecting the central issue of PTSD. Notations in his diary clearly indicated that he was struggling with the symptoms of PTSD but did not know where to turn for help. The diary also reflected an introspective and sensitive man who had strong feelings for other people. Although the veteran had used drugs intermittently over 10 years, his substance abuse was not accompanied by criminal behavior. In fact, he was never arrested, convicted, or incarcerated for a felony during the 12 years following his discharge from the Marines. Mr. E was no paragon of virtue, but he did not have an Antisocial Personality Disorder.

The Trial

During the trial in federal court, Mr. E's attorney utilized the insanity defense, asserting that the veteran, as a result of his combat experiences in Vietnam, had developed a PTSD and at the time of the alleged criminal act was not criminally responsible because he was experiencing a dissociative reaction. The federal court operates under the ALI test, which states that "a defendant is not responsible for criminal conduct, if at the time of such conduct, as a result of mental disease or defect, he lacks substantial capacity, either to appreciate the wrongfulness of his conduct or to conform his conduct to the requirements of law." The U.S. Attorney placed two physicians on the stand, one of whom was a psychiatrist, and both testified that the defendant, Mr. E, was not insane and did not meet the criteria for insanity as spelled out in the ALI test. They also testified that the veteran had an Antisocial Personality Disorder and a Substance Use Disorder and disavowed any possibility that he was suffering from a PTSD. The defense placed two psychiatrists on the stand. Both testified that Mr. E was suffering from PTSD and at the time of the alleged criminal conduct appeared to be suffering from a dissociative reaction. Although not psychotic in the usual sense, the defense psychiatrists agreed that the veteran seemed to fit the ALI standard and was not criminally responsible. Furthermore, Substance Use Disorder was a secondary manifestation and was an unsuccessful attempt to self-treat his PTSD. Although he had exhibited antisocial traits as a juvenile, Mr. E had not been involved in any criminal activity since his discharge from the Marines. In addition, he displayed a strong attachment to his family, which further made questionable the diagnosis of Antisocial Personality Disorder.

The jury, the final arbiter in this matter, was perhaps more persuaded by the villainousness of Mr. E's conduct and found him guilty. The judge, who disallowed introduction of the veteran's diary, records from the Vet Center, and most of the testimony of the defense psychiatrists, sentenced him to 10 years in a federal penitentiary. Mr. E's PTSD remains untreated.

REFERENCES

Adelstein, S.J. 1987. Uncertainty and Relative Risks of Radiation Exposure. *JAMA*, 258, pp. 625–657.

Agras, W.S., Leitenberg, H., Barlow, D.H., and Thomson, L.E. 1969. Instructions and Reinforcement in the Modification of Neurotic Behavior. *Am. J. Psychiatry*, 125, pp. 1435–1439.

Alberti, R.E., and Emmons, M.L. 1978. *Your Perfect Right* (third edition). San Luis Obispo, Impact.

Allodi, F. 1982, January. Psychiatric Sequelae of Torture and Implications for Treatment. Paper delivered at a symposium on "Torture, Medical Practice, and Medical Ethics," organized by the Clearing House on Science and Human Rights of the American Association for the Advancement of Science. Washington D.C.

Allodi, F. and Cowgill, G. 1982. Ethical and Psychiatric Aspects of Torture: A Canadian Study. *Canadian Journal of Psychiatry*, 27, pp. 98–102.

American Psychiatric Association Roundtable Meeting. 1960. Neurosis and Trauma. APA Convention, Atlantic City, N.J.

American Psychiatric Association Statement on the Insanity Defense. 1983. *Am. J. Psychiatry*, 140, p. 681.

Anisman, H. 1978. Neurochemical Changes Elicited by Stress: Behavioral Correlates. In *Psychopharmacology of Aversively Motivated Behavior*, edited by H. Anisman and G. Bignami. New York, Plenum.

Asher, R. 1951. Munchhausen's Syndrome. *Lancet*, 1, pp. 339–341.

Auerbach, D.B. 1982. The Ganser Syndrome. In *Extraordinary Disorders of Human Behavior*, edited by C.T. Friedmann and R.A. Faguet. New York, Plenum, pp. 29–46.

Bain, J.S. 1928. *Thought Control in Everyday Life*. New York, Funk and Wagnalls.

Baker, E.L. 1983. Neurological Disorders. In *Environmental and Occupational Medicine*, edited by W.N. Rom. Boston, Little, Brown and Co., pp. 313–328.

Barabanova, A.B., Baranov, A.E., Guskova, A.K. et. al. 1986. *Acute Radiation Effects in Man*. Moscow, National Committee on Radiation Protection.

Beck, A.T. 1976. *Cognitive Therapy and the Emotional Disorders*. New York, International Universities.

Beck, A.T., Rush, A.J., Shaw, B.F., and Emery, G. 1979. *Cognitive Therapy of Depression*. New York, Guilford Press.

Benedek, E.P. 1985. Children and Psychic Trauma: A Brief Review of Contemporary Thinking. In *Post-Traumatic Stress Disorder in Children*, edited by S. Eth and R.S. Pynoos. Washington D.C., American Psychiatric Press, pp. 3–16.

Berk, R.S. 1983. An Introduction to the World of Microorganisms. In *Microbiology: Basic Principles and Clinical Applications*, edited by N.R. Rose and A.L. Barron. New York, Macmillan Publishing Co., pp. 3–10.

Blackburn, A.B., O'Connell, W.E., and Richman, B.W. 1984. PTSD, the Vietnam Veteran, and Adlerian Natural High Therapy: Individual Psychology. *Journal of Adlerian Theory, Research and Practice*, 40, pp. 317–332.

Brend, W.A. 1939. *Traumatic Mental Disorders in Courts of Law*. London, William Heinemann.

Brende, J.O. 1981. Combined Individual and Group Therapy for Vietnam Veterans. *Int. J. Group Psychother.*, 31, pp. 367–378.

Brende, J.O., and McCann, I.L. 1984. Regressive Experiences in Vietnam Veterans: Their Relationship to War, Post-Traumatic Symptoms, and Recovery. *Journal of Contemporary Psychotherapy*, 14, pp. 57–75.

Brill, N.Q., and Beebe, G.W. 1951. Follow-up Study of Psychoneurosis. *Am. J. Psychiatry*, 108, pp. 417–425.

Bromberg, W. 1979. *The Uses of Psychiatry in the Law: A Clinical View of Forensic Psychiatry*. Westport, Quorum Books.

Buffler, P.A., Crane, M., and Key, M.M. 1985. *Environ. Health Perspect.*, 62, pp. 423–456.

Burgess, A.W. 1983. Rape Trauma Syndrome. *Behav. Sci. Law*, 1, pp. 97–114.

Burnside, J.W., and McGlynn, T.J. 1987. *Physical Diagnosis* (17th edition). Baltimore, Williams and Wilkins.

Burris, B.T. 1983. Symposium on Post-Traumatic Stress Disorder. American Psychiatric Association Convention, New York.

Cannon, W.B. 1929. *Bodily Changes in Pain, Hunger, Fear, and Rage: An Account of Recent Researches into the Function of Emotional Excitement* (second edition). New York, Appleton-Century-Crofts.

Caplan, G. 1964. *Principles of Preventive Psychiatry*. New York, Basic Books.

Caplan, G. 1986. Recent Developments in Crisis Intervention and in the Promotion of Support Services. In *A Decade of Progress in Primary Prevention*, edited by M. Kessler and S.E. Goldston. Hanover and London, University Press of New England, pp. 235–260.

Card, J.J. 1983. *Lives After Vietnam: The Personal Impact of Military Service*. Lexington, Lexington Books.

Cheek, D.B., and LaCron, L.M. 1968. *Clinical Hypnotherapy*. New York, Grune and Stratton.

Cloninger, C.R., Martin, R.L., Clayton, P., and Guze, S.B. 1981. A Blind Follow-Up and Family Study of Anxiety Neurosis: Preliminary Analysis of the St. Louis 500. In *Anxiety: New Research and Changing Concepts*, edited by D.Klein and J. Rabkin, New York, Raven Press, pp. 137–154.

Cohen, M.E., Badal, D.W., Kilpatrick, A., Reed, E.W., and White, P.D. 1951. The High Familial Prevalence of Neurocirculatory Asthenia (Anxiety Neurosis, Effort Syndrome). *Am. J. Hum. Genet.*, 3, pp. 126–158.

Cohen, R.R.L. 1970. *Traumatic Neurosis in Personal Injury Cases*. Washington D.C., Trial Lawyer's Service.

Cowen, E.L. 1986. Primary Prevention in Mental Health: Ten Years of Retrospect and Ten Years of Prospect. In *A Decade of Progress in Primary Prevention*, edited by M. Kessler and S.E. Goldston. Hanover and London, University Press of New England, pp. 3–45.

Crowe, R.R., Pauls, D.L., Slyman, D.J., and Noyes, R. 1980. A Family Study of Anxiety Neurosis. *Arch. Gen. Psychiatry*, 37, pp. 77–79.

Crump, L.E. 1984. Gestalt Therapy in the Treatment of Vietnam Veterans Experiencing PTSD Symptomatology. *Journal of Contemporary Psychotherapy*, 14, pp. 90–98.

Curran, J.B., and Gilbert, F.S. 1975. A Test of the Relative Effectiveness of a Systematic Desensitization Program and an Interpersonal Skills Training Program with Date-Anxious Subjects. *Behav. Ther.*, 6, pp. 510–521.

DaCosta, J.M. 1871. On Irritable Heart: A Clinical Study of a Form of Functional Cardiac Disorder and Its Consequences. *Am. J. Med. Sci.*, 61, pp. 17–52.

Dalessio, D.J. 1978. Hyperventilation, the Vapors, Effort Syndrome, Neurasthenia, *JAMA*, 239, pp. 1401–1402.

Davidson, H. 1965. *Forensic Psychiatry* (second edition). New York, Ronald Press.

Dawley, H.H., and Wenrich, W.W. 1976. *Achieving Assertive Behavior.* California, Bricks/Cole.

Diagnostic and Statistical Manual of Mental Disorders (second edition). 1968. Washington D.C., American Psychiatric Association.

Diagnostic and Statistical Manual of Mental Disorders (third edition). 1980. Washington D.C., American Psychiatric Association.

Diagnostic and Statistical Manual of Mental Disorders (third edition, revised). 1987. Washington D.C., American Psychiatric Association.

Diamond, B.L. 1956, Isaac Ray and the Trial of Daniel M'Naughten. *Am. J. Psychiatry*, 112, p. 651.

Dunner, F. 1983. An Evaluation of the Clinical Efficacy of Alpraxolam (Xanax) in Vietnam Veterans with PTSD. Presented at the Second National Conference on the Treatment of Post-Traumatic Stress Disorder (PTSD), Chicago.

Eisert, W.G., and Mendelsohn, M.L. (Eds.). 1984. *Biological Dosimetry.* Berlin, Springer-Verlag.

Erlinder, C.P. 1983. Post-Traumatic Stress Disorder, Vietnam Veterans and the Law: A Challenge to Effective Representation. *Behav. Sci. Law*, 1, pp. 25–30.

Eth, S., Pynoos, R.S. (Eds.). 1985. *Post-Traumatic Stress Disorder in Children.* Washington D.C., American Psychiatric Press.

Fairbank, J.A., and Keane, T.M. 1982. Flooding for Combat-Related Stress Disorders: Assessment of Anxiety Reduction Across Traumatic Memories. *Behav. Ther.*, 13, pp. 499–510.

Fairbank, J.A., and Brown, T.A. 1987. Current Behavioral Approaches to the Treatment of Post-Traumatic Stress Disorder. *Behavior Therapist*, 3, pp. 57–64.

Fairbank, J.A., and Nicholson, R.A. 1987. Theoretical and Imperical Issues in the Treatment of Post-Traumatic Stress Disorder in Vietnam Veterans. *Journal of Clinical Psychology*, 43, pp. 44–55.

Feindler, E.L., and Fremouw, W.J. 1983. Stress Inoculation Training for Adolescent Anger Problems. In *Stress Reduction and Prevention*, edited by D. Meichenbaum and M.E. Jaremko, New York, Plenum, pp. 451–485.

Fields, R.P. 1982. Research on the Victims of Terrorism. In *Victims of Terrorism*, edited by F.M. Ochberg and D.A. Soskis. Boulder, Westview Press, pp. 137–148.

Figley, C.R. 1978. *Stress Disorders Among Vietnam Veterans*. New York, Brunner/Mazel.

Fischer, V., Boyle, J.M., and Bucuvalas, M. 1980. *Myths and Realities: A Study of Attitudes Towards Vietnam Era Veterans*. Washington D.C., Louis Harris.

Fisher, E.B., Levenkron, J.C., Lowe, M.R., Loro, A.D., and Green, L. 1982. Self-Initiated Self-Control in Risk Reduction. In *Adherence, Compliance and Generalization in Behavioral Medicine*, edited by R. Stuart, New York, Brunner/Mazel.

Ford, C.V. 1982. Munchhausen Syndrome. In *Extraordinary Disorders of Human Behavior*, edited by C.T. Friedmann and R.A. Faguet. New York, Plenum, pp. 15–27.

Frank, J. 1961. *Persuasion and Healing*. Baltimore, Johns Hopkins.

Frank, J. 1978. *Effective Ingredients of Successful Psychotherapy*. New York, Brunner/Mazel.

Fredrick, C.J. 1981. Current Thinking About Crisis or Psychological Intervention in U.S. Disasters. In *Aircraft Accidents: Emergency Mental Health Problems*, edited by C.J. Fredrick. Rockville, National Institute of Mental Health, pp. 33– 42.

Freed, E. 1983. AIDophobia. *Med. J. Aust.*, 2, p. 479.

Freud, S. 1962. On the Grounds for Detaching a Particular Syndrome for Neurasthenia under the Description "Anxiety Neurosis." In *Standard Edition of the Complete Psychological Works of Sigmund Freud* (Vol. 3), p. 90. London, Hogarth Press.

Friedman, M.J. 1981. Post-Vietnam Syndrome: Recognition and Management. *Psychosomatics*, 22, pp. 931–943.

Gale, R.P. 1987. Immediate Medical Consequences of Nuclear Accidents. *JAMA*, 258, pp. 625–628.

Gallant, D.M. 1987. *Alcoholism: A Guide to Diagnosis, Intervention, and Treatment.* New York, W.W. Norton and Co.

Gallo, R.C. 1987. The AIDS Virus. *Scientific American*, 256, pp. 47–56.

Ganser, S.J.M. 1898. Uber Einen Eigenartigen Hysterischen Dammerzustand. *Arch. Psychiatr.* Nervenkr. 38, p. 633.

Gleser, G.C., Green, B.L., and Winget, C. 1981. *Prolonged Psychosocial Effects of Disaster: A Study of Buffalo Creek.* New York, Academic Press.

Glueck, S. 1962. *Law and Psychiatry: Cold War or Entente Cordiale?* Baltimore, Johns Hopkins.

Golden, S., and MacDonald, J.E. 1955. The Ganser State. *J. Ment. Sci.*, 101, pp. 267–280.

Goldstein, A., Kaizer, S., and Whitby, O. 1969. Psychotropic Effects of Caffeine in Man. IV. Quantitative and Qualitative Differences Associated with Habituation to Coffee. *Clin. Pharmacol. Ther.*, 10, pp. 489–497.

Goodwin, J. 1980. The Etiology of Combat-Related Post-Traumatic Stress Disorders. In *Post-Traumatic Stress Disorder of the Vietnamese Veterans*, edited by T. Williams. Cincinnati, Disabled American Veterans.

Gottlieb, M.S., Schroff, R., Schanker, H.M., Weisman, J.D., Fan, P.T., Wolf, R.A., and Saxon, A. 1981. Pneumocystis Carinii Pneumonia and Mucosal Candidiasis in Previously Healthy Homosexual Men. *New Eng. J. Med.*, 305, pp. 1425–1438.

Gottschalk, L.S. 1974. Self-Induced Visual Imagery, Affect Arousal and Autonomic Correlates. *Psychosomatics*, 4, pp. 166–169.

Grandjean, P., Arnvig, E., and Beckman, J. 1978. Psychological Dysfunctions in Lead-Exposed Workers. *Scand. J. Work Environ.* Health, 4, pp. 295–303.

Greden, J.F. 1979. Coffee, Tea, and You. *Sciences*, 19, pp. 6–11.

Grinker, R., and Spiegel, J.P. 1945. *Men Under Stress*. Philadelphia, Blakiston.

Guttmacher, M., and Weihofen, H. 1952. *Psychiatry and the Law*. New York, Norton.

Halpern, A.L. 1986. The APA Insanity Rule–Case Studies of a Metaphysical Subtlety. In *Crime and Punishment in Modern America*, edited by P.B. McGuigan and J.S. Pascale. Washington D.C., The Free Congress and Research Education Foundation, pp. 199–215.

Heath, C.W., Jr. 1983. Field Epidemiologic Studies of Populations Exposed to Waste Dumps. *Environ. Health Perspect.*, 48, pp. 3–8.

Heath, C.W., Nadel, M.R., Zack, M.M., Chen, A.T.L., Bender, M.A., and Preston, R.J. 1984. Cytogenetic Findings in Persons Living Near the Love Canal. *JAMA*, 251, pp. 1437–1440.

Hogben, G.O., and Cornfield, R.B. 1981. Treatment of Traumatic War Neurosis with Phenalzine. *Arch. Gen. Psychiatry*, 38, pp. 440–445.

Holland, B.C., and Ward, R.S. 1966. Homeostasis and Psychosomatic Medicine. In *American Handbook of Psychiatry, Vol. III*, edited by S. Arieti. New York, Basic Books. pp. 344–361.

Hollister, L.E., Greenblatt, D.J., Rickels, I., and Ayd, F.J. 1980. A Symposium: Benzodiazepines 1980, Current Update. *Psychosomatics* (Suppl.), 21, pp. 4–32.

Horowitz, M. 1974. Stress Response Syndrome, Character Style, and Dynamic Psychotherapy. *Archives of General Psychiatry*, 31, pp. 768–781.

Horowitz, M.J., and Kaltreider, N.B. 1980. Brief Psychotherapy of Stress Response Syndromes. In *Specialized Techniques in Individual Psychotherapy*, edited by T.B. Karasu and L. Bellak. New York, Brunner/ Mazel.

Horowitz, M.J., Wilner, N., Kaltreider, N., and Alvarez, W. 1980. Signs and Symptoms of Post-Traumatic Stress Disorder. *Arch. Gen. Psychiatry*, 37, pp. 85–92.

Imwinkelried, E.J., and Giannelli, P.C. 1986. *Scientific Evidence*. Charlottesville, Michie Company.

Institute of Medicine, National Academy of Sciences. 1986. *Confronting AIDS: Directions for Public Health, Health Care, and Research*. Washington D.C., National Academy Press.

Jack, W., Jr. 1980. The Vietnam Connection: Charles Head Verdict. *Criminal Defense*, 9, p. 7.

Jacobsen, E. 1974. *Progressive Relaxation: A Physiological and Clinical Investigation of Muscular States and Their Significance in Psychology and Medical Practice* (third edition). Chicago, University of Chicago.

Janerich, D.T., Burnett, W.S., Feck, G., Hoff, M., Nasca, P., Polednak, A.P., Greerwald, P., and Vianna, N. 1981. Cancer Incidence in the Love Canal Area. *Science*, 212, pp. 1404–1407.

Kadushin, C., Boulanger, G., and Martin, J. 1981. Long-Term Stress Reactions: Some Causes, Consequences, and Naturally Occurring Support Systems. In *Vol. 4 of Legacies of Vietnam: Comparative Adjustment of Veterans and Their Peers*. Washington D.C., U.S. Government Printing Office.

Kaiser, L. 1968. *The Traumatic Neurosis.* Philadelphia, Lippincott.

Kardiner, A., and Spiegel, H. 1947. *War Stress and Neurotic Illness.* New York, Hoeber:Harper.

Keane, T.M., and Kaloupek, D.G. 1982. Brief Reports: Imaginal Flooding in the Treatment of a Post-Traumatic Stress Disorder. *J. Consult. Clin. Psychol.*, 50, pp. 138–140.

Keane, T.M., and Fairbank, J.A. 1983. Survey Analysis of Combat- Related Stress Disorders in Vietnam Veterans. *Am. J. Psychiatry*, 140, pp. 348–350.

Keane, T.M., Zimering, R.T., and Caddell, J.M. 1985. A Behavioral Formulation of Posttraumatic Stress Disorder in Vietnam Veterans. *Behavior Therapist*, 8, pp. 9–12.

Kinzie, J.D. 1986. Severe Post-Traumatic Stress Syndrome Among Cambodian Refugees: Symptoms, Clinical Course, and Treatment Approaches. In *Disaster Stress Studies: New Methods and Findings*, edited by J.H. Shore. Washington D.C., American Psychiatric Press, pp. 123–140.

Klinger, E. 1970. *Structure and Function of Fantasy.* New York, John Wiley.

Kluznick, J.C., Speed, N., VanValkenburg, C., and Magraw, R. 1986. Forty-Year Follow-Up of United States Prisoners of War. *American Journal of Psychiatry*, 143, pp. 1443–1449.

Kolb, L.C. 1984. The Post-Traumatic Stress Disorders of Combat: A Subgroup with a Conditioned Emotional Response. *Military Medicine*, 149, pp. 237–243.

Kolb, L.C., and Mutalipassi, L.R. 1982. The Conditioned Emotional Response: A Subclass of the Chronic and Delayed Post-Traumatic Stress Disorder. *Psychiatr. Ann.*, 12, pp. 979–987.

Kosbad, F.P. 1974. Imagery Techniques in Psychiatry. *Arch. Gen. Psychiatry*, 31, pp. 283–290.

Krieger, D. 1983. Brain Peptides, What, Where, and Why. *Science*, 222, pp. 975–985.

Kroger, W.S., and Fezler, W.D. 1976. *Hypnosis and Behavior Modification: Imagery Conditioning*. Philadelphia, Lippincott.

Larsen, R.C. 1986, October. Psychiatric Workers' Compensation Claims. Paper presented at the 17th Annual Meeting of the American Academy of Psychiatry and the Law. Philadelphia.

Larson, A. 1972. *The Law of Workman's Compensation, Vol. I.* New York, Mathew Bender.

Laufer, R.S., Yager, T., Frey-Wouters, E., Donnellan, J., Gallops, M., and Stenbeck, K. 1981. Post-War Trauma: Social and Psychological Problems of Vietnam Veterans in the Aftermath of the Vietnam War. In *Vol. 3* of *Legacies of Vietnam: Comparative Adjustment of Veterans and Their Peers*. Washington D.C., U.S. Government Printing Office.

Lefford, M.J. 1983. Mycobacteria. In *Microbiology: Basic Principles and Clinical Applications*, edited by N.R. Rose and A.L. Barron. New York, Macmillan Publishing Co., pp. 223–234.

Levenson, H., Lanman, R., and Rankin, M. 1982. Traumatic War Neurosis and Phenelzine. *Archives of General Psychiatry*, 38, p. 1345.

Lewis, T. 1919. *The Soldier's Heart and the Effort Syndrome*. New York, Hoeber.

Lewy, E. 1941. Compensation for War Neurosis. *War Med.*, 1, p. 887.

Lifton, R. 1967. *Death in Life: Survivors of Hiroshima*. New York, Random House.

Lindstrom, K. 1973. Psychological Performance of Workers Exposed to Various Solvents. *Work Environ. Health*, 10, pp. 151–155.

Lindy, J.D., Green, B.L., Grace, M., and Titchener, J. 1983. Psychotherapy with Survivors of the Beverly Hills Supper Club Fire. *American Journal of Psychotherapy*, 37, pp. 593–610.

Linn, L. 1975. Other Psychiatric Emergencies. In *Comprehensive Textbook of Psychiatry*, edited by A.M. Freedman, H.I. Kaplan, and B.J. Sadock. Baltimore, Williams and Wilkins, pp. 2003–2009.

Lopez-Ibor, J.J., Jr., Soria, J., Canas, F., and Rodriguez-Gamazo, M. 1985. Psychopathological Aspects of the Toxic Oil Syndrome Catastrophe. *British J. of Psychiatry*, 147, pp. 352–365.

Mace, E.B., O'Brien, C., Mintz, J., Ream, N., and Meyers, A.L. 1978. Adjustment Among Vietnam Veteran Drug Users Two Years Post-Service. In *Stress Disorders Among Vietnam Veterans*, edited by C.R. Figley. New York, Brunner/Mazel, pp. 71–128.

Maeder, T. 1985. *Crime and Madness*. New York, Harper and Row, Publishers.

Mahoney, M.J. 1971. The Self-Management of Covert Behavior: A Case Study. *Behav. Ther.*, 2, pp. 575–578.

Mahoney, M.J., and Arnoff, D.B. 1979. Self-Management in Behavioral Medicine: Theory and Practice. In *Behavioral Medicine: Theory and Practice*, edited by O.F. Pomerlau and J.P. Brady. Baltimore, Williams and Wilkins, pp. 75–96.

Malone, W.S. 1951. *Louisiana Workman's Compensation Law and Practice*. St. Paul, West Publishing.

Malone, W.S., and Johnson, H.S. 1980. *Louisiana Civil Code Treatacy, Vol. 13, Worker's Compensation Law and Practice* (second edition). St. Paul, West Publishing.

Manchester, W. 1980. *Goodbye Darkness: A Memoir of the Pacific War*. Boston, Little, Brown and Co.

Manchester, W. 1983. *The Last Lion: Winston Spencer Churchill*. Boston, Little, Brown and Co.

Marks, I. 1981. *Cure and Care of Neuroses*. New York, Wiley.

Martland, H.S., Conlon, P., and Knef, J.P. 1925. Some Unrecognized Dangers in the Use of and the Handling of Radioactive Substances. *JAMA*, 85, pp. 1769–1776.

Masters, W.H., and Johnson, V.E. 1970. *Human Sexuality Inadequacy*. Boston, Little, Brown and Co.

Mavissakalian, M., and Barlow, D.H. 1981. *Phobia*. New York, Guilford.

McDermott, W.F. 1981. The Influence of Vietnam Combat on Subsequent Psychopathology. Paper presented at the American Psychological Association Convention. Los Angeles.

McGarry, A.L. 1986. Forensic Psychiatry Reports: Selected Clinical Topics and Models for Report Preparation. In *Forensic Psychiatry and Psychology*, edited by W.J. Curran, A.L. McGarry, and S.A. Shaw. Philadelphia, F.A. Davis Co., pp. 79–102.

McInnes, R.G. 1937. Observations on Heredity in Neurosis. Proc. R. *Soc. Med.*, 30, pp. 895–904.

McKinnon, J.A. 1984. Brief Psychotherapy of the Vietnam Combat Neurosis. In *Psychotherapy of the Combat Veteran*, edited by H.J. Schwartz. New York, SP Medical and Scientific Books, pp. 125–151.

McLean, A. 1975. Occupational (Industrial) Psychiatry. In *Comprehensive Textbook of Psychiatry* (second edition), edited by A.M. Freedman, H.I. Kaplan, and B.J. Sadock. Baltimore, Williams and Wilkins, pp. 2368–2375.

Meichenbaum, D.D. 1977. *Cognitive-Behavior Modification: An Integrated Approach*. New York, Plenum.

Meichenbaum, D., and Cameron, R. 1983. Stress Inoculation Training: Towards a General Paradigm for Training Coping Skills. In *Stress Reduction and Prevention*, edited by D. Meichenbaum and M.E. Jaremko. New York, Plenum, pp. 115–154.

Mettler, F.A., Jr., and Mosely, R.D., Jr., 1985. *Medical Effects of Ionizing Radiation*. New York, Grune and Stratton.

Milanes, F.J., Mack, C.N., Dennison, J., and Slater, V.L. 1984. Phenelzine Treatment of Post-Vietnam Stress Syndrome. *V.A. Practitioner*, 1, pp. 40–49.

Minnesota v. Saldana, 324 NW 2d 227, 1982 (Minnesota).

Modlin, H. 1967. The Post-Accident Anxiety Syndrome: Psychosocial Aspects. *Am. J. Psychiatry*, 123, pp. 1008–1012.

Modlin, H.C. 1980. Psychiatry and the Civil Law. In *Modern Legal Medicine, Psychiatry, and Forensic Science*, edited by W.J. Curran, A.L. McGarry, and C.S. Petty. Philadelphia, F.A. Davis Co., pp. 721–736.

Munoz, R.F. 1986. Current Issues in Prevention: Summary of the 1984 Vermont Conference on the Primary Prevention of Psychopathology. In *A Decade of Progress in Primary Prevention*, edited by M. Kessler and S.E. Goldston. Hanover and London, University Press of New England, pp. 391–399.

Noyes, R., Clancy, J., Crowe, R., Hoenk, P.R., and Slyman, D.J. 1978. The Familial Prevalence of Anxiety Neurosis. *Arch. Gen. Psychiatry*, 35, pp. 1057–1059.

Ochberg, F.M., and Soskis, D.A. 1982. Planning for the Future: Means and Ends. In *Victims of Terrorism*, edited by F.M. Ochberg and D.A. Soskis. Boulder, Westview Press, pp. 173–190.

Oppenheimer, B.S. 1918. Report on Neurocirculatory Asthenia and Its Management. *Milt. Surg.*, 42, pp. 7–11.

Parson, E.R. 1984. The Role of Psychodynamic Group Therapy in the Treatment of the Combat Veteran. In *Psychotherapy of the Combat Veteran*, edited by H.J. Schwartz. New York, S.P. Medical and Scientific Books, pp. 153–220.

Paul, G.L. 1968. Two Year Follow-Up of Systematic Desensitization in Therapy Groups. *J. Abnorm. Psychol.*, 73, pp. 119–130.

Pavlov, I.P. 1927. *Conditioned Reflexes.* New York, Liveright.

Pearson, N.A., Poquette, B.N., and Wasden, R.E. 1983. Stress- Inoculation and the Treatment of Post-Rape Trauma: A Case Report. *Behavior Therapist*, 6, pp. 58–59.

People v. Wood, 80–7410 (Cir. Ct. Cook County, Ill., May 5, 1982).

Public Law 98–473–October 12, 1984. 98STAT. 2057.

Quiroga, J., Deustch, A., and O'Grady, K. 1982. Medical and Psychological Sequelae in Latin American Survivors of Torture. Paper presented at the symposium on "Torture, Medical Practice, and Medical Ethics," organized by the Clearing House of Science and Human Rights of the American Association for the Advancement of Science, January, 1982. Washington D.C.

Raifman, L.J. 1983. Problems of Diagnosis and Legal Causation in Courtroom Use of Post-Traumatic Stress Disorder. *Behav. Sci. Law*, 1, pp. 115–130.

Rapoport, J., Elkins, R., Zahn, T.P., Buschsbaum, M.S., Weingartner, H., and Kopin, I.J. 1981. Acute Effects of Caffeine on Normal Prepubertal Boys. In *Anxiety: New Research and Changing Concepts*, edited by D. Klein and J. Rabkin. New York, Raven Press, pp. 355–365.

Rappaport, J. 1984. Studies in Empowerment: Introduction to the Issue. *Prevention in Human Services*, 3, pp. 1–7.

Ray, I. 1962. *A Treatise on the Medical Jurisprudence of Insanity.* Cambridge, Harvard U. Press.

Redfield, R.R., Wright, D.C., and Tramont, E.C. 1986. The Walter Reed Staging Classification for HTLV-III/LAV Infection. *New Eng. J. Med.*, 314, pp. 131–132.

Renshaw, D.C. 1982. *Incest: Understanding and Treatment*. Boston, Little, Brown and Co.

Resick, P.A., Jordan, C.G., Girelli, S.A., Hutter, C.K., and Marhoefer-Dvorak, S. 1985, August. A Comparative Outcome Study of Therapy for Sexual Assault Victims. Paper presented at the meeting of the American Psychological Association. Los Angeles.

Robitscher, J.B. 1966. *Pursuit of Agreement - Psychiatry and the Law*. Philadelphia, Lippincott.

Rosenbaum, A. 1986. Family Violence. In *Forensic Psychiatry and Psychology*, edited by W.J. Curran, A.L. McGarry, and S.A. Shah. Philadelphia, F.A. Davis Co., pp. 227–246.

Rosenheim, E., and Elizur, A. 1977. Group Therapy for Traumatic Neuroses. *Curr. Psychiatr. Ther.*, 17, pp. 143–148.

Rosenthal, T.L., and Bandura, A. 1978. Psychological Modeling: Theory and Practice. In *Handbook of Psychotherapy and Behavior Change: An Empirical Analysis*, edited by S.L. Garfield and A.E. Bergin. New York, Wiley, pp. 621–658.

Rosner, R. 1982. *Clinical Issues in American Psychiatry and the Law*. Springfield, Charles C. Thomas.

Sachse, H.R., and Scrignar, C.B. 1968. The Evolution of a Law and Psychiatry Program, *J. Legal Ed.*, 21, pp. 192–195.

Saigh, P.A. 1985. On the Nature and Etiology of Traumatic Stress. *Behavior Therapy*, 16, pp. 423–426.

Schultz, J.H., and Luther, W. 1969. *Autogenic Therapy (Vol. 1)*. New York, Grune and Stratton.

Scrignar, C.B. 1967a. The Physician and the Law. Determination of Mental Competency to Stand Trial. *JAMA*, 201, pp. 343–346.

Scrignar, C.B. 1967b. Tranquilizers and the Psychotic Defendant. *Am. Bar Assoc. J.*, 533, pp. 43–45.

Scrignar, C.B. 1968. Sex and the Underaged Girl. *Medical Aspects of Human Sexuality*, 2, pp. 34–39.

Scrignar, C.B. 1971. Maximum Security Hospitals: Where the People Are. Newsletter Am. Acad. Psychiatry. *Law*, 2, pp. 4–22.

Scrignar, C.B. 1974. Exposure Time as the Main Hierarchy Variable. *J. Behav. Ther. Exp. Psychiatry*, 5, pp. 153–155.

Scrignar, C.B. 1980. Mandatory Weight Control Program for 550 Police Officers Choosing Either Behavior Modification or "Will Power." *Obesity Bariatric Med.*, 9, pp. 88–92.

Scrignar, C.B. 1983. *Stress Strategies: The Treatment of the Anxiety Disorders.* Basel, S. Karger.

Scrignar, C.B. 1984. *Post-Traumatic Stress Disorder: Diagnosis, Treatment, and Legal Issues.* New York, Praeger.

Scrignar, C.B. 1987a. Post-Traumatic Stress Disorder. *The Psychiatric Times*, *Vol. IV*, No. 7, pp. 1, 8–11.

Scrignar, C.B. 1987b. Posttraumatic Stress Disorder and Sexual Dysfunction. *Medical Aspects of Human Sexuality*, 21, pp. 102, 104, 106, 111–112.

Scrignar, C.B., Group Therapy with victims of Post-Traumatic Stress Disorder. In M. Seligmen and L.A. Marsak (Eds.), *A Practioner's Guide to Interventions with Special Populations.* Orlando, Grune & Stratton (in press).

Scrignar, C.B., and Sachse, H.R. 1966. Tulane University School of Law-School of Medicine Training Program in Forensic Psychiatry. *Bull. Tulane Univ. Med. Faculty*, 25, pp. 311–315.

Scrignar, C.B., and Sachse, H.R. 1969. A Community and Action-Oriented Training Program in Law and Psychiatry, *J. Med. Ed.*, 44, pp. 52–56.

Scrignar, C.B., Swanson, W.C., and Bloom, W.A. 1973. Use of Systematic Desensitization in the Treatment of Airplane Phobic Patients. *Behav. Res. Ther.*, 2, pp. 129–131.

Selwyn, P.A. 1986. AIDS: What is Now Known. III Clinical Aspects. *Hospital Practice*, 21, pp. 119–126, 129–131.

Selye, H. 1946. The General Adaptation Syndrome and the Diseases of Adaptation. *J. Clin. Endocrinol.*, 6, pp. 117–130.

Selye, H. 1950. *The Physiology and Pathology of Exposure to Stress.* Montreal, Acta Inc.

Selye, H. 1956. *The Stress of Life.* New York, McGraw-Hill.

Server, M. 1972. Teaching the Nonverbal Components of Assertive Training. *J. Behav. Ther. Exp. Psychiatry*, 3, pp. 179–183.

Shader, R.I., Greenblatt, D.J., and Ciraulo, D.A. 1981. Benzodiazepine Treatment of Specific Anxiety States. *Psychiatr. Ann.*, 11, pp. 30–40.

Shapiro, D. 1977. A Monologue on Biofeedback and Psychophysiology. *Psychophysiology*, 14, pp. 213–227.

Shen, W.W., and Park, S. 1983. The Use of Monoamine Oxidase Inhibitors in the Treatment of Traumatic War Neurosis. Case report. *Military Medicine*, 148, pp. 430–431.

Shields, J. 1962. *Monozygotic Twins Brought Up Apart and Together.* London, Oxford University.

Sierles, F.S., Chen, J.J., McFarland, R.E., and Taylor, M.A. 1983. Post-Traumatic Stress Disorder and Concurrent Psychiatric Illness: A Preliminary Report. *Am. J. Psychiatry*, 140, pp. 117–179.

Silving, H. 1967. *Essays on Mental Incapacity and Criminal Conduct.* Springfield, Charles C. Thomas.

Skinner, B.F. 1938. *The Behavior of Organisms.* New York, Appleton-Century-Crofts.

Slater, E. 1943. The Neurotic Consitution. *J. Neurol. Psychiatry*, 6, pp. 1–16.

Slater, E., and Shields, J. 1969. Genetical Aspects of Anxiety. *Br. J. Psychiatry*, 3, pp. 62–71.

Slovenko, R. 1963. Psychiatry, Criminal Law, and the Role of the Psychiatrist. *Duke Law J.*, 3, pp. 395–426.

Slovenko, R. 1973. *Psychiatry and Law*. Boston, Little, Brown and Co.

Slovenko, R. 1984. The Meaning of Mental Illness in Criminal Responsibility. *Journal of Legal Medicine*, 5, pp. 1–61.

Sparr, L., and Pankratz, L. 1983. Factitious Post-Traumatic Stress Disorder. *Am. J. Psychiatry*, 140, pp. 1016–1019.

Spiegel, D. 1981. Vietnam Grief Work Using Hypnosis. *Am. J. Clin. Hypn.*, 24, pp. 33–40.

Spiro, H.R. 1968. Chronic Factitious Illness: Munchhausen's Syndrome. *Arch. Gen. Psychiatry*, 18, pp. 569–579.

Sprehe, D.J. 1984. Workers' Compensation: A Psychiatric Follow-Up Study. *International Journal of Law and Psychiatry*, 7, pp. 165–178.

State v. Heads, no. 106 126 (1st Jud. Dis. Ct. Caddo Parish) October 10, 1981.

State v. Marks, 647 P2d 1292, Kansas, 1982.

State v. Pullins, 145MICH APP 414 (1985).

Stuart, R.B. 1975. *Treatment Contract*. Illinois, Research Press.

Stuart, R.B. 1980. *Helping Couples Change*. New York, Guilford.

Stuart, R.B., and Davis, B. 1982. *Slim Chance in a Fat World: Behavioral Control of Obesity*. Chicago, Research.

Supplemental Studies for the National Commission on Workman's Compensation Laws. I(14). 1973.

Swan, R.W. 1985. The Child as Active Participant in Sexual Abuse. *Clinical Social Work Journal*, 6, pp. 62–77.

Taylor, J.G. 1963. A Behavioral Interpretation of Obsessive- Compulsive Neurosis. *Behav. Res. Ther.*, 1, pp. 237–244.

Titchener, J., and Kapp, F.T. 1981. Family and Character Change at Buffalo Creek. In *Aircraft Accidents: Emergency Mental Health Problems*, edited by C.J. Fredrick. Rockville, National Institute of Mental Health, pp. 23–32.

Torgersen, S. 1978. The Contribution of Twin Studies to Psychiatric Nosology. In *Twin Research, Part A: Psychology and Methodology*, edited by W.E. Nance. New York, Alan R. Liss, pp. 125–130.

Trimble, M.R. 1981. *Post-Traumatic Neurosis: From Railway Spine to the Whiplash*. Chichester, John Wiley.

Valliant, G.E. 1981. Natural History of Male Psychological Health X: Work as a Predictor of Positive Mental Health. *Am. J. Psychiatry*, 125, pp. 1435–1439.

van der Kolk, B., Boyd, H., Krystal, J., and Greenberg, M. 1984. Post-Traumatic Stress Disorder as a Biologically Based Disorder: Implications of the Animal Model of Inescapable Shock. In *Post-Traumatic Stress Disorder: Psychological and Biological Sequelae*, edited by B.A. van der Kolk. Washington D.C., American Psychiatric Press, pp. 123–134.

van der Kolk, B., Greenberg, M., Boyd, H., and Krystal, J. 1985. Inescapable Shock, Neurotransmitters, and Addiction to Trauma: Toward a Psychobiology of Post-Traumatic Stress. *Biological Psychiatry*, 20, pp. 314–325.

Walker, J.I. 1981. Vietnam Combat Veterans with Legal Difficulties: A Psychiatric Problem. *Am. J. Psychiatry*, 138, pp. 1385–1395.

Walker, J.I., and Nash, J.L. 1981. Group Therapy in the Treatment of Vietnam Combat Veterans. *Int. J. Group Psychother.*, 31, pp. 379–388.

Wallace, R.K. 1970. Physiological Effects of Transcendental Meditation. *Science*, 167, pp. 1751–1754.

Washington Post. July 12, 1986. "Navy Diver Remains Scared by Hijacking Ordeal."

Weston, D.W. 1975. Development of Community Psychiatry Concepts. In *Comprehensive Textbook of Psychiatry*, edited by A.M. Freedman, H.I. Kaplan, and B.J. Sadock. Baltimore, Williams and Wilkins, pp. 2310–2323.

Wettstein, R.M., Rogers, R., and Mulvey, E. 1986, October. Paper presented at the 17th Annual Meeting of the American Academy of Psychiatry and the Law. Philadelphia.

Wilson, J.P. 1980. *Forgotten Warrior Project*. Cincinnati, Disabled American Veterans.

Wolpe, J. 1958. *Psychotherapy by Reciprocal Inhibition*. Stanford, Stanford University.

Wolpe, J. 1982. *The Practice of Behavior Therapy* (third edition). New York, Pergamon.

Wooley, C.F. 1982. Jacob Mendez DaCosta: Medical Teacher, Clinician, and Clinical Investigator. *Am. J. Cardiol.*, 50, pp. 1145–1148.

Worthington, E.R. 1978. Demographic and Pre-Service Variables as Predictors of Post-Military Service Adjustment. In *Stress Disorders Among Vietnam Veterans*, edited by C.R. Figley. New York, Brunner/Mazel.

Yamagami, T. 1971. The Treatment of an Obsession by Thought-Stopping. *J. Behav. Ther. Exp. Psychiatry*, 2, pp. 133–135.

Yost, E.B., Beutler, L.E., Corbishley, M.A., and Allender, J.R. 1986. *Group Cognitive Therapy*. New York, Pergamon Press.

Ziskin, J. 1981. *Coping with Psychiatric and Psychological Testimony* (third edition). Venice, Law and Psychiatry Press.

Zuger, A., and Miles, S.H. 1987. Physicians, AIDS, and Occupational Risk. *JAMA*, 258, pp. 1924–1928.

Zunzunegui, V. 1982. Data Findings in the Examination of Torture Victims. Symposium on Torture, Medical Practice, and Medical Ethics, American Association for the Advancement of Science, Washington D.C.

Zusman, J., and Simon, J. 1983. Differences in Repeated Psychiatric Examinations of Litigants to a Lawsuit. *Am. J. Psychiatry*, 140, pp. 1300–1304.

ABOUT THE AUTHOR

C. B. Scrignar, M.D., received his training in medicine and psychiatry at Tulane University School of Medicine in New Orleans following which he joined the faculty in 1964. As director of social psychiatry, he guided programs combating juvenile delinquency, drug abuse, and consulted at prisons and a maximum security hospital. For over a decade he codirected the Tulane University School of Law — School of Medicine Training Program in Law and Psychiatry and was appointed an adjunct professor of law and psychiatry at Tulane Law School. By appointment of the governor, he has served as chairman of the Louisiana Narcotics Rehabilitation Commission and was appointed by the mayor of New Orleans as chairman of the Action Task Force on Juvenile Delinquency Prevention.

He has written extensively about forensic psychiatry, stress and anxiety disorders, drug addiction, human sexuality, crime and delinquency, behavior therapy and hypnosis. In 1981, his writing received recognition with a Milton H. Erickson Award of Scientific Excellence for writing in Hypnosis. His first book, *Stress Strategies: The Treatment of the Anxiety Disorders*, was published by S. Karger in 1983.

Currently, Dr. Scrignar is in the private practice of psychiatry and is a clinical professor of psychiatry at Tulane University School of Medicine and an adjunct professor at the Tulane University School of Social Work. He teaches courses on anxiety and psychosomatic disorders, behavior therapy, the diagnosis and treatment of sexual dysfunctions, and lectures on forensic psychiatry at the Tulane University School of Law. Several times each year he conducts seminars for lawyers and clinicians on PTSD and the psychological sequelae of trauma.